Gay Faulkner

Gay Faulkner

Uncovering
a Homosexual Presence
in Yoknapatawpha and Beyond

Phillip Gordon

University Press of Mississippi / Jackson

The University Press of Mississippi is the scholarly publishing agency of
the Mississippi Institutions of Higher Learning: Alcorn State University,
Delta State University, Jackson State University, Mississippi State University,
Mississippi University for Women, Mississippi Valley State University,
University of Mississippi, and University of Southern Mississippi.

www.upress.state.ms.us

The University Press of Mississippi is a member
of the Association of University Presses.

First printing 2020
∞

Library of Congress Cataloging-in-Publication Data available

LCCN 2019030041
Hardback ISBN 978-1-4968-2597-1
Trade paperback ISBN 978-1-4968-2598-8
Epub single ISBN 978-1-4968-2599-5
Epub institutional ISBN 978-1-4968-2600-8
PDF single ISBN 978-1-4968-2601-5
PDF institutional ISBN 978-1-4968-2602-2

British Library Cataloging-in-Publication Data available

For the "quair" kids—and the queer kids—for all the kids who have known how certain labels are meant to exclude us. Never forget that this world is our world, this life our life. This book is dedicated to you.

Contents

Acknowledgments

This book would not have been possible without the generous support—academic, personal, and financial—of the following:

Thanks to Jaime Harker, Jay Watson, Annette Trefzer, Doug Robinson, and Ted Ownby for helping me find my way through the earlier versions of this project.

Thanks to Ben Fisher, for undertaking the huge task of helping me edit this project in its early stages.

To Roy Neil Graves, for the original image that became the cover of this book and for teaching me how to write. The best prose in what follows is a tribute to you; where flaws emerge, they are my own.

To the faculty and staff in Special Collections at Southeast Missouri State University, especially Bob Hamblin and Chris Reiger, for your generosity during my trips to your archive. You've opened your doors to many scholars looking for the real William Faulkner; I hope this book encourages others to find their way to your invaluable collection.

To the staff at the Howard Gottlieb Archival Research Center at Boston University. Also, to the Harry Ransom Center at the University of Texas-Austin, and particularly to Jennifer Shapland, a public service intern who happened to be assigned to my initial inquiry and went out of her way to help me track down and obtain materials for this project. And to Jennifer Ford and her wonderful staff in Special Collections at the University of Mississippi, for their help with documents relating to Hubert Creekmore.

To the family of Hubert Creekmore, for letting me get to know your uncle. Your memories of him are a blessing. May this book gain him some of the attention he deserves.

To Ann Marie Schott, Katharine Burnett, and Melanie Anderson, for listening to me, drinking with me, and letting me watch your projects grow and evolve so that I could figure out the right direction for mine.

To the Koeller family—Sara, Calvin, Gavin, and Michelle—whose support in the last stages of this project pushed it over the finish line, even when I was going a little bit crazy.

To Scout, for keeping my feet warm on the long cold Wisconsin nights of revisions.

No scholar is a (financial) island. This book would not have been possible without the generous financial support of the following:

The original draft of this project was written with funding from the Francis Bell McCool Dissertation Fellowship for Faulkner Studies, sponsored by Campbell and Leighton McCool, in honor of Campbell's mother.

Other funding came from a research grant sponsored by the Graduate Student Council at the University of Mississippi and a semester-long fellowship sponsored by the Graduate School at the University of Mississippi.

Finally, I am fortunate to have always had a loving, supportive family for this project, and in this greater project called life. Thanks to Mom, Dad, Steve, Meghan, Marty, and Jim (and Anna and Nathan).

Abbreviations

Certain titles are abbreviated in citations and notes as follows:

AILD:	*As I Lay Dying*
BP:	The Blotner Papers
CS:	*Collected Stories*
EP:	*William Faulkner: Early Prose and Poetry*
ESPL:	*Essays, Speeches, and Public Letters*
H:	The Hamlet
ID:	*Intruder in the Dust*
LIA:	*Light in August*
M:	The Mansion
MF/GB:	The Marble Faun and A Green Bough
NOS:	*New Orleans Sketches*
S:	*Sanctuary*
SLWF:	*Selected Letters of William Faulkner*
SP:	*Soldiers' Pay*
T:	The Town
Thinking:	*Thinking of Home*
US:	*Uncollected Stories*
Vision:	*Vision in Spring*

Introduction

What follows is a biographical study of the life and works of William Faulkner. It borrows its approach from a long list of critical biographies both on Faulkner and on other authors and belongs to the tradition of literary biography, a critical approach well established as a field of scholarly inquiry. The most significant predecessor from which this study grows are the two editions of Faulkner's biography by Joseph Blotner. Blotner met Faulkner at the University of Virginia, where Faulkner was a visiting writer and where his daughter Jill enrolled as an undergraduate and where Blotner worked as faculty in the English department. Blotner was named Faulkner's official biographer by Estelle Faulkner (neé Oldham), Faulkner's widow, shortly after Faulkner's death. He began a remarkable undertaking of interviews and archival research to reconstruct Faulkner's life. He published the first version of his biography in 1974. At over 2,000 pages and occupying two volumes, his monumental efforts became a touchstone of literary biography, but for all its encyclopedic knowledge, it was not a full account. As new information came to light after Estelle's death—including information on Faulkner's extramarital affairs and alcoholism—Blotner revised his biography to a one-volume edition that condensed the overwhelming detail of the first edition and added insights into how moments in that life might have influenced Faulkner's prolific literary productions. The significance of the first edition's detail transformed into the significance of the second edition's insights. Both are not only cornerstones of Faulkner Studies but also are paragons of the form.

These two works are not, however, the entirety of Blotner's biographical record. He collected every loose end and paper scrap of his research over a twenty-year period into folder upon folder ultimately stored away in egg crates in his garage in Ann Arbor, Michigan, where it was purchased by L. D. Brodsky to be curated as part of the Special Collections at Southeast Missouri State University by Dr. Robert (Bob) Hamblin. Hamblin had enrolled for graduate work at the University of Mississippi in fall 1962, less than three months after Faulkner's death, and he served in the National Guard that protected James Meredith, the university's first African American undergraduate, whose integration caused a riot on campus that October. With Brodsky's financial support, Hamblin proved a worthy caretaker of Blotner's notes and oversaw their addition to the Brodsky Collection at Southeast Missouri State University as the Blotner Papers. The Blotner Papers can be described in three words: fascinating, complex, and, for lack of a better adjective, beautiful. The detail they hold is a rabbit hole worth falling into. They do not unclutter a simple narrative of Faulkner's life but represent the multiplicities and contradictions of any life story. For a scholar who wants to explore the possibilities such a life story might contain, to touch each page of the original documents and follow them to their conclusions is like feeling electricity bristle through one's fingers and tickle down one's spine.

Blotner and all biographers must make numerous decisions to unwind the myriad threads that make a whole life and braid them into a narrative. This study follows the lead laid down by Blotner, but in those Blotner papers, a few loose threads expose other passages back out of the labyrinth. There is evidence in the Blotner papers that suggest our understanding of Faulkner's sexuality might not be what we have generally assumed.

In this study, I explore the shape and scope—the possibility—of gay Faulkner. By exploring his interactions with gay men, his immersion in gay subcultures throughout his life but especially between 1918 and 1929, and his deep and meaningful relationships with specific gay men, especially his lifelong friend Ben Wasson, a part of Faulkner's life emerges that has heretofore been at best marginalized if not outright denied about his identity, his sense of self, and his public performance. Set alongside the development of gay identity from the latter nineteenth century and through the first half of the twentieth, Faulkner's life can be read as a kind of gay history, certainly for Mississippi, probably for the South, and maybe even for America. This coterminous history and his immersion into gay life directly influenced his fiction, and we can see that influence both in specific texts and in broad patterns throughout his writings.

There are a few things this study is, but also things it is not. First, this is a study of gay Faulkner, and while I explore some of Faulkner's lesbian-themed writings from the 1920s, this work is primarily male, white, and cisgender in focus. The reason for this focus is that Faulkner seems to have understood different identities differently, and he was not as generous to non-male, nonwhite, and what we would call non-cisgender experience. I do not mean to suggest that there is no lesbian Faulkner or trans Faulkner or nonbinary Faulkner, or, for that matter, room for a study that explores bisexual Faulkner as a coherent identity, not as simply two birds (gay and straight) knocked out of the sky by one stone attempting to fuse separate heterosexual and homosexual elements into a general category. Each of these approaches to Faulkner would require their own perspectives to shape them into a meaningful overview of his writing, and an honest assessment of them would likely struggle to praise Faulkner's depictions of these identities or his thoughts about the people to whom these identities belong. Nonetheless, I hope one day to read these studies, even if their conclusions must frankly assess bigotry, misogyny, transphobia, or worse in the life and works of William Faulkner.

Second, this study is not an assessment of the major novels of the 1930s, including *Absalom, Absalom!*, *Light in August*, and *Sanctuary*, nor does it turn its focus to the bookends of the so-called matchless times of Faulkner's great creation, *The Sound and the Fury* and *Go Down, Moses*. The reason for this omission is that these works have been the focus of such extensive critical conversation that I have decided to turn a light on other works to bring into focus themes that have not yet been deeply explored, though *As I Lay Dying* and the Snopes trilogy are fundamental to understanding gay Faulkner, are key works examined in this study, and certainly belong among his major works. Also, while some scholars have sought homosexual themes in these works, especially in *Absalom, Absalom!*, that no scholar has uncovered a smoking gun of representation suggests that, while gay themes circulate in them, those themes do not manifest as coherent identities. In other works, they most certainly do. Perhaps this study will allow other scholars to reevaluate Quentin and Shreve or Henry and Bon, Gail Hightower and Joe Christmas, and maybe even Popeye through lenses less fraught with paradigms of psychosis and neurosis if not outright reliance of structuring queer desires as deviance and Faulkner as only interested in them for being grotesque or perverse.

Finally, the question at the heart of this study is not "*Was Faulkner gay?*" Despite the number of midnights I have sat by Faulkner's grave with a bottle of bourbon, looking for inspiration, he has not spoken to me from whatever cosmos all his own he now inhabits. Nor did I ever get permission to dig holes around Rowan Oak in search of Faulkner's hidden box of illicit photos or salacious letters which would have been useful in answering that question, but which are not necessary for what this study really seeks to address: *Is there a gay Faulkner?*

You will find the answer to that question on the subsequent pages. Henceforth, I must allow that this ill-formed offspring of the last ten years of my life find its own legs to stand on, that by them it may stand or fall.

Gay Faulkner

Chapter 1

"Quair" Faulkner

William Faulkner never quite fit in. Despite the odds stacked in his favor as the oldest son of an established white family in a small southern town in the first half of the twentieth century, he never could inhabit the single, easy role of insider, or "one of us," in the town that would so entirely define him. The dynamic of feeling different, of feeling like an outsider and defining himself as one in opposition to the mantle of expectation readily available for him to don, most particularly defines the life—especially the young life—of this great, established, canonical icon of American literature. This dynamic has multiple facets; among these facets is one that results from the coincidence of time and place. William Faulkner, American writer, came of age and entered the maturity of his artistic vision over a sixty-year span of history during which difference, or *queerness*, was taking on a new meaning, and a subculture was forming into which he would find himself immersed, though few scholars have examined the details of his life in such a way as to reveal that beneath the mask of his multiple performances of identity, at the heart of Faulkner's sense of self, is a narrative of gay American history. From the earliest stages of his life and in his earliest efforts at self-definition, the shadow of this history cast itself onto his self-performance and greatly influenced the direction of his life and the creative impulses that generated his early prose and poetry. It remained with him even until the final novels of his prolific career. What is so remarkable is the degree to which Faulkner did not fear this shadow. He embraced it.

This study is devoted to understanding what it means that Faulkner fashioned for himself a gay identity, among the many other performances in which he often engaged. He knew about homosexuality, he knew homosexuals, and he could perform homosexual identity in ways far more complex and personal than as homophobic reactions and displays of psychosexual angst. In his life, he crafted what I am calling an apocryphal gay identity, or an apocryphal homosexuality. This study will explore the multiple manifestations and meanings of this identity in his life and in his writing. Understanding the ways in which he apocryphized gay identity—in his own performances of difference and in the fiction and poetry he produced from his observations and experiences—sheds profound light on the William Faulkner we know and, as is often the case with apocrypha, the William Faulkner we so far do not.

William Faulkner was the firstborn son of a union between two families whose histories course like blood across even contemporary maps of north Mississippi, quite literally in the case of Falkner, Mississippi, a town north of Ripley named after Faulkner's grandfather, the "Old Colonel" William Clark Falkner, whose railroad passed through the town on its route between Middleton, Tennessee, and Pontotoc. That same Old Colonel still stands as the most prominent marble citizen of a stiller town, the cemetery in Ripley, where he gazes over his nearby railroad to the west, country just purchased from the Chickasaw Indians when he came to Mississippi as a young man in the 1840s. The Falkners cannot quite be called the most prominent settlers in the area, certainly not equal to the Jones-Thompson family and its large holdings on the Tallahatchie River in Lafayette County before the war, or the Longstreet-Lamar family, which saw local and national political prominence both before and after the war. Rather, the Falkners rose to prominence only *after* the war, benefiting from not being large landowners with the majority of their capital invested in slaves but instead businessmen and lawyers, the prototypes of industrious and opportunistic individualists who would ride the waves of the postwar southern economy to establish themselves as the ersatz inheritors of the planters whom the ravages of war and emancipation had usurped.[1] These Falkners would stretch across the landscape of north Mississippi along the rail lines to Oxford and New Albany, where though they could never be considered equal to the great robber-barons of the late nineteenth-century American landscape, they would carve for themselves at least local prominence and relative wealth in their little notch of native soil. Despite the declining postwar southern economy, William Faulkner grew up in Oxford down the street from "The Big Place," owned by his grandfather J. W. T. Falkner, the Young Colonel. If he never met the Old Colonel, he still likely knew that the Old Colonel's house had been on "Quality Ridge" in Ripley before the Old Colonel was gunned down in the streets of that town by his former business partner.[2]

More significant to the young William Faulkner's sense of place and identity may well have been the maternal line he inherited from an equally industrious family but perhaps one with less romantic appeal than the legendary Old Colonel of Faulkner's paternal line. Joel Williamson relates the story of Maud Butler Falkner's father absconding with the yearly tax revenues of Oxford in the late 1880s; Dean Faulkner Wells has confirmed that he also took with him his octoroon mistress and likely settled with her for a time somewhere in Arkansas. On the one hand, as Williamson argues, though it may never have been openly spoken of at the dinner table, young William surely knew this story and likely felt a keen stigma from it. On the other hand, the name Charles Butler—shared by Faulkner's maternal grandfather *and* great-grandfather—would not necessarily have brought shame in Oxford. His great-grandfather, Charles Butler, is memorialized in contemporary Oxford on a historical marker in front of the First Baptist Church on Van Buren Avenue, leading downhill from the Square toward the old depot.³ This Charles and his wife, Berlina, along with Lelia Swift, Maud's mother, are all buried in a family plot in St. Peter's Cemetery in Oxford in the shadow of the central grove of cedar trees surrounding the graves of the Jones-Thompson family, who gave the land for the cemetery to the town but provided the highest (and metaphorically the most important) ground in it for their posterity. The prominence of other "old" Oxford families can largely be measured by their proximity to those cedars, including the Butlers, Kings, Shegogs, and Isoms.

This same older Charles Butler is directly responsible for the actual geography of the Oxford in which his great-grandson would grow up. Charles Butler Sr. surveyed the land that is now Oxford and laid out the grid pattern that marks the streets of the original town. The younger Charles Butler was responsible for the construction and upkeep of the sidewalks and street-lamps of the town, for which he was collecting the tax dollars with which he absconded.⁴ In a completely nonmetaphorical sense, when young Billy walked around Oxford, he followed in the paths of his forefathers, his world their world, his life and its patterns preset by theirs. In a metaphorical sense, perhaps he could understand the duality of that path and the different ways his forefathers negotiated it: the Charles Butler of civic virtue, the Charles Butler who ran away.

Young William Faulkner never quite assimilated into the Victorian regularity of his hometown. Writing from New Orleans in 1925, he would claim that his youthful interest in poetry sprang from the double compulsions "firstly, for the purpose of furthering various philanderings in which I was engaged, secondly, to complete a youthful gesture I was then making, of being 'different' in a small town" (*ESPL* 237). That Faulkner was "different" seems a true enough statement, but his claim that he intentionally affected this difference is more specious. Accounts of Faulkner in his teens collected by biographers confirm that, to some degree, Faulkner performed this difference, primarily sartorially. Frederick Karl explains that Faulkner's initial interest in books probably led him to his affinity for Estelle Oldham, but Karl continues, "what must be stated and even stressed was another side of Billy, not in sexual tastes, but in the desire to pass himself off as a dandy, or certainly someone different" (70), which he pursued through "a feeling for clothes and flamboyance [as of] someone who seeks roles, even at nine and ten; who, somehow, transcends his time and place and relocates himself with Charles Baudelaire, Oscar Wilde, and others like them who acted out" (71). Given the rigidly defined world he inherited, Faulkner would likely have put on these differences precisely for the reasons Karl suggests, to get out of (to transcend) his time and place for one not so stultifying; yet the reference to Oscar Wilde, arch-homosexual of the Victorian age, and "acting out" seem like slips in Karl's rhetoric, both of which register latent implications about the insistence that the "side of Billy" that wanted to act out was not indicative of "sexual taste." Karl also ascribes to the young Faulkner agency for acting different, as if his difference was intentionally affected and not the result of the way others perceived his identity against the local standards for belonging.

Not all the roles that Faulkner would play were necessarily self-created, and one of the ubiquitous biographical anecdotes from Faulkner's youth implies something far less intentionally affected in his youthful difference. Joseph Blotner relates this revealing anecdote:

> [William] and his brother [Murray] shared a taste for comic novels, just as his mother liked the serious novelists he did and Estelle enjoyed some of the same poetry that moved him. But it would be two years before a new friendship [with Phil Stone] would provide a mind as keen as his own to supply the excitement of a sympathetic response to new literary experience. And before that would happen [. . .] his alienation would prompt some students at the Oxford High School to tease him and call him "quair." (39)

Williamson relates the same story, pausing to clarify that the colloquial spelling of the word Blotner supplies "means 'queer'" (169), in case readers tone deaf to the peculiar timbre of that word find themselves unable to decipher it. *Queer* is a strange but powerful word, one which may sound very different to individual listeners, and one whose history was undergoing much change in the period of Faulkner's adolescence. But then, what might the word *queer*, or more properly "quair," have meant to William Faulkner?

Jay Parini expands a bit on what he thinks the word "quair" might have meant when applied to Faulkner: "According to Blotner, it was about this time that his fellow students referred to him as 'quair,' *in part because of his dandyish dress and in part because he shunned the company of athletes and those students who led more active social lives*" (30, italics added). The italicized portion of Parini's assertion is his interpretation of why Faulkner might have been called queer, not Blotner's. Parini owes his interpretation largely to Frederick Karl, who does not relate the story about Faulkner being called "quair," but does repeatedly ponder the significance of what he calls Faulkner's "feminized life" (86). Regarding Faulkner's early life, Karl describes as "feminine" his artistic pursuits—drawing, writing—in a town with clear demarcations between appropriate activities for young boys and young girls. In his later life, Faulkner's own perspicuous understanding of these same gendered divisions manifests in some of his best-known stories. After all, Emily Grierson briefly trains young girls to paint china dishes but no young boys are ever sent to her house. In his psychoanalytically informed biography, Karl also suggests that Faulkner's later love of horses and keenness on male activities such as hunting and on spending time in all-male spaces such as the hunting camp stem directly from his need to compensate for the other, more "feminine" pursuits of his youth, or at least feminine in the eyes of the community in which he needed to define himself.

That what made Faulkner "quair" might be associated with his gender or sexuality is no minor point for a young man growing up in the 1910s. As Marilee Lindemann points out in her biography of another famous queer writer, Willa Cather, of whom Faulkner was a younger contemporary, the cultural "moment—from the 1890s to the 1920s," when Cather and Faulkner both experienced their "sexual and literary coming[s]-of-age" was "a period when 'queer' became a way of marking the differences between still emerging categories of 'homosexuality' and 'heterosexuality,' and the word acquired a sexual connotation it had lacked in nearly four hundred years of usage" (2). Teenage boys calling teenage Faulkner "quair" is not the same as their calling him *homosexual*, nor equivalent to our contemporary term *gay*. At that precise cultural moment when Faulkner was called "quair," the word would have been in too much a state of connotative flux to pinpoint precisely what it would have meant, though it seems unlikely it would have registered the same note as the more contemporary slight "that's so gay" does among teenagers a hundred years later. But somewhere on the periphery of its connotations, the word *queer* had already begun to acquire its homosexual associations; that we feel it strike a chord in our contemporary acoustics is not an altogether unjustified feeling.

Reference to our contemporary usage might seem out of place in a discussion of small-town gender politics in the dusty Mississippi of the 1910s, but I include it here to highlight a point about acoustics. As recent anti-bullying campaigns (and recent highly publicized teenage suicides) demonstrate, this expression in our contemporary context has a distinct but layered resonance. Whereas people use the expression almost thoughtlessly as just an acquired and general way of demeaning any number of things that they find trifling, annoying, or disgusting, to kids who already feel "different" and may even be contemplating their own developing sexual identities, these words sting and feel far more directly derogatory than the off-hand ubiquity of their use is purportedly meant to imply. Though separated by time, the label "quair" and our contemporary expression "that's so gay" bear similarities in the degree to which someone already sensitive to their sexual identity in relation to their peers may hear such language much more acutely than most people would. We can understand the import of the term by way of a syllogism: If Faulkner had any nascent or latent homosexual desires, and since the word "queer" was gaining a homosexual connotation during this period, then it follows that Faulkner would hear the term as a derogatory statement about his perceived (homo)sexuality. In this regard, the experience of contemporary teenagers facing antigay bullying may serve as a germane model to understand how "quair" might have sounded to Faulkner and the reaction he might have had to it.

Parini is the only one of Faulkner's major biographers willing to posit that "[i]t is not outlandish to suppose that Faulkner himself had homosexual feelings at this time" (31). He explains as his basis for this supposition that homoerotic interests are not uncommon in adolescent boys. Though Faulkner by the latter half of the 1910s was no longer an adolescent (had he been born in 1997, not 1897, by the 2010s, a teenage Faulkner would have had access to a growing genre of LGBTQ-themed young adult, not adolescent, literature) his particular consciousness, noted for its profound depth, could certainly have stored away those nascent feelings and been able to access them for roles he would play in his later life. Of course, there is something outmoded in the notion that many boys have childish homoerotic feelings but, naturally, grow out of them, for we now generally acknowledge that homosexuality is not simply an experimental stage of childhood development that disappears with maturity. Such reasoning follows in the path of Freud and other late nineteenth- and early twentieth-century psychological theorists or their intellectual descendants in the 1940s and 1950s, including Alfred Kinsey. In the early 1970s, the psychiatric community began a long and still evolving process of revising this basic maturation pattern to a more realistic understanding of sexual identity. By the early 2000s, the condescending dismissal of homosexual desire as "just a phase" has been replaced by reminders that "I can't change, even if I try," to borrow from Mary Lambert, and "Baby, you were born this way," to borrow from the indomitable Lady Gaga. We should read even a relatively recent biographer such as Parini with a more open mind than some of his rhetoric would seem to allow about homosexual development and the maturation of natural or normal sexual desires. One does not grow out of homosexual desire as one grows out of old clothes. Nonetheless, Parini stands alone in making so bold a pronouncement about Faulkner's youthful identity, and there is little reason to believe Faulkner threw off this queerness just because he happened to grow up. Faulkner seems to have nurtured this identity, primarily in response to an event that would crystalize his developing sense of place and expectations: the marriage of Estelle Oldham, the girl who was supposed to be his promised bride.

Two Roads Diverged

The square regularity of the streets of Oxford bears metaphorical connection to the Victorian order pervasive in the South in which Faulkner grew up. Daniel J. Signal traces the influence of this Victorian order on Faulkner's generation that was coming of age in the dawn of the Modernist period, and he singles out the South from the rest of the country for the distinctive way in which its Victorianism "was certainly not riddled with morbid introspection" (5) but rather linked proper values to the attainment of rewards for industry and labor via clear and direct lines. Though Signal does not light directly upon what this worldview means for queer sexuality, he nonetheless outlines in broad terms the trajectory (and rewards for proper performance) that a boy such as William Faulkner was implicitly meant to travel to his maturation and societal fulfillment as a "man" with certain rights, privileges, and familial obligations. Joel Williamson asserts that "[i]n regard to gender roles" this Victorian order "was exceedingly clear" for young Faulkner as for all his peers "born into a Southern world that had a vision of itself as an organic society with a place for everyone and everyone, hopefully, in his or her place" (365). Faulkner's dandy dress and interests in arts put him at odds with this vision and resulted in his being labeled "quair" as a teenager, though as Williamson's use of the word "hopefully" implies, this vision that southern society had of itself was a vision—a normative vision—which not everyone managed to attain. Still, that Faulkner was a "quair" youth does not mean his attainment of a southern/Victorian ideal was hopeless. Youth, in this vision, could serve as protection against the full force of the word "queer," ameliorating it into a colloquial form with, surely, its own peculiar sting but also its own exceptions. So long as the young Faulkner would someday put away his childish things and mature to manhood, his "quair-ness" could be written off as the idylls of youth, which would allow its presence in the community to remain unthreatening.

To put a metaphorical spin on it, we might say that Faulkner was given to cutting across yards and through alleyways, tracing crooked pathways off the grid of the streets his great-grandfather surveyed, but the streets remained intact, and the owner of a violated garden or jumped fence could take consolation in knowing that one day the young man would understand the value of the plan the community had laid for itself; one day the young man would learn to stay on the sidewalk and walk along the preordained streets. Joel Williamson succinctly describes the plan Faulkner's life was *meant* to take (*meant* in the sense that convention, not necessarily any personal desire, dictated it) as following a preset "progression of love, marriage, and sex; family, clan, and community" (365). Of these steps, marriage is the most crucial because, if not the initial step, it is the most legally, morally, and communally binding. As for the initial step, love, Faulkner was safe being "quair" as a teenager because he had Estelle Oldham, the girl from down the street whom he supposedly wanted to marry, safeguarding his place in the social milieu of Oxford regardless of his being a little different from everyone else.

Williamson narrates the prescribed premarital progression in the southern/Victorian community:

> In the Victorian mind, God had so arranged the world that there was one certain woman ideally created for every man and one man for every woman. When they found one another they would recognize their destiny instantly and intuitively. There would be a sequence—rituals of recognition, love, courtship, engagement,

and marriage. Before marriage the woman would be a virgin. After marriage
would come sex and then children. (365)

The extent to which this progression describes any actual courtship is suspect, but it is not meant to describe the real. It describes an ideal, which, when
imposed upon members of a community as what they are *supposed* to obtain,
becomes the normative goal of those members, in this case the outline of heteronormativity. Following this path—or at least appearing to follow it—makes one
belong to the community and makes one incapable of ever truly being "queer."
What might actually happen in the privacy of the heteronormative bedroom
or, more broadly, within the confines of those discreetly squared-off lots filling
the gaps between the surveyed streets may be very queer indeed, but it does not
register as such so long as the porch is swept and Sunday service attended, the
right political affiliations maintained and the servants paid in a timely manner.

Estelle's presence has long been the grace allowed to Faulkner's early life to fit
it into a heteronormative telling, perhaps in his own time and certainly from the
vantage point of our own, but the truth behind this fated courtship is less solid
than it superficially appears. Though Estelle's picture appeared in the *Ole Miss*,
the student annual for the University of Mississippi, as a sponsor for Cornell
Franklin as early as 1913, Faulkner supposedly still pursued her as if they were
fated to be together and had long understood their mutual destiny (Blotner 41).
In interviews shortly after Faulkner's death, Estelle seems to have offered proof
that she felt the same. By these accounts, a seven-year-old Estelle once declared
of a boy, who happened to be William Faulkner, riding by her house on a pony
that "I'm going to marry him when I grow up" (17). Biographers starting with
Blotner use this story to demonstrate how fated both Estelle and Faulkner felt
their marriage was, even as that sense of fate weathered the eleven years between
Estelle's marriage to Franklin and her eventual union with Faulkner in 1929.
Williamson, though, ventures that "[l]ater evidence suggests that Estelle might
have said the same about several boys" (149). In her biography of Estelle, *Faulkner
and Love*, Judith Sensibar describes an interview shortly before Estelle's death in
1972 where she claimed that she fell in love with Faulkner when she was sixteen,
an age which coincides with her leaving for boarding school in Virginia. Though
inconsistent, these narratives of fated love come to approximate the image of
the idealized love these two children of Oxford were supposed to have for each
other in the sexual economy of their hometown. It is, however, unlikely that the
course of their love—or any love, for that matter—ran as smoothly as Estelle's
hindsight remembered it. What Faulkner and Estelle understood as "love" for
each other must be viewed in its proper context as a revision of the course their
love did, in fact, run. With such stories, we come to view the eleven-year lapse in
their relationship while Estelle married and had two children with another man
as essentially a waiting period without any challenge to the ultimate narrative of

their clearly defined, heterosexual identities and union. Faulkner's "quair" pursuits are excusable in this version of his youth so long as his ultimate desire resided in the right object of sexual attraction even as he rummaged off the sidewalks and trampled across yards.

A perfect example of the cover Estelle offers Faulkner are stories from the dances they often attended together when they were teenagers first entering their local sexual economy, the dances being the rehearsals for proper gender relations and the discipline of courtship, though in the case of Estelle and Faulkner, apparently, sometime after the "recognition" phase of their storied romance. Though Estelle danced with many boys and young William either refused to dance at all or danced very poorly when he did feel compelled to try, Estelle nonetheless made time to "sit and talk with him. They had an 'understanding,' she later said" (Williamson 174). This minimal degree of attention seems to have allowed for tremendous maneuvering on Faulkner's part, and that any biographer cites it at all implies a general acknowledgment that Faulkner's fundamental desires were heterosexual, even if he was not (or perhaps amplified by the assurance that he was not) a very good dancer. Of course, we can just as easily read these interactions as a mark of friendship as we can assume that they say anything at all about the feelings of two young love-birds with a sense that one day they would marry and all would be right with the world. After all, if other teenage boys at these dances simply took the time to talk with Faulkner on the sidelines of the dance floor, few scholars would read so heavily into *their* intentions as to assume it must mean that they were secret lovers with an "understanding" of their own. The interactions between Faulkner and Estelle seem perfectly plausible in a narrative of their devotion to each other that searches for patterns in the glance of hindsight, and may well have served in the moment to pass Faulkner off as excusably "quair." However, they do not offer any conclusive proof of the full range of Faulkner's nascent selfhood nor do they preclude further development of his "quair-ness" into something less excusable in his community.

Nonetheless, in the sexual order of Oxford, Faulkner could pursue Estelle through the rose-tinted glasses of a courtier, and her later accounts of these years mostly verify our assumptions that they long felt connected to each other, despite her decision to marry Franklin when pressed to do so by her parents. Before that other marriage and the damage that it did to Faulkner's prescribed path in life, whatever less-than-linear "quair" pursuits he might entertain would be rounded off so long as he arrived at that appropriate marriage with the perception of the appropriate courtship intact. Estelle's accounts serve the purpose of excusing all the misdirections along the way, and can easily be construed to mean that Faulkner, as far back as the 1910s, was a heterosexual, even if he was a bit different at times, since clearly, later in his life, he married a woman and had a child (and had affairs with Meta Carpenter, Joan Williams, and Else Jonsson).

With Estelle, Faulkner could only be "quair," never "queer." Perhaps he still can only be "quair" to this day in the eyes of most scholars and biographers because of the well-crafted narrative of his fated heterosexual life. The community could (and still can) overlook his youthful difference thanks to Estelle's presence, even if that presence was far more tacit and complex than most biographical accounts assume.

Into this picture of his youth, two influences hover that would later have profound effects on Faulkner's life. First, he befriended Phil Stone. Scholars often question Stone's possible homosexuality, questions I do not find intriguing both for lack of evidence and because trying to find evidence that Stone was gay can easily overshadow inquiries into the numerous other openly gay men with whom Faulkner found friendship, mentorship, and even, perhaps, intimacy. What Stone did irrefutably provide Faulkner was reading material not found in the local library. Stone plied Faulkner with the latest poetry in the most avant-garde literary magazines and provided him with the great French symbolists and imagists. His reading list for Faulkner included Mallarme and Pound, among many others, and it is likely that Faulkner's exposure to Eliot and Aiken originated with Stone as well.[5] Also, though Stone may not have introduced Faulkner to Swinburne, they shared an affinity for his poetry. Several of these shared authors would detail queer sexual practices in their works, especially Mallarme, Swinburne, and Aiken. Those queer practices would include various nonnormative sexual desires, among them lesbianism and male homosexuality. The young Faulkner would read these works and later experiment with their themes in his early poetry after Estelle's marriage to Cornell Franklin.

The other influence of this period would be a less thematic one: the flesh and blood example of the gay writer Stark Young, another Oxonian who preceded Faulkner by not quite a generation.[6] Faulkner met Young through Phil Stone sometime in 1914 when Young returned to Oxford for a visit. In 1914, Young was teaching in Texas, though he would soon move on to Amherst College and, by 1921, would be living in New York in Greenwich Village. According to Parini, Young "was as openly homosexual as one could be in those days," and his "urbane manner [. . .] attracted Faulkner, who found the bluff, swaggering models for male behavior on display around him rather stifling" (31). I would pause here to consider the double-sidedness of Faulkner's feeling of being different during this period in relation to Young's "difference." Faulkner affected his own difference—or made his own "youthful gesture" toward it—and his appreciation for Young surely stemmed from a shared sense of difference in their small town for reasons of literary interests and less-provincial worldviews. However, Faulkner was called "quair" and here was a man who was openly "queer." Thus, their affinity for each other, while little evidence suggests it was physical, cannot be reduced to a purely intellectual appreciation (in fact, Young's taste for the poetry of Gabriel D'Annunzio did not accord with Faulkner's poetic taste at all).[7] Parini describes the appeal Young held for Faulkner as, "Young, like [Phil] Stone, represented an alternative way of being in the world that included literate conversation and a love of books" (31). Of course, what rises to the surface of expressions such as "alternative way of being" is not just the interest in art and literature that made one "quair" but the additional implications of homosexuality attendant to that interest in the gendered world in which these men came of age and encountered each other. Young's presence highlights the fine line at this moment in American cultural history between being queer and being *queer*, or between being just "different" and being homosexual. Faulkner's friendship with Young and sense of mutual difference blurs the contours of these connotations.

To understand Young's homosexual identity, we can turn to his contemporary from Greenville, Mississippi, William Alexander Percy. Percy was born in 1885, Young in 1881.[8] The short gap between these two men and Faulkner's generation was one of quick change and lasting implications. In his biography of Percy, Benjamin E. Wise explores the complex and changing codes of gay identification in the latter nineteenth century, with obvious direct relation to the northern and western edges of Mississippi that Faulkner and Young also inhabited. Wise traces a long history of same-sex intimacy in Greenville, beginning not with William Alexander but with his uncle, William Armstrong Percy, yet another short generation further back in the chronology of emerging gay identity when the practice of living as and self-identifying as "queer" met the psychological theorizing of the Foucauldian "species" of the late-Victorian mind. Faced with the various tragedies of his generation of the Percy family, "William Armstrong took comfort in a romantic friendship with a neighbor, Henry Waring Ball," Wise writes (25). Though William Armstrong did not keep a diary of this friendship, Ball did. In that diary, Ball charts a string of such friendships: "Will Percy was my first love, my original Damon and Pythias. There has been a long line of them since—Will Percy, Will Mays, Sam Bull, Will Van Dresser, Tony Russell, and now Eugene" (qtd. in Wise 25). Wise is quick to clarify that the numerous relationships Ball recounts occurred from the 1870s to the 1890s, at a time when "homosexuality was not yet conceived as an identity, an either/ or sexual preference, [and] men were free to share romantic love without the stigma of *being* homosexual" (25). Therefore, the expression "romantic friendship" became a way to express numerous relationships that hovered in the gray areas of non-definition, some physically sexual, others not, all possibly homosexual, but only possibly and so safely assumed to be something else possibly, too. William Alexander Percy would not have such freedom. By the time of his young adulthood in the first decade of the twentieth century, terms such as "effeminate" and "sissy" had become less ambiguous as markers of difference, and the cover of societal ignorance no longer protected young men from accusations, even if the term "homosexual" was not the preferred way to identify "the love that dare not speak its name" (Wise 7). Wise is emphatic to assert throughout his biography that Percy negotiated his identity against a paradigm we can now identify as "gay," and he argues that Percy's negotiations, and those of others from his generation, are the source for our contemporary understanding of this identity in the latter half of the twentieth century and now into the early years of the twenty-first. He means to assert that men like Percy (and Young), men of the generation prior to Faulkner's, are the originators of the performance of gay identity with which subsequent generations would contend and that they would emulate.

The two William Percys, Armstrong and Alexander, are not merely convenient examples of a moment in gay history somewhat tangential to Faulkner's life. Ben Wasson, a friend of Faulkner's born in Greenville in 1900 and himself gay, knew William Alexander Percy and even introduced Faulkner to him. Faulkner read Percy's poetry and reviewed it in the University of Mississippi campus newspaper, *The Mississippian*. Faulkner would not meet Percy (or read his poetry) until long after establishing a relationship with Stark Young, but the themes of Percy's work and the pattern of Percy's life mirror Young's. Young was also a pioneer negotiating his sexual identity in a time when what we now clearly recognize as homosexual was a less-well-formed system of signs and was not as discreetly coherent a self-performance. However, Young, along with Percy, would be the type of influence to *set* the paradigm. Faulkner, younger than Percy and Young, would observed that paradigm as if it were an established mode of being, a category of person—homosexual—with a history and a sense of community antecedent to Faulkner's life and therefore seemingly part of an indefinitely older pattern that had always existed, even if that community and members of it would also seem to be always elsewhere, as a kind of oppositional identity in relation to the expectations of small-town southern life. Unlike Percy, who traveled often to Europe but also, according to Wise, felt a strong connection to his home in Greenville, Young left Oxford rarely to return after he graduated from the University of Mississippi. When Young was home, though, he would spend time with Stone and Faulkner. Young's influence on the young man sixteen years his junior would prove significant.

When Faulkner met Young, he was crafting his own sense of difference through literature and clothing. For Young, his actual homosexuality exacerbated his difference from the realm of accusation to that of practice. That Young embraced his homosexuality put him at considerable odds with the life patterns that Oxonians envisioned themselves pursuing. Karl explains of Young, "As a homosexual in a small town, he was obviously under restraints" (80). What those restraints might have been, Karl, in impressive understatement, does not detail; but if we envision, say, the out gay lifestyle described by George Chauncey in *Gay New York* and consider that Young eventually moved to Greenwich Village, we can begin to see an outline for visible gay life in the early twentieth century, at least in certain social spaces. As Chauncey explores, such social conventions as gay bathhouse culture, cruising, and a range of vocabulary for the varieties of homosexually inclined men that circulated in the Village (wolves, trade, etc.) created a communal atmosphere for men to act out their desires there, with at times crackdowns by the authorities but nonetheless with a general sense of freedom that openly soliciting sex from a stranger would not result in immediate imprisonment. Faulkner, who spent many of his visits to New York throughout his life in Greenwich Village, would eventually write in 1957 that the Village is "a place with a few unimportant boundaries but no limitations where people of any age go to seek dreams" (*T* 652). He would amend this description in 1959 to "[a] place without *physical* boundaries," as if suggesting that the freedom found there was not merely emotional or psychological but "physical" as well (*M* 814, italics added). In the smoldering aftermath of Estelle's marriage, Faulkner would make his first trip to Greenwich Village to room briefly with Stark Young. The boundless sexual freedoms there stand in marked contrast to the stifling fixity of sexual mores in the Oxford of Faulkner's youth.

Still, prior to Estelle's marriage, Faulkner had at least a chance of falling into the inertia of the set patterns of an expected, normative life. Young, on the other hand, would not find a place for himself on the square streets of his hometown. Rather, he would move beyond those streets, into a road something like the one that leads Joe Christmas onward for fifteen years in *Light in August*, not in that Young led a life of poverty and violence similar to Christmas's but rather in that he lived a life beyond the Victorian heteronormativity of his hometown and, by extension, opposed to it. I would underestimate the remarkable diversity of southern gay life to assert that for "queer" southerners, they have two options: stop being queer (physically and psychologically) in order to stay in the South or leave the South in order to be queer. But, *in extremis* and under the right set of circumstances, these two paths may present themselves as the only available options. Stark Young seems to have felt enough of a sense of difference for his homosexuality to want a different space to pursue his life. Faulkner, at least until 1918, did not seem to feel so moved.

As just the local "quair," such extremes seem a stretch for Faulkner as he ended his teen years and moved into his early twenties. He had Estelle, or could at least believe he had her (or at least we can believe that he believed as much). He had a friend in Phil Stone, plying him with reading material. He had met, so far mostly in passing, a young man who would come to exert tremendous influence on him, Ben Wasson, but his influence would mainly manifest after Estelle's marriage. Nothing in this earlier moment of Faulkner's life lends itself to an extreme worldview beyond the typical youthful ennui of small-town life, southern or otherwise. But it is also important to note that, with the right catalyst, the course maintained by tacit inertia can easily be swayed. In his teens, Faulkner had before him two paths: the path of the queer, represented by Young and his decision to live beyond the confines of Oxford, or the path of expectation and marriage within those confines, as represented by the supposedly fated sense of commitment to Estelle. It seems clear that Faulkner wanted to choose the latter and marry Estelle, but when she asked him to elope with her, he refused because he would not marry her without first asking the permission of her father.

Philip Weinstein marks this refusal as a—if not *the*—seminal experience in Faulkner's young life. Working in Honolulu, Cornell Franklin found himself employed and established and ready for a wife. He wrote to his mother in December 1917 that he wanted to marry Estelle when he returned to Mississippi the following April. His parents and her parents agreed that this was a good match. Thus, Estelle found herself engaged to Franklin, a circumstance that left her, according to Weinstein, "both unsurprised and dumbfounded," but also "[d] esperate" (67). Weinstein continues,

> [S]he turned to Faulkner for a way out, but he felt as hemmed in as she did. It had taken him, also, a lifetime of becoming who he was to find himself in this trap. The trap of who he was: a brooding poet yet to publish poems, a young man without a high school diploma, a frustrated cashier in his grandfather's bank, someone easily identifiable as one of the town's aimless and heavy-drinking youths; in short, a bad bet. He had no prospects, no counter-argument to propose. What he wanted most was getting ready to happen—not despite who they were but because of who they were. She could not bear it. "I supposed I *am* engaged to Cornell now," she told him, "but I'm ready to elope with you." "No," he answered, "we'll have to get your father's consent." (67)

Here was the moment when Faulkner could have married Estelle and did not. Other biographers focus more intently on the day of Estelle's actual marriage to Cornell Franklin, 18 April 1918, as the climax of this rupture in Faulkner's prescribed trajectory through the expectations of his community, but by 18 April, Faulkner was already in New Haven with Phil Stone, trying to avoid, it seems, facing the reality of losing his ideal of Estelle as his destined wife. This avoidance included watching men return to the campus from service in the war.

Of course, while various biographers focus on various moments, they also unanimously concede that the several months surrounding this wedding are, generally, the critical junction in Faulkner's life. Still, Weinstein's pausing to consider Faulkner's rejection of the offer of elopement draws into relief that Faulkner did not just want to marry Estelle; he wanted to marry her in a certain way that followed a preset series of rituals (and possibly because those rituals gave him an easy way to avoid saying yes outright). When the moment to marry her presented itself, he held to those rituals at the expense of his would-be bride.

She married another man. Faulkner was left as just the town "quair," so he left town as seemingly the best and only path available to him.

Estelle's marriage to Cornell Franklin ruptured the progression of Faulkner's life. He was a dandy and an artist, he wrote poems and drew pictures. His classmates called him "quair," but that did not matter because he had Estelle to pursue, a proper path awaiting him. Then that path was foreclosed. His other option was also something of a given: he would follow the example set by Stark Young, the other queer, and step out onto the open road. It was a road that would last eleven years.

Chapter 2

Queer Faulkner

In the spring of 1918, Faulkner left Oxford for New Haven, Connecticut, where he shared a room with Phil Stone, who was completing a degree at Yale. While there, he hatched a plan with Stone to join the British Royal Flying Corps and eventually moved to Canada to begin flight training. The war ended before he completed this training, and in December 1918 Faulkner returned to Oxford; but notably this Oxford did not have Estelle. From 1918 to 1929, Faulkner would leave and return to Oxford in a series of attempts to find a place for himself beyond his hometown. At the same time, he often found himself in his hometown, as a student at the University of Mississippi, originally, then as something of the town bum called "Count No 'Count." The basic arc of his life for these eleven years is outlined in numerous biographical studies: Oxford, New York, Oxford, New Orleans, Europe, New Orleans, Oxford. Estelle also made regular trips home to Oxford in a trajectory that mapped the deteriorating path of her marriage. Faulkner would often be in Oxford for Estelle's visits, but Judith Sensibar cautions that, at least for the first five to six years of that marriage, Faulkner would not necessarily have had his eye on his own eventual courtship of her. Rather, he courted Helen Baird in New Orleans in the mid-1920s, even devoting a novel and a collection of poems to her. He may have engaged in other "courtships" during this period as well.

When Faulkner got off the train from Canada in 1918, he returned a changed man in that he had begun to fashion for himself a series of new identities. As James G. Watson details, Faulkner played the part of the wounded soldier, despite having neither fought in the actual war nor been injured in it or even in his training. This performance, though important in his life, was not his only guise. In *The Origins of Faulkner's Art*, Judith Sensibar details another mask that he often wore, that of the poseur, or the Pierrot figure of the impostor, a literary trope with which he was fascinated. A more prosaic way of expressing this identity, following Williamson, would be that Faulkner took on the pose of a would-be bohemian after his return from the war. He wore old, ragged clothes and affected a detached attitude; he wrote adaptations of the imagist and symbolist poets he so deeply admired; and he experimented with pen-and-ink drawings clearly inspired by Audrey Beardsley. To an extent, he modeled his notion of the bohemian on decadent and other fin de siècle luminaries such as Oscar Wilde, whose "art for art's sake" commitment to aesthetic pleasure greatly influenced Faulkner as he made his first forays into being an "artist," the bridging identity that links these other manifestations of Faulkner's developing sense of self.

Faulkner's performances all deserve the critical attention that has been paid to them. In particular, his performance of the wounded soldier, and how that performance would work its way into his fiction, bears great relevance to this study and its search for gay themes in Faulkner's writing, but to understand the deeper implications of that performance, we first need to consider another performance that so far has not received the critical attention it deserves but is also at the heart of this nexus of identities that Faulkner appropriated in the wake of World War I. Taken as a whole, Faulkner's various performances speak to the degree to which he wanted to set himself apart from his hometown; he wanted to be different. One way in which he did this was through a performance of an emerging "queer" identity that extends from his earlier "quair" designation. Beginning in 1918, Faulkner began to pose as a homosexual.

Faulkner was, apparently, keenly aware of the cultural value of the various roles he played and how, at that moment in history, the signs of these other performances also bled into a "queer" identity that was coming into focus as a discernible "gay" identity. We know that Faulkner embraced this identity because of the multiple times he placed himself directly into the milieu of gay subcultures and surrounded himself with gay men. We also know that he embraced this identity because of the way that he treated it in his writing. When Faulkner returned to Oxford in 1918, he returned not as the youth with a degree of freedom allowed him until he embraced expectations but as the queer man who had failed to follow the natural progression of life via the Victorian pathways recognizable to his hometown. His reaction to his new role in town was to enroll in the university, write queer poems and stories, and befriend—in fact court—a young man he met before the war, Ben Wasson.

Ben Wasson, who would prove to be one of Faulkner's few lifelong friends, was a homosexual, though he was not the only homosexual on the campus at Ole Miss in the late 1910s. He was simply the one whom Faulkner chose to court. We could almost intuit that in a social space such as a university that attracted young men and women from all over the state and the South, we would find a greater diversity of people in the student population than the local town population (though at Ole Miss, that population would not include any racial diversity until 1962). That greater diversity would seem, we might hope, to allow that homosexuality surfaced on the campus. Unfortunately, intuition fails in this matter, thanks largely to the degree to which homosexuality was, as Eve Sedgwick terms it, an "open secret," but it was perhaps still more secret than open. What was generally known on campus then has largely disappeared

over the gap of time as memory has consolidated into the erasures of hindsight. Nonetheless, proof for such an intuition does exist. It comes from a series
of letters that Joseph Blotner received from an Ole Miss alumnus named Paul
Rogers, a contemporary of Faulkner's and Wasson's from their undergraduate days. Rogers took it upon himself to write Blotner after the publication of
his original two-volume authorized biography of the late William Faulkner. As
Blotner was composing his revisions for his one-volume edition of the biography in early 1980, he exchanged letters with Rogers, who insisted that, despite
the evidence of Faulkner's publishing lesbian-themed homoerotic poems in *The
Mississippian* in 1919, homosexuality was neither known nor discussed on campus. He also insisted repeatedly in his letters that Wasson was not gay, though
Rogers also claimed that he never knew Wasson intimately. However, what
Rogers claims that no one knew sketches in outline what seems to have been
well known on the Ole Miss campus at the time: the open secret of homosexuality. At numerous points in his letters, Rogers's denials function as a kind of
backhanded admission, as if his rhetorical gestures are escaping his control to
occlude in his version of early 1920s undergraduate life the actual state of affairs
at the university.

The first letter in this series relevant to campus homosexuality arrived from
Rogers in April 1980. In it, Rogers constructed an imagined campus innocence
as he ruminated nostalgically,

> The University of Mississippi is the one place where I have lived as an adult that
> homosexuality was a theme of no interests to the students. In fact, I never heard
> that word during the four years I was there. There was another, but so seldom
> heard that it is fair to say that the matter was almost never discussed. I wish it
> were that way now.[1]

First, "it" is not that way now, and we might question to what extent to which it
was "that way" then. Second, that Rogers offers this information about homosexuality at all implies a degree of anxiety that suggests a closeting of what was,
perhaps, more well known than Rogers wants to remember. Thus, his letter
reads like a kind of revisionist nostalgia, a purifying attempt to make his memories of Oxford great again.

To Blotner's credit, he did not buy Rogers's version of events. In his reply
from May 1980, he gently pushed back by addressing Wasson's homosexuality
more explicitly than he ever allowed himself to address it in published form in
either of his two biographies. To Rogers's denials, Blotner replied:

> A propos of "Sapphics" and homosexuality being a theme of no interest to the
> students at Ole Miss, do you think they were naive about it, or would the conven-
> tional gentlemanly code have precluded such attention to it? A couple of recent

books have tried to assess WF's sexuality, along predictable and, I think, somewhat unlikely lines. I do remember, though a Charlottesville doctor, a member of the Farmington Hunt, asked me about it obliquely, because of his own orientation, I think. I don't know if you knew Ben Wasson. It has been suggested to me that Ben was homosexual. Do you recall how he was regarded on the campus. One man said as a boy he was beautiful, angelic, taken up by older students and perhaps spoiled by them.[2]

Rogers responded in June to deny that Wasson was a homosexual, while simultaneously denying that he knew Wasson very well except by reputation for his striking features. In his efforts to defend the reputation of his alma mater, however, Rogers produced one of the most striking statements of the letter exchange: that Faulkner, not Wasson, was more "sophisticated" in regard to gay life. Rogers wrote, "I would suspect now that WF [William Faulkner] himself was more sophisticated about homosexuality than any student at Ole Miss, if only because of his numerous trips to Memphis and his acquaintance with the Victorians."[3] With this statement, Rogers effectively placed homosexuality in close proximity to Ole Miss—in this case in nearby Memphis, Tennessee—but only by way of reiterating the basic premise of the myth of homosexuality: that it is urban (Memphis) in relation to the rural (Oxford). Rogers, also, firmly placed Faulkner into this myth. Faulkner did, in fact, travel to Memphis often in the early 1920s with Phil Stone. The "Victorians" in Rogers's letter probably refers to Swinburne and other poets whom Faulkner imitated in his early published poems in the campus newspaper. Finally, to justify his nostalgia, Rogers effectively constructed another myth about homosexuality: it comes from elsewhere or is somehow a foreign infection, such as one that a soldier might be exposed to when he goes off to war and returns, bringing the infection with him.

Most striking in Rogers's letters is his dichotomy of urban and rural. The rural, including the pristine Ole Miss campus, inevitably transforms in these letters into the only place in Rogers's adult life not infected with the viral homosexuality apparently so rampant in the rest of society. Elsewhere, Rogers would go so far as to provide, "In 1925, I was a graduate at Cornell University. This was the time, and almost the very year, in which homosexuality burst, so to speak, upon the country and became a subject of open interest and conversation."[4] His sense of the timing is considerably off, historically speaking, as is, again, his geography, but his nostalgia in these passages is tied to a larger myth of gay life.[5] The proximity of Cornell to the cityscape of New York would make it, mythically at least, more susceptible to the gay influences found therein. Meanwhile, Mississippi could never harbor native homosexuality, or so the myth goes, at least not until it has had the insidious opportunity to spread itself slowly southward. This myth of isolation, best epitomized in John Howard's study *Men Like That*, traces gay history as a history of urban spaces, originally New York,

San Francisco, and Los Angeles, that over time extends to the hinterlands of Memphis, New Orleans, Atlanta, and even Birmingham. Howard implicates gay historians as complicit in upholding this historical pattern that gay life means urban life: as he says, "Where many are gathered, there is the historian" (12). He means to imply that where homosexuals live in less robust and discernibly coherent communities, historians often disregard that they exist at all, or, put more plainly, where few are visible, historians fear to tread. This pattern leads to a perpetuation of a variety of myths of rural gay life, including themes of isolation, suicide, and self-loathing, as if the lack of a gay community in small towns, particularly in Mississippi, the focal site of Howard's study, self-eradicates any gay presence that might rear its head therein.

At another point, Rogers claimed that the word "homosexual" had no currency at Ole Miss during the early 1920s. He instead supplied the expression more common on campus:

> But one thing is certain, the subject of homosexuality was not [a]t that time of much concern, as it is now and has been for the last fifty years. In fact, at the university there was only one word for it (indicated by the two letters C & S), and the male student's pundonor, or point of honor, was phrased as follows, "If one ever approaches you, sock him."[6]

If homosexuality was not of much concern, then why were the boys on campus trading a phrase to remind each other to defend their honor with their fists if they were ever confronted with it? Despite Rogers's attempts to other homosexuals into a different species from the rest of the undergrads with the derisive "If *one* ever approaches you," clearly the students had to know *a priori* to "one approaching you" that "one *might* approach you," and "you" better know what "one" is before "one" does. Also, to call gay men "Cock Suckers" (the letters C & S) instead of "homosexuals" hardly makes them disappear. But then, even Rogers could not fully reconcile the myth to the reality. While wishing in his earlier letter that it "were that way now," he admitted that "the matter was *almost* never discussed" back then before claiming that it exploded into the national consciousness in 1925 while he was a student at Cornell. "Almost never discussed" is quite different from saying "never discussed"; furthermore, things exist in the world that are never discussed, which does not mean that they do not exist. Finally, as I will discuss in more detail in chapter 6, the word *queer* had acquired its homosexual connotations as early as 1915; the *Oxford English Dictionary* credits this earlier date as when those connotations had so saturated uses of the word as to be worth recording as part of its definition.

In these small ways, Rogers's letters give away clues to the open secret of homosexuality on campus and Faulkner's proximity to it, but Ben Wasson's memoir better serves as the source for why other students thought Faulkner was more "sophisticated" about matters of homosexuality than most fellow students would/should be. Read with Rogers's comments in mind, Wasson's memoir outlines what looks a lot like his courtship by William Faulkner, a courtship that certainly would seem to have been noticed by the other students milling about on the grounds of campus as these two young men read poems to each other in the plush grass in the historic Grove or wandered off into the woods north of campus together.

As Blotner and Rogers exchanged their letters in 1980, Wasson was composing his memoir, which he would finish as a rough and unedited draft just before his death on 10 May 1982. Wasson first met Faulkner before the war, though only briefly, in that period which Rogers insisted was free of homosexuality on campus. In his memoir, Wasson particularly revised his account of first meeting Faulkner. This first meeting set the stage for the friendship that followed. Close inspection of this first meeting is useful because we have two versions of it, which, read together and through an appropriate frame of reference, demonstrate the keen level of sophistication in Wasson's own rhetoric about homosexuality in that distant past. Wasson described this first meeting in two places: first in an essay that he wrote for the *Delta Democrat-Times* in Greenville, Mississippi, on 15 July 1962, in the days following Faulkner's death, and later, right before his own death, in his memoir *Count No 'Count: Flashbacks to Faulkner*, published posthumously in 1983. As with Estelle's accounts of her first seeing Faulkner and falling instantly in love, Wasson's accounts have the advantage of hindsight to fortify them in a larger narrative of his and Faulkner's relationship. As with Estelle, Wasson also seems determined to reconstruct a narrative of shared understanding and, possibly, love. Wasson, however, admits in his memoir that he is telling stories based in truth but that are not necessarily perfectly accurate. He seems as well to have preferred to adhere to his own "gentlemanly code," which participates in a long history of such coded language in memoirs, letters, and other documents that recount gay life. Despite revisionist histories and cultural predilections for silence, the love that dares not speak its name has long found ways to express itself.

Writing about the history and structure of gay memoirs, Bertram J. Cohler explains that "[h]istorical and social change enters into the individual life story but in somewhat different ways for life-writers of different generations" (13). We can couple this general assessment with his other observation: "Being part of [a] hidden world," as gay men were until very recently,

> gave [these] men an identity counter to that of the larger social world order. [. . .]
> Gay men tell about these experiences in coded narratives, which [. . .] are often
> told or written as a kind of confession. Writing about these experiences provides a
> way of remembering and making sense of the past and helps these men overcome
> feelings of shame. (12)

Though Cohler's study focuses on memoirs written by gay men born after 1930, his assessment of the form of these memoirs seems to hold true for earlier periods, at least for the first decades of the twentieth century when gay men would have had some sense of identity and community forming in the world around them different from the sense of identity in the mid-nineteenth century or before. For Wasson's memoir, the "feelings of shame" in conflict with his sense of making a "confession" might explain the lack of an explicit declaration about his sexuality or saying openly what he and Faulkner might have done together. Also, Wasson wrote his memoir at the end of his life, nearly sixty years after the events on campus that he describes in its pages, so in addition to "feelings of shame," the lingering "gentlemanly codes" of campus from that earlier moment may explain Wasson's lingering reticence, even though he wrote at a much later date when gay men were experiencing a modest degree of openness and cultural acceptance relative to their previous decades of pariah-status. However, sodomy was still criminalized in the early 1980s and would remain so emphatically until 2003, and Mississippi is one of several states that have kept antisodomy laws on the books to this day despite the Supreme Court ruling them unconstitutional in *Lawrence v. Texas*. Outing himself explicitly in the early 1980s may not have felt wise for Wasson as that period may have felt more stultifying for Wasson coming to them from the 1920s than they appear when looking back on them from the 2010s and beyond. Or perhaps, at the end of his life, Wasson wished to record a story focused on the heart, not the glands, following the advice of his former courtier from a speech that courtier once gave in Sweden for an award he had recently won. Nonetheless, there is more to Wasson's account than meets the eye.

Although Wasson's account is a memoir, reading it as a highly coded, perhaps even purposely manipulated, account is also justified by its preface and by its publication history, which serve to bolster the impressionistic, as opposed to factual, nature of Wasson's memories. The publication history is complicated. Wasson drafted the manuscript of the memoir shortly before his death, and he died before its editing was complete. Final revisions fell to the staff at the University Press of Mississippi, which published the memoir, and primarily to then-editor-in-chief Seetha Srinivasan, Martha Lacy Hall, a freelance copy editor, and marketing manager Hunter McKelva Cole, all of whom worked to clean up the manuscript to meet the approval of Wasson's surviving sister, Mary Wilkinson. As he completed his one-volume revision of Faulkner's biography, Blotner wrote to Cole to ask to see the manuscript (a quick glance at the notes from that biography demonstrates that he not only saw it but also used it extensively in his revisions). In his response, Cole provided a photocopy of the manuscript in its then-current form along with a note to explain its unfinished state and how the editors had worked to revise it. He explained that the UPM team worked from "a photocopy of a very poorly typed version in cursive script" complete with handwritten marginal revisions from Wasson and additional editing by an unnamed third party. Cole noted that, even after Mary Wilkinson approved the manuscript, problems remained, but he also explained:

> In its present state, although it has many stylistic flaws, it retains both Wasson's rhetorical mannerisms and the accounts as he presented them. He made few attempts to pinpoint dates. The preface was created from extracts taken from rambling explanatory passages at the beginning and ending of various accounts.[7]

Stylistic flaws and inexact dating aside, the memoir "retains [. . .] the accounts as he [Wasson] presented them." Thus, the preface constructed by the editors highlights a single rejoinder. In it, Wasson stresses that "the reader will understand that I make no pretense at recalling Faulkner's words exactly as he spoke them, but I do say that our conversations—and those we had with others—are substantially factual and are faithfully reported" (x). Wasson explains that he hoped his memoir would "creat[e] a truthful portrait of William Faulkner in the days I knew him" (x). From Wasson's perspective, we can infer that the dates do not matter; rather the accounts that Wasson wished to present and the way he presented them without fleshing out selected details prove to be the central value of the book.

A perfect example of how the substance of the account meets with Wasson's hopes to relate faithfully the import of his story can best be seen in Wasson's recollection of his first conversation with Faulkner. What follows is a look at how we might read for "truth" beneath the elisions in Wasson's account of his life with Faulkner, starting with a comparison of the two versions of his first meeting with the man who would be so important to him throughout his life.

In his first account of their meeting, from the *Delta Democrat-Times*, Wasson explained that he was sixteen, had just arrived on campus, and was walking with "a newly made friend" whom he identifies as a senior but never explicitly names. Robert Farley, a fellow student, would tell Blotner in an interview that the young neophyte Ben Wasson "looked seraphic like a seraphim when he first came to Old Miss. He was a sweet kid and was taken up by upper classmen. He was as pretty as he could be."[8] On the one hand, in all his recorded memories of his first few weeks at Ole Miss, Wasson fails to account for what made him so popular with the older boys on campus. On the other hand, in his first telling, he did offer that his unnamed senior friend "gave me a special sense of sophistication."[9] The senior and Wasson encountered Faulkner, and the senior and Faulkner began to talk about clothes and then moved into a discussion of poetry. Wasson recalls Faulkner's "neatly trimmed mustache which struck me as quite worldly and daring." Wasson admits to being mesmerized by the conversation, which enhanced his already romantic feeling for the early autumn atmosphere of the campus, when "the world then seemed mostly green. Everything was so alive, so vital, and now I had met a fellow-man who was green with fresh thoughts, full of a love for creative things." Then, in his mesmerized state, Wasson realizes he has not yet actually spoken to Faulkner; he has only watched him talking to his senior friend. So, naturally, Wasson spoke up and "told him in over-flowering politeness that I was glad to meet him," to which Faulkner "turned to me and his eyes held amusement." Wasson thus elicited from Faulkner the bemused response: "'Ah,' he said, 'we seem to have a young Sir Galahad on a rocking horse come to our college campus.'" Wasson concludes the story by reporting that a few days later Faulkner "in kindly fashion, looked me up: me, a lowly freshman." Their friendship had begun.

On the surface, this version and the later version of the meeting in Wasson's memoir appear virtually the same, but Wasson's later memoir version shifts the timing of the meeting to create an even more sophisticated account of the subtle interactions he means to implicate. A perplexing subtext permeates the original 1962 version. Wasson is mesmerized and spends moments just watching Faulkner, taking in his clothes, his appearance, and his voice. When he finally does speak, Faulkner is amused, as if Wasson's attentions had not gone unnoticed. The story could have ended there; Faulkner could have been amused by Wasson's obvious crush but moved on, uninterested in having a love-struck freshman tag along after him around campus. In this light, we can read "Sir Galahad on a rocking horse" as possibly a slight on Wasson, whose angelic charms stood out at this moment as a bit naive and childish. The image of a handsome, courtly knight riding a rocking horse—a child's toy—offers a rather humorous take-down of Wasson's youth. Still, Faulkner looked up Wasson a few days later, so clearly the comment was not intended to dismiss Wasson and might very well have been a way to compliment him.

Innocent though this meeting seems, it teems with subtle markers that Wasson would later embellish with more detail in his memoir and which point to a code of gay encounter on the Ole Miss campus in the years surrounding World War I (and notably, Faulkner never "sock[ed] him," as Rogers explained to Blotner, which was how boys at Ole Miss were expected to act around a "cocksucker" like Wasson). The new details that Wasson included in his memoir retelling of this first encounter change the tone in important ways. Wasson dates his first meeting with William Faulkner to the fall of 1916, his first semester at Ole Miss. Wasson, a freshman, had made friends with some upperclassmen, "one among them, to my great pride, a senior," when "Bill Falkner" strolled along (Wasson 24). Faulkner was wearing clothes that Wasson later learned were meant to look "regimental," though Wasson found them "quite British" (25), descriptions that align Faulkner's self-presentation before the war with his faux-soldier act from after it. Also, Faulkner was already known as "Count No 'Count" on campus and around town. That he had this nickname *before* the war aligns this slight on his personality given him by Ole Miss students among whom Faulkner circulated after World War I with Faulkner's "quair" self-pre-sentation from before Estelle's marriage; thus, we can trace some consistency in his prewar and postwar performances—he was always a little queer and would amount to nothing. While Wasson considered Faulkner sartorially, the senior student in whom Wasson took such pride introduced Wasson to "the Count" and quickly rejoined, "You two fellows should get along fine," before adding after a pause, "You both like to read poetry and highbrow books. Don't you?" (25). We may not be mistaken to hear something accusatory in that final question.

The subtext of this exchange merits attention. Ben Wasson was a homosexual. He was also, in 1916, a sixteen-year-old freshman finding himself surrounded by older boys who included him in their group. One can easily interpret the "pride" that he takes in his senior friend as a coded reference to a crush, though the gentle but razor-sharp teasing that follows when Faulkner arrives on the scene leaves a reader with no real sense of the extent of that relationship, whether it was acknowledged but unreciprocated or was reciprocated to some degree, perhaps along the lines of what Howard delineates as "men like that" (Wasson, the homosexual) and "men who like that" (the senior, who may have had a sex-ual interest in the boyish and attractive Wasson but did not identify as gay). The clues in the story do suggest that the senior at least tacitly acknowledged Wasson's attentions, as it is the senior who cuts so deftly into Wasson's pride with the assertion, "You two fellows should get along fine." The implication here is that Wasson and Faulkner are both "men like that." That Faulkner may not have actually been a "man like that" would in no way prevent the senior from mak-ing that accusation, given Faulkner's reputation as the town "quair." Of course Wasson and Faulkner will get along, the senior implies; they both like poetry and books, those less-than-manly pursuits that marked Faulkner as "quair" in Oxford in the first place and now take on a different and more pointed signifi-cance in relation to Wasson and the other boys in the group. Thus, the senior is quick to throw a punch toward Wasson, a recognition of what he is, in that final question: "Don't you?" To paraphrase the senior, he is stating that Wasson and Faulkner will like each other. Why will they like each other? Well, the books and poetry, right? Only by adding that final question, the senior turns the previous assertion on its head. Maybe it is not the books and poetry at all. The final ques-tion implies that maybe it is something else.

The cracks in Wasson's storytelling show. Indeed, Wasson seems to want to let us know that Faulkner was, proverbially, in on the sly rhetorical coding in that first meeting. If there were subtexts abounding between Wasson, the lone fresh-man, and the group of older upperclassmen surrounding him, we can imagine that Faulkner, already acquainted with Stark Young and so not a completely sheltered novitiate entering a larger world, could have easily inferred those sub-texts himself. Just to be sure, however, that we understand Faulkner's sophisti-cated understanding of the situation, Wasson separates Faulkner's compliment, delivered on the spot in the earlier newspaper account, from the moment of their original meeting in his memoir, making it not a spur of the moment off-hand comment but a calculated phrase passed through a messenger and meant to take the measure of this angelic young man. In his memoir version, Wasson explains:

> A few days later, my *special senior friend* stopped me on campus as I was hurrying to class.
> "Saw the Count [Faulkner] in town yesterday. You know what he said about you? Man alive!"
> "What?"
> "Said you looked like a young Galahad who's just gotten off a rocking horse. I told you he's nuts." (26, italics added)

Wasson never explains why the senior friend from the previous anecdote has become, over the course of "a few days," a "special senior friend." That the cutting recognition of a few days prior has become "special" is highly suggestive, but Wasson, magnificently opaque, leaves the word to hang in the sentence, alliterative but undefined. He does, though, admit that "I took [Faulkner's] remark as a compliment" (26). How could he not have! Faulkner's comment describes a carved, boyish face on the body of the (sexually) purest knight of Camelot. In this version, the "rocking horse" becomes a positive reference to his youthful beauty, not a slight on his immaturity. Furthermore, by adding the passage of time for the patient and star-crossed lovers to communicate with each other via messenger, Wasson takes a loaded exchange and puts it into the terms not of male bravado and challenge but of knightly courtship a-la Castiglione.

Given Wasson has already established his literary pretensions—he reads poetry and highbrow books just like Faulkner, right?—we can read this literary reference in its most purely literary way as a high court romance with shades of Arthurian chivalry. According to Wasson, Faulkner described him as an idealized beauty, all the more for his sexual purity. Wasson stages this meeting and Faulkner's compliment in terms of high romance; it is a courtship. In fact, it even occurs over time, not in any immediate passing moment, and requires a messenger to exchange a message between the two "lovers" separated by time and distance. Whether or not these were the actual words exchanged between these men is suspect, but what we are left with as the *truth* of the story is that Wasson and Faulkner, from their earliest meeting, deeply understood each other. They can communicate on this high literary (and courtly) level, but the "special senior" can only exclaim, "I told you he's nuts."

The dichotomy Wasson sets up with this transference of timing is marvelous. The messenger is the very same "special senior friend" from a few days prior, but whatever the extent of the relationship between that "special friend" and Wasson, the senior does not understand the higher sophistication of Faulkner's remark. He thinks it is just "nuts." Wasson establishes that what follows with Faulkner is a relationship that is more meaningful because it is a relationship of the minds of these two men, not merely a sexual attraction. Wasson figures the senior as something of a clod. He lacks the sophistication and charm, or what might best be described as the courtliness, of Faulkner. To prove his own sophistication, Wasson used his memoir, more than half a century later, to return to Faulkner the compliment paid to him all those years before. If Wasson is Galahad, then Faulkner is himself a "Count" of some account; Wasson's memoir serves, over its own span of time, to account for his courtly friend and the special relationship they formed in the past and that Wasson, who outlived Faulkner by twenty years, still acknowledged and respected like fire carried in a horn across a lonely and distant mountain but still burning and capable of creating warmth. Unlike the senior, Faulkner played the part of the errant knight out to defend the honor (the sexual purity) of a maiden, though in this case the "maiden" was a young male with an angelic face, not a (female) virgin guarded by variously colored knights as in Malory's famous version of the old round table stories or the poetics of the Victorian Tennyson in his verse retelling.[10] Therefore, Faulkner is a better partner and more deserving of Wasson's "pride" and love than that senior, and will, in fact, win Wasson's devotion. As a courtship, Faulkner's initial salvo into Wasson's heart worked. Before his death, Wasson used the title of memoir to reclaim Faulkner's Count No 'Count nickname as a point of honor, not local ridicule for his pretentions. In a more immediate sense, just after World War I, and some three years after their first encounter, they would continue their friendship and move it into a performance of intimacy that even their classmates would call "queer."

The brief meeting and exchange of compliments before the war blossomed into a full-fledged courtship when Faulkner returned from Canada and reencountered Wasson at Ole Miss in the fall of 1919, which is also when Faulkner became a member of the Sigma Alpha Epsilon fraternity and began to spend intimate time with Wasson both on campus and off in the private setting of the Stone family home. I would offer this courtship as the primary example of Faulkner's actively and intentionally acting out a homosexual identity. Unlike the "quair" dandyism of his youth and his wounded soldier and bohemian personae, this performance is not merely a suggestively or latently, or even metaphorically, homosexual identity—though it is, alas, apocryphal. With Wasson, Faulkner played at an actual homosexual relationship with a homosexual in a model courtship. Nor was this courtship a minor incident but a long, drawn-out affair of true minds (and maybe even true hearts); and let us not unto the marriage of true minds admit impediments. The sophistication of these men allowed them to meet each other on a higher level than as merely co-literary companions. After recounting his first meeting with Faulkner, Wasson proceeds in his memoir to detail with sophisticated suggestion to rival any coded narrative of gay love the intimate bonds of his and Faulkner's mutual affections.

Wasson epitomized his courtship with Faulkner through two examples from after Faulkner's return from the war. The first began privately but culminated in a public display on campus as they began to be reacquainted through their fraternity. Wasson confesses to having loved the ritual practices of the fraternity, "especially that of initiation," which he considered "to be almost holy" (31–32). The bonds that Faulkner forged in their fraternity would have long and, at the time, certainly unforeseen effects in his later life. In the immediate moment, however, Faulkner's primary bond in the fraternity was with Wasson. Wasson had been initiated in SAE at Sewanee, where he transferred after his freshman year at Ole Miss; he returned to Ole Miss in 1919 for a law degree. Faulkner's own initiation in the fall of 1919 at Ole Miss left him less impressed than his starry-eyed companion. After his initiation ceremony "at the country home of Jim Stone," Faulkner asked Wasson to walk home with him some "three miles" to his parents' house on campus. Wasson narrates:

> It was a dark night, and the way led through a thick wood of leafless trees. Bill was completely familiar with the terrain. I was filled with awe, imbued by the performance and words of the ritual, the ceremony having left an almost hypnotic effect on me. I said to Bill what a splendid choice the goddess Minerva had been for our patron.
> "Don't you think the ritual's beautiful?" I said.
> "All that mythological hash?"
> "You're joking." I scarcely believed him.
> "Can't you tell when Roman gods enter or Greek gods crash the scene?" It's almost uncanny how those exact words remain in my memory when much more important things have long since faded.
> "I miss flying," he said, cutting off further discussion of the ritual. (32)

If these are the "exact words" that Faulkner spoke, there is much to them. In this scenario, Wasson plays the initiate, Faulkner the guide, even as Wasson describes attending Faulkner's initiation into the fraternity of which Wasson has been a member for two years. Wasson allows himself to be led, playing his part in this performance. Faulkner scoffs at the other performance at the fraternity initiation, but perfectly fulfills his role in the woods. He is sure-footed and never loses his way. He pretends he is a pilot who misses flying; he plays the part of the war hero for the eyes of his captive audience of one. These "exact words" place Faulkner in the role of teacher to Wasson's wide-eyed innocence, a relationship bolstered also by Wasson's assertion that Faulkner "was completely familiar with the terrain" of his hometown, whereas Wasson is not. These woods represent a kind of in-town isolation away from prying eyes, though the actual distance from the site of the original Stone home to campus was, at best, a mile or so, and likely followed closely the railroad tracks and the edges of the local Freedman's Town where a bike path runs today. Amplified sense of distance and isolation aside, they "continued [their] stroll to the campus through the dark woods, with [Faulkner] leading the way" (32), and their relationship changed after this intimate time together. Each had played his part in the relationship accordingly, and the relationship, accordingly, began to grow.

"In a day or so," Wasson continues, Faulkner "came to my room and held up a slim book, then handed it to me. The author was Conrad Aiken. Titled *Turns and Movies*, the book recounted in an unconventional manner moments in the lives of some people in the worlds of music and the stage" (32). This book proved an apropos selection given Wasson and Faulkner's later collaborations in the campus theater troupe that they founded together, the Marionettes; like Aiken's subjects, they are men interested in the world of music and the stage, right? To read the book, Faulkner led Wasson out of his room and to "a place near one of the ubiquitous Confederate monuments" on campus where they "sat there together in the grass, and he read the book aloud to me as students passed to and fro, glancing questioningly at us" (32–33). A conversation ensued between them over the merits of Aiken's poetry with Faulkner as his proponent, Wasson as his detractor in favor of Keats and Shakespeare. Their talk was surely very high-minded and literary, or so it would seem on its surface.

As is often the case with Wasson, he has implied more in his description of this day of reading than might immediately meet the eye. Those passing students, we are told, "glanc[e] questioningly" at Wasson and Faulkner reading to each other from a book of poems. Perhaps those students passed at just the right moment to hear Faulkner read aloud from "The Apollo Trio" about a group of traveling actors described as "damned degenerates" who have "women's hips, With penciled eyes, and lean vermilioned lips" and who "eat up cocaine" and "[simper] sweetly in falsetto tones" (lines 4–6, 13, 20). Perhaps they recognized Aiken's allusions to drag culture and effeminate homosexuality. Or perhaps, just in passing, they overheard Faulkner reading from "Gabriel de Ford," a poem about a ventriloquist, "a grotesque manikin" with "fixed and smiling lips" (lines 5, 7), a poseur in mid-performance and a fitting description of Faulkner himself whose reputation as Count No 'Count preceded him on campus and raised its own set of questions about this strange local and his strange ways. These students may even have slowed enough in passing to hear Faulkner finish the poem:

And since he always sings and never talks,
And flits by nervously, swinging his cane,
Rumors are thick about him through the circuit.
Some say he hates the women, and loves men:
That once, out West, he tried to kiss a man,

Was badly hurt, then almost killed himself.
Others maintain a woman jilted him. (lines 14–20)

As a matter of purely passing detail, after the war, Faulkner often walked around
with a cane for an injury he claimed he got in the trenches, though the other
details of the poem likely caught the attention of passing students just as much
as the mention of the cane would. It should come as no surprise that the other
students would "glance questioningly" at these two young men reading Aiken's
poems to each other.[11] Also, as another passing detail, Faulkner, at nearly this
same time, was publishing poems in *The Mississippian* inspired by Mallarme
and Swinburne, among other writers. Later he would claim to have used his
poetry to "further various philanderings" of his youth. Scholars may be guilty of
misidentifying the object of Faulkner's philandering.

The other example appertains to what can best be described as a series of private dates between the two men, sequestered dates away from the public eye of
campus. "There were nights," Wasson recounts, "when [Faulkner] would invite
me to go to the family home of Phil Stone, where Bill was apparently welcome
at all times," even when the Stones were not home, as is the case with this story
in Wasson's memoir (33–34). Faulkner led Wasson into the family library where
"he watched me read the book titles, and waved a hand to a brown leather chair
where I sat down." Then he offered Wasson "the treat [he'd] been promising,"
a private concert of several Red Seal records the Stones owned, including one
Faulkner claimed as "maybe [his] favorite—Beethoven's Fifth," which Wasson
had never heard (34). Wasson and Faulkner, intimate and alone on an evening
in the Stone family library, "were caught up in the spell and surge of the great
musical composition" and listened in complete silence to the recording a second time through (35). Wasson recalls that they "had several such music sessions when the Stone family was away" (35), though he pauses to address this
relationship in terms other than as a simple mentorship:

> I doubt he felt he was acting the role of mentor; it was more a sharing. There
> wasn't anyone else, other than Phil Stone, who cared deeply for things like litera-
> ture that were thought on the campus to be quite far afield, outré, and, probably,
> effeminate. He had found in me a young malleable person who liked the things he
> liked. He wasn't, and never became, a gregarious man. But maybe by being with
> me and talking with me, there wasn't so much loneliness for him. (36)

We could pause here and consider what Wasson means by "sharing" and tease
out the possible euphemism of the "several such music sessions" that he and
Faulkner enjoyed together at the Stone house while the Stones were away. After
all, this space has loaded implications. Wasson lived on campus with a roommate, Faulkner with his parents, but in the privacy of the Stone house, they

could create an intimate setting for a type of exchange that coeducational institutions strive to prevent occurring on campus grounds among members of the
opposite sex and must turn a blind eye to in all-male dormitories. In this case,
lacking a shared room on campus, they retreated to an off-campus site, specifically, according to Wasson, to assuage Faulkner's "loneliness."

Whatever might have happened at the end of these nights together, to label
these interactions *homosexual* is a fair assessment of them. In general, it is reductive to assume that this relationship—or any relationship—can only be homosexual if it progresses to the stage of physical sexual intercourse. Homosexuality
is not a purely mechanical function, and throughout the twentieth century, and
especially as men took on performed identities for homosexuality in the early
twentieth century, the sense of *being* homosexual has long superseded simply
doing "homosex" for men who apply the term to themselves as a marker of
identity, as Wasson did, though he avoided such explicit words in his memoir.[12]
Nonetheless, this homosexuality is, in multiple ways, *apocryphal*. First, evidence
for it relies on context not explicitly spelled out in print (Wasson never formally
outs himself). Second, Wasson's various accounts are not necessarily part of an
authorized account of Faulkner's life, even if Blotner chose to include some of
Wasson's memoir anecdotes in his revisions of the authorized biography. Third,
as I said at the beginning of this discussion of Wasson's memoir, we need to
consider alongside Wasson those claims in Rogers's letters, which are part of the
archive but, until now, have not been included in the published scholarly record;
just as the Bible has its apocryphal gospels, so, too, it appears does the life of
William Faulkner. To reconstruct Faulkner's performances of homosexuality is
to dig into the ephemera that never made it to final print.

In the case of this apocryphal homosexual relationship with Wasson, there
is as much to be said about the public perception of this relationship as about
Faulkner's private performances of it. As Wasson points out, the interest he and
Faulkner had in literature and the arts was perceived by many as "far afield,
outré, and, probably, effeminate." To be blunt, there is nothing "probably" about
it. These public and private performances did not go unnoticed on campus
nor did their implications remain unremarked. As Louis Cochran, a friend of
Faulkner's from this period and a fellow student at Ole Miss, noted of Faulkner
in an interview with Joseph Blotner: many on the Ole Miss campus "thought
him queer" (qtd. in Blotner 80). Blotner does not inflect the word here to signal some type of local or colloquial usage like "quair." The word is pure and
pointed: queer. The people calling Faulkner this word are not just the locals of
Oxford anymore with their peculiar "quair," but the students at the university,
twenty-somethings from around the South, New Orleans to Memphis, and in
some cases veterans of a foreign war. This crowd is a more cosmopolitan and
educated group, more familiar with broader national slang terms and their uses.
Such a distinction matters because the word itself in the early 1920s was far

less nebulous than just a few years previously; *queer* was coming into its own and taking on a specific denotative meaning in government documents and elsewhere to refer specifically to homosexuals. By 1920, *queer* meant *gay*. The students on campus were calling Faulkner a homosexual.

As this relationship between Wasson and Faulkner also highlights, the performance of these elaborate courtship rituals between these two men would give Faulkner ample experience of a homosexual perspective as a mode of being and living in the world, not simply as an act of two bodies touching with no context or larger implications for the lives of the men who claim those bodies as their own. With or without sexual intercourse (Wasson is not one to kiss and tell), Faulkner would prove himself capable of producing fictions the profound truths of which are not hindered by the minutiae of his experience but by his understanding of the all-encompassing whole of how one defines their life. In this private setting, Faulkner could have learned much about what it means to be gay, to define oneself as gay, and to perform that definition of self as a means of interacting with the world. For Faulkner, just this much could easily become more than enough for his fictions. Wasson's stories are not, however, the only evidence for Faulkner's apocryphal homosexuality.

Faulkner only spent a little more than a year enrolled at Ole Miss. He withdrew from the university in the fall of 1920, but after his withdrawal, he stayed in Oxford doing little except adding to the impression that he really was just a count of no account, though he would continue to publish poems, stories, and even reviews in the campus newspaper. Among those reviews was one of William Alexander Percy's volume of poetry *In April Once*. Percy read the review and did not appreciate it. When Wasson introduced Faulkner to Percy in Greenville in 1921, the meeting did not go well (Blotner records that Faulkner was also thoroughly drunk when he met Percy, which did not help mitigate any cool reception between the two). Seeing his friend wasting away in Oxford, Stark Young inserted himself into Faulkner's life in the fall of 1921. Faulkner accepted his intervention.

The *Oxford Eagle* social column ran an announcement in September 1921 to say that, after studying a year in Italy, Stark Young would be returning to Oxford briefly on his way to his teaching post at Amherst College, though Young was effectively in the process of resigning that post to move full-time to New York to work as a drama critic.[13] The *Eagle* also reported on 8 September that Dr. A. A. Young, Stark's father, had fallen off a ladder at his home and was hurt. In his notes, Blotner connects the two items to conclude: "So he [A. A. Young] was home at this time; so Stark could come to visit him & find WF [William Faulkner] 'discontented.'"[14] Emily Whitehurst Stone, Phil Stone's wife, would also remember that Stark Young "rent[ed] a room over the Square to write, over New's Drug Store [. . .]. One hot summer day there, PS [Phil Stone] and WF were laughing at D'Annunzio, when SY [Stark Young] said, [']But you know he still has quite a following.' WF and PS laughed and SY was furious."[15] The version of this account that makes its way into Blotner's one-volume biography—Blotner merely says that Faulkner and Young did not agree on the merits of D'Annunzio's poetry—omits the jovial intimacy of Emily Stone's telling. In the full version of the story, the men are joking around in Young's upstairs rented room. Young's fury does not eclipse the comradery of the setting and circumstances. Seven years after being introduced to Young, Faulkner clearly maintained a good relationship with him and enjoyed his visits home to Oxford.

Blotner was not unaware of the bonds among Young, Stone, and Faulkner. Emily Stone also mentioned in her interview the critiques of Young's writing by the citizens of Oxford, including by his own father, "who talked about his writing" and, noting the details that appeared in it, "would only wonder how he could remember all that."[16] In an undated note to himself concerning Emily Stone's comments, Blotner added:

> WF once remarked to me (perhaps to FLG [Frederick L. Gwynn]) wryly, that Mr. Stark Young once told him that people in his home town (Oxford?) wondered how he could remember so much (his Dr. father too?) as appeared in his stories. WF sardonic about the fact that they couldn't understand imagination or writing fiction so true it would be what people would do, perhaps people the writer never knew of. (This last unspoken by WF, but part of what he meant I'm sure).[17]

Blotner is conceding in this note that Faulkner's ability to turn the actual into apocryphal might have had a source more directly in Young's tutelage than is often credited, though Blotner's note also implies that Faulkner felt that all writing—Young's, Balzac's, Dostoyevsky's, or that by any number of other authors considered influential to Faulkner's development—comes from precisely this process of apocryphization. Still, Young's proximity to Faulkner would have made Faulkner, perhaps, more attuned to the criticisms that the local population laid against Stark Young. In fact, regarding *The Hamlet* in 1939, Faulkner would claim that he faced almost the same criticism from his fellow Oxonians. In a letter to Malcolm Cowley, 16 August 1945, Faulkner would claim that his character V. K. Ratliff/Suratt left many in Oxford wondering, "How in the hell did he remember all that, and when did that happen anyway?" (*SLWF* 197). Maybe in his letter to Cowley, Faulkner was not repeating actual criticisms made of his own work but was remembering and appropriating the criticisms made of his former mentor and wishing the same could be said of his writing as well.

In his notes, if not in the published editions of the biography, Blotner would continue pondering Young's influence on Faulkner. At one point, Blotner summarizes an announcement from the *Oxford Eagle*, 6 March 1924, about Young's two new books, *Three Fountains* and *Italian Sketches*. The same announcement also says that Young would be "staging" the play *Welded* by Eugene O'Neill. Appended to this summary, Blotner comments,

> He [Young] must have been an example for F [Faulkner] long before Sherwood Anderson. F may very well have been thinking of Y [Young] in those reviews he did for the MISS [*The Mississippian*], reviewing those plays, O'N's [O'Neill's] among them, thinking maybe of making a career for himself as a reviewer at the same time that he was writing his plays.[18]

Later in Faulkner's career, after winning the Nobel Prize, numerous writers and literary figures would remember connections to the great writer that are, at best, suspect; even many Oxonians would suddenly recall having been Faulkner's biggest fans all along. Young, on the other hand, was accused of *not* caring for Faulkner in those earlier, formative years. To this charge, he would respond in the *Eagle* in 1950 that he had long been a friend of Faulkner's and long had faith in Faulkner's brilliance.[19] Young, it appears, was not merely an ex post facto hanger-on. His influence on Faulkner was older and more involved than many contemporaneous (and contemporary) observers presumed.

In 1921, when he returned home to Oxford, Young would accordingly make an offer to Faulkner that would have tremendous ramifications for his developing career. Earlier than his comments in the *Eagle* in 1950, Young wrote an essay for the *New Republic* in 1938 about his connections to Faulkner. Worried that Faulkner was "bruised and wasted" in his provincial hometown, Young "suggested that he come to New York and sleep on my sofa till Miss Prall, a friend of mine, could find him a place there and he could find a room" (qtd. in Blotner 102).[20] Elizabeth Prall managed a bookstore in New York where Young found a job for Faulkner. This same Elizabeth Prall later married Sherwood Anderson and moved to New Orleans, where she would be instrumental in Faulkner's migration to the Vieux Carre in the mid-1920s. In 1921 Faulkner did not realize the lasting effect this advantageous trip would have on him; rather, he just wanted out of Oxford. He accepted Young's offer and traveled north, though he spent the majority of October in New Haven with friends whom he had met while living there with Stone in 1918. Faulkner would not return to New York until November to rendezvous with Young.

Blotner coyly says of Young that he was a "rare bird in the eyes of the average Oxford resident" and a "true exotic" (102). Frederick Karl offers a more explicit rendering of the tension to which Blotner obliquely refers: "Given his sexual preferences, Oxford was clearly not the territory for [Young]. He needed large cities and travel abroad, where he could blend into the landscape and escape unnoticed" (174). Karl's comments establish the same mythic geography as Paul Rogers in his letters to Blotner. In this myth, the rare bird Young does not belong in Oxford; he does find a place for himself in New York, specifically in

Greenwich Village. *If* Oxford was a rural space completely nonconducive to gay life (and that is a big *if*), Greenwich Village certainly was its opposite. Young would be the first of two known homosexual roommates of Faulkner's in the 1920s: Young in Greenwich Village, William Spratling in the French Quarter in New Orleans. Both locations have long histories of being associated not only with artistic communities, but also of functioning as gay enclaves in the larger American landscape. Greenwich Village functions as a kind of white elephant in discussing Young and Faulkner; it delineates against an otherwise homogenous background a distinctive shape, a feature of the landscape that, to say the least, stands out. Greenwich Village, even in 1920, had already established its place as a gay haven. If Young was gay in Greenwich Village where he could live his life more openly than he felt he could in Oxford, then Faulkner's moving in with him in the Village would have put him into gay living quarters with an openly gay man. Perhaps even Young's sense that Faulkner needed a change of place was predicated off his sense that Faulkner, like Young himself, would thrive in the less (sexually) repressive atmosphere of gay Greenwich Village. These two queer men needed a space outside of the rigors of the normative boundaries they perceived in their hometown.

Jay Parini has been willing to suggest that Young's "interest" in Faulkner "was, also, perhaps, a sign of sexual attraction: he relished the company of younger males, especially those with an artistic bent, like Faulkner, who either had no explicit knowledge of Young's sexual inclinations or didn't much care" (58). There is no reason to believe that Faulkner was unaware that Young was a homosexual, so it follows that he "didn't much care," or, a third option, cared and appreciated Young the more for his "inclinations" and his openness about his sexual orientation. Of Faulkner's life in New Orleans in later years, Parini concedes that "[o]ne sees that Faulkner was clearly at ease with homosexual men" (76) and that "I suspect that he identified with homosexuals as outsiders and considered himself—as an artist—an outsider as well" (77). We can easily apply these statements retroactively to Stark Young and Faulkner's brief time in 1921 in Greenwich Village and even earlier, to Faulkner's friendship with Young from their first meeting in the mid-1910s all the way back in the low hills of north Mississippi.

Faulkner's stay with Young proved minimal, lasting only a few days. According to the postmarks on his letters home, he went to New Haven, writing his mother from there on 6 October 1921. Evidence in the letter suggests that he had stopped in New York first, as he explained, "Mr. Stark hasn't come yet, so I left an address at his office in New York so he can tell me when to come down to get work" (*Thinking* 144). The letters from New Haven continue through 1 November 1921. After a nine-day hiatus, Faulkner's next letter home, dated 10 November, is postmarked from New York. In the interim, he had come to New York, moved in briefly with Young, and met Elizabeth Prall. "Mr. Stark,"

Faulkner wrote, "lives in Greenwich Village, a lovely basement room where you can be lulled to sleep by the passing of the subway trains. I stayed with him last night and spent today looking for a room of my own" (156). Faulkner stayed with Young for only a night or two, and his letter very clearly explains that Young's apartment consisted of a single basement room. His letter otherwise describes the crowds of New York and briefly details the eccentricities of style for its denizens, notably all in the Village. "Miss Prall" wears "[h]orned rimmed glasses, bobbed hair, and smocks," style choices that elicited from Faulkner the observation: "Styles are queer" (157). He also noted that the first important poet he met, Edwin Arlington Robinson, is "a real man," which is to say he is "not a Greenwich villager" (157). At some point in Faulkner's journey through Greenwich Village, William Alexander Percy came by to visit him, apparently all in good faith as a friend from down South, any transgressions for Faulkner's drunkenness in Greenville or his review of Percy's poems forgiven (Blotner 108). Young, it seems, was not the only gay Mississippian who acted differently in New York than he did at home.

That Faulkner arrived in New York on Young's invitation only to stay a night with him and wanted to find his own place certainly seems odd, at least on the surface, and leaves one to wonder if something happened to drive Faulkner away from Young's home. In a later interview now collected in *Lion in the Garden*, Faulkner would claim of his stay with Young, "He had just one bedroom so I slept on an antique Italian sofa in his front room. It was too short. I didn't learn until three years later that Young lived in mortal terror that I would push the arm off the antique sofa while I slept" (14). Young would recall the situation differently. Along with saying that he had only a one-room apartment, which Faulkner's 1921 letter verifies, he also noted that the sofa was just "a homely denim sofa, bought at a sale" and quite different from what Faulkner claimed was "an antique I so preciously feared would be ruined by the wild young genius!" (qtd. in Blotner 104). Faulkner's embellishment of this brief stay strikes an odd note for the degree to which it participates in a coded homophobia almost to the point that it sounds like an inside joke. First, Faulkner seems reluctant to admit that he shared *one* room with a man, a known gay man no less, in Greenwich Village. He places himself in a front room, not in the bedroom, even though the apartment, by both Young's account and the admission of Faulkner's earlier letter, allowed for no such spatial differentiations. Second, despite making sure that no one thought he slept in the same room with Young, much less on the same bed (or sofa), Faulkner alludes to his sleeping habits enough to suggest that he is a rambunctious sleeper given to breaking the bed during his nightly tumbling. Though the sofa is "too short," Faulkner himself was a very short man and often felt self-conscious about his height. Finally, in much the same way that "sleeping with" someone is a euphemism for sex, Faulkner's fear of breaking the sofa in his sleep comes across as a humorous euphemism for other nocturnal activities as well, and at the least suggests that, if he was actually sleeping, he was tossing and turning the whole night through. One can only speculate why.

I am reading so much into Faulkner's anecdote not because I believe that he is trying to cover up the truth about having sex with Young but committing numerous Freudian slips that reveal something about his "real" sexuality but because the evidence clearly suggests that he is telling a fiction about his stay with Young that deserves to be read for its deliberate ironies and subtle implications. In this case, in an interview from 1931, ten years after his night with Young, he creates an apocryphal homophobia and plays his part splendidly, though in actuality he is simply admitting that he understands what connotations might arise from his admission—in a letter to his mother—that he slept, even for just one night, in the same room as gay Stark Young in gay Greenwich Village. Though one need always be careful about reading Faulkner's letters from the late 1910s and early 1920s too literally—these are, after all, the letters that Faulkner used to craft his apocryphal wounded soldier identity—the letters do offer some understanding of Faulkner's real motives for moving out from Young's apartment so quickly. In his second letter home from New York, postmarked 12 November, he begins right away by assuring his mother, "I am settled at last," in an apartment near Central Park (*Thinking* 158). While he does not like it, since it is "about ten miles from Mr. Stark" (159), he allows that "[i]t will do until I find a place I like better" (158). "I want," he makes clear, "a place down toward Greenwich village where Mr. Stark lives, but rents are cheaper in this part of town" (158). Faulkner did eventually move to the Village, finding an apartment at "35 Vandam Street" (161).

There is ample circumstantial evidence in these anecdotes to claim that Faulkner was comfortable around, knew about, and lived with and among homosexuals, even preferring to live in their neighborhood rather than elsewhere in the city where rents were cheaper. He also seems particularly devoted to "Mr. Stark." George Chauncey dates the gay reputation of the Village to the 1910s and 1920s when the neighborhood "constituted the first visible middle-class gay subculture in the city [. . .] even though its middle-class and bohemian members are better remembered" (10). Blotner says of the Village that it was a place "to try free expression and perhaps free love, but also to try to paint, sculpt, compose, and write" (105). Gary Richards offers as well that Faulkner's next *habitue*, "the bohemian Vieux Carre of the 1920s was one of the few urban areas of the United States outside Harlem and Greenwich Village with a significantly open homosexual population" (22). Though no evidence survives that Faulkner ever "slummed it" in Harlem to take in a drag show in the early 1920s, he would hardly need so overt a homosexual escapade to experience the gay life of the city and of one of the preeminent and most openly gay subcultures in the country (also, he would slum it in Harlem in 1932 with Ben Wasson to visit a drag bar along with Carl Van Vechten and his boyfriend).

The existing record of this digression from a life firmly planted in Oxford points to Faulkner's desire to find a place for himself in the world beyond the Victorian, and implicitly heteronormative, confines of his hometown. He did not want to live *with* Young; instead, he wanted to live *like* Young, unfettered by tradition, expectation, and convention, the free life of an artist in a brave new world. These desires implicate a homosexual life, at least when laid against the expectations of his upbringing and alongside the model he followed to find this different way of being the person whom he wanted to be. Although he was invited by Young to New York, the invitation of a place to stay only lasted until Faulkner could find a place of his own. He did so quickly, having some money from home to live on and having landed a job with Elizabeth Prall shortly after he arrived. Faulkner attempted this trip to New York to forge his own life, not merely to flop on a friend's couch like a bum. He does not seem interested in courting Young in the way that he courted Wasson nor sharing an intimate emotional relationship with him. His excursion was mostly professional; as Young had moved beyond the confines of Oxford, so would his friend, William Faulkner. That the path that he would follow was forged by a homosexual whose trailblazing is related to his sexual identity is mostly a coincidental result of time and place. At that time and in that Oxford, gay life appeared unbearable, so Young sought a new life elsewhere. That time and that place are Faulkner's as well as Young's, and Faulkner followed in Young's footsteps. There is no reason to believe that he was blind to where this path led; in fact, his 1931 recounting of the trip, in which he plays with the implications of his one-night stand in Young's apartment, suggests that he knew perfectly well the multiple levels of meaning in his following in the footsteps of Young's attempt to escape the confines of home and in spending the night with him. Though other options did exist, Faulkner saw a choice between two options, the same options understood by Stark Young: the (heteronormative) life of Oxford or this (queer) life in a different city with a different set of standards to mold his sense of self. He chose Young's path, and with it he inherited its accoutrements. Rather than shun them, he embraced them and let them become part of his sense of self and, later, a part of his fiction.

Unfortunately, this sojourn only lasted until Christmas 1921. Worried about Faulkner, Phil Stone, with the help of Estelle's father, Lem Oldham, secured Faulkner his infamous job as university postmaster in Oxford. After a brief stay in New York, Faulkner agreed to come home to accept the job, making this foray to the Village something of a failure. He would stay in Oxford until 1924, where he would continue his friendship with Ben Wasson. Though Wasson graduated with his law degree in 1921 and moved home to Greenville, he often returned to Oxford, and one of his visits, which coincided with one of Estelle's visits, offers further insight into Wasson and Faulkner's interactions in the elaborate performance of their courtship and lifelong relationship.

In December 1924, Faulkner was preparing a permanent move to New Orleans; he had made numerous trips to the city from 1921 to 1924 with Phil Stone and the Clarksdale gangster Reno DeVaux, but in late 1924 he went to New Orleans to meet Elizabeth Prall, now Elizabeth Anderson, Sherwood Anderson's new wife. The trip convinced Faulkner to move to New Orleans, which he would do in early 1925, but first, he found himself in Oxford with Wasson and Estelle. While in Oxford, Wasson stopped by the Oldhams' home for a party. Faulkner chose not to attend so he could continue working on a poem. After the crowd left, Estelle invited Wasson to stay and showed him into the music room, where she played the piano for him, in a setting that closely approximates the "musical sessions" Wasson and Faulkner shared at the Stone home while they listened to Red Seal records. "She finished the piece," Wasson explains in his memoir, "then rose from the piano stool, put her arms around my shoulders, and we spontaneously kissed" (81). Notably, the subject (Estelle) of the sentence performs the verbs "finished," "rose," and "put." Wasson changes the subject to "we" for the verb "kissed," putting himself into the situation as an acting agent, not merely the recipient of an unwelcome advance. The kissing lasted until Cho-Cho (Estelle's daughter Victoria) interrupted. Wasson quickly exited, and after stumbling around town for a while, confused, he went to Faulkner to confess what had just happened. "Bud," Wasson recalls Faulkner saying, "Eve wasn't the only woman who handed out an apple, just the first one" (81). Then Faulkner gave Wasson the poem he had just finished and never mentioned the incident again, though Wasson would believe a similar incident in *Flags in the Dust* between Belle Mitchell and Horace Benbow was based on this transgression.[21]

That Wasson grants himself agency in this kiss seems odd, though it does help to mitigate the erroneous assumption that Estelle is a wanton provocateur. Had Wasson depicted Estelle as throwing herself on him despite his resistance, she would come across as a hussy acting out uncontrollable sexual impulses when, ultimately, Wasson means to depict a far more nuanced and intentional interaction. That Wasson must confess to Faulkner seems odder. Estelle was still married to Cornell Franklin, and Wasson claims in his memoir that he did not at the time know that Estelle and Faulkner had feelings for each other prior to that marriage and possibly over the course of its duration. That Faulkner forgave Wasson so easily is odder still. Did he not still secretly love Estelle or have any plans to marry her someday himself? By 1924 Faulkner had likely surmised that Estelle's relationship with Cornell was in extreme turmoil; Sensibar points out that Estelle's many trips home to Oxford would have made most observers aware that something was amiss. Yet Faulkner still left for New Orleans, despite her presence and any slight suggestion that she might become available. In New Orleans, Faulkner even went so far as to court another woman, Helen Baird. Not until 1927, when he returned from living in New Orleans, did he begin moving in the direction of courting Estelle and solidifying a life for himself in Oxford. To an extent, his forgiveness of Wasson follows from his assumption that, despite her troubled marriage, Estelle was still not his to feel slighted by. We might also wonder to what degree did Faulkner not see Wasson as a threat. That Faulkner's gay best friend kissed a married woman whom Faulkner might or might not have been currently interested in pursuing does not seem to ruffle any feathers for any of the people involved, except Wasson's, whose shame seems to flow from his sense that by kissing someone else (a woman), his best male friend (Faulkner) might be disappointed or upset with him.

It is tempting to try to read Estelle's motives in this incident. She knew that Wasson and Faulkner were very good friends, but later, in Hollywood when Faulkner tried to pass off Meta Carpenter as Wasson's girlfriend rather than his own, Estelle would see right through it. Estelle likely knew that Wasson was a homosexual from his reputation on campus and in Oxford. At least from the time that she sponsored Franklin in the yearbook, she had participated in the social scene of university life where, we can easily assume, she would have learned the basic social categories on campus, including the markers for and rumors about male homosexuality. Did she kiss Wasson despite his homosexuality? Did she kiss him knowing he would tell Faulkner? Did she mean to make Faulkner jealous? Or did she kiss him because, by kissing him, she was kissing the one who replaced her as the object of his affections? Was kissing Wasson a much deeper act, a confused moment when Faulkner's two "beloveds" came together, only awkwardly since the two were themselves bound to gender codes and protocol? Arguably, in this incident we see Estelle bonding with Wasson, her would-be lover's would-be beloved, only that bonding occurs as a misplaced kiss since Estelle and Wasson, a woman and a man, do not know how else to articulate this bond, of which Wasson claims he is ignorant and, as a homosexual, would not seem likely to pursue in the first place. If we could unsex all three of these individuals, we would see triangles of exchange and interaction not too dissimilar from those Eve Sedgwick explores in nineteenth-century literature as "homosocial bonding," in *Between Men*. But these bonds are not between *men* only to be mitigated by the ameliorating presence of a woman. Wasson and Estelle, a man and a woman, are negotiating their shared love for another man, but Wasson and Faulkner seem to have had little trouble expressing their devotion to each other. In the nineteenth-century paradigm that Sedgwick explores, such blatant homosexuality must be mitigated by the presence of the woman, but in this case, the homosexuality is not the problem. Rather, the heterosexual desires of this triangle are having a difficult time articulating themselves and seem, frankly, excessive. There need be no woman at all mitigating the circumstances between Wasson and Faulkner. They get along just fine by themselves without a woman between them.

Questions about what motivated Estelle at this moment reside in the realm of speculation because they seek to understand motivations that are fundamentally inarticulate. This incident is told to us by Wasson. No record survives in which

Estelle confirmed or denied this incident or commented on her motivations, though Wasson remained her friend throughout her life as much as he remained Faulkner's. Wasson's motives do deserve our consideration. This incident culminates in his confession. He worries about *his* relationship with Faulkner, and Faulkner, ever the courtier, forgives Wasson's transgressions. It is Wasson, not Estelle, whose virtue in the eyes of his lover is imperiled. The two figures in direct contact are two men. Estelle is the lover whose desires are vague and peripheral. She might court Faulkner through Wasson, but Faulkner does not court Wasson through her. Wasson may kiss her, but he also does not court Faulkner through her; he goes directly to Faulkner to confess. An incident like this shows up in Faulkner's fiction, though not in *Flags in the Dust*, but in "Divorce in Naples," when George forgives Carl for his brief tryst with a woman. In the story and in this real event, the wronged lover forgives his beloved. Wasson remains steadfast. Galahad's purity, though imperiled, remains true.

If he failed to escape Oxford in 1921, Faulkner was considerably more successful in attempts to escape in 1924 and through 1927. In New Orleans, Faulkner would begin writing prose and eventually compose his first two novels. He would fail to court Helen Baird, though he certainly made every effort to succeed, and he would share a room with another openly gay man, the architect and artist William Spratling. He would travel to Europe. He would visit Oscar Wilde's tomb. Spratling would have a homosexual affair in a jail cell in Europe, for which Faulkner would forgive him as he had forgiven Wasson. They would return to New Orleans and continue living with each other in another of America's historically gay spaces: the Vieux Carre. In fact, the one place in his biography where scholars have excavated Faulkner's gay influences relatively extensively is New Orleans.

In his 2012 study *Dixie Bohemia*, John Shelton Reed attempts to outline the sexual otherness and bohemian liberation of the French Quarter in the 1920s. He quite naturally places Faulkner and Spratling in the center of this world, largely because their coauthored book *Sherwood Anderson and Other Famous Creoles* offers the most extensive listing and firsthand published accounting of the people so instrumental in creating the sexual and artistic freedom there. However, when Reed wanted to flesh out the sketches in that book and understand the extent of sexual liberation—and particularly the homosexual presence—in the Vieux Carre, he turned to Joseph Blotner's extensive interview notes that he collected for his biography, because those notes, if not the biographies produced from them, teem with rich, gossipy details of the sexual habits and sexual openness of the people with whom Faulkner surrounded himself, including gay men such as Lyle Saxon, William Odiorne, and the unconquerable William Spratling. Prior to Reed's study, Gary Richards laid out the most detailed biographical groundwork necessary to understand the gay influence of the French Quarter on Faulkner's early prose.[22] Richards redirects the traditional pattern of the conversation about Faulkner's time in New Orleans, arguing not that Faulkner lived in New Orleans and happened, while there, to meet a few openly gay men but that New Orleans was itself a center of gay life into which Faulkner immersed himself and that these men are the characters most prominent in the life he led in that immersion. Of Faulkner's life in New Orleans and the fiction he produced from it, Richards writes that, despite Faulkner's attempts to minimize the influence that these gay artists had on him, "he repeatedly betrays his admiration of these figures and implicates himself in multiple strategies that reinforce links between artistic production and male same-sex desire" (21). Richards ultimately posits that Faulkner, whose artistic pursuits were in his life labeled effeminate, "quair," and queer, found in the French Quarter a community of "queer" (homosexual) artists who not only showed him that such associations of art and sexuality have merit, but that those associations are nothing to be afraid of. However, looking at the entirety of Faulkner's life up to his arrival in New Orleans, I would slightly alter Richards's assertion: Faulkner did not discover this association between art and homosexuality in New Orleans. He was aware of it before he arrived in New Orleans, and his arrival there may have been predicated on this very association.

In the stories of Faulkner and William Spratling's exploits in New Orleans, and later in Europe, we can find evidence that if ever Faulkner openly embraced a gay life, he embraced it with William Spratling. According to Spratling's memoir, while drinking overpriced Pernod and bathtub gin that they made in their shared apartment, he and Faulkner passed the time by shooting a BB gun from their window at passersby and awarding points based on the exoticism of their targets: a "butcher boy" was worth fewer points than if one of them "pink[ed] a Negro nun" which "rated ten points (for rarity value)" (Spratling 28). Spratling also recounts a joke that he and Faulkner pulled on Robert Anderson, Sherwood's son, who stopped by too often and wore out his welcome at their apartment: "The kid was so difficult to get rid of that finally, one day, we grabbed him, took his pants off, painted his peter green and pushed him out on the street, locking the door" (28). According to Richards, both Blotner and Parini give misleading accounts of this incident when they reduce it to childish game-playing; Robert Anderson was nearly twenty when the two Williams did this to him, "suggesting that adult sexual currents rather than those of ostensibly desexualized childhood impacted this scenario" (Richards 24). Also, in one of the sketches Faulkner wrote for the *Times-Picayune* while he was living in New Orleans, "Out of Nazareth," the narrator, David, a stand-in for Faulkner, recounts joining a character named Spratling in Jackson Square for some cruising. Spratling scores a young vagrant who loves Housman's collection *A Shropshire Lad*. In this cruising scene in New Orleans, referring to *A Shropshire Lad* is no random allusion. Faulkner uses the volume as a signifier of the gay theme of the story, which is everywhere inferred but carefully never explicitly stated. By naming Housman's volume, he is tipping his hand, in case his readers miss that the story is about two men cruising a park for young "lads."

Faulkner's original purpose for being in New Orleans, other than to meet Anderson, was ostensibly so he could sail to Europe. Instead, he spent the first half of 1925 writing *Mayday*, later titled *Soldiers' Pay*, when he was not out cruising with Spratling or writing his sketches for the *Times-Picayune*. Spratling would later claim his influence on this period of Faulkner's creative life, specifically regarding the novel that Faulkner wrote in their apartment. He explains that *Soldiers' Pay* is "a novel in which I am 'reflected' as one of his characters," though he never specifies which character he means and the term "reflected" leaves open to interpretation the degree to which he influenced Faulkner's novel and his other literary output at the time (Spratling 31). A clearer example of Spratling's influence may be the letter that Faulkner submitted to the *Item-Tribune* about marriage and the difficulty two people of opposite sexes have in relating to each other.

On 4 April 1925, the "poet, philosopher, and student of life William Faulkner" responded to an editorial column in which the writer had queried: "What is the matter with marriage?"[23] The editorialist, Barbara Brooks, was paying ten dollars for the best response of no more than 250 words. Faulkner, whose picture was published with his response, offers that marriage is not the problem; the people who enter it are. He admonishes those who become consumed by "[t]he first frenzy of passion, of intimacy," which he claims "is never love." He worries that "man invariably gains unhappiness when he goes into a thing for the sole purpose of getting something. To take what he has at hand and to create from it his heart's desire is the thing." Significantly, since Faulkner's response faults the people—the man and the woman—who enter marriage but does not fault the institution, his response might measure the depths of his own heart and implicate himself for his refusal to marry Estelle as much as it could also be admonishing Estelle for marrying Franklin. Perhaps, after six years, an older Faulkner is recasting his refusal and her subsequent action as products of the "frenzy" of youth. After all, he had marriage to hand with Estelle in 1918 and refused on a technicality that he may have easily come to regret as a spur of the moment impulse that costs him his promised bride. As a young man he had wanted to marry Estelle, or so the posthumous mythology of his early life suggests. Writing from New Orleans in 1925, he positions himself as an advocate for the institution of marriage, and he could be reprimanding himself for not understanding what Estelle needed from him at the time—an alternative to her parents' choice of a husband whom she did not love.

Despite the failings of marriage, Faulkner maintains that the union of two people is not the problem. He even specifies: "Two men or two women—forming a partnership, always remember that the other has weaknesses, and by taking into account the fallibility of mankind, they gain success and kindness." Though

Faulkner does not call it a "marriage," what he means by a "partnership" more accurately describes the "marriage" to which he believes heterosexual partners should aspire. He advocates for love, "a fuel which feeds its never-dying fire," rather than for passion, "a fire which burns itself out." The conceit of his response is that same-sex partnerships maintain a higher degree of purity than the base passions of heterosexual affairs (perhaps he is also drawing on his courtly interactions with Ben Wasson, who records the high pomp of knightly virtue displayed by Faulkner without the lusty passions that might—just might—also have sparked their interests in each other). Same-sex partners understand each other. Faulkner takes this conceit so far as to make it the model on which all successful (heterosexual) "marriages" should be built—not on the institutions of societal expectation but on the partnership of like minds. That Faulkner would turn his attention to the question of marriage at this juncture in his writing and argue for same-sex partnerships as a model for happy married life is no minor diversion. The influences that shaped his opinion in this editorial are fundamental to all the creative output in these critical years of his intellectual development, especially in both novels that he wrote in New Orleans.

Faulkner eventually made his trip to Europe. He and Spratling traveled together after Faulkner had submitted his manuscript for *Soldiers' Pay* to Boni and Liveright, which accepted it for publication. The two Williams arrived in Genoa on Sunday, 2 August 1925, and immediately got themselves into trouble. Sometime after midnight, Spratling, admitting that he "had reached that stage where everything seemed irresistibly amusing," approached a woman and a man whom he describes as "her 'business manager'" and proceeded to toss coins on the floor while dancing on a table (Spratling 32). In his drunken state, he had convinced himself that he had found a pimp and prostitute and was delighted that they both "scrambl[ed] after the coins" (32). The fun lasted until he was arrested for stomping on the coins and therefore defacing the image of the king on them. He spent a night in jail. In his memoir, Spratling describes very little about his prison experience except to say that he spoke to other prisoners, including "a young kid" and an "Italian hero who had escaped the French Foreign Legion in Africa" (32). Spratling does report that, in the morning when Faulkner came to retrieve him, Faulkner was "distant and gloomy" and seemed mad at Spratling. When Spratling pressed him about "seem[ing] a little sore," Faulkner rebutted "why shouldn't he be sore, having missed such an experience himself" (33).

Blotner remained faithful to Spratling's account when he recounted it in his biography in its proper chronological place.[24] Blotner then included that Faulkner shared this incident with Ben Wasson in a letter in which "he made himself the protagonist" (Blotner 156). Whether or not Blotner ever saw this letter is unclear. This letter has not survived in the archive, but Wasson reported in his interview with Blotner that Faulkner had written him "from Europe saying *he* had been jailed in Italy obviously and characteristically he had appropriated

Bill Spratl[ing]'s story." In his interview notes, immediately following this sentence, Blotner added, "Ben says Bill Sprat[ling] introduced the Riveria [Riviera] to America whatever that means," but for reasons also unclear, Blotner crossed this sentence out.[25] Such simple facts belie an important detail in the story, which appears in the revised edition of Blotner's biography but nowhere in the first two-volume edition nor in either of Spratling's published accounts nor in either the handwritten nor the later typed versions of Blotner's interview notes with Spratling from January 1965, though Blotner would cite that interview in his one-volume revision as the source for a profound piece of information about Spratling and about Faulkner's appropriation of his night in jail.

According to Blotner, during his interview Spratling admitted that "[t]here in the dark cell, another prisoner had begged for his sexual favors, and Spratling had brusquely granted them" (Blotner 176). When Blotner added this detail to the 1984 revised biography, he quite pointedly did *not* include it in its proper chronological place with his recounting of the Genoa material in chapter 18. Rather, he added it later, in chapter 20 with a general overview of some of Faulkner's fictional output from his European trip—far removed from the reference to the identity switch that Faulkner made in his letter to Wasson. Joel Williamson followed Blotner's lead (and his notes and his sources) and included that Faulkner related the incident to Wasson and changed the incident to say "that it was he [not Spratling] who got into difficulty and was thrown in jail" (202). Williamson also placed the incident from the jail immediately in context with Faulkner's appropriation of the story. He explains, "Apparently, Spratling told Faulkner that while he was in jail, he participated in a homosexual act," though Williamson also adds, "Presumably, however, Bill did not tell Ben about a sexual encounter," only that he, not Spratling, had spent a night in jail (202). Williamson declined to include any interpretation of this strange identity switch beyond the adverbs "Apparently" and "Presumably," both of which likely stem from the fact that he was following Blotner's published comments in the revised biography but could not confirm those comments in the archived interview notes, where no record of this homosexual encounter appears. We must assume that Blotner would not have included this information had Spratling not told it to him, but he did not write it down in his notes, though perhaps something of this story explains Wasson's reference to the "Riviera" that prompted Blotner to write "whatever that means."[26]

That Faulkner took a story about a sexual encounter from his gay friend in Europe and told it to his gay friend in America creates a chain of gay erotics between these men and implicates Faulkner's sense of continuity in his relationships with them. It is tempting to read Wasson's ambiguous statement about Spratling bringing the Riviera to America as a coded reference to his knowledge of Spratling's gay exploits in Europe and his return to America afterward, but the dearth of detail in the interview makes such a reading difficult to support.

As a matter of apocrypha, the incident and its suggestive implications seem so nearly to be the smoking gun that does not smoke, but obviously it would be intriguing to find a handwritten letter by William Faulkner in which he told Ben Wasson that he had a homosexual encounter in an Italian jail, even if Faulkner was just faking it. Despite the items missing from the proverbial evidence room of archived materials on Faulkner's life, Williamson does draw attention to the curiosity of the incident and Faulkner's interest in and appropriation of it. It is not a stretch to wonder aloud if the fun that Faulkner regrets missing was Spratling's homosexual encounter in a foreign jail, but solid proof eludes us. Scholars are left only with inference and deduction, the old ellipses familiar to all biographers of LGBT lives.

After arriving in Europe, Spratling and Faulkner separated to make their own tours, but met in Switzerland after only a few days and traveled together to Paris, arriving on 13 August 1925. While there, Faulkner began working on material that would become his heavily psychoanalytical though never completed novel *Elmer*, which Blotner would later publish after Faulkner's death in its most nearly completed form as "A Portrait of Elmer."[27] Faulkner toured the Luxembourg Gardens, source of inspiration for the final scene in *Sanctuary*, and toured some World War I battlefields, gaining copious firsthand information to include in his World War I stories set in Europe. In addition to this incident in Genoa with Spratling, the European trip is marked by other equally homosexual performances and experiences. On 16 August, Faulkner wrote home to his mother that he had gone sailing down the Seine, "past Auteuil and Meudon, to Surenes" (*SLWF* 11), saw the Arc de Triomphe, and "walked down the Champs-Elysees to the Place de Concorde" (12). He also took in the Bastille and made his way to Pere Lachaise Cemetery where he "went particularly to see Oscar Wilde's tomb" (12). James Polchin remarks that "[t]he fact Faulkner respected Wilde and his work underscores the young writer's interest in a certain sexual decadence" (149), and that "[f]or Faulkner, Wilde's life and work probably provided a means of creative social criticism. Wilde's plight as the persecuted homosexual and outcast of Victorian England may have served as a model of the effects of repressive social morals" (150). Wilde's influence on Faulkner probably mostly accords with Polchin's assertion. Unfortunately, Polchin uses Wilde's story to argue that Popeye from *Sanctuary* was inspired by Faulkner's knowledge of sexual deviance, thus constructing homosexuality as sexual deviance with no pause to consider that Faulkner might have had—in fact, he did have—objective and actual experience with real homosexuals that would allow him to see this particular "difference" as more than just perversion, deviance, decadence, or any other in a string of adjectives that denigrate homosexual desire as simply outré. Faulkner saw himself as different, found an interest in literary modes of the late nineteenth century in which Wilde participated and which Wilde greatly influenced, and probably appreciated Wilde's willingness to explore sexualities outside of the accepted norm, an appreciation that does much to explain Faulkner's regard for another poet who challenged Victorian mores, Algernon Charles Swinburne. However, Faulkner did not visit Swinburne's grave, or for that matter any other graves while in Europe, or at least none that he wrote about in his letters home to his mother.

Faulkner did not explain his sentiments concerning Wilde's grave beyond noting that he "went particularly" to see it, a pilgrimage Wilde's fans still make to this day to kiss his tombstone. Faulkner never confessed to having kissed the tombstone, but he did likely read the inscription on the tomb from Wilde's *The Ballad of Reading Gaol*:

> And alien tears will fill for him
> Pity's long-broken urn,
> For his mourners will be outcast men,
> And outcasts always mourn. (qtd. in Ellman 589)

Certainly, Wilde's outsider status appealed to Faulkner, and these lines register the power of Wilde's exiled life and the struggles he endured for his iconoclasm. In Europe we find Faulkner on his most successful endeavor to kick the dust of his small town off his feet and escape to a life less rigid in its expectations. Faulkner led a queer life. Wilde did, too, but Wilde's queer life was not only a performance of mannerisms that bothered the gender categories of his society. Wilde had sex with men and was tried for it as a crime. The most famous of those men, Lord Alfred Douglas, did little to hide the evidence of his affair with Wilde, a sexual affair, and Faulkner would have been as aware as anyone of his generation of the sensational trial that accompanied Wilde's downfall and imprisonment and, of course, his writing of the poem that Faulkner read on his tombstone.

Whether or not Faulkner would have known that the prime piece of evidence used against Wilde was a letter that he had written to Douglas that Douglas allowed, through carelessness, to fall into the hands of blackmailers is less certain. In that letter, Wilde referred to Douglas by the pet name Hyacinthus. Back in New York, Boni and Liveright were reading a manuscript of Faulkner's first novel, wherein a hyacinth becomes a critical symbol in understanding what has happened to Donald Mahon. For now, it suffices to say that Faulkner knew what made Wilde an outcast: his homosexuality. Faulkner fashioned his own identity of difference and "went particularly" to visit Wilde's tomb. Faulkner must have been aware of the implications of his own performance at this moment. We see in this visit, especially in context with Spratling's exploits in Genoa, a view of William Faulkner very intentionally and precisely posing as a gay man and even writing home to his mother about it.

In the same letter in which he mentioned visiting Wilde's tomb, Faulkner also mentioned "hav[ing] met one or two people—a photographer and a real painter" (*SLWF* 12). The photographer was William "Cicero" Odiorne, whom Joel Williamson describes as "a highly talented photographer and mysterious person from New Orleans" but who was also "homosexual, and, sadly, limped because he had a club foot" (205). The friendship that Faulkner and Odiorne began in Paris would continue in 1926 in New Orleans when Faulkner returned there. Spratling and Faulkner would even include a sketch of Odiorne in *Sherwood Anderson and Other Famous Creoles*. Odiorne's pictures of a bohemian Faulkner strolling the streets of Paris have become iconic images of the author, and Odiorne seems to have made an impression on Faulkner beyond just being good with a camera. "Odiorne and Bill [Faulkner] were very good friends," writes Williamson, "Bill allowed Odiorne to read some of his current work, always a sign of respect and affection on his part" (215). This friendship remains relatively unexplored by Faulkner biographers, but its extent does seem mitigated because though Faulkner continued his friendship with Odiorne in New Orleans, he still preferred rooming with Spratling after their trip to Europe together ended in December 1925. Faulkner would spend Christmas in Oxford, and then returned to New Orleans for much of 1926 and resided there primarily until 1927 with Spratling as his roommate for the entirety of his stay.

When Faulkner returned to New Orleans, he immersed himself into the gay subculture there, an immersion that would not go unnoticed by the local inhabitants, worldly wise denizens of a gay landscape with limited need for denial or double-talk about the men who inhabited their city. In notes for his biography concerning Faulkner in New Orleans, Blotner recorded several decidedly gossipy interviews with former residents who knew Faulkner and Spratling in the mid-1920s. One interview with Harold Levy captured Levy digressing about Odiorne. Levy explained, "Odiorne limped because of a club foot—a homosexual too. Odiorne had a coldwater walkup in spite of this."[28] While surely Levy meant that Odiorne had a "coldwater walkup" despite his club foot, the syntax of Blotner's notes leaves some interpretive room about the proper antecedent for "in spite of *this*." There is a certain humor in imagining Odiorne had a "coldwater walkup" despite his homosexuality.

In his own interview, Spratling told stories about numerous artists, sculptors, and writers from New Orleans, often offering brief accounts of them, such as for Sam Gilmore, who "had come to NO in 1921. He wrote exquisite poetry, was a homosexual."[29] About himself, however, Spratling was evasive, if playfully so. Spratling began his interview by teasing Blotner about Faulkner's sexuality and the discussions that ensued because of it. Blotner typed up Spratling's comments as:

> WF [William Faulkner] didn't seem highly sexed. He was certainly not homosexual, but he seemed interested in what was going on inside here. (the head.) Mrs. Levy [Harold Levy's wife] said Oliver LaFarge defended WS [William Spratling] against charges of homosexuality by saying, Anyone who sleeps with as many

women as he does! Who keeps a douche bag in his bathroom. Jas. K. Feibleman said he thought WF started out being interested in women but eventually the bottle took over.[30]

Spratling's bravado comes through in this account; he later even claimed Faulkner stole Helen Baird from him, as he was "interested" in her first. Blotner relates in his biography that "Spratling good-naturedly said that he had been interested in [Baird] first and Faulkner had taken her away from him. Spratling was probably exaggerating both his own interest in Helen Baird and Faulkner's appeal to her" (142). Coy Blotner is showing his own abilities at understatement here. The homosexual Spratling did not lose Helen Baird to Faulkner. The real story seems to be that, to the extent to which Faulkner paid unreciprocated homage to her in poetry, Baird stole Faulkner from Spratling. While in none of his written or typed notes does Blotner ever directly refer to Spratling's homosexuality, the clue that Spratling told Blotner about his sexual encounter in a Genoa jail suggests that he and Blotner openly discussed homosexuality during Spratling's interview beyond just this story about Oliver LaFarge defending Spratling because of his douche bag. This story is simply the one that survives in the archive. Spratling's explicit confession has disappeared. Both that unrecorded confession and this story about a douche bag function as their own kinds of apocrypha.

Reading Spratling's account of his *own* charge of homosexuality—or, more properly, his secondhand account that someone else told him that another person had defended his reputation when yet another person had called him a homosexual—is, to say the least, loaded. Why would anyone accuse Spratling of such a thing? Especially if he were courting women, such as Helen Baird? Why is it important to establish that Faulkner was not highly sexed? The accusation that Spratling is a homosexual is mitigated by the hyperbolic response that he sleeps with a lot of women and has a douche bag in his bathroom. Fortunately, the man with whom he shares that bathroom and with whom he shares his apartment is *not* "highly sexed," lest we might wonder if that douche bag is for all of Spratling's female company or for other purposes. Objectively speaking, a douche bag can be used to rinse any body cavity. For sexually active gay men, douching and other cleaning methods are standard hygienic practices often performed both before and after sex. The douche bag, a red herring in Spratling's interview, was just as likely used for homosexual purposes as it could have been for heterosexual ones. If Spratling or his roommate *were* highly sexed—which, thankfully, Spratling claimed was not the case at least for the roommate—we might have to consider that the douche bag actually belonged to Faulkner or Spratling and probably got a lot of use.

If Spratling was accused of being a homosexual, the accusation was very likely much broader than that: that is, that he and Faulkner were lovers. That they lived together makes this a likely assumption for their circle of friends to deduce. If there really was a douche bag hanging in Spratling's bathroom, its presence implies at the very least that he was engaged in an active sex life of which Faulkner, his roommate and fellow bathroom user, would have been very aware. The other option would be that the two roommates carried on an active sexual relationship together for which they needed a douche bag as a standard accoutrement of male same-sex practices. Since we know Spratling was gay and since we have no records or accounts of Faulkner's own engagement in a sexually promiscuous parade of women during this period, these two deductions are the most reasonable we can make: the douche bag was Spratling's for all his lovers, of whom his roommate Faulkner was aware; or it was Faulkner and Spratling's because they were lovers. Thus, the douche bag serves as the perfect metaphor for Faulkner and Spratling's relationship and the open living situation they shared in their halcyon New Orleans days. It both does and does not seem to mean anything, which is why it is so marvelous.

Even without this metaphor, other scholars have already considered the homosexual implications of Faulkner and Spratling's relationship, at least as far as assuming that other members of the New Orleans community must have prodded the two men about being lovers. Despite not citing Spratling's interview, Gary Richards deduces this general assumption about Faulkner and Spratling's relationship purely from the circumstantial evidence of their cohabitation and close friendship. Of course they would be seen as lovers. Of course Faulkner would be aware of that perception among their friends. Richards ponders if perhaps this perception would have led Faulkner to some anxiety, and it might have, but it did not cause Faulkner enough anxiety to make him move out of Spratling's home. In fact, the circumstantial evidence from the entirety of this period of Faulkner's life seems very clearly to imply that the homosexual implications of his relationships caused him no anxiety at all.

The evidence suggests that Faulkner and Spratling shared more than just a mutual living space. They performed together a model of gay identity that struck their own friends as gay, though the hyperbole of LaFarge's defense of Spratling also suggests that no one was taking these accusations too seriously. Faulkner could safely perform a gay identity in the Vieux Carre with Spratling, and if that identity included sex with Spratling as a lover, so be it, though gay identity exceeds the actions of the bedroom. In the generation after the coming-of-age of men like Percy and Young, gay identity had long since left the isolated confines of a single action men might perform but otherwise not associate with any sense of self. It had become a mode of being, an identity, that encompassed many facets (sometimes all facets) of a person's life. Considering all these stories together, much of Faulkner's life from 1918 to 1928 is readily identifiable as homosexual. Evidence of the degree to which Faulkner engaged in this performance and was consciously aware of its implications can be seen in the fiction and poetry he produced during these years.

Though homoerotic and queer undertones can be found in almost all of Faulkner's texts, the prose he began to generate in New Orleans and Europe, including his first two completed novels and the abandoned novel *Elmer*, along with stories generated in response to his European trip, such as "Divorce in Naples," and the World War I fiction he produced in the 1920s up to and including *As I Lay Dying*, and even his early commercially successful Yoknapatawpha story, "A Rose for Emily," abound with homosexual representations that rival the canons of out gay authors producing explicitly gay works of their own. Before New Orleans, in the brief fiction that he wrote and certainly in the poetry that most centrally occupied his attention, gay themes abound. Coupled with his New Orleans material, these chart a narrative of Faulkner's appropriation of his apocryphal gay identity and detail its multiple stages of expression and experience as he converts his (actual) performance of it to his (apocryphal) creative treatment of it. He lived in New Orleans, at least primarily, until 1927 but even after he returned to Oxford, a move that very nearly coincides with Estelle's return there and her filing for divorce, he continued to explore homosexuality as a theme right up until and even after the first years of married life with Estelle. At the end of his eleven-year road, he may have found heterosexual marriage and its expectations, but before that marriage and in its immediate aftermath, his fiction and poetry would teem with the inspiration of the eleven years of an apocryphal gay life.

Chapter 3

Gay Faulkner

Faulkner's immersion into gay culture and his crafting of a gay identity greatly influenced his writing during the years 1918–1929 and into the first year of his marriage to Estelle and the first stories and novel he wrote after his marriage. On the one hand, Faulkner converted his experiences with gay men and in gay settings into surprisingly sympathetic and complex depictions of gay characters with gay sensibilities. On the other hand, the influences of queer themes in his poetic models also led him to explore lesbian themes in his early poetry, themes he would revisit in his second novel, *Mosquitoes*, alongside a provocative representation of a gay male relationship. He did not, however, treat lesbian themes and gay male themes equally, though the influence of William Alexander Percy's "Sappho in Levkas" seems to have given him at least a modest capacity to show a degree of sympathy for all same-sex desires, not just male-centered ones.

First Fiction: "Moonlight"

Faulkner vaguely identified "Moonlight" as "about the first short story I ever wrote" (Meriwether 87). Blotner provides that the earliest version of the story is probably from "around 1919 or 1920 or 1921," though it was not until 1928 that Faulkner submitted it to a magazine, in substantially revised form, only to have it rejected (*US* 706). The story was never published in Faulkner's life, only posthumously in *Uncollected Stories*. The story that eventually reached print focuses on an unnamed protagonist preparing to rendezvous with his girl, Susan. The previous evening, Susan's uncle, also identified as her "guardian" to emphasize his role in surveilling her sexual coming-of-age, comes upon Susan and the protagonist in a swing in her yard, right at her curfew. By sheer size and authority, the uncle runs the protagonist off, leaving him feeling emasculated. In response, Susan sends him a note asking to meet again, when "I will be yours tonight even if tomorrow not goodbye but farewell forever" (*US* 497). Skeet, the protagonist's friend, is employed to arrange a new rendezvous in hopes of fooling the uncle that the protagonist is not making an inglorious return.

The protagonist assumes Susan means that she wants to have sex with him. He is sixteen, as is Skeet, but Skeet has already been initiated into the mysteries of sex. He and "most of the others would go down into Nigger Hollow at night sometimes and they would try to make him come, but he never had. He didn't know why; he just hadn't" (498). Though he thinks to himself, "*Maybe I ought to practice up on niggers first*" (498), and worries, "*It's like I'm going to miss out now*" (496), he also confesses, "*That's all I want [. . .] I just want to seduce her. I would even marry her afterwards, even if I ain't a marrying kind of man*" (500). In these semi-stream-of-consciousness asides, the protagonist conflates sex and seduction, the former the physical act, the latter the courtship that proves so problematic for him. The former seems not to trouble him, but without the latter, the former will not take place as far as he understands. Notably, he seems to believe that Skeet's trips to "Nigger Hollow" involve seduction, rather than assertions of white male authority. Skeet's sexual initiation is antithetical to the one the protagonist seeks, but the protagonist misses this distinction. He wants to seduce somebody, the sex being a consequence of that seduction but not necessarily the end that he most desires. Skeet's end is physical sexual gratification *sans* seduction. The protagonist's inability to differentiate between the two explains his inability to articulate why he has not gone with Skeet and "the others" on their excursions, where, try as they might to make him come, he, alas, does not. The other unarticulated element of his desire is *whom* he wants to seduce. He repeats that he wants to seduce "somebody." He never specifies who that somebody is, nor even that person's gender. He also "ain't a marrying kind of man." Faulkner will use this same phrase to describe the eternally certified bachelor, Homer Barron, in "A Rose for Emily."

The protagonist offers Skeet some of his father's whiskey in exchange for Skeet's help. Skeet agrees, but when he and the protagonist meet to carry out their plan of sneaking Susan out to meet the protagonist, Skeet immediately demands his whiskey first, even "grasp[ing] at the bottle inside [the protagonist's] shirt" for it (500). When Skeet does finally bring Susan to the protagonist, she wants to go to the movies, which is where she has told her aunt that she is going. She probably did not say she was going to the movies with anyone, especially a boy, but that is all she has in mind. The protagonist proceeds to fondle her, though "his hands felt queer and clumsy as they touched her" (501). He offers her whiskey, which she rejects as she "curiously" asks him, "What's the matter with you tonight?" (501). They manage a kiss, "the cool uncomfortable unlustful kissing of adolescence" (501). He then proceeds to take her to his aunt and uncle's house. They are out of town, but he has convinced himself that their bed is preferable not merely for its availability but because it is "*where laying has done already took place, maybe just two nights ago, before they left*" (499). When Susan realizes his intention, she cries out and begs him to stop. He immediately complies, feeling stupid and "like wood," and can only say to himself, "*I wouldn't have hurt her. All I wanted was just to seduce somebody*" (503). In light of his failure, the pronoun switches from "her" to the ungendered "somebody," a switch that corresponds to his unclear desires throughout the story.

Although the protagonist of the story has not successfully acculturated to the communal practices of sexuality as his peers have, the story does not seem too particularly promising for a gay reading even until these final moments when the seduction fails. At this point, Faulkner adds another paragraph that, as will the final paragraph and revelation of "A Rose for Emily," calls for a complete revision of the signs to which the story has pointed from its first words. After the protagonist apologizes to Susan for scaring her, the story concludes, "He held her. He felt nothing at all now, no despair, no regret, not even surprise. He was thinking of himself and Skeet, lying on a hill somewhere under the moon with the bottle between them, not even talking" (503). The protagonist feels no passion for seducing a woman; he only wants to seduce "somebody." In the wake of his failure, his thoughts turn to an easier, pastoral romance that requires no fretful seductions. His thoughts turn to Skeet. Skeet, of course, participates in sexual acts with a girl/woman, or so it seems right to assume that he does. The sex of whomever he is seeking in "Nigger Hollow" is never given, but that "others" go with him makes it unlikely that they are all gay and all seeking male companionship. The focal point of the narration, though third person, is limited to the unnamed protagonist, so whatever is happening in "Nigger Hollow," the narration only provides readers with the perspective of the protagonist. That the narration never identifies what is happening there not only suggests that the protagonist does not know but also that he prefers not to find out. The narration leaves us with his pastoral ideal of an intimate space to share with Skeet: all we know and all we need to know. The bottle *between* them may seem as if it is a barrier, but Skeet has already felt inside the protagonist's shirt for that very bottle, reaching his hands to touch the protagonist and crossing any barriers that the bottle might seem to impose.

The easy reading of this story would focus on the failed "seduction" in the context of Faulkner's failure to win Estelle's hand in marriage. Early versions of the story lend credence to this impression, but Faulkner's revisions imply that such a directly autobiographical reading was not his intention. Writing about early draft versions of the story in which the protagonist rejects his female lover without turning his thoughts to a male companion, Frederick Karl claims that the ending, through a similar twist in the final paragraph, allows the protagonist to turn the tables on his rejection. The "twist of the story," Karl claims, "is of interest; for it places control in the hands of the young man, not the girl, and he finally rejects her" (178). Karl continues that "[i]f Faulkner did indeed write this in the Fall of 1921, when he was just past twenty-four, the story memorializes a young man building his defenses against rejection" in the wake of Estelle's recent return to Oxford and subsequent removal to the Far East with her husband (178–79). On a biographical level, it seems likely that Faulkner wrote some of his own emotions concerning Estelle into the story, but Estelle is not all the story. Estelle was absent for much of those crucial years from 1919 to 1921 when the story was first written. In the face of her loss, Faulkner centered his attention on Ben Wasson in the courtship that he enacted with him by reading him poetry on campus, escorting him through the dark woods, and spending evenings alone with him in the front parlor of the Stone's house, when the Stones were out of town. That house represents a preferable, private place where maybe laying has also occurred just a night or two prior to Faulkner and Wasson's visits.

The evolution of this story from its first version in 1919–1921 to its final form in 1928 demonstrates an author reworking and playing with his material in a cogent, perhaps even intentional, fashion, not as a subconscious upwelling of anxieties about a woman whom Faulkner felt that he had lost. As Blotner reports in his two-volume biography, the original story focused on two friends, Robert Binford and George, carousing at a drugstore and cruising the passing women. "They are superficially hard and cynical," Blotner describes, and "[i]n the dark shade of the courthouse trees they drink corn whiskey and smoke cigarettes" (Blotner 2 Vol. 322). When George meets his girl Cecily and attempts to get her into an empty house, she resists him, just as Susan will resist the unnamed protagonist in the later version of the story. In the earlier version, though, Cecily eventually relents, at which point "George changes his mind" about having sex with her (322). The two walk back downtown together, their tryst unconsummated.

For the earlier version of this story, Karl reads George as the stand-in for Faulkner who takes charge and controls the outcome of the seduction to seize the power of rejection from the woman who rejected Faulkner in his actual life. As Faulkner revised the story, the woman (Cecily/Susan) regains that power. At the end of the original story, Cecily and George return downtown. When Susan rejects the protagonist of the later story, that protagonist imagines fleeing to the countryside with Skeet. As Robert Binford becomes Skeet over the course of the revision process, he takes on elements of both Ben Wasson and Phil Stone. Skeet's sexual initiation mirrors the one that Stone "confessed to his wife" about his own adolescent experimentation, according to Susan Snell (37), though the girl in Stone's confession lived "up the railroad tracks" and was named, improbably, Dewey Dell. Her race is not specified, though "up the railroad tracks" from the Stone house would likely accord with the location of the Freedman's Town in Oxford and that she was a girl whom Stone felt comfortable experimenting with implies, in the southern racial/sexual hierarchy, that she was probably black. If Stone also confessed this story of his sexual initiation to Faulkner—the name Dewey Dell implies he did as it appears in a later novel—then certainly, Stone's influence informs the development of Skeet's character.

Faulkner's friendship with Stone, however, does not accord with the youthful homoeroticism of the pastoral romance that the protagonist imagines with Skeet at the end of the revised story. That homoeroticism rests, most likely, on an apocryphization of Faulkner's courtship of Wasson. Skeet is a translation of elements of both Stone and Wasson, part the friend, part the object of sexual interest who is so naturally a part of the protagonist's world that he need not be seduced with all the difficulty attendant upon seducing a member of the opposite sex in the elaborate rituals of proper heterosexuality. They can simply lie upon the grass together, without reading Conrad Aiken poetry in this case.

We see elements here of what Faulkner claimed in his editorial to the *Item-Tribune*, that when two men form a partnership, "they gain success and happiness," whereas a man and a woman are always at odds. Perhaps Faulkner's successful courtship of Wasson laid the groundwork for the editorial Faulkner wrote while living with Spratling in New Orleans. Faulkner's general impression of male-male courtships in the 1920s would account nicely for the revisions of "Moonlight" from its early draft version in 1919–1921 to its final version in 1928. Over the course of his revisions, Faulkner made multiple substitutions, involving Estelle and Wasson, to turn his actual experience into an apocryphal narrative. In the final version of the story, Faulkner assimilates basic biographical details from his life and overlays them onto a basic plot involving readily identifiable literary types: wooing suitor finds his attentions unrequited by a dismissive woman so he turns to a friend for consolation. Susan/Estelle functions similarly to the bodiless female voice from T. S. Eliot's "The Love Song of J. Alfred Prufrock," explaining to her would-be lover, "That is not what I meant at all." Skeet/Wasson becomes the surrogate for the unrequited love for that woman. Having a surrogate for his unrequited affections better serves to alleviate the sting of rejection than for the protagonist/ Faulkner to pretend the power to reject Susan/Estelle had been his all along. The (male) surrogate allows the protagonist to imagine seducing somebody successfully, regardless of his earlier rejection, much as Faulkner successfully courted Wasson in place of Estelle in the early 1920s, in and around the time that the story was originally written. But Faulkner's process of creating his fiction is not always so directly a matter of scratching out one person's real name and substituting a pseudonym (the one-to-one substitutions that seem apparent in this reading of "Moonlight" oversimplify the creative process of any artist, and certainly one as talented as William Faulkner). Faulkner's making the actual into the apocryphal involves a more complex process of assimilation, not just substitution, to refigure a given scenario into something vaguely recognizable as autobiographical but still fundamentally its own unique telling of events.

Poetic Complications

"Moonlight" aside, Faulkner originally fashioned himself a poet. In his poetry, we see the problem that Faulkner encountered when translating his idealized same-sex partnership into a lesbian context. Three of Faulkner's earliest writings contain variations of lesbian themes: "L'Apres Midi d'un Faune," his very first publication; "Sapphics," an early poem he published in *The Mississippian* while a student at Ole Miss; and an imitation of Sappho, "o atthis," that he wrote in 1919–1920 but would not publish until many years later in *A Green Bough* (1933). The first two he apparently wrote as individual poems but later included them, along with "o atthis," in his unpublished sequence *The Lilacs*, which he gave to Phil Stone in January 1920 as a handmade volume. None of these three poems is a fully original creation. "L'Apres Midi" is an imitation of the symbolist poem by Stephane Mallarme, which was also translated by Sergei Diagalev's Ballets Russes—and specifically by Diaghilev's male lover Vaslav Nijinsky—into a famous ballet in Paris in 1912. "Sapphics" is an imitation of Swinburne's much longer poem from his collection *Poems and Ballads* (1866); "o atthis" is apparently an imitation of translations of the ancient Greek poetess, the so-called tenth muse, Sappho, though Judith Sensibar suggests that it has a more direct antecedent in a poem of the same title by Ezra Pound published in September 1916 (*Origins* 69). As an imitation of Sappho in the wake of late nineteenth-century Victorian poetry, it is not unique regardless of its pedigree; but it is worth contextualizing its content, if not its form, not with its Victorian ilk but with its Mississippi cousin, William Alexander Percy's "Sappho in Levkas," published in 1915.

Though seemingly the apprentice works of a developing poet, these poems are not purely imitative. For both "L'Apres Midi" and "Sapphics," Faulkner greatly reduced the scope of his antecedents, and in his distillation of the earlier, longer poems, crafted content decidedly different from Mallarme's and Swinburne's and decidedly his own. Faulkner's distillation specifically revises the representations that his antecedents made of lesbianism and its relationship to art. In Mallarme's original, his faun is led into the woods by a nymph and comes upon two other nymphs sleeping together. The faun is a projection, or an "illusion" as Sensibar calls it, but the erotic voyeurism of the faun's vision inspires the creation of the poem as the faun "realizes that illusions are powerful agents capable of generating real and deeply felt emotions. Such emotions, if listened to objectively and carefully perceived, may be used, in Mallarme's faun's case, to make music and poetry" (*Origins* 71). Swinburne employs a similar frame. The speaker of his poem "Sapphics" dreams that he is following Aphrodite across the seas to Lesbos. Aphrodite feels a compulsion to journey to Lesbos on "reluctant / feet" (lines 12–13), but once there, she comes upon Sappho, "Ah the tenth [muse], the Lesbian!" (line 30), singing her songs in praise of her love for women. Aphrodite wants to reject this vision and weep, but she keeps turning toward it in order to see "the Lesbians kissing across their smitten / Lutes with lips more sweet than the sound of lutestrings, / Mouth to mouth and hand upon hand, her chosen, / Fairer than all men" (lines 49–52). Despite her distaste for what she sees, Aphrodite witnesses it and is inspired by it. The speaker adopts the image of Sappho for the creation of his own poem. In these poems lesbian sexuality is productive; it produces, as if in a kind of procreative erotic fire, the poetic voice of both speakers and is fundamental to the creation of art. It is tempting to believe that Faulkner might appropriate imagery from both poems and revise it in accordance with the idea that (female) same-sex relationships extend beyond prurient sexual expression to deeper kinship and understanding. He does not so revise said imagery.

Faulkner appropriates both poems, but his versions change the procreative, generative element of lesbian sexuality from the originals. Led into the woods by a nymph, Faulkner's faun giddily "follow[s] through the singing trees / Her streaming clouded hair and face / And lascivious dreaming knees" (*EP* 39).[1] The faun is fascinated by the beauty of this one nymph and becomes increasingly enraptured by it. In this regard, Faulkner's faun is not different from Mallarmé's, but before Faulkner's faun can come upon the two sleeping nymphs, "some great deep bell stroke" wakes the speaker from his vision (*EP* 40). Faulkner removes the lesbian scene from his version of the poem. Sensibar argues that, whereas Mallarmé's "faun experiences an erotic sensation that arises from fantasizing about the nymphs" sleeping together, "Faulkner, unable still to be a disinterested observer of his own emotions, excludes this daring suggestion from his poem" (*Origins* 71). It is, however, that exclusion that is, perhaps, more daring and suggestive than Sensibar admits.

The main interest of Faulkner's speaker is in chasing the illusion of the nymph's erotic calling. He wants to be titillated by the singular nymph leading him through the forest. He does not want to witness a lesbian encounter between two nymphs; one nymph is enough for him. Before he stumbles too far into his vision, he wakes up, but the nymph's eroticism still inspires him. The fantasy is still erotic, if not homoerotic and fixated on a lesbian scene. In terms of lesbian representation, Faulkner's use of it in this poem is his omission of it. He read Mallarmé's original, complete with its lesbian representation. He chose not to include that lesbian representation. The source of his poem is good old-fashioned heteroeroticism: a male speaker is sexually aroused by a feminine nymph and makes art from his arousal. In his poem, the lesbian scene that we do not witness is subordinated for the ideal nymph whom we do see and who inspires the creation of the poem. The chase becomes the central inspiration; the lesbian encounter becomes excess waste, unnecessary to the creation of art. The poet discards it. The speaker does not need to acknowledge that women can be lovers. His inspiration rests entirely in his one muse; his poetic vision rests entirely between her "lascivious dreaming knees." Faulkner is turning away from any interests in lesbian same-sex desire. He focuses instead on a heterosexual fantasy. But if all of this is an illusion, then it might well amount to simple onanism. The poem lacks a scene of coupling as the inspiration for creation. It is tempting to say the poem is about nothing, to borrow an Elizabethan pun. At the least it is prurient for its mild pornography. The speaker is focused on what is between a woman's knees. He leaves out any details that might attain something higher and more meaningful than his lusting.

In his imitation of Swinburne's "Sapphics," Faulkner allows the scene of lesbian sexual encounter, but he changes Aphrodite's perspective. Sensibar acknowledges this concise but deeply telling change of perspective. In Swinburne's poem, Aphrodite "Saw the Lesbians kissing" (line 49); in Faulkner's version, "She sees *not* the Lesbians kissing" (*Origins* 81, italics added). Faulkner cuts tremendously from Swinburne's poem, removing the name Sappho altogether and reducing Swinburne's twenty-stanza poem to his own six-stanza version. He adds the word *not* twice in his poem, so that whereas Swinburne records what Aphrodite witnesses, Faulkner records what she turns away from. Faulkner then concludes his poem with a stanza of unremitting despair:

Before her go cryings and lamentations
Of barren women, a thunder of wings,
While ghosts of outcast Lethean women, lamenting,
Stiffen the twilight. (*EP* 52)

Sensibar explains that the "Lethean women," another of Faulkner's additions not in Swinburne's original, are meant to suggest that this scene of lesbian sexuality is best forgotten, not remembered at the end of the vision as an inspiration for art. In Faulkner's version of the poem, lesbianism is the source of "cryings and lamentations." The women who practice it are "barren."

Here, though, as in "L'Apres Midi," what we do *not* see becomes central to the meaning of the poem. Though Aphrodite turns away from the scene of kissing lesbians, the speaker of the poem does not. He goes right on recording it, implying that he is watching it and taking note of it, even if Aphrodite refuses to look herself. Unlike his version of "L'Apres Midi," in "Sapphics" Faulkner does not actually omit the lesbian scene. What the speaker sees but declares that Aphrodite turns away from becomes a record of omission that reminds us of what has been omitted. Conversely, in all his fiction, Faulkner never once shows two men kissing; even George and Carl in "Divorce in Naples" only manage a dance or two while the narrator of that story observes them. Though we know they are lovers, we are never privy to a sex scene. In "Sapphics," the lesbian scene we are meant to forget is the focal point of the poem, laid bare and out in the open for the reader as exactly the thing we are not supposed to see. This playful element of the poem, to say by *not* saying and to show by *not* showing, allows the reader to participate in the speaker's illicit voyeurism. Though an audience may be troubled by the sound of loud weeping over the barrenness of lesbianism, we are still allowed the fantasy of watching two women make out. The speaker enjoys this scene, even if Aphrodite is troubled by it. He records it in a poem.

Certainly, Faulkner had a different understanding of lesbianism than he had of male homosexuality, and Sensibar correctly points out that Faulkner was troubled by lesbianism despite his early interest in depicting it. In her biographical study *Faulkner and Love*, Sensibar considers these two poems and the collection *The Lilacs*, a gift of which Faulkner made to Phil Stone. She then posits that Faulkner must have given Stone these poems as a way of acting out, psychically, his own anxieties over his increasingly close relationship with Stone, a man. Sensibar goes as far as claiming that "Stone was the first of a long series of very bright men, many of them either bisexual or homosexual, who served, as Stone self-mockingly put it, as Faulkner's 'wet nurse'" (242). Though she can provide no evidence to verify that Stone was either bisexual or homosexual, Sensibar asserts this implicit connection between Stone's sexuality and Faulkner's supposed response to it not as evidence that Faulkner was troubled by lesbianism but as evidence that he was troubled by all homosexual and homoerotic desire, including that between men. As she states,

> In both of these poems, written before self-censorship resulting from the Wilde trials, Mallarme and Swinburne are celebrating the myriad forms of sexuality— homosexual acts and fantasies in particular—from which they, as mature poets, derive imaginative inspiration. In contrast, Faulkner appears threatened by the underlying emotional currents in these poems. (312)

Sensibar is conflating too many sexualities here, and then using that conflation as the basis to argue that Faulkner's reaction to homosexuality must be fundamentally anxious, despite there being ample evidence to the contrary in his writings and in the biographical record.

The preponderance of evidence from Faulkner's life suggests a more nuanced sense of sexual orientation and gender roles. First, regardless of Stone's sexuality, Faulkner never demonstrated any sense that he was "threatened by the underlying emotional currents" between himself and Wasson, himself and Young, or, later, himself and Spratling. Why he would feel anxious about Stone and then respond to that anxiety with poems about lesbianism is not altogether clear, but his reading explicitly male homosexually themed poems to Wasson on the pleasant autumnal grounds of the Ole Miss campus undercuts any impression that these lesbian poems might have functioned as a homophobic release valve between himself and his other friend. A more accurate reading might be to say that Faulkner and Stone bonded over titillating discussion of female bodies in much the way that lesbian-themed pornography has long been a staple of male heterosexual fantasy, whereas with Wasson, Faulkner chose poetry appropriate to their (nonheterosexual) relationship. Second, lesbianism and male homosexuality are two different sexual identities and should be considered in a more discreet context than as simply "myriad forms of sexuality" with no distinction for larger codes of gender and uses of sexual representation in literature. It is possible for a gay man to feel at odds with lesbianism and possible for lesbians to have no deep love for gay men. Gertrude Stein even once explained to Ernest Hemingway that male homosexuality was disgusting, but lesbian sexuality was beautiful.[2] Clearly, Faulkner's generation saw queerness as a rainbow with many stripes. The gender of the speaker and his/her own sexual orientation could produce gradations of acceptance that disappear when we overgeneralize queer desires.

In Faulkner's two poems, as in the originals on which he modeled them, lesbianism is presented as a variety of heterosexual male fantasy, not as a means of voicing closeted male homosexual desires or angst. Mallarme and Swinburne wrote about sexual acts between women as part of a tradition of heterosexual Sapphic-themed poetry from the Victorian period and late nineteenth century. Their titillation at seeing women together is mildly pornographic but still het-erosexual. Though he changes the lens of each sex scene, Faulkner is also thor-oughly invested in the voyeuristic fantasy of these poems, with limited interest in the lesbianism at their core. A man viewing women for the sake of erotic pleasure does not at all imply that same man would receive erotic pleasure from viewing other men. Faulkner is not threatened by his own interest in viewing, or *not* viewing, lesbian sex; so long as he receives the sexual gratification he associ-ates with female sexuality, lesbianism is acceptable. Faulkner's understanding of lesbianism does not bear on his perception of male homosexuality except to the extent that his chosen models demonstrate his awareness of sexualities beyond purely heterosexual ones, for men as well as for women. In fact, he seems aware of the difference between the appropriation of Sapphic themes for voyeuris-tic heterosexual fantasy as opposed to utilizing them for coded homosexual representations.

In his adaptation of Sappho, "o atthis," Faulkner offers a more nuanced understanding of lesbian sexuality with considerably more empathy than his other two lesbian-themed poems. As an imitation of Sappho's scattered verses, Faulkner's version is purposely slim on detail and imagery and reads as if it is itself a fragment of a longer poem, but the poem contains the seed of a full idea and, much as with Pound's "In a Station of the Metro," captures a still image of a singular instant that is complete in itself despite its minimalist design. Atthis is the famed woman on whom Sappho showered her desires and to whom she seems to have written some of her poems, though Atthis had a male lover and abandoned Sappho, who shortly thereafter killed herself in despair, according to tradition. Basically, Atthis is to Sappho as Laura is to Petrarch, Beatrice to Dante. Sappho, as poet, creates a female speaker in her poems who is recording her erotic attachments to another woman; therefore, her poems record same-sex desire and have long belonged to the canon of gay and lesbian literature. Faulkner's imitation of this Sappho serves a purpose beyond mere apprenticeship. He is appropriating Sappho's illicit same-sex desire and making it his own heteroerotic love poem to an idealized female. In so doing, he demonstrates the power of same-sex desire to convey universal emotion. As they (lesbians) love, so he loves. In this regard, "o atthis" differs from "L'Apres Midi" and "Sapphics," which remain heterosexual fantasies with no regard for the subjectivity of those engaged in same-sex relationships.

When Faulkner, a male poet, appropriates the voice of Sappho to praise Atthis, he infuses that voice with heterosexual desire that, if coded, is heterosexual nonetheless, and only minimally coded. As Swinburne and Mallarme can record their voyeuristic encounter with lesbian erotics and still stay safely in the realm of heterosexual fantasy, Faulkner's inhabiting the voice of Sappho also safely remains in the same realm. One could argue that his interest in imitating this style is to find a way in his poetry to cry out for Estelle. According to Sensibar in *Faulkner and Love*, he wrote the poem before January 1920, at a time near to one of her visits to Oxford after her marriage. It is not unreasonable to read the poem as Faulkner making himself Sappho and cleaving his/her chest over the loss of Estelle/Atthis to another man (Cornell Franklin), though as with all his apocryphal creations, this poem is an imitative experiment in style about Estelle's loss, not necessarily a measure of Faulkner's actual emotional depths as much as a measure of his acute perception of how to make real events into aesthetic creations. For Faulkner, "o atthis" is not a very lesbian poem at all in that the male author can easily be seen as simply appropriating a female voice to lament his female lover, but the subversive same-sex desires at the heart of the poem do not transform easily into voyeuristic fantasy. We are not watching lesbians kiss; we are hearing a person grieve, who happens to be a lesbian. The reason for this remaining element of same-sex subjectivity may result from the influence of William Alexander Percy.

In November 1920, Faulkner published in *The Mississippian* a review of William Alexander Percy's volume *In April Once*. Comparing Percy to Swinburne and noting that Percy "obscures the whole mental horizon" (*EP* 73), he dwells on the pagan and Latin influences in Percy's poems to claim that Percy "suffered the misfortune of having been born out of his time" (71). Overall, the review attempts to make room for Percy's antiquated poetic forms; saying that Percy is a poet out of his time is not intended as an insult. Nonetheless, when Ben Wasson introduced Faulkner to Percy in Greenville, the review had stung Percy enough to mitigate any jovial meeting between the two, though in New York in 1921 Percy befriended Faulkner as if untroubled by the review after all. Percy's *In April Once* is not his only work that seems out of its time. The title poem of Percy's first collection, *Sappho in Levkas*, also harkens back to the

Victorians in its extreme coding of same-sex desire. As Faulkner read Percy's second volume, we may assume that he was familiar with the first, and possibly familiar with the criticisms directed toward it.

Benjamin Wise discusses the critical reaction to Percy's earlier volume, citing specifically the review of Harriet Monroe in the *Memphis Commercial Appeal*, which hit the same notes as Faulkner's later review of *In April Once*.[3] Monroe argued that the book "represented certain tendencies which the modern poet should avoid with every fibre of his being and every effort of his art" (qtd. in Wise 136). What Monroe missed, however, is that Percy was not writing in the modernist tradition but in a classical one in line with coded homosexual works by the likes of "Walter Pater, John Addington Symonds, and Charles Kains-Jackson, among others," and that Percy was "trying to portray homosexual relationships not as sodomy but as love" (Wise 137). To accomplish this end, in "Sappho in Levkas" Percy wrote from the point of view of Sappho crying out to her spiritual father Zeus. Percy's poem is not a fragment; it is hundreds of lines long. As Sappho, the speaker laments not the loss of Atthis or an idealized female, but rather confesses her attraction to and her affair with the young shepherd boy Phaon. The eroticism in the poem remains homoerotic; Percy may have written as a woman, but he was a man, and the speaker uses *her* gender to praise the beauty of a man *she* wants but cannot have. As will his female counterpart Atthis, Phaon abandons Sappho, leaving her to the despair that becomes the impetus of her lament. The loss of love, not the erotic titillation of viewing two nymphs in loving embrace or two lesbians kissing, is the source of poetic inspiration.

Faulkner's far gentler critique of Percy's later volume of poetry suggests that he understood the deeper meaning in Percy's poetry better than other contemporary reviewers. Faulkner's review of *In April Once*, in which Faulkner focused on the classical instead of the modernist nature of Percy's poems, was quite possibly his way of responding in code to Percy's coded poetry. He recognized Percy's "tendencies," and if they are not "modernist," then Faulkner was still willing to grant that they belong to a tradition worthy of respect, even if they were formally outmoded. Possibly, too, Faulkner was aware of the deeper codes of a poem such as "o atthis," his own imitation of Sappho, though his poem is a far more formally modernist adaptation than Percy's. In content, however, both Faulkner and Percy display similar techniques. Percy, a gay man, parrots Sappho, a lesbian, to praise the beauty of Phaon, a shepherd boy, and to lament Phaon's loss and the transgression against her own same-sex desires that he caused her (a coded way for Percy to confess his own transgression against heterosexual expectations). To ferret out the intricate layers of same-sex desire in the poem requires a highly astute understanding of the way in which the poem is structured. In his imitation of Sappho, Faulkner parrots the lesbian to lament the loss of Atthis, a woman. Faulkner is still partaking of a heterosexual tradition of appropriating lesbian themes for heteroerotic ends, but the poem is far tamer than his previous two lesbian-themed poems in that it at least tacitly acknowledges the universal applicability of Sapphic love. Percy's gay-male-themed Sapphic poem offered a model to Faulkner of how to move beyond the purely voyeuristic appropriation of lesbian themes.

Faulkner would not write only lesbian-themed poetry during this period. Shortly after these early poetic experiments, he published a provocative poem in New Orleans that draws heavily from his experiences with Wasson. In June 1922, the *Double Dealer*, a magazine out of New Orleans that also published Hemingway and other major voices of American Modernism, published "Portrait," by William Faulkner. The poem consists of six quatrains, each with an individual ABCB rhyme scheme. The action in the poem revolves around a speaker who refers to himself as "I" and a partner whom the speaker refers to as "you." The two are returning from a night out together, "tonight's movie" (*EP* 99). The speaker sounds like a gentler, less mortified Prufrock than Eliot's original as he directs: "Let us walk here, softly checked with shadow, / And talk of careful trivialities" (99). The setting recalls the one described by Wasson in his memoir after Faulkner's initiation into SAE at the Stone house. Faulkner guided Wasson back through the dark woods, Wasson trailing in Faulkner's wake and brimming with awe at the rites of initiation. Faulkner is not the speaker, necessarily, nor is he transcribing exactly the events of that walk through the woods, but the imagery of the poem, the situation it describes, and the relationship between the "you" and the "I" seem greatly influenced by this or a very similar memory.

Much in the poem suggests parallels to Wasson's later account, both in the minute detail that Faulkner uses and in the way in which Faulkner presents the relationship between the speaker and his companion. The speaker recalls, "The darkness scurries, / And we hear again a music both have heard / Singing blood to blood between your palms" (99). Perhaps the music is Beethoven, whom Faulkner shared with Wasson on their "several such music sessions when the Stone family was away" (Wasson 35). Also, the intimacy of the poem brims with delicate but heavily erotic connotation:

> Come, lift your eyes, your tiny scrap of mouth
> So lightly mobile on your dim white face;
> Aloofly talk of life, profound in youth
> And simple also. (*EP* 99)

The "tiny scrap of mouth" and "dim white face" suggest images of feminine beauty, but though the speaking subject of the poem might feminize the object of his gaze, that does not mean this is a "Portrait" of a lady. The feminine features might be female, but they also recall descriptions of Wasson, famed for his angelic features and youthful beauty. That the speaker wants this object of his affection to talk of life "aloofly" in a way "profound in youth and simple also" will later be echoed in the speaker's partially admonishing, "You are so young" (99), which recalls the rocking horse on which Faulkner once placed Wasson, his Sir Galahad. The sting of the admonition is minimal, for the tone of the poem suggests a nurturing, paternal quality in the speaker. He is enamored with the youth of this person walking with him. Emphasizing the youth and femininity of the "you" in the poem are ways that the speaker establishes the hierarchy of their relationship. He is older and wiser, the youth younger and more impressionable. He leads, the youth follows. He literally looks down on the youth, who has to "lift your eyes" to the speaker. The tiny, feminine mouth serves both as synecdoche for all the youth's tiny, feminine features and as a contrast to the unstated manliness of the speaker, whose mouth is not so tiny, nor the rest of him we would presume. Faulkner was never a tall nor imposing man in real life, but he relies on the dichotomy of small/large, feminine/masculine to establish, structurally, the nature of the relationship between the two bodies in the poem.

The tone is similar to the one Wasson attempts to impart to Faulkner in his memoir as Faulkner gently admonishes him after the SAE initiation for being "filled with awe, imbued by the performance of words and rituals, the ceremony having left an almost hypnotic effect on me" (Wasson 32). That memoir would not be published for nearly sixty years after "Portrait" first appeared, but the similar treatment of this shared memory bridges those years, suggesting that the evening had a similar impact on Faulkner. Wasson seems to think that Faulkner was dismissive of the initiation, but "Portrait" suggests that Faulkner recalled the details of that night both intricately and evocatively, not dismissively nor judgmentally. In the poem, Faulkner allows his speaker to dwell on the naivete of his protégé:

And frankly you believe
This world, this darkened street, this shadowed wall
Are dim with beauty you passionately know
Cannot fade nor cool nor die at all. (99)

The speaker also ends the poem by calling on the youth to "Profoundly speak of life, of simple truths, / The while your voice is clear with frank surprise" (100). The speaker is implying in this imperative that his own voice has lost the sense of wonder that he sees in his young protégé; but as that wonder inspires the speaker, even if sorrowfully, it serves as the impetus for the creation of the poem. The speaker envies this youth and is moved by his faith in beauty.

"Portrait" originally belonged to the unpublished collection *Vision in Spring*, which in her edition of the collection, Sensibar dates to 1921 as a gift Faulkner gave Estelle while she was in Oxford before Cornell Franklin came to retrieve her. Sensibar also considers the volume a sequence, much as the unpublished volume *The Lilacs* (1920) and the later published volume *The Marble Faun*. In light of the entire sequence, the object of the speaker's attention in "Portrait" would seem to be female. Though the poem does not contain a single gendered pronoun, the other poems in the volume have a clear sense of sexed characters: the male Pierrot, the female Columbine. At times throughout the sequence, the speaker addresses "you," speaks as both "I" and "we," and refers to "he," or Pierrot. While much ambiguity derives from this constantly changing perspective—even Sensibar claims, "*Vision in Spring* is difficult to read" (*Vision* xix)—the essential interaction seems to be between a male figure and a female figure.

Taken out of the context of its larger sequence, a context in which it was not originally published, the feminized "you" does not retain a definite sense of being "female" and could easily be the object of a different kind of erotic attraction. The poem offers little evidence to suggest that the feminine youth is, in fact, female. The only phrasing from "Portrait" that describes the physical body of the object of the speaker's attention beyond its face and mouth is from the fourth stanza:

> Young and white and strange
> You walk beside me down this shadowed street,
> Against my hand your small breast softly lies,
> And your laughter breaks the rythm of our feet. (*Vision* 34, spelling from original)

How, precisely, the speaker can both walk *beside* the "you" of the poem and have "your small breast" lying "[a]gainst my hand" makes for a strange contortion. Perhaps the speaker's arm is draped over the shoulder of this other person, and so the hand is resting in the vicinity of the breast? This is an awkward image in an awkward line, but clearly the "breast" is singular. Even the verb "lies" verifies the singularity of "breast," as it is the breast that is grammatically doing the lying "against my hand." The first and third line of all the stanzas are unrhymed; the line could just as easily have been "Against my hand your small breasts softly lie," but "breast" is singular, not the plural "breasts" used to name part of a female body Faulkner will later call "mammalian ludicrosities," also plural, in one of his more famous novels (*AILD* 164). The poetic "breast" of the poem is not a sexual innuendo; it refers to the chamber wherein resides life, wherein resides the heart, a universal organ. Otherwise, in the text of this one poem, no other evidence sexes the object of the portrait except imagination and inference.

"Portrait" was published individually in New Orleans and marks Faulkner's entrance into New Orleans as a poet long before his actual arrival there to mentor under Sherwood Anderson. By reading the poem out of sequence, the sexuality of the poem reveals itself as far less heterosexual than the longer sequence would seem to suggest that it is. Armed with Wasson's memoir account of this same period, we can easily see the details of Faulkner's poem as a reworking of his experiences with Wasson, which would imply that the intimacy of the poem, if not the sequence to which it belongs, is homosexual. Without conflating too many varieties of sexuality here, if we were to follow Sensibar's lead in her assertion that Faulkner's gift of *The Lilacs* to Stone was an enactment of homophobic anxieties (though it was not), then we could assume conversely that Faulkner's gift to Estelle of *Vision in Spring* with its poem inspired by his courtship of Wasson links the two courtships. This assumption would imply that Faulkner courted Wasson, a man, as a means of practicing his later courtship of Estelle. Such an assumption does not leave much room for homophobic anxieties on Faulkner's part. This moment could also serve as a measure of Faulkner's own profound negative capability. He could use one poem to court two different lovers of two different genders with no thought of the contradictions implicit in such a double-minded purpose. Such a negative capability would not necessarily imply that Faulkner is bisexual. Rather, he could be homosexual and not homosexual at the same time. We are, after all, talking about performance. To impart to Faulkner this degree of negative capability would imply that his sexual identity was permeable, contextual, and contingent, a move commensurate with much of the current modus operandi of sexuality studies; but to impart this capability to him also implies that he understood what being a homosexual entailed and that he understood homosexuality *as* an identity, not simply as an action. Indeed, at no point in the poem do the two bodies in it have sex.

The lone publication of "Portrait" in 1922 highlights its homosexual elements by clearing away the surrounding ambiguities of the longer sequence. Placed in a chronology building to the publication of his sketches in the *Times-Picayune*, which have numerous gay (male) themes, the homosexuality of this first New Orleans publication accords with Faulkner's general development as a writer in the early 1920s. Nor does the poem, as a purveyor of gay male themes, wince or flinch in its depiction of intimacy, nor make its depictions voyeuristic.

More Short Fiction

By 1924, when Faulkner moved to New Orleans with a copy of his recently self-published *The Marble Faun* in hand, Wasson's central place in Faulkner's apocryphal gay imagination was shifting, and naturally so. "Portrait" was likely written before Faulkner's sojourn to New York in late 1921, though published in New Orleans afterward. In New Orleans Faulkner would find a different experience of homosexuality than what he knew in Oxford. With Wasson in Oxford, there is a certain insularity to Faulkner's gay depictions as the private walk on a dark lane with his one companion or the romantic escapism of a failed courtier dreaming of an isolated space on a hillside with his one true love. New York, and definitely New Orleans, would introduce Faulkner to a

much larger gay world wherein such isolation would not have been the readily available and recognizable place for queer identities. In these communities,
homosexuals abounded *as* communities. The influence of these communities
on Faulkner's writing was the new narrative perspective that he developed to
record those communities as an observer and a commentator on the ways in
which homosexuals integrate into and interact in their social settings. Also,
often the central narrator or character in his New Orleans writings participates
in the homosexual interactions being recorded. In "Out of Nazareth" the narrator is out cruising with a character named Spratling and only desists from
courting the young vagrant whom they both approach because "Spratling saw
him first," so he had dibs we might say (*New Orleans Sketches* 47). Such a defer-
ral allows the narrator to back out of the direct courtship and record the gay
life around him, whereas the unnamed protagonist in "Moonlight" and the
speaker in "Portrait" do not have a perspective that allows them to see beyond
their immediate moment or outside of themselves. Beyond the intimacy of
their encounters, their experiences are isolated from their larger world; their
desires are insular, their place marginal, their state alone. In New Orleans, gay
men are everywhere, and Faulkner would gleefully record the gay life he witnessed all around him there.

The three stories that best epitomize Faulkner's recording of the gay life
of New Orleans are "Jealousy," "Out of Nazareth," and "Don Giovanni." Gary
Richards offers the most thorough overview of these stories and the gay
themes they present, though his treatment of these themes often ventures into
a common trope prevalent in scholarly attempts to place Faulkner in proximity to homosexuality: anxiety must rule the day. The source of the anxiety
model of Faulkner and (homo)sexuality has roots deep in the creation of the
accepted biography of Faulkner. Richards, like most scholars, uses published
biographies, not the archived notes on which those biographies are based. The
image of New Orleans and its gay community is anything but tight-lipped in
Blotner's archived notes, as demonstrated by John Shelton Reed's preference
for those notes to construct the "bohemian" atmosphere of New Orleans in
the 1920s. Unfortunately, when Blotner chose to exclude those details from
his published biographical record, he inadvertently set in motion an erroneous (because incomplete) understanding of Faulkner and sexuality. As later
studies have attempted to reconstruct an understanding of Faulkner's life in
relation to homosexuality but without access to the full record of Faulkner's
gay life, the distortions of that life move toward increasing grotesquery, to borrow a term from Sherwood Anderson, an apropos borrowing from Faulkner's
time in New Orleans. The grotesquery that has developed is that the one truth
of Faulkner's sexual life must be his anxiety about it. Using Anderson's terminology from the opening section of *Winesburg, Ohio*, we might say that this
"truth," formed of a great many vague thoughts, loses what inherent "beauty"

it might have had as it becomes the sole item of focus. Perhaps we could better state this distortion as that this original idea loses whatever potential it might have had to shed new light on the work and the man; instead it becomes a *falsehood*—or a misinterpretation that perpetuates and distorts itself through repetition, much like Wing Biddlebaum's hands in the first story in Anderson's collection overwhelm him and perpetuate his self-hatred. Thus, what started as a conclusion deduced from the consideration of certain evidence—which, as it turns out, was not all the evidence, only certain selective evidence—has become an *a priori* assumption directing subsequent discussion to look basically something like this: sex freaked Faulkner out, and particularly anything even remotely queer, much less gay, surely caused him endless anxiety that boiled over in his writings. That Faulkner might have immersed himself as an observer and fellow traveler in a sexual subculture, as many of Blotner's interviews suggest, is a detail lost to the distortion. The anxiety model flourishes unmitigated by the biographical evidence of Faulkner's comfort among gay men. Certainly, Faulkner may have had his anxious moments, but those moments are only part—and I would argue a small part—of the larger narrative of his (apocryphal) gay life.

Beyond Blotner's archived notes, the relatively recent addition of the letter from the *Item-Tribune*, "What's the Matter with Marriage," could help mitigate the near-ubiquity of the anxiety model. James Meriwether included the essay in his 2004 re-edition of *Essays, Speeches, and Public Letters*. Faulkner's thoughts on marriage and the basis of a successful relationship suggest far less anxiety about same-sex "partnerships" than most scholars apply to his works. As a measure of his response to his surroundings when he wrote the letter, Faulkner's advocacy for same-sex relationships does much to assuage the notion that he felt anxiety over his gay life in New Orleans. Read alongside his New Orleans sketches, the editorial points to a more complex understanding of gay life and activities than one saturated with anxiety and aversion.

"Jealousy" demonstrates the tension that arises when readings of Faulkner's stories suffused with the notion of his sexual anxieties run headlong into the greater, if apocryphal, influence of his immersion in a gay community. In the story, a restaurant owner, Antonio, tries to convince himself that a young waiter is flirting with his wife. The root cause of his tension is that the waiter's friendliness with his wife, if it is *not* flirting, must be a kind of effeminate gay chumminess and is, therefore, threatening to Antonio's manhood much more deeply than if the waiter were merely trying to cuckold him. In a fit of rage, he threatens to kill his wife, only to have her dismiss him as "insane" and recall him to his duties as host while patrons arrive for dinner. Antonio then approaches the waiter with the same accusation, that the waiter is having an affair with his wife. Richards narrates the exchange that follows:

If anything, the waiter seems stereotypically gay. Consistently flashing his "white satirical smile," he flatly denies the husband's accusations with bitchily overprecise diction—"You are already mad. Had you not been I should have killed you ere this. Listen, tub of entrails, there is nothing between us; for her sake whom you persecute, I swear it. I have said no word to her that you have not seen, nor she to me. If she be attracted to someone, it is not I"—and the confrontation culminates when he prissily slaps the husband. (Richards 29, interior quotations *New Orleans* 34, 37–38)

Richards notes other details about the waiter, who is described in the story as "a tall Roman god in a soiled apron," marked by his "supple grace" (*NOS* 34, 36). Richards proceeds to read the story as an indictment of "unenviable heterosexuality" (Richards 30) in which Faulkner uses the "courteous and efficient" (*NOS* 36) waiter as a juxtaposition to the clod-like owner who sells his restaurant to the waiter rather than continue to expose his wife to whatever it is that seems to be bothering him. For Richards, the story is primarily about Antonio's fear of emasculation (which can certainly produce homophobia), and the focus is squarely on Antonio rather than the waiter, who is "bitchily overprecise" and "stereotypical."

Richards does not, however, include in his discussion the waiter's response to Antonio that if Antonio wants to kill him, he would have to do it "from behind" (*NOS* 38). John Duvall appropriates similar imagery from Faulkner's World War I stories to discuss "male homosexual panic" over the prospect of anal penetration and emasculation. If we apply that anxiety here, that doing it "from behind" is a kind of Freudian slip on the part of the waiter about anal sex, the tensions between the waiter and Antonio amplify to something more than what Richards deems "simply the husband's projections" of his homophobia onto the waiter. That something more manifests in extreme violence when Antonio attempts to shoot the waiter in the back of the head at the end of the story only to have the gun explode in his hands while the waiter "crashe[s] forward into a glass table, then to the floor" (*NOS* 40). Standing at point-blank range, the waiter is at the very least seriously injured, possibly killed by the "husband's projections," which are considerably more violent and dangerous than the metaphorical projection of anxiety at the beginning of the story over perceptions of possible queerness or cuckoldry. This story represents no mere "irony [. . .] in the scenario of triangulated desire that evinces a pronounced homoerotic connection between the two men," as Richards describes it (29). The metaphorical injury to Antonio's heterosexual masculinity may be unfortunate, but we cannot ignore that the "stereotypically gay" waiter is seriously injured, too. When perception induces violence, we should not fault the victim for being stereotypical (any more than we would fault a rape victim for daring to wear a nice dress or an abused spouse for daring to talk back to his partner). The story is not about the woes of heterosexual angst. The story documents a hate crime.

The two opposing forces in Richards's reading are "stereotypically gay" and "unenviable heterosexuality." That the unenviable heterosexual severely wounds if not kills the stereotypical homosexual does not find a place in his reading; rather, the "near-constant anxiety about heterosexuality" that Richards finds in the *New Orleans Sketches* comes to elide considerations of homosexual representation (Richards 29). The waiter does appear to be crafted to pique the reader to believe he might be gay, perhaps stereotypically so. His actions may well be "bitchy" and "prissy," and his entrance into the story as a "tall Roman god" offers a quick if superficial way to suggest that he attracts the eye. Antonio notices him and "knotted his hand into a fist upon the desk and he stared at his whitening knuckles as at something new and strange" (*NOS* 35). Clearly, what he sees troubles him, but Antonio's feeling hyperbolic anxiety does not mean that Faulkner felt the same degree of anxiety over prissy gay men himself.

The real tension in the early scenes of the story is between seeing and reacting: the appearance of someone who looks gay and the reaction of someone troubled by his own perception that someone else is a homosexual. Given that reaction, what consequences might result? We might imagine Faulkner sitting in his own Vieux Carre cafe, observing the patrons and the waiters in that gay space and imagining the confrontation that he describes between a waiter and an owner, arguing bitchily and prissily with each other, in public no less. Faulkner's genius is in taking us from that superficial moment and into the personal lives of these two men all the way to the violence at the end of the story. The story offers no real clues as to the nature of the relationship between these two men beyond being a rancorous business partnership infused by jealousies that at times almost surface but ultimately remain elusive and unclear. Out of that ambiguity, Faulkner apocryphizes a scenario that is not a spilling over of his own heterosexual anxieties, but is, rather, an indictment of heterosexual anxiety that is taken to the grotesque extreme of becoming irrational. Antonio is mad; Faulkner uses him to demonstrate how dangerous such madness and panic can be. Indeed, even if the waiter is "stereotypically gay," Antonio is no more justified in trying to kill him than if the waiter were gay but less flamboyantly so. Faulkner is not the homophobe in the story. In his observations about the dangers of overreacting to a person who might be perceived as gay, this story is an indictment of homophobia.

Seemingly the diametrical opposite of "Jealousy" is the sketch "Out of Nazareth." The setting is Jackson Square. An unnamed narrator is wandering the streets with his friend Spratling. They are talking about art and the use of light in paintings, but this conversation is a cover; the two men are cruising the park together, a gay practice as common then as now. After the exposition, the action in the story begins not with jealousy, but with an abnegation of it. Upon seeing a young man in front of St. Andrew's Cathedral, Spratling exclaims, "'My God,' he said, clutching me, 'look at that face'" (*NOS* 47). Since "Spratling saw him first," the narrator allows him to do the courting, which in turn allows the narrator to record the courtship, but not before the narrator dwells upon the nature of this particular beauty:

> And one could imagine young David looking like that. One could imagine Jonathan getting that look from David, and, serving the highest function of which sorry man is capable, being the two of them beautiful in similar peace and simplicity—beautiful as gods, as no woman can ever be. And to think of speaking to him, of entering that dream, was like a desecration. (47)

The "desecration" of "entering that dream" is probably less noble than it sounds (a prurient mind might read such language as a poetic way of referring to penetrative anal sex). Thankfully, this "desecration" is also "beautiful as gods" and beautiful in a way "no woman can ever be." Meanwhile, more a painter than a man of words, Spratling says hello. Spratling and the narrator take the young man to eat, where they learn that he is effectively a hobo traveling cross-country from migrant work camp to work camp, but that he also writes.[4]

The innocence of the exchange seems, as the narrator suggests, almost a desecration to read for its deep and loud homosexual undertones, as if to do so would break the delicacy of a love that dares not speak its name. Therefore, rather than directly admit his feelings, the young man hands over his copy of A. E. Housman's *Shropshire Lad* and explains that he "like[s] it because the man that wrote it felt that way, and didn't care who knew" (49). Neither Spratling nor the narrator bothers to ask "what way" Housman felt. The crux of the story is that one either knows or does not know. Spratling and the narrator know. We, as readers, are invited to test our own wits. Just as the young man will not state aloud what they all three know, the narrator refuses to name what he, too, does not care if his reader knows. The "secret" of the reference is that careful readers would recognize Housman's interests in "lads" in the volume as an elaborate coding of his homosexual desires. No less a critic than Paul Fussell even claims of the volume that few readers were unaware of what was effectively Housman's open secret: the suffering lads were his way of depicting his (at the time) illicit homosexual desires in a form that allowed him to praise their beauty and valor. Faulkner's narrator in this story appropriates Housman's book of poetry to accomplish the same end.

The young man wants to pay for his meal, but Spratling will not allow it. As an alternative method of payment, he suggests that the young man come to his apartment the next day so Spratling can use him as a model for a painting. If Spratling wants to sketch the young man for a painting, then the narrator writes his "sketch," so he gets his own kind of gratification from the exchange. The multiple types of sketching occurring in this exchange allow for the word *sketch* to expand to the realm of euphemism. To "sketch" the young man means alternatively to draw him, to write about him, and to make sexual advances toward him, at least to the degree that both forms of artistic sketching involve paying tribute to his beauty. Spratling absolutely insists that the young man "call on *us* tomorrow" (49, italics added), implying that he and the narrator will be present for what ensues at the euphemistic "sketching." The invitation to an intimate, private "sketching" suggests that Spratling intends for the young lad to pay for his meal with sex (or at least pose for a nude).

Instead, the young man hands over a story he has written, before "confid[ing] to Spratling and me, blushing, that he is seventeen" (*NOS* 53). The narrator, accordingly, reprints that story in the frame of his larger sketch. Gary Richards rightly calls the story written by the young man a "powerful Whitmanic narrative" (35). The short piece seems actually to be a prose revision of "Pioneers! O Pioneers!" with the longer frame narrative serving as a kind of explanation of its powerful homoeroticism. The full sketch "Out of Nazareth" almost seems like an extended trope of stanza eighteen of Whitman's poem:

> I too with my soul and body,
> We, a curious trio, picking, wandering on our way,
> Through these shores amid the shadows, with the apparitions pressing,
> Pioneers! O Pioneers! (lines 69–72)

The narrator, acting as a kind of sexual pioneer, channels to great effect both Whitman and Housman in this sketch set on the "shores" (or banks) of the Mississippi River. Jackson Square specifically, but by extension the Vieux Carre of which it is the heart, serves as a space to act out the powerful homoeroticism of Whitman's poetry in the specific homosexual context of the gay life of New Orleans. One cannot help but note two key features of the sketch: the narrator is implicating the degree to which he participated in, not just observed, that life, and he puts that life out in the open, in the public Jackson Square in the middle of the afternoon, as if for the world to see. As for Whitman's "amid the shadows," the only shadow cast in the story is the narrator's refusal to state clearly that which can be reasonably inferred. Alas, to think: Faulkner—or at least his narrator—might have felt this way and does not care who knows! Next to "Divorce in Naples," the sketch "Out of Nazareth" is Faulkner's most overtly gay text. For all its suggestive silence, it is also arguably the most celebratory.

Both "Jealousy" and "Out of Nazareth" were published in the *Times-Picayune* in 1925, on 1 March and 12 April, respectively, dates congruent with Faulkner's publication of his editorial on marriage in the *Item-Tribune* on 4 April. The third gay narrative from Faulkner's pre-European New Orleans period was never published in his lifetime, at least not in its original form. Joseph Blotner dates "Don Giovanni" to "the first half of 1925" and notes that its original type-script includes under Faulkner's name the address "624 Orleans Alley/ New Orleans," the address he shared with Spratling beginning in March of 1925 and where he also wrote *Soldiers' Pay* (*US* 705). "Don Giovanni" resembles a more mature version of "Moonlight" in that the plight of the protagonist, Herbie, mirrors that of the unnamed protagonist from the earlier story. Herbie, however, is a thirty-two-year-old widower with thinning hair who married early in life with hardly any courtship, only to have his wife become an invalid and die. Herbie's age makes him exactly twice as old as the protagonist from "Moonlight." Now, much older, Herbie wants to court a woman. Skeet becomes Morrison, a more worldly-wise and patient friend whom Herbie consults for tactics to woo a woman. Morrison lives upstairs from an unnamed writer who represents a new element in the story. Blotner suggests that the basic premise of the relation-ship among Herbie, Morrison, and the unnamed writer is modeled upon that of Faulkner, William Spratling, and Sherwood Anderson.

This story epitomizes Faulkner's move from the insular gay themes of his earliest writing to the communal gay themes of his New Orleans material. Herbie spends the first half of the story explaining his plans to court his date not to his date but to Morrison. The story implies that such lengthy discus-sions between Morrison and Herbie are common. The first implication that something is amiss comes from the unnamed writer. When Herbie first tries to find Morrison to go over his game plan for his date, Morrison is asleep. Herbie yells up to him from the street only to have the unnamed writer complain about the noise and ask Herbie if "you think this is a bathroom?" (*US* 481). The writer does not know what Herbie wants to talk about, but his equating Herbie's actions to something one does in a bathroom strikes an odd note. To get rid of Herbie, the writer wakes Morrison, essentially allowing whatever is going on between Herbie and Morrison to happen so long as it does not inter-fere with his work. What ensues is a conversation about the planned courtship longer than the courtship itself. Morrison approves the plan, though with a slightly ironic tone as he seems to understand how hopeless Herbie's plan is. Part of the conversation turns to the weight of Herbie's "artillery" and its lack of recent use (483–84). Still, rather than dash Herbie's hopes, Morrison encour-ages him. The communal aspect of these three men helping each other over-shadows the homoerotic subtext in Herbie and Morrison's conversation. The conversation does not stand out as odd in this context, even if it should belong in a bathroom.

Such is not the case *after* the date, when Herbie seeks out Morrison again. Herbie's courtship fails. He finds out that his planned conversation, calculated to elicit very precise responses from his date, does not elicit the responses he expects. Courting a woman proves to be far more difficult than he imagined. We do not witness any of the date firsthand. Rather, "[p]erhaps three hours later," Herbie returns to call again on Morrison. The writer intercedes. Herbie finds himself talking at length about the date to the writer, explaining how his date deserted him for a younger, rougher man. The writer would find the story humorous if he did not find it so pathetic. He expresses his stupefied rage by exclaiming aloud, "'God, regard your masterpiece! Balzac, despair! [. . .] Get to hell out of here,' he roared, 'you have made me sick!'" (487). He suggests that Herbie "go to a brothel, if you want a girl" (487). Herbie, though, does not seem to want an actual girl. He really seems to want to seduce somebody, nothing more. Unable to rouse Morrison and thrown out by the writer, he wanders the streets and considers a new plan: he will talk rough and be rough! This, he is sure, is the secret. Needing to tell Morrison, he calls him and, rather than let Morrison get in a word even in greeting, as soon as Herbie hears the phone pick up, he dives into his new plan: "I will be cruel, hard, and brutal, if necessary, until she begs for my love. What do you think of that?" (488). Here, as he did in "Moonlight," Faulkner turns the story on its head in a single line. Rather than Morrison being on the other end, Herbie finds that he was talking to the operator, a woman, who responds in kind: "You tell 'em, big boy; treat 'em rough" (488). In the story, Herbie gets no closer to a courtship than this.

If in "Moonlight" the pastoral romance imagined by the narrator seems melancholy and wishful, in "Don Giovanni" Faulkner elevates a sense of homosexual longing to the level of farce. In "Moonlight," there is no one to identify that what the protagonist is feeling when he longs to be with Skeet on a hillside is a homosexual desire. In "Don Giovanni," the female operator's response immediately brings to the fore the intense eroticism that has colored Herbie and Morrison's interactions all along. Herbie courts Morrison. Though the writer might see it at first, so long as it does not interfere with his work, he does not care. When Herbie forlornly explains his failures to the writer, then the writer dismisses Herbie and even claims that Herbie makes him sick. Undeterred, Herbie continues to seek out Morrison, whom he clearly feels is his one companion in the world, from whom he seeks understanding, solace, advice, and company. When Herbie finally does muster the courage to speak openly about what he wants, his pure impatient rush to talk to Morrison mucks up the whole affair. Indeed, Morrison should have been on the other end of the line; Herbie wants to say these things to Morrison in the first place. Faulkner does not, however, lament the farce of the pseudo-homosocial conventions keeping Herbie and Morrison from speaking openly to each other (they do enact their courtship through a woman, if only by telephone and accidentally). He makes the farce humorous; no harm comes to anyone. The writer keeps writing, the operator hangs up to take another call. Herbie is embarrassed. Morrison is still out there waiting to listen patiently to Herbie's woman troubles, to hear Herbie "treat 'em [them? him?] rough," and to enact varieties of courtship rituals with him until Herbie finally gets that courtship right.

Mosquitoes, Both Ways

Though Faulkner never published "Don Giovanni," he used it as the framework on which to build his second novel, *Mosquitoes*, about the inanity, artistic pretensions, and sexual ambiguities of New Orleans bohemian life. Faulkner transforms Herbie into Ernest Talliaferro, Morrison into Dawson Fairchild, a writer, and the unnamed writer into Gordon, a sculptor. Herbie's date, identified in "Don Giovanni" as Miss Steinbauer, becomes Jenny in the novel (*US* 705). These changes and the expanded length of the novel gave Faulkner a canvas on which to paint much more broadly and intricately developed characters. While most of the commentary about homosexual themes in the novel appertains to its lesbian content, there is also material in the novel appertaining to themes of male homosexuality, most notably in the character of Dawson Fairchild. One could reasonably suggest that the novel is just a longer version of "Don Giovanni," in which Faulkner changed the names of the principal characters and to which he added roughly three hundred pages of banal artistic banter that takes place over four days on a boat. Faulkner also added some clarity to the original scene in "Don Giovanni." Expecting to hear from Talliaferro/Herbie after his failed courtship of Jenny, Fairchild/ Morrison laments, "I wish Talliaferro could find him a woman. I'm tired of being seduced," and so explicitly names the type of relationship that he and Talliaferro have (*Mosquitoes* 313). Though the novel leaves much ambiguity in Talliaferro's character, his double courtship, first with the older rich widow Mrs. Maurier and then with Jenny, makes him seem ultimately heterosexual, but he maintains at least a latent desire to prefer the company of men. On the other hand, Fairchild does not need Talliaferro to seduce him. Faulkner's other central addition to the novel is Julius Wiseman, Fairchild's friend, who is often identified as "the Semitic man" and who joins the cast as Fairchild's constant companion.

Minrose Gwin explores gay male themes in the novel, but her emphasis rests squarely on Talliaferro in her essay "Does Ernest Like Gordon? Faulkner's *Mosquitoes* and the Bite of 'Gender Trouble.'" The question of her title is apt; she finds evidence of Talliaferro's interest in Gordon in the first scene of the novel, perhaps an outgrowth in the added material of residual gay themes from "Don Giovanni." Ernest spends time "watching [Gordon's] hard body in the stained trousers and undershirt, watching the curling vigor of his hair" (*Mosquitoes* 10). At the end of the novel, Talliaferro calls Fairchild in a repeat of the ending scene from "Don Giovanni." We could not, however, rephrase her question "Does Gordon Like Ernest?" Gordon is described in the novel as the "queer shabby Mr. Gordon," so he clearly elicits a strange response from people, but he proves to be the most hypermasculine figure and only successful courtier of women on the boat. Gwin reads these incidences as evidence of "gender trouble," using Judith Butler's concept from her book of the same name, rather than as evidence of male homosexuality.

In the revision of "Don Giovanni" into *Mosquitoes*, Faulkner's most consistently gay male character is not Talliaferro, but Dawson Fairchild, with a little help from his friend/lover Julius Wiseman. Unfortunately, the impression that Sherwood Anderson served as the model for Fairchild seems to have precluded such a discussion of Fairchild's homosexuality. Blotner suggests that Morrison in "Don Giovanni" is based on Sherwood Anderson, a connection he carries to its logical conclusion in relation to *Mosquitoes* to claim that Morrison becomes Dawson Fairchild. This flow chart roots Fairchild in Anderson as well (*US* 705). Frederick Karl supports Blotner's character genealogy and claims in his introduction to the most recent edition of the novel that "Dawson Fairchild stands in, in many ways, for Sherwood Anderson" (1). This genealogy seems logical if we assume that any single character in one of Faulkner's novels functions in a 1:1 correlation with a real-life person, but the problem is that if Fairchild is Anderson and Anderson was a heterosexual, then considering Fairchild to be a homosexual would seem to be rather *illogical* as having no biographical basis. If *Mosquitoes* evolved out of Faulkner's life in New Orleans in such a directly correlative way, then the family tree of each character implicitly limits interpretations of those characters beyond the confines of reasonable poetic license. Indeed, could a homosexual suddenly appear in the branches of any family tree with no predecessor or genetic origin, as simply a completely original mutation? Or must there always be genetic precedent? Thankfully, this study is not designed to determine the root cause of homosexuality as something one is born with, achieves, or has thrust upon them. Rather, wherever homosexuality might have come from, this study seeks to understand if Faulkner coded this fictional character as homosexual. If so, how? And, maybe also, why?

Faulkner transferred actual characteristics into his apocryphal creations more complexly than as 1:1 correlations, and there might be other DNA than just Sherwood Anderson's that informs Fairchild's genetics. If we consider that Spratling may also inform Fairchild, then we might be able to see the degree to which we can read Fairchild for his heavily suggestive homosexuality. Morrison in "Don Giovanni" is *not* a writer. The writer in the original story has no name. He is too busy to put up with Herbie's games of courtship. Meanwhile, Herbie and Morrison forge ahead with their courtship and leave the stodgy old writer to grumble in despair and disgust at what he perceives as man's degradation. As in "Out of Nazareth," we see Herbie and Morrison effectively "cruise" together, though not in the specific context of two men on the prowl for a sexual partner in Jackson Square but as two men trading ideas about how to secure a partner, ostensibly a woman of course. Blotner also suggests that the unnamed writer becomes Gordon (*US* 705). Gordon, the sculptor, seems likely kin to Spratling, a visual artist and architect as opposed to a writer; but the unnamed writer that links the actual Spratling and the apocryphal Gordon certainly makes for an unclear genealogy. In *Mosquitoes*, the unnamed writer appears in the epilogue in sections 5 and 10 as a character in addition to Gordon. If there is any genetic kinship between Gordon in *Mosquitoes* and the unnamed writer in "Don Giovanni," that kinship results from Faulkner splitting the original character to create two new characters, not merely renaming one character as someone else. Into one of those new characters, Faulkner infused elements of William Spratling. Similarly, Fairchild is not 100 percent Sherwood Anderson. In his revisions, Faulkner included a great deal of Spratling in Fairchild as well. Blotner and Karl are not wrong to explicate genealogies between real-life figures in Faulkner's life and his fictional creations, and certainly Anderson informs Morrison and Fairchild. Their genealogies, however, only tell part of the whole that Faulkner so deftly apocryphized for his fictional creations. If Spratling was right, that he is reflected in a character in *Soldiers' Pay*, then he is very likely reflected in characters in *Mosquitoes* as well. Much of Fairchild may have roots in him, and much of Fairchild seems to owe a debt to his homosexuality. Out of these multiple origins, a gay character appears.

Evidence abounds in *Mosquitoes* to suggest that Fairchild is a homosexual. Early in the novel, when Talliaferro asks Fairchild to keep him company and give him advice, Fairchild responds that "Julius and I are spending the evening together," implying that Talliaferro would be a third-wheel (44).[5] Later, Julius and Fairchild run into Gordon by a row of warehouses near the dock and discuss the impending boat party. Speaking of the value of having friends with boats and cars, Fairchild explains, "If you can neither ride nor drive the beast yourself, it's a good idea to keep it in a pasture nearby" (50), but his "beast" is no longer purely boats and cars. It morphs into a metaphor, ostensibly, for having a woman available "to ride" as needed. Gordon does not respond, but Julius does, calling out Fairchild for his faux-heterosexual reference: "But you've got your simile backwards [. . .] You were speaking from the point of view of the rider" (50). Julius's zinger is meant to remind Fairchild that men can be kept and ridden just as cars and women can (in contemporary gay parlance, Julius is distinguishing between a "top" and a "bottom" and implying that Fairchild is the latter). If Julius is Fairchild's lover, then this line is the wink-and-nod acknowledgment between them. They trade increasingly metaphoric barbs in front of Gordon before moving on without him. Fairchild and Julius then wander the banks of the Mississippi River and watch "[t]wo ferry boats [which] passed and repassed like a pair of golden swans in a barren cycle of courtship" (53). These boats (designated with a pun on "ferry") mirror Fairchild and Julius, though if their "cycle of courtship" is "barren," they still stand together on the banks, "remove their hats," and watch peacefully and without speaking the coming and going of the boats in their courtship, a ritual with significance to them, "barren" or not. This mutual watching is one of the only unspoken moments in a novel dedicated to conversation and serves as a metaphor that needs no words; it dares not speak its name.

Life on the *Nausikaa* provides further evidence for Fairchild's homosexuality. Fairchild leads the men below deck at every opportunity to partake of the bootleg whiskey that he has smuggled on board. These retreats ruin Mrs. Maurier's plans for dancing and cards since her goal is to balance the number of men and women as part of her sense of social order. Playing and dancing with uneven numbers unnerves her. By default, then, Fairchild represents the loss of the heterosexual balance (men to women) of Mrs. Maurier's efforts, though we should expect nothing less of him since "Fairchild was not that sort: social obligations rested too lightly upon him" (103). When Fairchild does come above deck to engage in the sexual banter, he does so only to poke fun at heterosexual practices. Of sex between a man and woman—after marriage of course—he sneers, "If the husbands ever saw the comic aspect of it . . . But they never do [. . .] There'd sure be a decline in population if a man were twins and had to stand around and watch himself make love" (185). While this bit of wisdom implicates the ungainliness of the male as well as the female body, the "husbands" are, notably, the ones who would find it "comic." The twin husband would not necessarily find his twin the ungainly partner but rather the way that his twin, coupled with a woman, looks simply foolish. The first twin, while in mid-coitus, has the advantage of being too distracted by what he is doing to realize objectively how comical the contortions of heterosexuality are. Were the one twin to look at the other, however, he might forego the comic ugliness of "woman" altogether for the narcissistic enticement afforded by the appearance of his twin and the promise of symmetry as opposed to the comic coupling of different parts.

Returning to this theme, Fairchild calls himself "a purely lay brother to the human race" (241), implying that his only interest in heterosexuality is for its reproductive necessity, a kind of labor for the layman to perform for utility, not for enjoyment. He then goes so far as to claim of women, "After all they are merely articulated genital organs with a kind of aptitude for spending whatever money you have" (241). Fairchild prefers the company of men and dismisses the sexual appeal of women as anything more than breeders. At his side, ever present, is his friend and fellow dismissive misogynist Julius. In fact, when Mrs. Maurier has enough of Fairchild and boots him off the boat in Mandeville, he still wakes up, hungover, beside Julius and "tried to rouse the Semitic man, but the other just cursed him from his slumber and rolled over to face the wall" (302). Fairchild has gotten out of his bed to wander the room before attempting to wake Julius, and the novel leaves unclear whether the bed in which Julius sleeps is the same bed Fairchild has just exited. Then, at the end of the novel, when Talliaferro calls Fairchild to repeat the dirty-talk scene from "Don Giovanni," Fairchild is not merely out; he is out with Julius.

Fairchild and Julius partake of their share of what readers might find to be unnecessary misogyny. One could not fault Richards were he to apply to Fairchild and Julius his characterization of the gay waiter from "Jealousy"; they are a pair of "bitchy queens." There is, however, a fullness to their characters that saves them from the depths of a flat onerousness. They stay above the fray of the sexual politics onboard the *Nausikaa*, and much of their misogyny surfaces only when they are confronted with the banal sexual economics of their fellow passengers, who are not themselves particularly praiseworthy specimens of humanity, regardless of Fairchild's commentary. On land in the prologue and epilogue, Fairchild and Julius wander through the disconnected lives of the other characters as a form of social glue, generous in their friendships and untroubled by the perils of the New Orleans social/sexual scene. They suggest much about Faulkner's experiences in gay New Orleans, as their unencumbered lives prove by far the most enviable of all the characters and those characters' various attempts at their largely unsuccessful heterosexual courtships. Fairchild and Julius remind us of Faulkner's earlier concession: men and women struggle to understand each other, but two men can connect.

On the other hand, the misogyny that permeates Fairchild and Julius's relationship exceeds into Faulkner's depictions of lesbianism in the novel. His handling of lesbian sexuality—alongside his sympathetic portrayal of gay men, no less—regresses to the perspective of his early voyeuristic poetry in which he denies lesbian desire the marriage of true minds that he allows for his gay male characters. In *Mosquitoes*, Faulkner returns to Swinburne's "Sapphics." The two "lesbians" kissing from that earlier poem become Pat Robyn and Jenny Steinbauer. Aphrodite becomes Eva Wiseman, Julius's sister, only in this case she is not appalled by but pruriently participating in the heterosexual voyeurism of the supposedly homoerotic scene. That scene proves to be bona fide Faulkner apocrypha in that it was cut from the final version of the novel for reasons not altogether clear, though metaphorically the excision of the scene bears striking parallels to Faulkner's earlier handling of lesbian material in both "Sapphics" and "L'Apres Midi," where we see by not seeing. Minrose Gwin provides the excised scene, which occurs on the second day of the voyage, at the end of the "eleven o'clock section" (*Mosquitoes* 156) and briefly explicates it in relation to its surrounding context. Eva Wiseman has put Mrs. Maurier to bed and stumbles upon Pat and Jenny kissing in their bunk. The two have been alone together since the beginning of the "ten o'clock" section, undressing in front of each other and talking about their virginity for nearly fifteen pages of verbal foreplay.

Homoerotic material in the "ten o'clock" section remained in the final published version of the novel. "Jenny had the cabin to herself" (*Mosquitoes* 136) when Pat arrived. Jenny is undressing; Pat comments, "You've got a funny figure" (139), as Jenny combs her hair with the only luggage she brought—the comb. "Her hair," the narrator tells us, "lent to Jenny's divine body a halo like an angel's" (139). Pat is surprised that Jenny makes no effort to re-dress and asks aloud, "Don't you wear any nightclothes?" (140), though Jenny reminds Pat that she had promised to lend her some of her own, which Pat never supplies. As Pat lays down to sleep, "Jenny's angelic nakedness went beyond her vision and suddenly she stared at nothing with a vague orifice vaguely in the center of it, and beyond the orifice a pale moonfilled sky" (140). If we imagine that Faulkner is given to puns, then "nothing with a vague orifice vaguely in the center of it" is an indirect way of saying that Pat is staring at Jenny's naked vagina in the pale moonlight from the open port window. They discuss Pat's brother Josh, change positions in their shared bed several times, make mention of a "black man" from Mandeville named Faulkner (145), and eventually light on their mutual virginity as the scene ends and returns the reader to the upper deck and Mr. Talliaferro and Mrs. Wiseman.

With this provocative foreplay as the setup, sometime after eleven o'clock Eva Wiseman puts Mrs. Maurier to bed and comes to Jenny and Pat's cabin. The excised passage describes "the two young women, Jenny and Pat, in their shared bunk, and commences to describe explicitly and in highly erotic language their sexual contact" (Gwin 134). That passage, reprinted nearly in full in Gwin's essay, includes descriptions of Pat "stroking [Jenny's body] lightly" and Jenny "sigh[ing]" and "ma[king] a soft wet sound with her mouth" (qtd. in Gwin 134). Finally, they kiss. Gwin stops quoting the scene and proceeds to summarize what happens next:

> At this point Pat jerks away and accuses the working-class Jenny of kissing in a common way. Pat says that she will teach her how to kiss properly. As she proceeds with this undertaking, Eva Wiseman opens their door and watches them "with dark intent speculation." And here the scene, which has been framed by the lesbian presence of Eva Wiseman, ends. (135, internal quotation from *Mosquitoes* typescript)

Though she is Julius's sister, Eva Wiseman never merits the odd title "the Semitic [wo]man." Rather, the narrative and the other characters refer to her most commonly as simply Mrs. Wiseman, an honorific usually reserved for married women or, more likely in her case, for older women in a group who are not generally part of the sexual economy and are, therefore, considered off the market. Eva Wiseman is the proverbial "old maid" of the boat party, the female equivalent of a man who "ain't the marrying kind." Jenny and Pat are the objects of male sexual desire in a reiteration of the heterosexual fantasy from "Sapphics." Gwin labels Eva Wiseman a lesbian, though the novel never makes so explicit a point of naming her sexual identity. If the gay male material in the novel tropes on the unstated love that dares not speak its name, the lesbian material is simply unstated, as if to emphasize what is not seen so as to titillate with prurient innuendo the pornographic voyeurism that Faulkner prefers for lesbian bodies.

In the excised scene, the old maid Mrs. Wiseman is depicted as more than just an unfortunate woman who could never find a husband. She is, instead, the old, prurient lesbian, similar to Swinburne's Aphrodite only in what she sees, lesbians kissing, not in her reaction to it. Mrs. Wiseman is quite pleased with what she discovers. Later, "Jenny found Mrs. Wiseman in their room, changing her dress" (*Mosquitoes* 178). This encounter opens a very short scene from the "eleven o'clock" morning sequence from the Day Three chapter, so, temporally, roughly twelve hours after Eva Wiseman watched Jenny and Pat kissing. While briefly talking about Mr. Talliaferro, "Mrs. Wiseman paused and watched Jenny curiously" (178). In a much shorter rehearsal of the foreplay from the night before,

Jenny looked at her reflected face, timelessly and completely entertained. Mrs. Wiseman gazed at Jenny's fine minted hair, at her sleazy dress revealing the divine inevitability of her soft body.
     "Come here, Jenny," she said. (178)

The scene ends, fraught with implications that what follows is another kissing lesson. There is, however, no excised material from this encounter. Whereas Faulkner had his young lesbians flirt and then kiss, and then later removed the description of the actual kissing, when the older, predatory lesbian Eva Wiseman beckons Jenny, there is no scene to excise. Faulkner never intended to show his audience their kissing. This scene lacks the two nubile young bodies that make Pat and Jenny's foreplay so titillating. Also, to say the least, none of this viewing inspires the production of art. With the exception of Gordon, all the other artists and characters in the novel only talk about art but never actually produce it. In this regard, everyone's erotic output is onanistic and "barren."

Pinning down precisely why the lesbian kissing scene between Pat and Jenny was cut from the final version of the novel proves difficult. Gwin explains that, among the existing letters between Faulkner and his publisher, the crucial one in which the publisher explains the excision has not yet been found by archivists, which makes it bona fide as apocrypha as well. Ben Wasson would explain to Blotner that "[t]he book was badly cut or rather was cut badly by the publisher. The business about the lesbian attraction between Jennie and the other woman shocked the publisher."[6] Wasson's comments establish both that the excised scene was "lesbian" and that Faulkner was not responsible for its removal; his publishers were. Using the existing letters in the larger archive, Gwin offers a reasonable deduction for the removal: "that to be published in the mass market, [Faulkner learned that] he would need, at least in part, to muffle and veil explicit same-sex eroticism" in his fiction (122), though his publishers, not the mass market, seem the ultimate source of the cutting. Gwin cites as corroborating evidence for this claim the trial for obscenity of Radclyffe Hall for her lesbian-themed novel *The Well of Loneliness*, which occurred in November of 1928, roughly a year after

Mosquitoes was published, to suggest that publishers in general were nervous about material that might embroil them in costly legal proceedings.

At the risk of being too elliptical, Gwin's deduction is both true and not true. Certainly, publishers deleted gay and lesbian material from texts prior to publication to avoid costly court battles and lawsuits for obscenity. That Boni and Liveright, Faulkner's publishers, preemptively excised material that would later so trouble the publication of Hall's novel suggests that the late 1920s saw a general crackdown on certain sexual material. Homosexually themed material did not, however, *always* lead to such drastic editorial decisions nor costly court battles. Mann's *Death in Venice* and Proust's *Cities of the Plains* were not banned outright for their depictions of male same-sex desire, nor would later fiction from the early 1930s with overt gay (male) themes find itself in legal limbo. Conversely, Faulkner had previously written and published lesbian-themed poems, "L'Apres Midi" and "Sapphics," though both in a much more limited "market" on the campus at Ole Miss. In 1933, he would publish "o atthis" as part of a volume for national release. Furthermore, just prior to his working on *Mosquitoes* in the wake of his European trip, he had written "Equinox," later to be published as "Divorce in Naples," which sympathetically portrays a gay male relationship. Gay male themes also abound in *Mosquitoes*, even in the edited version. To claim that Faulkner felt the need "to muffle and veil explicit same-sex eroticism" seems only to hold for lesbian, not gay male, eroticism, and only in 1927. Also, *The Well of Loneliness* is more famous for the way in which Hall appropriates psychoanalytical models of lesbianism to paint a sympathetic portrait of her lesbian characters and to give Stephen Gordon a degree of subjectivity that those very models were meant to preclude. Hall's novel famously lacks a sex scene. Faulkner's lesbian material in *Mosquitoes* is voyeuristic heterosexual fantasy. Faulkner's and Hall's depictions of lesbianism are not equal nor are the reactions to them (excision prior to publication versus an obscenity trial afterward). As an item of Faulkner apocrypha, it would be worth a lot to find the letter Boni and Liveright wrote to him to explain their decision to cut the kissing scene between Pat and Jenny. As the record currently stands, the reason for these excisions proves elusive, but Gwin may be right to offer these excisions as Faulkner's first experience with having explicit homosexual material edited from his work. The experience may well account for his decision to move away from such explicit themes so that by the mid-1930s, the homosexuality he includes is significantly more coded and latent.

Return to Short Fiction

Between "Don Giovanni" and *Mosquitoes* Faulkner wrote his most overtly gay story, "Divorce in Naples," originally titled "Equinox." He would not publish the story for several years, but Blotner dates its original composition to just after his return from Europe.[7] Much of Faulkner's European sojourn informs his early fiction, especially the Genoa jail incident, which greatly influenced "Divorce in Naples," but Faulkner combined two incidences from 1924 to 1925 to create the dynamic of the story. First is the Wasson/Estelle incident for which Wasson confessed and sought Faulkner's forgiveness; second is the complex and partially apocryphal encounter that Spratling had in a Genoa jail when he and Faulkner first arrived on the Italian coast. From both, Faulkner took the two primary characters, two male lovers whose bond is threatened by a third party, and substituted Spratling's night of adventure for Wasson's transgression with Estelle. The protagonists of the story, George and Carl, substitute for Faulkner and Spratling, but Carl and George are crewmen on board the ship, whereas Faulkner and Spratling were passengers. The final substitution in the story proves most intriguing: the woman in the story with whom Carl cheats on George for the man in the jail with Spratling.

In the story, the sexual encounter occurs offscreen. George returns to a table in a bistro to find that his lover Carl has disappeared with one of the women with whom they were having drinks. The narrator describes these women as "of that abject glittering kind that seamen know or that know seamen" (CS 877). The pun in this description, in the first sentence of the story no less, establishes the double-talk of all that follows. Thus, when another crewman, Monckton, admonishes George for bringing his "wife to a place like this" when he brings Carl to the bistro in the first place, we are justified to read the marital terminology as evidence of George and Carl's homosexual "marriage" (or "partnership" to use Faulkner's expression from his *Item-Tribune* letter), not just as witty banter. Carl is gone for days. When he does return, George is gloomy and keeps his distance until they can make up.

The girl is Faulkner's substitute for Spratling's time in jail and his sexual encounter with a male. Faulkner converted that homosexual encounter into a heterosexual encounter at a house or hotel to which George has no access. The jail/house/hotel is a space beyond his purview. Outside of their shared space, his lover is cheating on him. What specifically occurs out of George/Faulkner's sight or with whom it occurs matters very little, as there is little to limit the imagination of a jilted and jealous lover of any orientation when they feel cast off and wronged. Even though he may have wished himself the protagonist in Spratling's escapade, Faulkner easily created a story from his disengaged and "jilted" role in whatever happened in Genoa from his perspective, not Spratling's. Indeed, Faulkner played a central part in Spratling's one-night affair as the jilted lover of a homosexual relationship. Such a series of intricate and provocative substitutions speaks to Faulkner's ability to take the actual details from his experiences and make them the apocryphal material of his stories. This explicitly homosexual story may be one of the best demonstrations of how complex (and brilliant) that process was for a young writer finding his way into his literary output for the next twenty-five years.

If Spratling and Faulkner are Carl and George, the primary (sexual) relationship is between them and does not tarry on the unnamed third party, whether it be a male prisoner or a woman of the town. As with Wasson's confession to Faulkner about Estelle, wherein the two main characters were Wasson and Faulkner, not Faulkner and Estelle, we see the focus of the story coming back to Faulkner/George, his gay male partner Wasson/Carl, and *their* relationship. We also see Faulkner/George performing his role in that relationship as he should, as the typecast jilted lover who happens to be gay. Any anxieties that the protagonist experiences appertain to his sense of betrayal by his male lover, not to his sexual orientation as somehow wrong or loathsome. Nor is the protagonist looking for a third party to help mediate his latent homosexual desires. The homosexuality is overt. The third party hinders the otherwise good relations between the two (gay) men, but they end up back together in the end.

Though "Divorce in Naples" is clearly a gay narrative, not all commentators can divorce themselves from a heterosexual reading of it. A full assessment of Faulkner's apocryphal gay life revises no less than Blotner's brief but significant overview of the story from the revised biography. When Blotner succinctly summarizes "Divorce in Naples," he includes not only key details but also his impression of the eventual outcome of George and Carl's relationship and what might happen in their future.[8] That impression only follows from the details of the story if Blotner is making an *a priori* assumption about the supposedly natural progression of sexual development, which subordinates homosexual desire as a youthful dalliance for the full maturity of proper heterosexuality. Blotner's error in reasoning is not an example of his incidentally regressing to an anxiety model. Rather, he simply misses the mark because of a general assumption about homosexuality that saturates much of post-Freudian Western culture, and certainly saturates literary criticism. The error is not Blotner's; the error is bigger than any one man. Blotner summarizes the story as follows:

> The story deals with two crew members on a thirty-four-day ocean crossing. George is a large dark Greek, whose beloved Carl—a small blond eighteen-year-old Philadelphian of Scandinavian descent—betrays him with a female prostitute. *Their reconciliation is shadowed, however, by an indication of future heterosexual betrayals by Carl.* (175, italics added)

The first two sentences accurately relate the events of the story, and George and Carl reconcile, as the third sentence says. There is, however, no reason to read "Divorce in Naples" as a story of developmental homosexuality on its way to sexual maturation as heterosexuality. There is, quite frankly, no "shadow" of "future heterosexual betrayals" haunting the conclusion of the story. There is an indication that Carl is still growing, actually physically growing; thus, he wants George to buy him "a suit of these pink silk teddybears that ladies use. A little bigger than I'd wear, see?" (*CS* 893). Blotner reads this passage as evidence that Carl intends to cheat on George again as soon as they make landfall in some other port-of-call. Thus, Carl wants the pink teddy for his possible future female sexual partners to wear, who will be bigger than him because of his small frame (in contemporary slang, Carl is a "twink").

The end of the story, however, is far too ambiguous for such a definite reading. The problem with Blotner's reading is one of perspective about the basic development of homosexual/heterosexual identity. If, as Jay Parini claims, "[i]t is not outlandish to suppose that Faulkner himself had homosexual feelings" during his youth (31), then Blotner's reading of "Divorce in Naples" may explain the ending of the story. Parini implies that if Faulkner had those feelings, then he grew out of them. "Certainly, by the time he reached adulthood," Parini continues, "his homoerotic feelings were safely repressed" (31). I have serious doubts that repressing homosexual desire in any form is ever safe; quite the opposite, the repression of desires leads to far more psychic damage for gay men than anyone should be expected to bear. To borrow from a later William Faulkner, "Some things you must always be unable to bear" (*ID* 201). Among them should be that society thinks it safest to deny normal, natural, and even beautiful desires. Blotner is, perhaps unconsciously, applying the same basic premise to the fictional Carl. Carl will also "safely repress" his "feelings," after his gay lover buys him a pink teddy for his promiscuous heterosexual liaisons. Unfortunately, George—the Greek, of course—is beyond saving, but Carl will mature and abandon his childish dalliance. Following the same line of reasoning, Faulkner would eventually "grow out" of his homosexuality and marry Estelle, though he also maintained close friendships with openly gay men who never put away their childish feelings for proper (hetero)sexual relationships. But what if Faulkner was skeptical of such a narrative of proper development? "Divorce in Naples" does not have to offer heterosexual futurity to have a well-articulated, meaningful conclusion.

The story centers upon a young and sexually inexperienced Carl who is taken in by the older and more sexually experienced George. They are lovers, as the first-person narrator of the story makes clear when he relates that the other members of the crew call Carl George's "wife" and then throughout his narration of the key events of the story, including their reconciliation and dancing together on ship. The narrator, however, is just an observer, limited to what he sees and hears. While he may provide details about George and Carl's affair and does serve to verify that they are lovers, he is not privy to the most intimate exchanges of their sexual lives. He can only record their dancing, their fighting, and their eventual reconciliation after Carl's Neapolitan tryst. In Naples, Carl does disappear with a young woman, likely a prostitute, a woman who "know[s] seaman" (*CS* 877). George is despondent, even after Carl returns to the ship. For days after leaving Naples, the two avoid each other. Finally, the narrator observes Carl performing a kind of purification ritual:

> He undressed swiftly, ripping his clothes off, ripping off a button that struck the bulkhead with a faint click. Naked, in the wan light, he looked smaller and frailer than ever as he dug a towel from his bunk where George had tumbled his things, flinging the other garments aside with a kind of dreadful haste. Then he went out, his bare feet whispering in the passage.
>
> I could hear the shower beyond the bulkhead running for a long time; it would be cold now, too. But it ran for a long time, then it ceased and I closed my eyes again until he had entered. Then I watched him lift from the floor the undergarment which he had removed and thrust it through a porthole quickly, with something of the air of a recovered drunkard putting out of sight an empty bottle. (*CS* 888)

After this ritual, Carl speaks to and reconciles with George. Since he just threw away the unclean undergarments of his sexual tryst with a woman, he quite naturally needs new undergarments. As a sign that he is more committed now to George and, from experience, more certain of his homosexual preferences, he wants a pink teddy. He wants his lover to buy it for him. He wants one that will last as he grows up and stays with George. He asks his lover to buy him a pink teddy just a little bigger than he is so that he can grow into it.

My reading of the story parallels Blotner's and should challenge his, but not necessarily supplant it. A reading that contends that Carl means to turn heterosexual and betray George again is based on the same two premises as my reading, only the former is inverted. First, to believe that Carl means to move toward heterosexuality is to assume that his homosexual affair with George is a product of his immature sexual curiosity, a childish experiment that, on becoming a man, he puts away. Such a reading is based on a simple, and possibly subconscious, reiteration of a basic model of psychosexual development. If, however, sexuality is something that develops, then the opposite development must also hold true. Carl is experiencing stages of his sexual development. He has a tryst with George. As a childish experiment, he tries sex with a woman. Realizing a heterosexual life is not what he wants, he returns to his rightful sexuality, more mature for his experience and more prepared for the committed love that a mature relationship requires. The older and more experienced of the two, George understands and accepts his lover's transgression. Yes, the story charts a psychosexual development, but there is no reason to privilege heterosexuality as its natural outcome.

Second, the basic sexual economy in the story is not a reiteration of a homosocial economy where two men "have sex" with each other by triangulating their desires through the ameliorating presence of a woman. George and Carl express their desires to each other, and at least on the boat, they are a couple, and everyone knows. The woman George had his affair with is not even named in the story. She is not a wedge that separates them, but she may well represent the transgression that helps pull them together. In Faulkner's actual life, he and Wasson were not deferring their true feelings through Estelle when Faulkner forgave Wasson for kissing her, nor was Faulkner necessarily angry at Spratling because he, Faulkner, did not have sex with the third party to his and Spratling's relationship in an Italian jail. Spratling knew that he was gay, as did Wasson; Faulkner knew that Spratling and Wasson were gay. The relationships they formed did not need to be triangulated through someone else to make them safely homosocial rather than explicitly homosexual. Their relationships existed in the open "between men" in a twentieth-century context, when being homosexual had become a possibility that earlier periods may not have been able to articulate so clearly. As Faulkner apocryphized his actual experiences, what comes to the fore of his narrative is the love between two gay men, not the anxiety between two straight men who are worried about being gay and so transfer their desires through women. The story is not afraid to name them lovers (Carl is George's wife), but it leaves unnamed the woman because the focus is George and Carl and their "partnership."

Yet for all of Faulkner's acceptance of and even celebration of gay male bonds, anxieties do enter his fiction, even if they are not the sole controlling force for it. The gay community of his early New Orleans sketches becomes the ambiguous ending of "Divorce in Naples" and then the misogynist banter of *Mosquitoes*. The open space of New Orleans becomes the utopia of the ship on which Carl and George work, an idyllic space roving an empty, formless, and unconfined ocean. In *Mosquitoes* and "Divorce in Naples," ports are dangerous because they represent a reentry into the confines of society. "Divorce in Naples" begins on land but ends at sea. The ship from "Divorce in Naples," with its crew holds and open decks for dancing, becomes the *Nausikaa*, with an upper and a lower deck on which different interactions take place, also roving open waters, but mostly stuck near shore for the greatest part of the novel, which begins and ends on land. The next, and final, story pertinent to the development of gay themes in Faulkner's early writings goes one step further and confines the homosexual within the prison and tomb of heterosexual expectations (aka: the marriage bed). After *Mosquitoes*, Faulkner literally and figuratively returned home: to Oxford and to Yocona/Yoknapatawpha County, to Estelle and to marriage. There he wrote one of his most famous stories, "A Rose for Emily," about a man who rejects marriage because of his ambiguous—and possibly gay—sexual identity only to die and rot for thirty years in the bridal chamber of his "wife." The anxiety that seeps out of this story is not homophobic. Rather, it muses on the cost incurred by that *baronial* person, the Count of

No 'Count, when he returns *home* to a life that forces a difficult repression of the life he led in gay New York and New Orleans for so much of the 1920s. The homeward- (Homer?) bound baron (Barron?) is marching to his tomb.

Faulkner wrote "A Rose for Emily" after he married Estelle. He published it very quickly for a minimal but welcome financial gain alongside his deliberate "tour de force," the novel *As I Lay Dying*.[9] Along with the later "Barn Burning," "A Rose for Emily" has become his most widely read short work, often taught at the high school level where even high school students recognize the details that suggest Homer Barron is no ordinary suitor for Miss Emily's hand. The narrator, something of the town scribe who speaks from a timeless omniscience and employs the royal "we," offers tantalizing clues about Homer's sexuality. "Little boys would follow him in groups to hear him cuss the niggers," the narrator tells us; one always knows where Homer is by the laughter of boys and men around him (*CS* 124). Though minor details, this homosociability of Homer's character is what later confuses the town when they realize that Miss Emily intends to marry him. Homer's male orientation serves as one of two pieces of evidence to explain the reaction the narrator reports:

> When she had first begun to be seen with Homer Barron, we had said, "She will marry him." Then we said, "She will persuade him yet," because Homer himself had remarked—he liked men and it was known that he drank with the younger men in the Elk's club—that he was not a marrying man. (126)

This remark, "that he was not a marrying man," is lifted almost verbatim from the protagonist in "Moonlight" when he explains "*I ain't a marrying kind of man*" (*US* 500). The town understands the implications of this statement based on their observations that "it was known that he drank with the younger men in the Elk's club" and "[l]ittle boys would follow him in groups." From these details, they deduce that "he liked men." This deduction does not actually mean that Homer "likes men" in a homosexual sense; rather, it means that the town thinks that he does. The opinion of the townspeople shifts over the course of the story with their consideration of these details. Originally, they assume that Homer and Emily will marry, but they also quickly concede that, actually, "she will [have to] persuade him yet." On closer inspection, the townspeople deduce that Homer is *queer*, to sum him up in a word not used to describe him but that was used to describe Faulkner, whom Estelle once tried to persuade into marriage, too, but failed. Rather than poison Faulkner (fact and fiction do, alas, sometimes fail to align), Estelle married someone else and Faulkner went on an eleven-year queer odyssey. His return coincided with his writing "A Rose for Emily."

Homer's sexuality has consternated Faulkner scholars at least since Hal Blythe, in 1988, identified him as a homosexual, claiming that "Faulkner has painted a picture of a modern pederast that helps the audience penetrate the chivalric illusion and see that Miss Emily's beau is gay" (49). Scholars should be wary of this claim, not because Blythe argues that Homer is gay but because Blythe considers homosexuality a form of "modern pederasty." Faulkner wrote the story in the late 1920s/early 1930s, and the story is set entirely in the post-bellum period. The Grierson house was even built "in the heavily lightsome style of the seventies" (CS 119), being the 1870s, after the word homosexual was first coined by German psychologists and became a "species," according to Michel Foucault. "Pederasty," even modified by the adjective "modern," is not the appropriate framework through which to view the story. Faulkner's life and its historical context are better touchstones. Faulkner—with Wasson in Oxford, Young in New York, and Spratling in New Orleans and Europe—witnessed, participated in, and, in his fiction, articulated twentieth-century homosexual desires and identities. The matrices of sexual orientation in this story are products of the 1920s when it was written, not ancient Roman or Greek sources. In fact, we can easily trace the *racial* matrices of Faulkner's lifetime in the story to verify its proper historical context. Homer is only in Jefferson because, during the postwar period, numerous northern investors and workers, such as Homer, "invaded" the South. The story, however, was written much later, well into the twentieth century by a twentieth-century author who crafted a more-or-less contemporary narrator speaking of events across time but firmly rooted in the story's present. Thus, it is important that the little boys who follow Homer do so "to hear him cuss the niggers." Faulkner does not intend Homer to represent some antiquated chivalric tradition. Homer, the Yankee carpetbagger, represents the complicity of all Americans, North and South, in the racial superiority that produced Jim Crow laws and brought about that era that Joel Williamson describes in his book *The Crucible of Race* and African American scholars have generally labeled as the nadir of the black experience in America, that dark period from the 1890s to the 1930s when black life was all but untenable, north and south. This period coincides with the action of the story, which documents its contemporary racial politics. It documents the sexual politics of that period as well.

The consternation on the part of scholars interpreting Homer's sexuality deserves mention because Homer is one of a small number of Faulknerian characters whom scholars have attempted to discuss as gay in an extended conversation, though that conversation is largely problematic.[10] On the one hand, the argument for his homosexuality is marred by the anachronistic application of paradigms that fail to account for the realities of gay life *in the present as well as in the past*; indeed, for all the praise heaped on Faulkner as a chronicler of southern *history*, his works are actually far more significant for their insights into his contemporary scene than for recording antebellum plantation life or giving an accurate depiction of the realities of Reconstruction and/or

Reconciliation, periods from before Faulkner was born. On the other hand, the backlash against gay readings such as Blythe's is conservative to the point of being reactionary and, under the auspices of protecting the fragile and marginal space of nonnormative identities, denies a voice to one of the very identities it supposedly seeks to protect. One notable response to Blythe has gone so far as to claim that gay readings of Homer are "errors of interpretation" and "misreadings" because they are dangerous for the young high school minds that encounter the story as their first introduction to Faulkner and his southern themes (Fick 99). I would offer that the average gay reader may find such errors, if they are errors, more felicitous than troubling because even an erroneous gay misreading is better than no gay reading at all. Fortunately, a more productive approach does emerge from the pitfalls of these readings: not whether Homer is gay or not, but rather *how* his sexuality is perceived and *what* that perception might mean for how we interpret the story.

The central issue relevant to gay themes in "A Rose for Emily" is not what Homer does but how the town reacts to him, including how Emily acts toward him and what she does to him to keep him in her life. We know that Faulkner knew gay men in many different environments with varying degrees of freedom and confinement placed on them by their immediate surroundings. Notably, Homer is not in New Orleans; he is in Jefferson. Faulkner's apocryphal courtship of Wasson speaks more to Homer's plight in the story than Faulkner's experience of the gay life of New Orleans; thus, it is marked more by insularity and isolation than gay communal bonds. Whatever happens between Homer and Emily happens in private, and the town can only speculate about their relationship. If Homer is gay, that too does not "happen" out in the open. The narrator may describe his drinking with young men and his boisterous male companionship, but the narrator very specifically does not directly state what these details mean except to say, open-endedly, that Homer "liked men." James Wallace notes that "[t]o believe that the narrator here reveals something true about Homer is to become exactly like the narrator and his society of gossipy, nosy neighbors" (106). Wallace believes that the real focus of the story is the propensity of the town to gossip and that Faulkner uses his narrator to draw readers, unaware, into the cycle of that gossip in his apocryphal small town (107). Readers become complicit in the speculation and rumor-mongering familiar to many LGBT people under the surveilling eye of a society determined to see what they otherwise want to remain private. The closet may not be the ideal place for gay existence, but it has often served as a safe space in a society that rarely affords one. It is, unfortunately, also a convenient centerpiece around which prying eyes can circle, like fake Hollywood Indians stalking around movie-set wagons, looking for a clear shot for the kill.

Wallace's claim, which he derives from a close reading of the text, actually rings true—possibly truer—when the story is contextualized with Faulkner's "queer" life in Oxford before and after Estelle's marriage and the gay life he explored through the 1920s in New Orleans and New York. In many ways, Homer's plight reflects Faulkner's own situation as he wrote the story and from his experiences growing up as the town "quair," a term applied to him by his fellow townspeople in much the way the Jeffersonian populace determines that Homer is different as well. Faulkner understood the value of gay representation and could use it to great effect in his stories, as he does here (and as he did in the short sketch "Jealousy"), to indict homophobia and to critique the stifling expectations of a heterosexual social order. The town is complicit in what happens to Homer. His imprisonment is a natural product of the expectations of the town that can only see him as one way (straight and married) or another (gay and disappeared). In this regard, Homer approximates the same vulgar dichotomy represented by Stark Young, a man who seems to have had a tremendous influence on the young William Faulkner. Young would not marry a woman, so he fled to Greenwich Village to make a life for himself. Faulkner did not marry Estelle, at least not when she first wanted him to, so he followed Young to a different life. But Faulkner came back to marry after all. He reappeared in Oxford after his travels to New York, New Orleans, and Europe. Though the dichotomy of presence/absence for straight/gay life is simplistic, it nonetheless seems to be a powerful divide undergirding Faulkner's sexual identity and perspective on the world, especially in his apocryphal chronicling of it in his early fiction. This dichotomy structures nearly all his gay-themed fiction, and the novel written alongside "A Rose for Emily" explores the same dichotomy only ending in the removal of the gay man to an asylum rather than disappearing him into the less brick-and-mortar institution of marriage. Neither ending offers an affirmation of the expectations of a small southern town. Both were written at the mid-point of the author's life. "A Rose for Emily" even eerily predicts the length of Faulkner's actual marriage, as well. The thirty years of Homer's captivity approximates the thirty-three years of Faulkner's marriage before his death in 1962.

Ultimately, in "A Rose for Emily" we are left with an image of sheer horror—not in favor of homosexuality but certainly against the confinements of a heterosexual marriage. We must remember that at a point in Faulkner's life he faced two reductive but no less palpably "real" options: he could either marry Estelle and gracefully slide into the life of Oxford or he could reject that life for the "queer" life he first witnessed in the person of Stark Young. Evidence suggests that he was mildly interested in the former, preferring marriage to Estelle with her parents' permission to eloping with her. When that plan did not work, the quair/queer young man ran off to fight a war, failed, came home, courted a gay man in the confines of his hometown, learned much but decided he needed a bigger world, moved to gay Greenwich Village, failed, came home, worked at a miserable job in the university post office for three years, failed, moved to gay

New Orleans, toured Europe with a gay man, moved back to gay New Orleans to live with that gay man, and became the novelist who would go on to win the Nobel Prize. Then he came home to marry Estelle. He did not fail in New Orleans, or so it seems. He did fail to woo Helen Baird while he was there. He did fail to publish his third novel, *Flags in the Dust*, at least without significant revisions, but that novel itself reveals his interest in stories about returning home and his having a seemingly endless supply of stories to tell about the home one returns to. He finally married Estelle, correcting an earlier failure of sorts, which brought him home, but not necessarily as a failure. Then he spent the next twelve years producing a series of literary works that would change the world.

But all was not well. That strange and ill-defined man, Homer Barron, comes to town. He can play a part in town that makes men laugh. He can drink with the boys. The town thinks he is a bit odd, certainly "not the marrying kind," but that Homer Barron disappears. Only later does the town realize what happened to him. He got *married*, in a decidedly metaphoric sense. Emily's powers of persuasion involved rat poison. She killed *that* Homer Barron who wanted the freedom to drink with the men at the Elk's Club and tell jokes to the boys. She confined him to her bedroom, away from the temptations of that former life and its implication of homosexual desires. She made Homer a heterosexual. Over the course of thirty years, Homer decayed beyond recognition, the "still unravished bride[groom] of quietness" forever sequestered to the bridal chamber, but certainly no longer fair even if he is eternally chaste. "A Rose for Emily" apocryphizes something deep in Faulkner's psychic life, a purging of a self that can no longer walk freely through the backlots and alleyways but must conform to the rigid expectations of the streets, indeed the bedroom, of his very small and very stifling hometown. After all, Homer Barron is in town to oversee the building of sidewalks, those strictures that direct where the townspeople should walk, the rigid pathways to guide them where they should be going. In a larger sense, he is laying the path for a queer young man to walk to his grave.

With "A Rose for Emily," Faulkner's apocryphal gay life abroad mostly came to an end. The new life he embraced in marriage produced a new set of challenges for how to articulate gay identity, apocryphal or otherwise. Yet, this narrative of his apocryphal gay life is only half complete. Simultaneous to this identity, Faulkner also performed another identity, the apocryphal soldier returning from World War I. His out-and-out lies about his war experience have long fascinated scholars, and certainly Faulkner's World War I themes permeate much of his fiction. Especially in his handling of those themes from 1918 until the publication of *As I Lay Dying* in 1930, his performance of war and his performance of homosexuality bled into each other, for reasons largely beyond his control. Rather than cordon off the two, he began to assimilate them into his representation of a "queer" wounded soldier returning home to an untenable peace. He would find literary precedent for this assimilation, and he would also find the wounded soldier motif a much more productive means of bringing homosexuality into a small-town context to face its rigid heterosexual expectations, though it would take Faulkner the entire eleven years of his apocryphal gay life to find the best means to articulate the conflict at the heart of these apocryphal identities.

Chapter 4

Cadet Faulkner

Faulkner's wartime experiences long baffled scholars, especially his early biographers. The first major collision between his self-created myth and the reality of
his experiences happened in the mid-1940s. In 1944 Malcolm Cowley wrote to
Faulkner for permission (and information) for a study of his works, out of which
would eventually grow *The Portable Faulkner*, the volume perhaps most significant in establishing the critical place of Faulkner with which we are now so
familiar. Faulkner, whose literary reputation remained high even while his popular readership dwindled from its already anemic numbers, could not have helped
being delighted by Cowley's attention. The mid-1940s found Faulkner in his first
serious dry spell as a writer. The 1942 publication of *Go Down, Moses* marked
the end of that "matchless time" in which he produced what John Pilkington
has called "The Heart of Yoknapatawpha." After 1942, Faulkner found himself
somewhat spent creatively, producing only the occasional, and often forgettable,
short story in response to the New Deal, "The Tall Men," or World War II, "Shall
Not Perish," and making his first tentative scratches at a new World War I novel,
A Fable, that would take him over ten years to complete and that would be vastly
different from his previous World War I novels about soldiers returning home
to rural, southern spaces. Enter Malcolm Cowley, courting the old writer for a
biographical essay and envisioning a collection of Faulkner's work that would
expose the scope and history of his great apocryphal creation.

All seemed well and good in the collaborative process between the two men,
or so one would be led to believe by the letters Cowley eventually collected
in *The Faulkner-Cowley File: Letters and Memories 1944–1962*. All seemed well,
that is, until Cowley pushed Faulkner for more information about his service in
World War I. In a letter from 8 December 1945, Faulkner willingly outlined his
life for Cowley, including reference to his supposed service in World War I, but
with a notable rejoinder that the dearth of details about his time in the service
was not unintentional:

> I graduated from grammar school, went two years to highschool, but only during
> fall to play on the football team, my parents finally caught on, worked about a year

as a book-keeper in grandfather's bank, went to RAF, returned home, attended
1 year at University of Mississippi by special dispensation for returned troops,
studying European languages, still didn't like school and quit that. Rest of educa-
tion undirected reading.

The above I still hope can remain private between you and me, the facts are in
order and sequence for you to use, to clarify the whos who piece. The following
is for your ear too. What I have written is of course in the public domain and the
public is welcome; what I ate and did and when and where, is my own business. (67)

Cowley did not take the hint. Being an eager suitor in pursuit of Faulkner's
legend—aware as he was of reports that Faulkner had a metal plate in his head
from a war wound and had once crashed a plane into a barn—Cowley mis-
took Faulkner's coyness for humility rather than cover. When he subsequently
sent Faulkner a draft of the essay that included how Faulkner had "been trained
as a flyer in Canada, had served at the front in the Royal Air Force, and, after
his plane was damaged in combat, had crashed it behind the British lines,"
Faulkner's response was more direct (72). He excised the war material in his
revision of Cowley's original paragraph and asked that Cowley make "no mention of war experience at all" in his biographical piece (74). When Cowley continued to include the information—after all, Faulkner provided no reason for
his redactions—Faulkner became increasingly belligerent in his demands that
details about his service be excised. He admonished Cowley that "[i]f you mention military experience at all (which is not necessary, as I could have invented a
few failed RAF airmen as easily as I did Confeds) say 'belonged to RAF in 1918'"
(77). Cowley still failed to take the hint and sent the war material to the typeset-
ter. At this point, Faulkner boiled over: "You're going to bugger up a fine digni-
fied distinguished book with that war business" (82). He wanted the description
of his service removed. He offered to pay to reset the typeset himself.[1]

Finally, Cowley "saw the light" (83), and from the perspective of 1966 when
he compiled his memoir, he could finally ask himself, "Why didn't he say flatly
that he hadn't served in France during the war?" (75). Indeed, even when
Cowley agreed to cut the material about the crashed plane, Faulkner responded
at length to explain that perhaps he crashed the plane through pilot error or
that, whatever really caused the crash, he did not deserve credit when so many
other brave pilots had never gotten any. That there was never any crash, that
there was, in fact, no service in France or in the war beyond at best a few mea-
ger flight hours at a training facility in Canada, Faulkner failed to admit to
Cowley. The truth will out, however, and after Faulkner's death Cowley outed it.
Cowley seemed bemused, if somewhat chagrined, at his ignorance during the
letter exchange from the mid-1940s. After all, he assumed that the stories he had
heard about Faulkner were true; he thought that he knew and understood the
man; and he thus pursued his misconceptions to the breaking point. Cowley's

error is a common one to any biographer or scholar: to take at face value from the subject of inquiry what might actually be a complex pose.

Faulkner was a man of many guises, and he held to few stories throughout his life more steadfastly than he did to his persona of being a wounded World War I veteran. He often repeated the story when it suited him, such as when he was courting Meta Carpenter. He sometimes displayed his very own RFC uniform, such as when his daughter Jill was born and "he expressed his pride" by wearing it while visiting her in the hospital (Williamson 240). These instances of using his apocryphal invention of his war experiences were clearly meant to further decidedly heterosexual ends; in one case, his persona helped him court a woman, in another he used it to represent his pride at having fathered a child with his wife. However, such clear heterosexuality was not the case before Faulkner married Estelle. When Faulkner returned from Canada in December 1918, he fashioned for himself an apocryphal sense of difference in his hometown, based on performances as a bohemian poet, a gay man, and, most famously, a wounded veteran of the first World War. He had begun fashioning these identities even before he left, the residue of his youthful gestures becoming the conscious efforts of a man forging his own way through the backlots and alleyways of small-town southern convention inherited from Victorian forefathers and their grand designs. His false claims of having been a soldier who was wounded in aerial combat in France have occupied much of the biographical interests in Faulkner's life and his creative output in his early years as a writer, but there is more to this soldierly persona than has heretofore been explored.

Faulkner's soldier persona was not mutually exclusive of his apocryphal gay identity, largely owing to the same cultural context in which a "quair" boy would become a "gay" man in the first quarter of the twentieth century. As Marilee Lindemann explains of Willa Cather, Cather (and Faulkner by extension) came of age during a crucial juncture in the history of *queerness* as the concept assumed connotations that we today recognize as "homosexuality." Cather and Faulkner also devoted significant effort to producing narratives of queer soldiers that bear striking similarities to each other, as Merrill Maguire-Skaggs has established, including his borrowing extensively from Cather's queerly inflected martial novel, *One of Ours*. Whether or not it was originally Faulkner's goal to muddle the two personae—the soldier and the homosexual—when he first returned to Oxford remains unclear, but by the time he wrote *Soldiers' Pay*, he seems to have become aware of the links between the two. By the time he married Estelle and wrote *As I Lay Dying*, he would directly confront the duality of these modes of difference in one character, Darl Bundren, and removed him from his postage stamp of native soil because of his being "queer," a word applied to him—and only him—five times in the novel.

The true history of Faulkner's wartime experience is short and relatively uneventful. He enlisted in Canada in June 1918. On 11 November, armistice was declared, ending World War I. On 5 December, William Faulkner's corps of flight cadets in Toronto was demobilized. By mid-December, Faulkner was at home in Oxford. He spent 179 days in the RFC, all of them in Canada, at best only a few brief hours of them even in a plane, much less flying one, and he possibly accumulated no flight hours at all. Blotner graciously offers that Faulkner did gain something important from this experience: "The product of his 179 days—part of the triad he would cite so often: imagination, observation, and experience—would last him a lifetime" (67). What Faulkner did not gain were his wings, a head wound, a leg wound, or even the uniform he wore when he got off the train in Oxford in December 1918, posing as a war hero. By the time Faulkner descended from that train, however, he had already established and elaborated this fictional persona. He even affected a limp when he first arrived, but it is unclear at what point in the following months he began adding that he also had a metal plate in his head.

The triumph of Faulkner's apocryphal persona did not begin on that December day. Rather, it began even before he left Oxford for New Haven, before Estelle's wedding, when he began telling stories about his failure to enlist in the American armed services as a pilot for being too short, though no evidence supports that he ever tried to enlist at all (Blotner 60). At this point, he was still William Falkner. He might even have still envisioned some life with Estelle. He would enlist after her marriage, in Toronto. To do so, he would pose as a British national from Finchley, England (on his mother's side), affecting an English accent from his heavy Mississippi drawl. He would also lie about his age, making himself eight months younger than he really was. His most significant affectation, though, was that he "misspelled" his name with a "u," becoming for the first time William *Faulkner* in his attempt to remake himself as something other than *that* boy from *that* town. These elaborations would take time to perfect, time his brother Murry (also called "Jack") actually spent in the trenches in France, serving in the United States Marine Corps. Even surrounded by the real heroics of other men from his hometown, Faulkner's lack of time in the trenches himself in no way prevented his self-presentation as a soldier with an exciting and noble martial history.

The main prop of Faulkner's apocryphal persona when he returned to Oxford was his uniform. During flight training, Faulkner was just a cadet and wore a poorly cut cadet's uniform, which was nothing as grand as the officer's uniform he would wear on his return to Oxford. In *William Faulkner: Self-Presentation and Performance*, James G. Watson analyzes the early images of Faulkner in his actual cadet uniform, an "ill-fitting costume" which Faulkner wore with no "sense of ironic self-presentation" and "no gesture of selfhood" (18). Faulkner called this his "rookie" uniform and complained about it—and drew pictures of it—in letters home to his mother in July 1918 (24). Upon demobilization, Faulkner had the right to wear this uniform when he returned home. By August, however, Faulkner had already

assured Murry [his father] and Maud he would have a real officer's uniform in
eight weeks—"my sure enough uniform," he called it—and concluded the letter
with still another drawing of himself to counteract the Cadet image, this one in
the classic uniform of a flying officer in garrison cap, belted tunic, breeches, put-
ties and stick. (24)

Faulkner would not achieve a higher rank or its attendant uniform in eight
weeks. Roughly twelve weeks later the war would end. Sixteen weeks later would
find him home, where he would "present himself to his family [. . .] wearing
the uniform he had drawn in his August letter" (Watson 27). Despite his never
having attained the uniform or a commission, Faulkner accomplished his apocryphal transformation from cadet to officer for two reasons. First, he used the
money paid to him by the RFC for his honorable discharge to buy an officer's
uniform (Blotner 66). Second, he had already established for his audience (his
parents directly, the city of Oxford by extension) that he would have earned that
uniform in the time that elapsed between his drawing of it in August and his
reappearance at home in December.

Though Faulkner could not have foreseen the armistice that would prevent
his actual commissioning, he laid the groundwork for his apocryphal officer's
status months in advance of any fruition of his goals of returning to Oxford as
a wounded war hero. He clearly had some grand mission in mind as a way of
removing himself from obdurate sameness at home to become someone different, perhaps even praiseworthy. Key to this deception would be that he did
not enlist anywhere near Mississippi nor even in the American armed services.
He created a foreign identity to bring back to Oxford, a sign of difference to
declare that, as Joel Williamson explains, "[h]e had not been simply another
American 'doughboy' in a rough cut, ready-to-wear, ill-fitting uniform," but that
he had been "truly cosmopolitan in his military career, transcending provincial
Mississippi, the South, and even America" because he served for the British RFC
(185). Of course, the prospects of dying in war would have lent to this effort at
deception the grandeur of myth. Since he never died (or even fought), he simply found himself at home playing a role that his hometown would find quite
queer indeed.

In her study of Willa Cather, Marilee Lindemann notes not only the changing connotations of the word *queer* to mean "homosexual" during the 1910s and
1920s, but she also explores the degree to which the term came to signify dissonance with American national identity as a new sense of "American" emerged
during this period to replace more regionalist identities and foci in American
literature, thought, politics, and public life. Lindemann explicates multiple
uses of *queer* in Cather's fiction to show that, sometimes at least, "queer" was a
marker for foreign-ness, often applied to characters who retained the marks of
their foreign origins (Scandinavian, German, Czech) and had not yet assimilated themselves into their contemporary American scene. At the same time, for

Cather *queer* also meant "homosexual," and she even employed *queer* at times self-referentially in letters when she clearly meant to refer to her lesbianism. Lindemann's study seeks to synthesize the connotative dissonance of the terms *queer* and *American* at a time when both terms were "sites of contestation, up for grabs in the game of the nation's emergence as a modern industrial, imperial, and cultural power in the late nineteenth and early twentieth centuries" (4). The "cultural power" Lindemann refers to is a sense of likeness—in appearance, tastes, origin, etc.—as the fundamental tenet of American-ness. Lindemann then proceeds to argue that Cather's work "queer[s] 'America' by examining the axes of difference—psychosexual, racial/ethnic, economic, and literary— that made the nation [at that moment] a space of vast energy and profound instability" (4). Her argument foregrounds the ways in which a localized identity—citizenship, or a sense of self bound to a place for the likeness one has to other natives of the place—created an understanding of "normal" or "American" against which one could be measured as queer.

If we apply this understanding of *queer* to Faulkner when he returned from "the war" (or at least returned from Canada) in December 1918, in full-on British officer drag no less, then we can begin to understand the deeper significance of this self-performing apocryphal identity and its relation to a larger narrative of Faulkner's life. The "quair" Faulkner was becoming more "queer," in terms very much sartorial again, though this time with a vague sense of foreign-ness, that he had been somewhere outside the confines of his hometown, touched new and queer things, and had now returned, affected by (though in reality only affecting) a queer identity. Understanding Faulkner's deep roots in Oxford (Mississippi, not England) allows one to grasp the utter irony of this queer performance; after all, no amount of sartorial display could ever shake the thoroughly ensconced like-you-ness that marked the reality of Faulkner's place in his hometown and home region. But we see him in these performances seeking marks of difference to set himself apart. Apparently, he felt he was apart from, not a part of, that town, though in the case of his soldier drag, as with his dandy dress while a teenager and his interest in literature and art, this marker of difference (foreign/queer soldier) carries strong connotations of a homosexual identity that in the 1920s would infuse the fictions produced from this apocryphal pose. As youthful gestures at being different in a small town, Faulkner seems to have discovered that all markers of difference carry many of the same basic connotations.

Clothes alone do not a costume make, however, and there was more to Faulkner's self-presentation as a wounded World War I veteran that implicates it in sexual—and especially homosexual—difference. While William Faulkner was writing letters home to his mother about his flight training, his brother Jack saw action from September to just shy of the November armistice in 1918, was gassed on the front, and suffered from shrapnel in his right knee and in his skull from a German shell. From early November to mid-December, after Faulkner returned home, the family had no word from Jack and assumed he was dead. These dates matter. When William Faulkner got off that train in December 1918, he faked a limp. Sometime later, he also lied and claimed that he had a metal plate in his head from an old war wound. The latter lie may have come directly from his brother's actual stories, but clearly the former lie, the limp, was his own creation, for at the time of William's return, he would not yet have heard from his brother nor known about his brother's wounds. Both of William Faulkner's apocryphal wounds become central to the wounded veterans he created, though the limp is the most telling and suggestive for the origin of the connotations for the "head wounds" that his later fictional soldiers suffer.

World War I fiction abounds with veterans returning home effectively sterilized by the war. Rather than narrativize the war in stories of triumphant warriors returning home, secure in their masculinity and guaranteed (sexual) futurity for their victorious homelands, the highest brows of Modernism figured the returning soldiers as so many hollow Prufrocks scouring for moral sustenance in a dry and barren world waiting for the unfulfilled promise of rain. Sometimes authors expressed the sexual metaphor in emphatic ways, such as Jake Barnes in Ernest Hemingway's *The Sun Also Rises*, whose only war wound is his impotence though he is otherwise healthy. Others crafted veterans whose wounds were more encompassing, though fundamentally still sexual, such as Clifford Chatterley in D. H. Lawrence's *Lady Chatterley's Lover*, who has been paralyzed from the waist down, is in a wheelchair, is accordingly impotent, and therefore cannot gratify his wife sexually. Others forego explicit sexual injury for the completely metaphorical wound, for example in Ford Madox Ford's prescient novel *The Good Soldier*, where the wounds are purely psychological, or in Part II of Eliot's *The Waste Land*, where even fertile (hetero)sexuality loses its potency because of an abortion. We can easily connect Faulkner's World War I narratives to these narratives and draw comparisons between the (sexual) wounds suffered by Faulkner's veterans. More significant, though, is the degree to which Faulkner's apocryphal wounded veteran persona was already participating in these narratives when he exited the train in the immediate aftermath of the war.

Faulkner's war "wound" was his loss of the path to proper heterosexuality when he turned down Estelle's offer to elope. He manifested this wound by faking a limp caused by a leg wound. A leg wound as a metaphor for sexual frustration or impotence has a long literary history from classical and Renaissance literature that World War I fiction adapted in male figures such as Jake Barnes and Clifford Chatterley. Their injuries "below the belt" merely reiterate the tradition of leg-wound-as-sexual-wound that has its roots in figures such as Shakespeare's Adonis, who dies when a bore drives its tusk into his leg while attempting to kiss his inner thigh, or Homer's Odysseus, who has a wound from a bore on his thigh that eventually helps identify him as he reclaims his proper role as husband after his twenty-year absence from the marriage bed (perhaps Faulkner's use of a passage from the epic journey of Odysseus to title his novel about the Bundren's journey to find Anse a new wife is purely coincidental, perhaps not). A limp is an easy injury to fake, and while most of Faulkner's wounded veterans would suffer from less physical wounds, with the notable exception of Elmer Hodge, the metaphoric leg/sexual wound is nonetheless the root for the mental/sexual traumas that Faulkner transformed and explored in characters such as Bayard Sartoris, Donald Mahon, and Darl Bundren. Faulkner took an old trope and expanded it in the new context of World War I, largely by observing another type of wound common to veterans of World War I: a head wound, or what he calls "shell shock" in a letter he wrote home to his mother shortly before his enlistment in 1918 (*Thinking* 48).

The synthesis of a leg to a head wound as a metaphor for sexual damage caused by the war likely had its basis in biographical details. Faulkner began his lie about the metal plate in his head much later than his return to Oxford in December 1918, very probably in direct response to Jack's actual war wounds, which far exceeded the apocryphal limp that Faulkner affected in his first per-formances of his soldier identity before Jack returned home. This injury bears a metaphoric significance much more contemporary to World War I, as the reality of returning soldiers with horrific injuries met the cultural imagina-tion of the country to which they returned. Faulkner observed this reality in New Haven in the person of a wounded veteran named Captain Bland, whom Faulkner identifies as suffering from "shell shock" though he bears no visible external wounds. The idea of a metal plate in one's head combined with the psy-chological trauma of shell shock melded in Faulkner's imagination as a singular consequence of war: the all-purpose head wound. He eventually linked the idea of a head wound to a leg wound and its sexual significance to create a metaphor for psychosexual damage caused by going off to war. In the image of the head wound, Faulkner could move beyond simple metaphors for sexual impotence and into more complex metaphors for war wounds as a measure of psychologi-cal damage. By synthesizing the idea of the sexual wound (the leg wound) and the mental wound (the head wound), Faulkner's war characters become tinged with psychosexual damage so that, returned to their native soil, they cannot find peace in hometowns that expect them to marry and settle down after the trauma of their wartime experiences.

This synthesis of physical wounds into deeply psychological sexual trau-mas took time for Faulkner to perfect, but his efforts represent one of the most profound insights of his particular literary genius. Through repeated experi-mentation with variations on a standard narrative of the wounded returning soldier, Faulkner would eventually create Darl Bundren, whose wound, what makes people call him, and only him in the entire novel, "queer," is not a limp nor even ostensibly physical nor purely the result of shell shock. Rather, he suffers a psychological sexual wound when the path of his life takes a turn beyond the boundaries of his experience and expectation, shows him a queer, foreign world, and then pulls him back into a local orbit that can only understand his new sense of self as "queer," or insane. He is purged from the novel that Faulkner wrote in the months immediately following his marriage and alongside his depiction of Homer Barron trapped in Emily Grierson's grotesque bridal chamber. In the novel, in the story, and in Faulkner's personal life, the journey—the Bundrens' funeral procession, Homer's carpetbagging, and Faulkner's travels—ends with marriage. Each journey also concludes with the repudiation of the queer, either through removing him to an asylum, killing him in the marriage bed, or suppressing him for a life with a wife, her two children, and the responsibilities of making a home. Not only would Faulkner raise Estelle's children, but he also had two of his own with Estelle (one, Alabama, would die hours after her birth; the other, Jill, survived). His actual story would resolve itself with a proper heterosexual union. His fictional creations would not find any such life when they returned from their wars. His fictional soldiers inherit the full weight of their literary precedents and never can find the guarantees of sexual futurity that the victories of battle should have promised them.

Faulkner began the process of experimenting with images of sexually damaged soldiers in his early poetry, but not until his first novel in 1925 while he was immersed in the gay subculture of New Orleans did he turn his full attention to those images and attempt to narrativize them. Though he was creating his apocryphal soldier identity even before the war ended, in New Orleans, affecting his limp and claiming that he had a metal plate in his head, Faulkner sat down to create a narrative—to make the actual into the apocryphal—out of his performances. From 1918 to 1925, Faulkner's performance of his wounded veteran identity was mostly a matter of his repeating it until it was accepted as true, whereas with his apocryphal gay identity, he courted and lived with gay men and even made efforts to submerge himself into gay communities. We can see how he blended his various apocryphal identities by considering four projects he had open on his desk at roughly the same time in early 1925. In the same brief period, he wrote his gay-themed sketch "Out of Nazareth," his essay on what is the matter with marriage for the *Item-Tribune,* his first novel, *Soldiers' Pay,* and an essay entitled "Literature and War." From this final item, we get a sense of the literary influences on which Faulkner drew to craft his World War I fiction. In that essay he does not include Cather's *One of Ours* though he seems likely to have read it very closely. Other well-known influences on Faulkner's work, namely A. E. Housman, appear in *Soldiers' Pay* and "Out of Nazareth." Not surprisingly, then, at this moment in Faulkner's life, as he began his experiments in World War I narratives, his chief influences from World War I literature were largely gay influences as well.

A starting point for understanding how these various aspects of Faulkner's life merge is in Faulkner's repeated use of A. E. Housman's heavily homoerotic ode to young soldier boys, *A Shropshire Lad*, a volume that Faulkner scholars have long identified as one of his favorites and as heavily influential on his early writing. In an essay from 1924, "Verse, Old and Nascent: A Pilgrimage" Faulkner himself named this particular volume as part of his efforts to "complete a youthful gesture I was then making of being 'different' in a small town" (*ESPL* 237). The youth of "Out of Nazareth" carried with him a copy of *A Shropshire Lad*. Early in *Soldiers' Pay*, just before he discovers that his son Donald is still alive, the rector pulls a tin box out of his desk in which he keeps a few of his son's treasured belongings. Its "sorry contents" include "a woman's chemise, a cheap paper-covered 'Shropshire Lad,' a mummied hyacinth bulb. The rector picked up the bulb and it crumbled to dust in his hand" (64). Readers later realize that the woman's chemise probably belonged to Emmy, with whom Donald had a brief but seemingly passionate affair before the war. In this tin box, though, the woman's chemise seems strikingly out of place. Given the other contents of the box, the chemise implies that Donald had a secret sexual life before the war, though not a heterosexual one. The third-person omniscient narration allows readers to deduce Don's heterosexuality through flashbacks of sexual encounters with Emmy, but other characters in the novel have much more limited access to Don's inner life to make confident deductions.

The copy of Housman could signify, broadly, war and death, but it also exudes a deeply homosexual significance that was not lost on contemporary readers before and after the war. Housman's volume predates the war by nearly twenty years, and Faulkner may well have read it before the war, but Paul Fussell establishes that the volume, though popular before World War I, came to have renewed significance and a large readership directly in response to the war. He also argues persuasively that the volume was a central influence on much of the later poetry written by actual veterans of the war. Fussell describes the increased popularity of *A Shropshire Lad* in the marketplace of World War I literature as sanctioning latently what was prior to the war unmentionable overtly but which was very much at the heart of Housman's martial iconography and at the heart of much war poetry inspired by it:

> But it might seem that the "increase in interest" [in Housman's volume] was less in poetry than in the theme of beautiful suffering lads, for which the war sanctioned an expression more overt than ever before. Homoeroticism was now, as it were, licensed. *A Shropshire Lad*, Brian Reade observes, "is like a beautiful ruin built over an invisible framework, and Housman obscured the framework so well that until recently not many readers of the poems seemed to guess that it was *l'amour de l'impossible* which haunted many of them. . . ." Whether or not readers were really that naïve—I think they were not—it is remarkable the way *A Shropshire Lad*

[. . .] anticipates, and in my view even helps determine, the imaginative means
by which the war was conceived. (282)

The volume shared by the youth in "Out of Nazareth" and Donald Mahon in
Soldiers' Pay links them to this "invisible framework" of "*l'amour de l'impossible.*"
Fundamentally, Fussell is describing what Sedgwick later termed the "open
secret" of twentieth-century male homosexuality. Donald's and the youth's preferences for Housman signify their homosexuality without uttering the love that
dares not speak its name. They speak in euphemisms rather than in explicit
declarations, thus avoiding criminal liability, a reality of Housman's England
and Faulkner's America until well into the twenty-first century. That within five
months of writing the sketch and the novel Faulkner would visit the grave of
the most (in)famous victim of an older Victorian order that would, through
incarceration, work to keep that name of that love unspoken and impossible
speaks to the degree to which the theme of unarticulated homosexual desire
was on Faulkner's mind in 1925. Of course, in "Out of Nazareth," Faulkner made
a game out of not saying what is clearly being shown. He seems to have understood both the "secret" and how "open" it was for readers. Faulkner used that
open secret to signify the homosexuality in the story and in the novel as well.

In *Soldiers' Pay*, the youth procured by Spratling in "Out of Nazareth"
becomes the young, prewar Donald Mahon, pulling his beloved book out of his
pocket and declaring his awe that someone could feel like *that* and not mind
who knows about it. If any doubt remains, however, about the implications of
the contents of the tin box, and the degree to which *l'amour de l'impossible* and
the "open secret" of homosexuality influenced Faulkner's depiction of Donald,
the flower that the rector pulls out—and crushes—screams those implications
in powerful metaphor. The hyacinth has long held an important place in gay
literary representation. Hyacinthus was a male beloved by Apollo and, of course,
killed in the prime beauty of his youth (the "bury your gays" trope common in
contemporary pop culture has roots considerably older than often acknowledged). From this story, the flower became the representation of the desire
between two male lovers, eventually becoming the nickname Oscar Wilde gave
to his beloved Alfred Douglas in a series of letters that Douglas carelessly misplaced and that subsequently fell into the hands of blackmailers and finally to
the solicitor charged with trying Wilde for his sexual conduct. Those letters
were used in Wilde's trial as the cornerstone of the evidence to prove that his
relationship with his Hyacinth was (homo)sexual.[2]

In early April as he began the novel, Faulkner also wrote his editorial to the
Item-Tribune in answer to the query "What Is the Matter with Marriage?" The
argument that two men or two women have a better chance at happiness than
heterosexual couples appears twice in *Soldiers' Pay*. First, when Cecily realizes
that Donald is still alive, she begins to fantasize that Margaret Powers has been

his lover. She then ponders, "How would I like to have a husband and a wife, too, I wonder?" (80), meaning a three-way marriage with one husband and two wives. Would the wives share the husband? Would the husband share his wives? Who would have sexual access to whom? Cecily continues, "Or two husbands?" (80). Would they sleep with each other and with her? Cecily fancies that she should get married at least once because, "I guess it's worth trying" (80), but she seems uninterested in a simple heterosexual marriage where she and one man are stuck unhappily with each other. A multiple marriage would provide more options and more mutual understanding according to the logic of Faulkner's editorial response, of which Cecily becomes a spokesperson.

Emmy has a similar moment, though hers is more clearly an indictment of heterosexual relationships despite the number of partners. As she recalls her childhood, she recalls her father, an alcoholic house painter, marrying "an angular shrew who, serving as an instrument of retribution, beat him soundly with stove wood in her lighter moments" (116). Of this unhappy marriage, Emmy's father advises his daughter: "Don't never marry a woman, Emmy. [. . .] If I had it to do all over again, I'd take a man every time" (116). Though on the surface this declaration appears to be folksy humor, the idea of her father "tak[ing] a man every time" to guarantee his happiness rings more emphatically when read beside Faulkner's assertion that "[t]wo men or two women—forming a partnership, always remember that the other has weaknesses, and by taking into account the fallibility of mankind, they gain much success and happiness" (*ESPL* 337). The problem, of course, is that Emmy "takes a man," in this case Donald. Her father is so mad that he disowns her, leading her to take refuge at the rectory until Donald returns from the war. Perhaps the father realizes the inverse of his own statement. He might need a man to guarantee his happiness. Emmy would logically need a woman. The opposite sex partner is the problem, not *all* women. His declaration misleads Emmy; she should "take a [woman] every time" or else she will suffer. Notably, when Donald returns, his injuries prevent him from recognizing Emmy or even acknowledging her existence. They do not understand each other any longer. War made him blind to her, but she should have known that their affair would only lead to heartache, as heterosexual love always does when it is a frenzied fire of passion. Same-sex couples fare better in this Faulknerian universe.

Reading from Faulkner's canon preceding his time in New Orleans also provides a fascinating source for Emmy's character. If Donald is outed by the contents of his tin box, he is saved by Emmy's being the likely owner of the woman's chemise. She was his last (known) sexual partner before leaving for the war. In her description of her night with Donald, Emmy draws on the imagery Faulkner also used in his short story "Moonlight" where the male narrator dreams of being alone on a hillside with Skeet as the ultimate source of joy. Faulkner revised that story through the 1920s with its final vision of Skeet and the narrator on a hillside together not completed until 1928. This evolution of the story generally allows for its revisions both to influence and be influenced by material in *Soldiers' Pay*. Emmy expands the details from that story, remembering how Donald came to her one night and whisked her away to a pond for some skinny-dipping, after which she lies down in the cool, damp grass, where she can "see him running along the top of the hill, all shiny in the moonlight, then he ran back down the hill toward the creek" and toward her (123). He returns to her and they make love.

The male author Faulkner describes the scene of Emmy's giving herself to Donald from *her* point of view. As a writer, he lets himself imagine "[w]hen he looks at you—you feel like a bird, kind of; like you was going swooping right away from the ground or something. But there was something different there, too. I could hear him panting from running, and I could feel something inside me panting, too" (123). This scene depicts Donald seducing Emmy but has links to the revision of the desired but never experienced seduction between Skeet and the protagonist of that earlier story. Faulkner expands the scene from the point of view of the seduced, not the seducer. In "Moonlight," seduced and seducer are men. In *Soldiers' Pay*, they are a woman and a man, but a man is writing the woman's part about what it must feel like to be seduced by a man and subsequently to have sex with him. One could reasonably suggest that Faulkner did not need to rely on his creative powers to imagine what Emmy might have felt at that moment. What she felt and what the protagonist of "Moonlight" imagines with Skeet seem to be revisions of the same basic scenario, only with differently gendered characters interacting in each final version.

Beyond his own immersion into gay culture and his references to gay themes in his own writings that reappear in *Soldiers' Pay*, other evidence demonstrates that by 1925 Faulkner had read much World War I literature and borrowed its "queer" themes to produce his own narratives. Merrill Maguire-Skaggs argues persuasively for the relationship between *Soldiers' Pay* and Willa Cather's *One of Ours* in her essay "Cather's War and Faulkner's Peace." She asserts that "Faulkner's novel begins where Cather's leaves off—with soldiers returning from the war" (42). The influence did not produce a one-to-one correlation between the main characters of both novels, but the elements that Faulkner borrowed for his novel are central to his apocryphal identities as a soldier and a homosexual. Maguire-Skaggs accounts for the difference in branches of service between the protagonists (Claude Wheeler is in the American infantry, Donald Mahon in the Royal Flying Corps) by siphoning that difference through Victor Morse, the American flying ace whom Claude first encounters on the *Anchises* on his crossing to Europe. Claude and his fellow bunkmates "were astonished to see that [Morse] wore the uniform of the Royal Flying Corps and carried a cane" (Cather 224), and are surprised to learn that he is, nonetheless, from the unglamorous town of Crystal Lake, Iowa, and is, therefore, not a dapper

British airman after all. Morse goes on to die in glorious air-born combat, which Claude only hears about secondhand but never actually witnesses. Maguire-Skaggs not only compares Morse with Donald (and with Bayard Sartoris from *Flags in the Dust*) but also notes that this description of him "matches the Bill Faulkner who wrote home about learning Morse code during aeronautical training" (47). Morse stands out because of his foreign affectations and his cane; Faulkner had attempted to emulate both in December 1918 when he returned from his un-fought war. Like the real Faulkner, Claude was fascinated by men like Morse, but neither Morse nor Claude would ever return home. Faulkner would return home, faking it.

Maguire-Skaggs argues that Cather's Claude becomes Faulkner's Donald, only the "clod" becomes more sophisticated, as if Claude progressed from the infantry to being an RFC pilot, then lived and came home. The connection between the two characters is that one is an account of the type of man who leaves for war, the other an account of the type of man who returns. If, however, Faulkner's Donald Mahon represents the continuation of the narrative of Cather's Claude Wheeler, or if, as Skaggs explains, "[e]ach writer seems to talk *at* the other directly" in their World War I fictions, then the debt Faulkner owes Cather should carry with it the imprint of Cather's interests beyond basic descriptions of soldiery and the ironies of war (46, italics added). In quite literally the first sentence of description of the world Claude encounters once he leaves home for the service, Cather details that Claude's new company now consists of "[a] long train of crowded cars, the passengers all of the same sex, almost the same age" (Cather 217). These "soldier boys" (218) fascinate Claude, and he spends time throughout his journey and wartime experiences describing the minutia of their faces and body types. Once in Europe, Claude encounters the deranged "star patient here, a psychopathic case" (272). The psychopath has forgotten himself, not unlike Donald Mahon in Faulkner's novel, but "[t]he queer thing is, it's his recollection of women that is most affected," from his memories of his mother to his betrothed. Donald's mother never appears in *Soldiers' Pay*; instead, Donald forgets his betrothed, Cecily, and his other lover, Emmy, the two women in his life.

Other latently homosexual material abounds in Cather's novel. The psychopath escaped once and was taken in by a French family whose son died in the war. Claude, accordingly, meets David Gerhardt, who leads Claude to the Jouberts, an elderly French couple who have lost both of their sons and so take in Claude and David as replacements. Claude quickly becomes infatuated with the urbane, sophisticated David and hopes to impress him. These two take their extended leave together, returning to the Jouberts' home. This idyllic break from combat fulfills Claude's otherwise inarticulate homosexual desires just before he and David return to the front to die. Claude comes to articulate this shared leave as "the period of happy 'youth' [. . .]. He was having his youth in France"

(331). Of David, he determines that, in his past, "he was always looking for someone whom he could admire without reservations [. . .]. Now he believed that even then he must have had some faint image of a man like Gerhardt in his mind" (332). At the end of the novel, Claude makes a bargain with God that if David can live, he will accept that he must die, but in the star-crossed irony of lovers in mortal danger, David dies, too.

No good homosexual awakening can go unpunished. Both men die in glorious battle. Claude, who could never quite fit in back home in Nebraska, is transformed in the minds of his mother and the family maid, Mahailey, into the son well lost but always transcendently near, perhaps even "directly overhead, not so very far above the kitchen stove" as the novel ends with perfect poetic irony (371). Marilee Lindemann notes of this bitter ending: "The women's devotion to Claude's memory and to one another and their ability to endure disappointment stand as an implied critique of a masculinity that seems to require the violence of war to realize itself" (72). She continues:

> In *One of Ours* war makes the queer a hero and gives him a space for love, allowing him to reconstitute a family, enter history, state his faith in his "wonderful men" (Cather 385), and die for a glorious cause, but all of this exaltation is predicated on the twin violences of war and misogyny, implying that men who love men do so because they feed on death and the hatred of women. (74)

I do not entirely concur with Lindemann's assertions of Claude's "misogyny," though his relationship with his wife, Enid—and her depiction in the novel—certainly give Lindemann grounds for her reading. The absolute contempt with which the narrator of *Soldiers' Pay* depicts Cecily Saunders makes the misogyny in *One of Ours* tame by comparison. Nonetheless, her critique of Claude's heroism—with or without the attendant misogyny—is one to which Faulkner seems to have been attuned.

For Lindemann, Cather's novel critiques masculinity by depicting a man who loves other men, a seemingly effeminate trait in its American context, but who proves his manhood by dying violently in a war. Claude's acceptance into society is based entirely on his proving that he is "man enough" for it, which requires his death since he is also "queer." That death is necessary—in a foreign war and far from home—because otherwise Claude's queerness, his homosexuality, threatens the fabric of a society that would extol his masculinity. He can be as non-heterosexual as he would like to be, so long as he is far from home, never comes back, and dies gloriously enough to overshadow the tainted reality of his life that leads to that death. If such a queer figure dares to live, the delicate balance of the home front cannot find a place for those unfortunate enough to return as survivors; the hero who returns is simply queer. Indeed, Donald Mahon was reported, quite thankfully, dead before he shows up, somewhat alive, on his father's doorstep. While he thinks that Donald is dead, the rector can go through the tin box of loaded signifiers of Donald's homosexuality without noticing their significance—he can even crush Donald's hyacinth bulb. He can narrate a life for his son that is unencumbered by the weighty connotations of the signs before him. Any sign that does not fit that narrative dissolves away into oblivion. Donald can be the man his father wants to remember him as. Unfortunately, at just the moment when the rector begins the process of editing his keepsakes of his son's life, that son reappears, alive but severely wounded by the war.

Maguire-Skaggs establishes Faulkner's novel as the second half of Cather's original in which Faulkner envisions Claude Wheeler returning home alive. Claude dies at the end of Cather's novel, and Cather offers as the final scene the transfiguration of Claude in the eyes of Mahailey and his mother into an ever-present memory always just above the stove or thereabouts. Claude becomes Donald in Faulkner's novel. Accordingly, Faulkner begins his novel with the "deceased" Donald coming back to life. The narrative flows forward from that moment until Donald does finally die, though throughout the novel, numerous characters concede that Donald is not really alive even if he is still present and breathing. The war killed Donald. The man who returns is just a shell to see to its grave. The Donald from before the war has died, metaphorically. The Donald who returns does not fit the narrative that his father and the rest of the towns-people want to tell themselves. If Claude's war experience allows him to articu-late homosexuality, his death allows society to repudiate his homosexuality and to accept him into the fold. If he does not die, however, that homosexuality becomes articulated but not repudiated. Thus, Donald Mahon might properly be read as the flesh-and-blood embodiment of that homosexuality, washing up on the proverbial shore back home. We should not be surprised that the goal of the various characters in the novel is to get Donald married to close any fissures in their narrative of his life that his reappearance opens.

Though certainly heavily influential, *A Shropshire Lad* and *One of Ours* do not wholly account for all of the gay themes in Faulkner's World War I fiction. As Faulkner wrote his novel, his sketches, and his essay on marriage, he also wrote a short but revealing essay on "Literature and War." Paul Fussell devotes an entire chapter to "homoeroticism" in literary depictions of the war. In his essay, Faulkner cited two of four authors whom Fussell singles out for their homoerotic writings. First, Faulkner's essay discusses Siegfried Sassoon, who mentored Wilfred Owen and who wrote in his war memoirs about his close relationship with a man named Dick. Fussell identifies two "Dicks" in homo-erotic war writing—the name of the idol of both Sassoon and Robert Graves. Faulkner named Margaret Powers's dead husband "Dick" in *Soldiers' Pay*. Second, the essay cites Rubert Brooke, whose handsome "special beauty" became iconic during the war and filled "needs" on the home front that "were as deeply homoerotic as they were patriotic" (Fussell 276). Combined with the influence of Housman and Cather and their "homoerotic" writings, it seems fair to suggest that Faulkner had access to and was aware of the homoerotic elements in war writings by his contemporaries. Also, since he named neither Housman nor Cather in "Literature and War," we can deduce that he read more than just the authors he listed in it. Perhaps the poet whom Faulkner did not name—Wilfred Owen—also served as an influence for his depictions of wounded soldiers.

Owen was a homosexual poet whose senseless death in senseless battle so domesticated him for an English-speaking readership as to make his poems some of the most powerful and well-known responses to the war. As Faulkner did in his poem "Lilacs" and in *Soldiers' Pay*, in "Disabled," written in 1917, Owen envisioned the life of the returning veteran who did not die in battle and thus cannot bear the so-called glory expressed in the old saying *Dulce et decorum est pro patria mori*, an expression Owen ironized in another of his famous poems. This soldier lives, and he now "[sits] in wheeled chair, waiting for dark, / And shiver[s] in his ghastly suit of gray, / Legless, sewn short at elbow" (lines 1–3). His physical disabilities remove him from the sounds of children playing in the park and the twilight attention of "girls [who] glanced lovelier as the air grew dim" (line 9). His once beautiful face, sought by artists, has grown "old" and pale since he "lost his colour very far from here" in the "shell-holes" of the battlefield (lines 16, 17, 18). Such was his zeal for war that he enlisted early, even lying about his age, so that he could hear the "drums and cheers" of the crowds as his train rolled away after he was called up to fight (line 36). He returned to fewer and more subdued crowds, and "[o]nly a solemn man who brought him fruits / *Thanked* him" for his service and sacrifice (lines 38–39, italics in original). He is destined to spend the rest of his life in institutions and as an object of pity to those who did not go to war and so did not return so wounded. The closing lines of the poem sound the refrain, "Why don't they come / And put him to bed? Why don't they come?" (lines 46–47). Even the speaker in the poem prefers that this invalid be removed from sight.

In addition to the physical wounds, his countrymen and women base their reactions to him on a deeper revulsion. As the speaker explains, "All of them touch him like some queer disease" (line 13). That word *queer* carries much weight in the poem and suggests that this soldier's "disability" refers to something far less outward than his missing arms and legs. Daniel Pigg challenges readers to consider the cultural context of the word *queer* at this historical moment to understand the poem, though his essay from 1997 makes use of an older version of the *Oxford English Dictionary*, which first cites *queer* as "homosexual" in 1922. A more recent edition of the *OED* establishes the currency of this usage as early as 1915. Pigg first argues that the soldier's disability is not simply a product of the war but of "oppression in society that has brought a soldier to this state." Thus, as the soldier imagines the hands of girls that will no longer touch him, Pigg continues that "[f]or the poet, the notion of queerness is connected not just with the loss of potential heterosexual contact but also with the great notion of the 'lie' [line 29] that has created him in this particular image." That lie is the same lie that Cather explores: dying in war makes one great and brave, but going to war also exposes one to queerness, which makes that dying necessary. In this sense, war makes a soldier queer; or, as Pigg explains it, "War creates the queer and the strange." Given the newly emerging use of *queer* concurrent to the war and the ways in which it shaped the world and artistic responses to it, I would assert that the war made the soldier *gay*. Now, having dared to live, his fractured form is untouchable.

I do not mean to suggest that exposure to war spreads homosexuality as if homosexuality *is* a disease, though that suggestion certainly seems to be at the heart of the homophobia so rampant in a society afraid of these men who return home alive. In fact, Faulkner's experience of the Spanish flu, a major world crisis contemporary to the war, would lend to him a sense that the effects of war and communicable diseases bear metaphoric connections. Cather also hints at a similar linkage: onboard the *Anchises*, Claude becomes a nurse during a devastating outbreak of the flu, which becomes his first exposure to the horrors of mass casualties and the irony of death taking those who seem least likely to die. In relation to homosexuality, if Claude Wheeler's narrative is any guide, the war opens a pathway by which men who feel as if they are outcasts can find a means to enter society. While going to war to find the label *hero* and receive the plaudits of the nation, these men also find that their otherwise suppressed or dormant homosexual desires that they could not express at home they can express abroad. These men are not diseased, nor do they catch homosexuality. Rather, they realize that societal conventions and expectations are relatively spatial and relevant only to a small space. Once they leave that space, they find that being gay is neither all that horrible nor all that rare. This gay literary narrative will be repeated in landmarks of gay fiction throughout the twentieth century from *Beebo Brinker* to *Tales of the City*: small-town boy/girl goes to big city; isolated homosexual finds community. This powerful narrative is one Faulkner would have found particularly appealing in 1925 as he moved away from the provincialism and confinement of Oxford to the freedoms of the Vieux Carre. Conversely, he might have found this spatial and mobile narrative particularly confining when he thought about returning home. For what happens to the man who finds expression for his desires in a foreign war, but who must return home afterward, never again to feel the hands of the girls back home on him or be the recipient of heterosexual attention because his "wounds" prevent him from joining those practices anymore? When he returns home, the people who never left in the first place can only treat him as if he has some queer disease. No one wants to catch what he brings back to the isolated hometown that would prefer to mourn him dead than face the reality of his life in the trenches and among all those other young men.

Faulkner saw both sides of this narrative, the freedom of leaving and the confinement and convalescence of return. When he did finally return home in 1927, he revised and reenvisioned this narrative and eventually repudiated its queer elements in the first novel of his domestic life, *As I Lay Dying*, which is really just a novel about a wounded soldier returning home from war. He wrote it after he had rehearsed many varieties of this narrative of the returning soldier through the latter 1920s.

Chapter 5

Queer Soldiers

On Sunday, 7 April 1918, before he had hatched his plan with Phil Stone to join the RAF but also in what would prove to be the final months of the war he planned so fastidiously to join, Faulkner wrote home to his mother from New Haven that he had met a "celebrity," Nicholas Llewellyn, a soldier most recently from the front near Rheims but bearing a wound from the first battle of Ypres (*Thinking* 48). That Faulkner calls Llewellyn a celebrity speaks to the awe he felt regarding those famous fighters of a war that he romanticized from the safe distance of the Yale campus. This romanticizing is strikingly incongruent with the perception of the war held by actual veterans at that late stage in its history. Paul Fussell traces elements of the irony so prolific in the poetry and memoirs written by actual veterans to as early in the war as the costly stalemate at first Ypres in November 1914, but Fussell also establishes that the tone of World War I literature emanates from seeds planted long before the war, in poetry by Thomas Hardy and A. E. Housman. In April 1918, Faulkner, a fan of both Hardy and Housman, had not yet attained the modern perspective on the war that came to define a generation of war literature. Rather, Faulkner's starry-eyed excitement about meeting Llewellyn reeks of the youthful detachment of one not involved in the war in any real way, a detachment verified by Faulkner's efforts to enlist and fly planes in the war to be like his other idols mentioned in his letters home: Major Raoul Lufberry, Victor Chapman, William Thaw, and Bert Hall (*Thinking* 56–57). Naturally, Faulkner insists in his letters that all these men died, though as James G. Watson points out, Faulkner's romanticizing of their deaths failed to mention that two would, in fact, survive the war (58, n2). We might consider these forgotten survivors as the first casualties of Faulkner's apocrypha and his oversight concerning their actual fates in his first World War I fiction.

These details in Faulkner's letters home from New Haven speak volumes about his impressions of "war" and its glories, but these letters, in hindsight, do more than enough to implicate how very far away from the actual war Faulkner's experience was. These letters, first from New Haven and then eventually from Toronto where he had begun basic training at flight school, do belong in a canon of his World War I writings, however, and not entirely for the clear fictions they contain. Indeed, if Faulkner did not experience the war, he did experience the other catastrophic event concurrent with it, the Great Influenza. His letters home from Toronto all came through quarantine. The base was shut down. The backdrop was the Spanish flu, a part of the narrative of World War I that Willa Cather also included in *One of Ours*. Nor was Faulkner's experience of this part of the war purely an abstraction through the veil of quarantine. On 21 October 1918, he began a letter home with the seemingly innocuous, though somewhat perturbed, statement, "The quarantine has not lifted yet, though one can parade for a pass to see a dying relative or some such thing," but then he turned to a much more personal loss; "That was rather bad about Vic. It's queer how the people one thinks would live for ever are the first to go" (*Thinking* 117). "Vic" was Victoria Oldham, Estelle's sister, who died of the Spanish flu. Her unexpected death is what he finds so queer. Faulkner's accounting of this death—his peculiar use of the word *queer*—in effect compliments Fussell's understanding of the irony that the war instilled into the larger literary consciousness of those who lived through it. War (and the flu) strike down those least likely to be its victims. So it goes.

There is a unifying motif in Faulkner's quarantine, Victoria's death, and the fictional experience of Claude Wheeler, hero in *One of Ours*, with the Great Influenza. A small-town boy from Mississippi, Faulkner found himself among a larger group of men from all parts. Victoria and her husband were living in Georgia at an army training camp—another instance of a local from a small town migrating to a new environment to be around men of all types. Claude Wheeler experiences the influenza on board a ship crossing the Atlantic to fight in the war. Thus, a man from a small, isolated Nebraska community confronts the disease when he, too, is moved into contact with a larger group of men from all over the United States. From the point of view of epidemiology, few situations could be more conducive to the spread of a viral contagion than the war, wherein millions of men and women from small, isolated communities encountered large, mobile populations. As the name *Spanish* flu implies, moreover, the movements of men back and forth between Europe and America—largely for the cause of fighting the war—provided the perfect path for the dissemination of the virus into American populations at a far more accelerated rate than would have been likely during peacetime. The flu and the war were both foreign, yet both reached back across the Atlantic to the American home front.[1]

The larger thematic influence of the Spanish flu is a subcutaneous aspect of Faulkner's World War I writings and would inform his ideas of what happens to a small-town man when he leaves his local sphere for the European theater and then returns. In short, that man will have been exposed to conditions that he will bring home with him and that have the potential to be quite dangerous in a small, local population unfamiliar with his new disease. Nor would Faulkner limit the potential for "infection" only to the flu. Years later, after he published

As I Lay Dying, in May 1931, Faulkner wrote a brief review for the *New Republic* of Erich Maria Remarque's novel *The Road Back*, an apt title for the thematic discussion of how Faulkner would depict the war in the 1920s and up until the publication of *As I Lay Dying* in 1930. In that review, Faulkner stated almost explicitly the types of war "contagion" his fiction describes. Speaking of the hope that the Remarque's novel would find a popular readership, Faulkner explained, "And if the United States had not got back its troops 50-percent intact, save for the casual cases of syphilis and high metropolitan life, [the novel] would not be bought (which I hope and trust that it will be) and read."[2] In 1931 Faulkner could clearly conceive of the war and the "50-percent intact" returning soldiers as having been exposed to diseases, namely syphilis in this case instead of just the flu, the former a sexually transmitted disease as opposed to the airborne influenza. But what could he mean by "cases of [. . .] high metropolitan life"? What contagion does this condition imply? What would a case of high metropolitan life look like?

The review from 1931 and the letter home about Victoria's death form bookends around Faulkner's treatment of war as a type of exposure and returning soldiers as contagious carriers of a peculiar/queer disease, like Wilfred Owen's disabled veteran. In between the two, Faulkner experimented with varieties of narrative predicated on this idea of contagion and the returning soldier, only the contagion his soldiers harbor always has an element of psychosexual "disease" in need of treatment by a "doctor" in *Soldiers' Pay*, by a matchmaking aunt in *Flags in the Dust*, by an asylum in *As I Lay Dying*, and by a wife—or at least the suggestion of a wife—in all three. The other telling detail from Faulkner's in-the-moment experience is from the letter from New Haven, 7 April 1918, in which he glamorized Nicholas Llewellyn, though this detail, like the full implications of war and contagion, would take time to saturate Faulkner's vision and infiltrate his apocryphal creations. After fixing on Llewellyn for a paragraph, Faulkner added the following observation, almost as an afterthought: "There are two other English officers here, Captains Massie and Bland. Bland is suffering from shell shock" (48). Though one might be tempted to believe that witnessing shell shock would give Faulkner pause in his pursuit of glorious battle fame, it did not (nor, for that matter, did the body count he recited for Maud in his letter about Lufberry and all the other dead pilots he could name). At this moment Faulkner may well have been of two minds like two blackbirds in one tree. On one level, he saw Bland and recorded his existence; on another level, he failed to recognize the deeper implications of what he was seeing. Putting this double vision in a Faulknerian context almost seems too easy because, of course, "Memory believes before knowing remembers" (*LIA* 119), or so Faulkner tells us in the first novel that he wrote after completing *As I Lay Dying*, and after realizing in one character the full apocryphal potential for the bare edges of the war he recorded in these early letters.

The "queer" elements of World War I literature did not inform Faulkner's first foray into his war-themed fiction. In 1919, he published a short story in *The Mississippian* entitled "Landing in Luck." The hero of the story, Cadet Thompson, is an American attempting to fly with the RFC. Though he is a slow learner and rather clumsy in the air, he has as much pluck as he has luck. After clipping the landing gear off his plane at take-off in his first solo flight, he manages to land successfully, which is to say that he survives even if the airplane does not. Despite the circumstances that do not portend his future success in flying, his landing earns him respect and a place at the table with the more accomplished British pilots. The story is fanciful and heavily influenced by Faulkner's hero-worship of men like Llewellyn. Much of Faulkner's supposedly "firsthand" experiences that he would relate about his "actual" adventures in the war (the metal plate in his head, his stories about crashing behind enemy lines) reek of romanticized images of war and its effects. His fiction, on the other hand, rarely returns to such fancy.

Written in 1920 but not published until 1933 in *The Green Bough*, the poem "Lilacs" signals a developing consciousness of the effects of war as horrible and tragic. The unnamed subject of the poem is a wounded pilot who has returned home to die. He had been "Raiding over Mannheim" when "Out of the bullet-tortured air: / A great black bowl of fireflies" swarmed up to engulf him (*MF/GB* 9–10). Wounded beyond repair, the pilot now finds himself in the midst of a garden party while around him women "[drink] tea / Beneath the lilacs on a summer afternoon" (7). The pilot is an object of pity. The only attention he gets from the women is to overhear them talking with other men at the party about him. The pilot overhears one of these men whose "voice has dropped and the wind is mouthing his words / While the lilacs nod their heads on slender stalks, / Agreeing while he talks, / Caring not if he is heard or is not heard" by the pilot who languishes in the mute silence of his Prufrockian internal monologue (10). The pilot's closing thoughts record his response to this overheard pity: "I hear their voices as from a great distance—Not dead / He's not dead, poor chap; he didn't die—" (11). The pilot is conscious of what is happening around him, but he cannot affect it. His life is internal, theirs external; he is the center of attention, but he is not a participant in the action of the poem. "Lilacs" bears a striking resemblance to Owen's "Disabled," only at the end we hear Faulkner's pilot reciting to himself the pity of the other partygoers rather than hear the speaker in the poem voice that pity by wishing someone would take the ruined invalid with his queer disease out of sight.

The "moral" that the poem conveys is that it would have been better for the pilot, the "poor chap," to have died in Europe in the war and thus to have spared himself the benign pity he experiences when he returns home figuratively dead. He certainly is no longer part of the coed socializing at the party, and one can reasonably conclude that "he will never feel again how slim / Girls' waists are, or how warm their subtle hands" (Owen 67).[3] The crowd looks at him, if they do not touch him, like some queer disease. Overall, the poem seems to propose that death would have been preferable to pity, or that between death and pity one should choose death. The glories of battle are meaningless, it seems, if they do not also kill the pilot or soldier. The poem stops short of critiquing the irony of glorious death in battle and instead fixates on the pilot's failure to die. Therefore, the poem maintains Faulkner's romantic sense of the fallen hero, whose failure makes him as much of a slow learner and just as clumsy as Cadet Thompson in "Landing and Luck" (a more skilled pilot would have died and earned a more vaunted status). By bringing the pilot home, however, to encounter the pity of "the women" instead of the tacit respect of his fellow pilots, Faulkner opened a door through which to direct his later World War I fiction to more mature ends.

Post-1920 and "Lilacs," Faulkner continued to perform his World War I wounded soldier persona to his friends and in various social situations, but his writing moved toward the imitative poetry explored in the previous chapters. That writing was heavily gay themed, but was not war themed. Faulkner also courted Ben Wasson, moved briefly to New York with Stark Young, and eventually moved to New Orleans and the gay scene of the Vieux Carre. In 1925, settled in New Orleans and still dutifully performing his outward role of having a limp and a metal plate in his head from war wounds, he began his first novel, which he referred to as his "mistress."[4] He also wrote occasional pieces for the *Times-Picayune*, such as "Out of Nazareth," and submitted the occasional letter to the *Item-Tribune*. He moved in with William Spratling. He was also reading the work of Siegfried Sassoon and Rupert Brooke. When he returned to World War I fiction in 1925, his output underwent a decided change from the hero-worship of men like Llewellyn to an awareness of that other figure from his encounter in New Haven so many years earlier, the shell-shocked Bland.

In *Soldiers' Pay* Faulkner returned to the image of the wounded pilot from "Lilacs," and, while introducing him, echoed the sentiment from that poem and its romanticized image of war. Cadets Julian Lowe and Joe Gilligan are trading wit and whiskey on a train meant to take them home from the war after they have been decommissioned. On the way, they encounter Donald Mahon, a name Faulkner intended as a double pun on "man" to universalize Mahon's condition and, conversely, to rob him of identity as just another "man," or body, sacrificed to the gods of war. Perhaps unintentionally, though, Mahon's name also implies a gendered distinction that reminds us that, when we look upon "Mahon," we are beholding a "man." Cadet Lowe beholds him thus:

> He saw a belt and wings, he rose and met a young face with a dreadful scar across his brow. My God he thought, turning sick. [. . .] Cadet Lowe pressed the bell, regarding with a rebirth of the old feud between American enlisted men and officers of all nations the man's insignia and wings and brass, not even wondering

what a British officer in his condition could be doing traveling in America. Had I been old enough or lucky enough, this might have been me, he thought jealously. (21)

Mahon's scar, his officer status, and his perceived foreignness repulse and attract Lowe, whose eyes regard not only Mahon's "young face," now scarred, but also take in his whole body, conveniently dressed in officer regalia. Mahon is actually from "Gawgia," as the black porter tells Lowe and Gilligan, but Gilligan insists, "Christ, I thought he was a foreigner" (21). Then, as Lowe's fascination increases and he begins questioning Mahon, Gilligan rejoins, "Don't you see he don't remember himself? Do you reckon you would, with that scar?" (25). He later declares, with significant ambiguity, "My God, it makes you sick at the stomach, don't it?" (25). The "it" has no clear antecedent and in context could refer to "the dreadful scar" itself or to Mahon's "face, young, yet old as the world, beneath [it]" (25); or *it* could refer more generally to the collision of the scar and Mahon's youth as what disorients and sickens these two men staring at him. Whatever *it* is, it makes Gilligan *sick* at the stomach when he sees it. This generic expression of revulsion carries much significance in relation to Donald's injuries, his proverbial queer disease.

While Gilligan gets sick, Julian Lowe almost seems to be aroused by Mahon's presence and perceived glories. Lowe provides too much excessive hero-worship in this scene in his "jealousy" of Mahon's scar. He represents an apocryphal version of the younger William Faulkner in New Haven, idolizing dead pilots and wounded soldiers without fully realizing the horrors of war that his novel in 1925 much more deftly handles than his earlier story and poem. Of course, Lowe also functions as Gilligan's partner, with both Lowe and Gilligan fascinated by and drawn to this "Mahon/man" in front of them. Their eyes take in the scene. Lowe explicitly wishes he was Mahon; Gilligan takes upon himself the responsibility of looking after Mahon. The scene almost articulates the implicit queer desires at work among these three men, but Margaret Powers intercedes into this queer triangulation of male desire before it can progress to more overt homoeroticism. Powers replaces Lowe in this queer triangle, a replacement early in the novel that effectively stunts any further implications that, minus Powers's arrival on the scene, Lowe and Gilligan would have been the (same-sex) partners who take Mahon home. Powers and Gilligan emerge as significantly more emotionally mature than Lowe by the end of chapter 1 and decide to take upon themselves the task of returning Mahon to Georgia to die.

After allowing Lowe a childish and idyllic (though unconsummated) courtship of Powers, Faulkner shuffles him off to his mother in San Francisco. He reappears throughout the novel via his dreamy letters to Powers about finding work and a home to support her, but his physical body—and the romanticism embodied therein—are shuffled away at the end of the first chapter to allow the real plot to unfold: Mahon's return, his death, and the efforts of Margaret Powers and others in his hometown to "save" him. That Faulkner allows this prologue with Lowe, however, ever so slightly hints that the subtext of the proceeding action is homosexually charged. The novel starts among men with their mutual idolization, jealousies, and sympathies for each other. Margaret Powers enters the scene just as the seeds are sown that might explicitly demonstrate the male-to-male attraction powering the interactions prior to her appearance. Whatever power might animate the interactions of Lowe, Gilligan, and Mahon, Margaret *powers* anew with safely heterosexual animus. Lowe subsequently turns his attentions to her; Powers and Gilligan encourage his courtship. Lowe never entirely disappears, though. His early presence in the novel permeates the rest of the action, an echo of male same-sex possibilities stunted in their progress by the necessity of getting the wounded "Mahon" safely and properly home.

After Lowe's exit, *Soldiers' Pay* turns fully to Faulkner's memories of Bland and begins to rely on his readings of other war literature to explore the implications of Mahon's return. In this first attempt to enter the larger conversation of World War I literature, Faulkner had to step very far beyond his experiences into the realm of artifice to present that life. The whole novel is artifice much more than it is merely apocryphal. Faulkner was not making his actual war experience into an apocryphal account in this novel; he was extending into the realm of fiction what was already an apocryphal persona. Faulkner traveled by train back to Oxford from Canada, but the closest character in the story to Faulkner's actual-experience-made-apocryphal is Julian Lowe, who never had a chance to serve and whom Faulkner quickly removes from the central plot to become a love-struck boy creating his own fantasy about Margaret Powers from the safe distance of California while the main action of the novel unfolds on the opposite coast. Lowe does not even function as a distant observer or narrator; he writes letters to Margaret that represent the sheer artifice of courtship, far more show than substance. Then he even disappears from his mother's house, to which he has returned and from where he writes his letters, a situation not unlike Faulkner's actual living arrangements upon his return to Oxford. After chapter 1, Faulkner turned his attention to experiences he could only assimilate through other World War I narratives and through the vicarious experiences of the war through others: Llewellyn, Bland, and his own wounded brother, though that brother returned in a far less catatonic state than Mahon. The novel is an extended performance, a stylized theater of the postwar South (Faulkner even selectively employed the structure of dramatic dialogue in it at times). Into this facade, Faulkner introduced another significant pun. If Mahon is the "man" returning from war, his father, who is an Anglican rector, becomes the "doctor" who will diagnose his disease and propose a cure for it. That the title "doctor" can refer to a clergyman may seem to be an innocent choice of words for the critical scene of diagnosis and recognition, but in the context of contagion and the larger experience of the war on which Faulkner could actually draw—the Spanish flu—calling the rector "doctor" signifies the double entendre of Mahon's condition. He is queer, but nobody wants to say as much explicitly. The townspeople can, however, diagnose his condition and prescribe treatment for it in a discourse of disease that quarantines the queer implications of Donald's return into the medical language of healing his "wounds."

In chapter 3, part 4, Mahon's father meets Cecily's father, Mr. Saunders, in a scene fraught with innuendo about Donald's sexuality. Donald's betrothed, Cecily, has rejected him when she sees his scar. He now appears different, or foreign, to her, and his new foreignness is too much for her to bear. She realizes that she cannot marry him. On a trip to town her father, Robert the elder, then encounters Donald's father, the rector who tends to his flock's moral health and so goes by the appellation "Doctor" in conversation. Deluded by the premise that his son *will* recover from his "scar," the rector/doctor begins to discuss Donald and Cecily's engagement. When Mr. Saunders tries to respond that his daughter cannot be expected to follow through, given the new circumstances, the doctor insists, "[H]e has a scar, you see. But I am confident this can be removed, even though Cecily does become accustomed to it. In fact, I am depending on her to make a new man of him in a short time" (109–10). There is something not quite right about what the doctor/rector is diagnosing. Donald Mahon has a physical scar on his face that has somehow produced in him a detachment from the world. At no point in the novel does anyone directly explain how the scar on Donald's face may be related to any deeper concussive injury that could cause his loss of memory. Still, he is no longer interested in participating in the world of his Georgia hometown and even fails to recognize Cecily, who in turn is repulsed by him because now when she looks at him, she sees something very different from the attractive young man to whom she was once engaged. Donald's father does not discuss his son's scar as a physical object, though, but as a psychological mark that has unmanned (un-Mahon-ed) him. Thus, he completely believes that the scar can be removed by the simplest of means: a woman makes him a new man/Mahon by instituting the treatment of marriage. Marriage is the treatment that the doctor recommends to cure his son's ambiguous disease. Mr. Saunders does not agree with the rector's plan of treatment and opts instead to try again the next day to convince the rector that Cecily cannot marry Donald, but the rector emphatically repeats his diagnosis and prescribed treatment. He continues that his son "is naturally a bit confused right now," though confused about what he never clearly says, "but care and attention, and above all, Cecily, will remedy that" (110). Notably, the rector/doctor even uses the medical term "remedy" to discuss what he hopes will occur when Donald is married. Precisely what is she supposed to remedy? What will marriage remedy? What is *that*?

At this point, Mr. Saunders's curiosity is piqued. He asks, "But what happened to him?" (110). The rector concedes, "He won't talk about it. A *friend* who came home with him assures me that he doesn't know and cannot remember. But this happens quite often, *the young man—a soldier himself—*tells me" (110, italics added). The "friend," who in this case is a "young man" and a fellow soldier touched, presumably, by the same experience even if he does not outwardly express the mark of that experience so plainly on his face, is Joe Gilligan, not Margaret Powers. That soldier friend is familiar with Donald's symptoms and can "assure" the "doctor" that those symptoms are quite common among soldiers. Echoes of Julian Lowe's reactions to Donald reverberate in the rector's statement. If *two* young male friends had brought Donald home, the homosexual implications of his ailment might overtake the narrative. Since Margaret Powers replaced Julian, the outward appearance of Donald's caretakers matches a discernible heterosexual pattern that mitigates the all-male aspect of Donald's war experience and the early stages of his return on the train. Mr. Saunders originally intended to tell the rector that the engagement was off, but after listening to the rector, he decides instead, "I wonder if I might stop in to speak to Donald" (110). Mr. Saunders realizes that Donald's "scar" is deeper than a superficial wound and that his daughter's reaction is not simply a product of his external disfigurement. Mr. Saunders wants to witness this un-manning himself.

At the rectory Mr. Saunders sees for himself what everyone except the rector sees, that Donald Mahon is "scarred" beyond repair. Nonetheless, the rector continues to play the role of doctor and insists, "But Donald is in a position to help himself now, provided he gets his medicine often enough," a statement that he directs to Mr. Saunders, concluding "with jovial innuendo" that "[w]e depend on you for this, you know" (113). When Mr. Saunders finally has the opportunity, he corners Margaret Powers and demands, "Why doesn't someone tell him the truth about that boy?" (113). The "truth" is most likely that Donald is injured beyond repair and will die, but at no point is this "truth" explicitly stated. Donald's true condition remains unstated, an open secret of implication and metaphor suggesting that his wound is an injury to his supposed heterosexuality since marriage seems to be the best way to fix whatever it is about him that has been damaged. It is not difficult to read Donald's story as that he has gone off to war and returned as a homosexual detached from all the surroundings that prior to the war seemed to suggest a very different truth about his life.

When Mr. Saunders demands to know what a real doctor has concluded, Margaret Powers answers that "[t]he man that was wounded is dead and this is another person, a grown child. It's his apathy, his detachment, that's so terrible" (114). Apathy and detachment are not related to any physical scar. The diagnosis, even from a real medical professional later in the novel, is that Mahon has removed himself from the expectations of society as much as he has been physically wounded by the mark he bears on his face. Therefore, Margaret Powers and Mr. Saunders decide to fake the engagement with Cecily long enough to let Donald die in peace. They reason for the virtue of this course because, "Remember, he might have been your son" (115). Mr. Saunders does, in fact, have a son, a miniature version of himself who even shares his name. Mr. Saunders is readily convinced that such a possibility—Donald could have been his son!—is so awful to imagine that he finds himself ready to sacrifice his own daughter to cordon off Donald's illness until he can die. Through this sacrifice, Donald may at least passably resemble the outward appearance of normality in the town, lest his still unnamed condition spread, possibly to other sons, like Young Robert Saunders.

Mr. Saunders will later explain to his daughter that "we expect you to be [Donald's] best medicine," though she counters, "He brought his own medicine with him" (137). This jab is ostensibly aimed at Margaret Powers, but Donald also brought Gilligan, his "friend," home with him, and nearly brought Julian Lowe as well. Cecily's primary resentment, though, is clearly for "that black woman" Margaret Powers (138), an easier target of jealousy than the young soldier who bears no outward wounds. Cecily eventually refuses to continue the charade of healing Donald with the balm of heterosexual convention, so Margaret Powers marries him instead, and Donald, never cured of his "apathy" or his "scar" despite the best efforts of his father and Margaret, dies anyway. The conclusion of the novel, Donald's death, is never in question. He has gone to the war. He has returned wounded. No woman can save him, not even Emmy, whom Donald slept with before the war but now does not even see. A real doctor, not the rector, proclaims that Donald is "practically a dead man now" (150). As this proclamation comes on page 150 in a novel of 315 pages, we might conclude that all the mercurial marriage planning that occupies so much of the action of the novel is purely sound and fury that accomplishes nothing, but the charade does accomplish quite a lot. The marriage planning maintains the proper heterosexual order of the town and keeps the townspeople free from Donald's queer condition, at least as much as possible given that so many people want to see Donald, which would expose them to his contagion if Gilligan and Margaret did not do their best to deny people admittance to Donald's room.

In the midst of the main narrative, Robert Saunders, the younger, swells the progress of characters on the stage of this small town. Robert is Cecily's kid brother, and his as-yet-formless sexuality streaks through the novel in brilliant flashes like heat lightning. He first appears on the evening of Donald's return. Cecily has fled to her home where her moaning histrionics sound in the background the melody of "Ooooh, don't, don't, mamma! I c-can't bear to think of it. [. . .] Not ever, not ever. If I have to see him again I'll—I'll just die. I can't bear it, I can't bear it" (92). Meanwhile, young Robert keeps asking her what Donald looks like. While Cecily's parents put her to bed, Robert sneaks off to the rectory to get a glimpse of the soldiers. As he slides down a fence to cut through the backyards between his home and the rectory, he rips the back of his pants and "sprawl[s] in the damp grass feeling a thin shallow fire across his young behind" (96). He considers this misfortune "rotten luck" but continues his mission (96). He is turned away by Gilligan, but he decides that he will have better luck in the morning. He stalks home, where his dinner and scolding parents are waiting; "[t]hen soaped and hungry he clattered into the dining room, accomplishing an intricate field maneuver lest his damaged rear be exposed" (98).

The brilliance of this interlude in relation to the larger action of the adults is a product of Robert's utterly guileless reaction to his *exposed rear*, notably a reference to combat and the rhetoric of war. He tears his pants and exposes his "behind" on his mission to see the returning soldier. He attempts to hide the damage by "accomplishing an intricate field maneuver." He is a little soldier in training, though he is unaware of the full implications of his exposure to the real soldier who just returned wounded from the war. Such details are rife for a homoerotic reading. Robert transgresses by sneaking out. He exposes himself in a way that would be distinctly horrifying to a homophobic reader on the lookout for signs of the emasculating power of anal penetration. Robert is unconcerned, however, except to the extent that he knows his parents will be angry that he tore his pants. He continues his mission, meets one soldier, though not the one he was looking for, and, despite having a "damaged rear," does not balk when asked where he was by his parents. He immediately tells them that he went to see the soldiers, his torn pants completely forgotten. He is sublimely unaware of himself as a factor in the sexual economy that drives the plot.

Young Robert later appears completely naked, skinny-dipping in a water hole with his friends. Gilligan and Margaret Powers are walking through the woods when they hear noises through the trees. They spy Robert poised "on a limb, balanced precariously to dive" (155). The narrator describes, "His body was the color of old paper, beautiful as a young animal's" (155). Gilligan calls out to Robert as he prepares to jump. Startled in mid-flight, he crashes into the water and reemerges long enough to swim out of view. Gilligan has called to him, but he directs his ire at Margaret Powers, who retreats into the woods with Gilligan because she feels that they have ruined his fun. Robert broods on her intrusion, "his malevolent face watching her retreating figure as he swiftly donned his clothes. 'I'll fix you!' he swore, almost crying" (155). Yet, Gilligan is ultimately responsible for spying on him and calling to him, and Gilligan has brought a woman into the space of his adolescent freedom wherein he can swim naked with other boys and feel no shame. A returning soldier himself, Gilligan has caused Robert's exposure, and in this case, Robert is all too aware that someone has seen him fully exposed.

His role in the novel remains so minor as to make a full psychosexual case study impossible, but this scene does suffice as a moment of awakening at which Robert understands his own body as sexualized, though his awakening is only to a transient knowledge. Later in the novel he is back prowling around the rectory, "bent on a seduction of his own" (214). Over lunch, he quizzes Januarius Jones about whether or not he served in the war. Robert is still looking for soldiers. They still elicit his curiosity in ways that need monitoring and censoring. Margaret Powers's warning that Donald "might have been your son" sounds an ominous note for young Robert Saunders. His interests in the soldiers and his intricate field maneuvers imply he will grow up to be a "soldier" himself one day if his parents are not careful to steer him on a more appropriate path. Mrs. Saunders finally intervenes in his adolescent machinations. When she notices that he has cornered Januarius Jones, she runs off Robert for his annoying inquisitiveness, thus interrupting his "seduction." Her intervention is well placed. Robert's curiosity implicates his nascent interests in the company of men. Mrs. Saunders intervenes to put an end to his attentions just as her husband has conspired to make Donald appear as if he is on the path to proper heterosexuality in the institution of marriage. Nonetheless, Robert's minor role in the novel could not be more crucial. He is the young boy, the "lad" of an A. E. Housman poem or any number of nineteenth-century authors from Walter Pater to Walt Whitman. His attraction is his sheer innocence. In a novel filled with floral imagery and the prepubescence of spring, he is the budding flower on the very edge of bloom. He is desperate to get a glimpse of Donald (Mahon/man), even going out of his way on his daily trek to school and bringing friends with him, a situation that bothers Gilligan so much that he comments to Margaret Powers, "We got to stop this [. . .] can't have these damn folks in and out of here all day, staring at him" (146). Young Robert's always exposed body becomes the contested site over which will play out the great lengths to which the adults will go to reestablish the heterosexual social order that Donald's reappearance has disrupted. He is the blooming youth whose sexuality must be protected, and he clearly wants to transgress and see Donald. The goal of the town is to put him on a proper path in life. His transgression must be denied.

If these details do not fully articulate a homosexual narrative, they also do not articulate a measure of Faulkner's homophobia. The reactions of the characters to Donald's "scar" may be homophobic, but the conclusion of the novel seems to be far more an indictment of a society for its expectations that refuse to admit queer sexualities into them. Yes, Donald's death is a foregone conclusion from the beginning of the novel, but there's the rub. Donald would have been better off had he actually died in the war. His father, Cecily, and everyone else in town had received word that he was killed in action, and they have been acting under that assumption for some time as the novel begins. They have recreated their ordered reality, putting Donald proverbially a few feet about the stove as a lost idol much the way Mrs. Wheeler and Mahailey do with their memories of Claude in *One of Ours*. Everyone is quite surprised when Donald suddenly returns with his "friend" and the "black" woman. The society to which he has returned does not have the capacity to revise their narrative and envision a place for him in their town except to force him into a marriage for the sake of maintaining order. The society back home, not the scar from abroad, ultimately sentences Donald to death. To that society, he was dead when he left for the war. By leaving, his fate was sealed and the townspeople could mourn and remember him in whatever capacity best suited them. His return forces the town to confront a reality for which they are unprepared.

Faulkner's life in gay New Orleans as an alternative to the confines of small-town Oxford offers an easy paradigm for the source of the geography of his novel set in small-town Georgia and in the larger European theater of war. Structurally, the binaries at work in the novel include urban to rural, elsewhere to home, open to closed, acceptance to rejection. The townspeople accepted Donald when he was gone. They reject him when he returns (or at least do not mind his dying so long as they can cover up any messy reality of his life). At the same time, these binaries are encumbered by the larger connotations of contagion and exposure, especially in the historical moment surrounding World War I. Small-town boy goes to the big city. When he comes back, he has acquired queer big-city ways. Or he goes across the ocean. The home front would seem to have an easier time imagining that homosexuality is bred on foreign shores. Foreign homosexuality poses no threat to the home front when it takes place in a battlefield in faraway France. What happens, however, if it comes home after the war has ended? Faulkner seems to have asked this question in *Soldiers' Pay*. He continued to pursue it in his World War I fictions for the next five years until he came home in his own real-life enactment of the apocryphal narrative of the returning queer.

In *Elmer*, "The Leg," "Ad Astra," and *Flags in the Dust*, Faulkner would experiment with various permutations of the basic elements of *Soldiers' Pay*. First, in his effort to bring Donald Mahon home, Faulkner invented a fictitious town in Georgia, a place at some remove from his little postage stamp of native soil. Much of the story is purely invented and represents a significant stretch beyond Faulkner's actual experiences of the war, and by moving the action to Georgia he robbed the novel of what minimal connection it might have had to his actual experiences, as if to suggest that, while first experimenting with such latently homosexual elements, he could not put his own identity, even apocryphally, too fully into the text. Estelle's sister died at an army base in Georgia. Perhaps his memory of that death prompted Faulkner to choose Georgia as a site for the exposure and attempts at quarantine that animate *Soldiers' Pay*. Second, Donald Mahon's catatonic inertia make him an *object* of pity, much like Owen's disabled soldier, but he never becomes a *subject* in the text. Donald is a distinctly flat and static character, minus small peaks at his personality before the war from Cecily Saunders, Emmy, and his father. Cecily's hyperbolic vanity and fickleness make suspect what little she might provide about Donald. Emmy's memory of her courtship and its consummation with Donald is told by her, not the narrator, and is distinctly her point of view, with no access to Donald's internal feelings. Donald's father is blind to the reality of his son's life. We are granted a brief glimpse of Donald's remembering being shot down, much as Faulkner's speaker in "Lilacs" recalls that pilot's experience over Mannheim, but otherwise Donald is a body around which we observe everyone else's actions and motivations, but never his. Neither of these elements represent flaws in the plot, but they do serve to limit the way in which Faulkner could tell the story of a returned soldier. Other permutations produced their own limitations but also their own insights.

Faulkner began *Elmer* while in Paris in the summer of 1925, though he would never satisfactorily complete it. He submitted a revised version of it to his publishers in the early 1930s as "A Portrait of Elmer" though plans for its publication never came to fruition. Despite other revisions, Faulkner maintained in the original manuscript and in the later story the material concerning Elmer's boyhood crush and adolescent homosexuality. In "A Portrait of Elmer," a third-person narrator attempts a psychological case study of Elmer Hodge. Never an excellent student, Elmer "developed a fine sexless passion for the teacher. But this year he was ravished away from that constancy by a boy, a young beast as beautiful to him as a god, and as cruel" (*US* 616). This first flame of desire dies quickly when the boy pushes Elmer down on the playground, causing Elmer to "transfer[] his sheeplike devotion once more to the teacher" (616). Faulkner includes this detail in Elmer's psychosexual development, but he also cordons it off as part of Elmer's adolescence, out of which Elmer matures to become a functional heterosexual. In the meantime, Elmer grows up and goes to war. He "entrained for Halifax" to serve for the Canadian government (627), but unlike Faulkner, who also enlisted in Canada, Elmer fights in the war. There he receives a horrible scar on his back from an intense burn and develops the ubiquitous limp of literary soldiers, including the apocryphal soldier William Faulkner. After the war, as a practicing heterosexual, he courts a woman in Houston "where he already had a bastard son" (612). His real passion, however, prefiguring Quentin Compson's later obsession, is finding his long-lost older sister Jo, for whom he harbors an incestuous desire that he has maintained since he was a child and she ran away to get married. He thinks once that he sees her while he is walking the streets of New Orleans, a city he returns to often and the city to which Faulkner returned after his own time abroad. The end of "A Portrait of Elmer" has Elmer, in Paris, fleeing wildly to his hotel because of a massive bowel movement that prevents him from courting yet another woman.

The elements of the story never come together. To tell in full a *Bildungsroman* of a wounded soldier did not work for Faulkner the way it did for Cather in *One of Ours*. In a *Bildungsroman* the details become too fixed and compartmentalized. Indeed, later critics—Parini in regard to Faulkner's actual life, Blotner in regard to "Divorce in Naples"—argue for versions of a cordoned-off homosexuality as a fleeting moment of one's youth, but no evidence suggests that

Faulkner saw homosexuality through the same lens. His inability to complete a satisfactory revision of *Elmer*/"A Portrait of Elmer" could well have been a product of his sense that a neatly partitioned, linear life study did not effectively account for the complexities of consciousness. In *Soldiers' Pay*, the effectiveness of Donald Mahon's character stems from his lack of history. That novel begins *in medias res* and offers only vague glimpses of the Mahon from before the war. The novel is primarily a limited third-person account of Donald's life in the immediate aftermath of the war. In "A Portrait of Elmer," an omniscient narrator employs occasional internal monologues, but Elmer has too much history, which is all laid out in precise moments and all in the past. Faulkner could not produce a holistic impression of Elmer from the disparate parts of his experience. As for the other element of his war narratives—location—Faulkner was more successful in this story than in his novel. Elmer Hodge returns from the war to New Orleans. In Europe, Elmer prefers Paris, which Faulkner also visited and where he first began writing *Elmer* before putting it aside and returning to it in the early 1930s. Faulkner put Elmer Hodge into spheres with which he was familiar, rather than create a fictional place removed from his actual life. This autobiographical geography represents an effort on Faulkner's part to assimilate his actual experience in the apocryphal details of his fictional creations and so represents a positive step toward his eventual realization of a gay-themed war narrative set in his native north Mississippi.

Faulkner seems to have written at least a draft of "The Leg" while he was in Europe in 1925.[5] In the story, two British soldiers court a girl before the war. In the war, one dies while the other is wounded and loses his leg. When the survivor returns, he continues his courtship, but he is haunted by his phantom limb and ghostly images of his lost companion, whom he comes to believe takes on bodily form and continues courting this one woman between them. The story is rife with queer elements, but the setting is entirely European. Structurally, Faulkner also seems to digress in his presentation of homosexuality in the story; the relationship between the two soldiers centers firmly on a single woman between them in a model of same-sex eroticism that muddies the waters of their desires. Such triangulations are common in pre-1850s literature, or so Eve Sedgwick has argued, but in other writings, Faulkner relied on more modern and more complex interactions to depict homoeroticism and homosexuality. Admittedly, the gothic elements of the text—the ghostly figure courting the woman and the phantom limb—seem to borrow from ghost story traditions firmly rooted in nineteenth-century horror tales and other gothic forebears wherein patterns of triangulated desires present in "The Leg" are not uncommon. Faulkner modernizes these gothic elements, however, by applying them to a World War I narrative and the trauma of the wounded survivor.

The ghostly figure is a visitation from a battlefield, the shadow of the lost heterosexual who returns as an apparition to continue his failed courtship from before the war. The surviving soldier has a leg wound, a metaphor for a sexual wound that complicates his courtship when he returns by reminding him of his loss, in this case both his leg *and* his male companion. The woman between them, through whom they mediate their desires, does not function to sanction their inarticulate homoeroticism through the safety of her female body. Rather, she finds herself literally haunted, alongside the surviving soldier, by the casualties of war and the relationships whose previously unfettered histories are decimated by it. In this story, Faulkner was experimenting with the elements of his World War I material to create a strikingly complex portrait of the psychology of desire and trauma. Before the war, the two men enact a version of a triangulated courtship similar to older models of same-sex desire between men with a woman in the middle. After the war, the loss of that past haunts and nearly kills those unfortunate enough to have survived. Obviously, the title is not coincidental: "the leg" is the missing member emblematic of a phantom desire (between the two men) beyond what we directly observe (between a man and a woman) that estranges and horrifies. When one man dies, the other is wounded irreparably in the leg. It is a sexual wound. It haunts him.

The origins of "Ad Astra" are somewhat unclear, though the narrator of the version Faulkner eventually published very clearly establishes that he is telling this story twelve years after it took place, or in 1930 (408).[6] Faulkner attempted to publish the story after his marriage in 1929, but the story possibly dates to earlier as Faulkner began to experiment with the character Bayard Sartoris, the central figure of his first Yocona/Yoknapatawpha novel *Flags in the Dust*. The Bayard who appears in that novel is clearly troubled by his experiences in the war. In "Ad Astra," Faulkner explored the events at the heart of Bayard's wartime experiences to understand what Bayard might have brought home with him and what could be the cause of his turmoil when he returns home without it. The thematic similarities between the novel and the story suggest that whichever one Faulkner wrote first, the other was on his mind at the same time. In the fictional chronology of Faulkner's nascent county, the events of "Ad Astra" immediately precede the events in *Flags*, even if Faulkner published it later.

Though Bayard Sartoris will eventually come home in the novel in a homecoming that apocryphizes Faulkner's return to Oxford to court and marry Estelle, "Ad Astra" does not quite bridge the gap between home and abroad. The story is set entirely in Europe immediately after the war has ended. In the story Faulkner provides three characters to perform the charade of masculinity requisite to the theater of war: Bayard Sartoris, Monaghan, and, intriguingly, a pilot named Bland. Bayard features as the protagonist of *Flags*. Monaghan will also appear in that novel in a telling moment that links the themes of the story to the queer subtext of the novel in surprising but powerful ways. For now, though, I will consider the story in isolation, as its own piece in the larger puzzle. In the story, Faulkner articulated a clear homosexual desire, but he simultaneously quarantined that desire away from the developing landscape of Yoknapatawpha County. The homosexuality in the story happens in Europe. Bayard and Bland make sure it stays there even though Monaghan will return home after the war and reappear in Bayard's story right as Bayard prepares for his violent death as a test pilot. Whenever Faulkner wrote the story, its connections to a letter from 1918—the pilot named Bland—and a novel published in 1928 thoroughly demonstrate that, in a Faulknerian universe, the past is not dead; it is not even past. The trauma of the war that Faulkner witnessed in New Haven informed his novel about Bayard, whose history he expanded in a story set just prior to Bayard's return home.

The genealogy of the letter, story, and novel proves illusive, however, though they do not inform each other in an isolated triangle. Other influences surface in the story and novel. In his essay "Faulkner's Crying Game," John Duvall describes the scene that fractures the heterosexual civilities of Faulkner's World War I fiction with an allusion to Faulkner's own queerly loaded reading of Conrad Aiken's poetry to Ben Wasson on the Ole Miss campus. Duvall relates this queer recitation to "Ad Astra." He describes how Monaghan, an American, has downed a German pilot and taken him prisoner. Monaghan then proceeds to "violate protocol by bringing his prisoner, who has a bad head wound, into the cafe where his comrades are 'celebrating' the end of the war" (56). Monaghan's intention is to get the man very drunk and "to take him home with me" (CS 412). Bland asks what Monaghan wants with the man, to which Monaghan responds that "he belongs to me" (412). Then Bland asks the German if he wants to go to America with Monaghan. Though he has a wife and child in Germany, he responds that, yes, he would like that very much. His head wound has apparently made him forget about his previous heterosexual life, much as Donald Mahon's head wound made him forget himself (and the psychiatric patient in Cather's One of Ours has forgotten himself as well). Needless to say, the French crowd in the cafe collectively responds with "shocked and outraged faces" (CS 412) because, as Duvall argues,

> Monaghan is not trying to make a *man* out of the German. Like Billy's reading poetry to Ben, something seems askew here that, if this were between a man and woman, the reader, like the Ole Miss students, would process as part of the natural and normal. That is, had Monaghan brought in a French woman, tried to get her drunk, and promised her a trip to America, who would think twice? The war's over; boys will be boys. But what happens in the cafe is a seduction that exceeds the boundaries of this homosocial world, and it is precisely that the war is over that leads to the homoerotic subtext of this scene. (57)

The premise of Duvall's essay is that in war a man's masculinity is measured by his ability to penetrate the bodies of other men with bullets. After a war, that very penetrative act takes on less glorious connotations: (sexual) penetration as the loss of masculinity. The dichotomy between penetrating with bullets and penetrating with a penis that Duvall constructs is somewhat inelegant but nonetheless metaphorically accurate. Marilee Lindemann's understanding of the larger context of battle and its Janus-faced creation of both an all-male (gay) space and a space in which to measure irreproachable masculinity offers a more nuanced version of the abrupt distinction Duvall isolates in the imagery of Faulkner's short story. Duvall echoes her assessment of war in identifying the homosexual subtext of the scene, even to the extent that he recognizes the source of homophobia in the story in the reaction of an affronted society, not in Faulkner's own fraught masculinity.

"Ad Astra" does not have the hate crime ending of "Jealousy," but the characters do attempt to eradicate Monaghan's blatant challenge to the reestablishment of postwar heterosexuality. Bland, Bayard, and the other pilots take the German soldier to a whorehouse where the masculinity established in war can be reestablished in the performance of hypermasculine heterosexuality. Unfortunately, Monaghan's impulses cannot be so easily removed. In particular, Bayard will find himself touched by Monaghan's queer disease when he finally returns home without his brother John. He watched John be shot down by German planes, their bullets becoming the penetrating penises of Duvall's reading. Monaghan's German lover only adds to Bayard's notion that Germans want to emasculate/ kill American men with their homosexuality. The horror of what he has witnessed haunts Bayard, primarily with the impression that he, too, as a pilot may suffer from the same emasculation represented by John's death and Monaghan's homosexual impulses. When he returns home, Bayard will act out his aggression and outrage. He will despise the rigid confines of home. He will dream of his brother. He will escape home finally, but only to die. His fate is hardly surprising and has been foretold in "Ad Astra." When Bland at one point asks another soldier, "And what will you do now?" since the war is over, the soldier responds, "What will any of us do? All this generation which fought in the war are dead tonight. But we do not know it yet" (420, 21). Faulkner bore out this idea in *Soldiers' Pay*. In his subsequent World War I fiction, he simply rephrased it. "Death" is the loss of heterosexual masculinity that these soldiers have suffered. If they die in war, they are lucky, for if they return queerly wounded, they face the long, drawn-out "death" of failing to find their way back into the heterosexual order of a home that no longer has a place for them.

Faulkner could never escape his home, however, and his fiction eventually found itself firmly rooted in those square streets and that small town of his ancestors. In *Flags in the Dust*, he turned his creative attention to a fictional county in north Mississippi that he named Yocona. He transferred the legend of the Old Colonel from Ripley to Jefferson and placed his monument high in a new cemetery. He also made the Jefferson Depot the central site of the

Sartoris family's lore and heritage, but young Bayard will not detrain there as a triumphant war hero. As Faulkner faked his return in RAF drag and with pomp, Bayard—an actual veteran—sneaks off the side of the train opposite the platform and disappears almost unnoticed. By faking a war wound, Faulkner wanted the glory he was not rightly due when he returned home. Bayard shuns the glory he has earned by fighting in dangerous air combat, largely because what he witnessed—his brother's death—has so shadowed his impressions of war that he does not feel heroic. Though ostensibly different, these two home-comings, the actual and the apocryphal, are merely inverted versions of each other, and to depict the returning veteran in such a familiar setting and with such heavily, if apocryphally, autobiographical overtones did cause Faulkner pause. Bayard not only marries Narcissa after the war. We also learn that he was married before he left for the war and fathered a son, though his first wife, Caroline White Sartoris, and that son died less than a month before the war ended. Cordoning off Bayard's war experience from his pursuits of heterosexual marriages both draws attention to the queer space of the war that falls between these two marital bookends and mitigates the homosexuality inherent in nar-ratives of the returning soldier by institutionalizing his sexuality as formed and set *before* his departure and *after* his return. If Bayard is an apocryphal ver-sion of Faulkner, then Faulkner does not want to cast him into his hometown with too much queer energy. This impulse does not mean that there is no queer energy surrounding Bayard, but only that it is cordoned off—quarantined from the rest of the town—or at least is meant to be. Perhaps this addition of a before and after heterosexual story by Faulkner represented his own move toward adopting a similar story for himself: before his queer digression in the 1920s, he had a heterosexual life, too, and would have one after. No worries about that queer interlude that he had so long pursued. Faulkner could quarantine the queer elements of his own life and, finally, properly marry Estelle, a fate that needed the revisions of his apocryphal life story to seem more fated than, per-haps, it really was.

That quarantine is not entirely successful. The details of Bayard's heterosex-ual life always carry some hint of other desires. When he returns home, on his first night back, readers encounter Bayard "lying naked between the sheets" and "wak[ing] himself with his own groaning" (45–46). His nightmare begins with him thinking about his wife and their last night together before the war and her death; but that thought can last only so long until his dead twin brother John overshadows her, haunting him and causing his groaning. Later, when Bayard finally courts Narcissa, he does so only after she watches "the long shape of him [lying] stiffly in its cast beneath the sheets," and he wakes up from his nightmares and "beg[ins] talking of his dead brother, without preamble, bru-tally" (257). The dead brother's presence is necessary to mediate the heterosex-ual courtship Bayard finally pursues with Narcissa. Aunt Jenny has worked to arrange Bayard and Narcissa's eventual marriage, but Narcissa can only sit by Bayard's bed and wait for him to accept her as the object of his desires by transferring the nightmares of his former life onto her and the promise of new life she represents (she will, in fact, bear his child). Narcissa must understand John's death for her courtship with Bayard to begin. Only after he has spoken to her plainly and "brutally" about John will he court and marry her.

That Faulkner chose to make Bayard's twin brother the object of his repressed homosexual desire also mitigates the articulation of that desire by binding it up with familial love and "the young masculine violence of their twinship" (45) that connects them as brothers, not lovers, except that the underlying "twinship" also mirrors a tradition of homosexual representation in the figure of Narcissus.[7] Faulkner's naming the female suitor meant to replace John Narcissa draws in stark relief the underlying homoeroticism of John and Bayard's relationship. John functions as a ghost-like figure whose image, and particularly whose "death," haunts Bayard much as the leg-less soldier in "The Leg" is haunted by his lost companion while he pursues his own courtship. Bayard, however, bears no outward wounds. Unlike Donald Mahon's and Elmer Hodge's, Bayard's trauma is entirely psychological, though he does succeed in seriously harming himself by attempting to ride a wild horse out of town only to be knocked off it by a tree. He is literally in a cast when he wakes up to tell Narcissa about his brother. Bayard has his own outward wounds when he begins to court Narcissa, and he must explain why they are so emblematic and significant.

Aunt Jenny is not unaware of the undercurrent of Bayard's devotion. She explains to Narcissa that Bayard "never cared a snap of his fingers about anybody in his life except Johnny" (52). This explanation necessitates her later realization that "[h]e needs a wife" to help him relieve the energies coursing through him and prompting what for all practical purposes seems to be his death wish (212). Notably, Aunt Jenny chooses a woman named Narcissa to fill in for the absence of John. As Bayard sees himself reflected in John, perhaps he will see something of himself reflected in her as well, only this obsession with his reflection will hopefully be free of the homoeroticism that brought the original Narcissus to his doom, but Aunt Jenny unwittingly misinterprets the story of Narcissus. Narcissus has a female enamored of him, the nymph Echo, herself a kind of reflection of her beloved but of a different type from the one that Narcissus fixates on. She is a voice, he an image; she is a woman, he a man. Narcissus does not return Echo's attentions. Her voice echoes futilely through the cave as she mourns her unrequited love. Furthermore, she only echoes other voices, much as Narcissus only loves his own image reflected back to him. Conversely, Narcissa does make progress with Bayard, even marrying him and having a son by him whom she wisely names Benbow Sartoris rather than naming him after Bayard or John, both old family names in the Sartoris family, both associated with violence and war. Narcissa's success effectively allows for a reflection after the war of the image of Bayard from before it, with a wife and son. The reflection is inferior to the original, though, and only a fetish object for the town, and specifically for Aunt Jenny, to allow them to believe that proper order has been maintained even after Bayard abandons his wife to pursue his violent self-destruction. Bayard is not cured by Narcissa's attentions or by reproducing his previous heterosexual life on the other side of the looking glass of the war, that prism that distorts reflections and alienates the image from the person desperate to see themselves there. His memories of John overwhelm him. He never sees his son but instead lights out for new territory before his birth. Narcissa is a reflection, but the wrong reflection, though unlike Echo, she saves herself if not Bayard.

Bayard can never find peace in Jefferson, but does find peace, at least briefly, in the surrounding Yocona County right before he leaves it, with the MacCallums, poor white hill country people living near what Faulkner will soon transform into Frenchman's Bend. The father there shares his name with Aunt Jenny, or Virginia Du Pre. He is Virginius MacCallum. If Miss Jenny is the shrewd matchmaker of Jefferson, Virginius is the detached patriarch of Yocona County, reflections of each other as well, though inverted reflections and each with his/her own distinctly inverted sense of the proper social order. Virginius works to comfort Bayard in a rural pastoral setting, a space Faulkner eulogizes as lost in the mad modernization of the world throughout his fiction. Virginius allows Bayard to stay at his home and room with his youngest son, Buddy, also a returned veteran from the war and younger than Bayard. Buddy and Bayard share a room where, as they prepare for bed, Bayard watches "Buddy undress in the lamplit chill" (340). The two soldiers talk easily and openly, even about John. Less troubled than Bayard by his war experiences, Buddy eventually "ceased talking and presently he sighed again, emptying his body for sleep" (342). He will not be the only returning soldier in Faulkner's canon who prepares for sleep this way; a neighbor in nearby Frenchman's Bend will also perform the same empty-ing in As I Lay Dying. Bayard stays with Buddy and the MacCallums as long as he possibly can. Though this interlude in the novel proves brief, especially in relation to the focus on Bayard and Narcissa, what it lacks in development it makes up for in silence, peace, and understanding. At least for the few weeks he is there, Bayard ceases to pursue his dangerous exploits and calmly partici-pates in the life of the MacCallum family, even though he has no blood ties to them and never marries into it. His primary relationship there is with Buddy. His fellow soldier provides Bayard with his much sought-after peace. Virginius provides Bayard what Virginia cannot. Her machinations to get Bayard a wife fail to comfort him. Virginius allowing Bayard to stay with his son offers Bayard the last peace he will ever know.

Bayard cannot maintain the peace that he finds with the MacCallums, however. The MacCallums pretend that they have not heard the news from town about old Bayard's death. They do not partake of town affairs, and so long as their home remains free of word from town, Bayard feels safe there. Unfortunately, at all moments the threat of this infiltrating knowledge shadows Bayard's stay. He knows that eventually the MacCallums will go to town and return informed about his transgression. His incessant need to speed around county roads in his car brought about his grandfather's death from a heart attack when Bayard momentarily lost control of the car and it spun off into the unregulated freedom of unbridled momentum and briefly left the road. The symbolism of the accident that cost old Bayard his life is rife for a metaphoric reading in relation to Faulkner's young life. Faulkner was a young man given, metaphorically, to cutting across back alleys and yards and not respecting the well-laid plan his forefathers had laid for him and all future generations in Oxford. Bayard kills his grandfather when his reckless pursuit of speed causes him to lose control and leave the defined path of the road. Old Bayard's death usurps all the well-laid marriage arrangements and future life young Bayard has tacitly made with Narcissa, under Aunt Jenny's direction. Bayard flees to the MacCallums. He eventually leaves Yocona County. Narcissa may bear his son, but this life is not his life, this world his world. He runs away.

Bayard never sees his son. Simon, the Sartorises' black retainer, best sums up Bayard's problem: "wid all dese foreign wars en sich de young folks is growed away fum de correck behavior; dey dont know how ter conduck deyselfs in de gent'mun way" (112). Though Simon's diction is an example of the incoherent *non-sense* of minstrelsy, a product of the banal racism that plagues the novel, his commentary at this moment proves an astute diagnosis.[8] Something has happened to Bayard abroad. When he returns home, he at best only suffers through the town, primarily driving his new car around its compact streets, the "[t] own among its trees, its shady streets like green tunnels along which tight lives accomplished their peaceful tragedies" (117). Bayard can barely make the city limit before he wants to slam down the gas pedal and high-tail the backroads of the county, desperate to escape the conformity and expectation of the tunnels and peaceful tragedies of the well-laid grid pattern of the town. He can barely suppress his contempt at having to stay in the defined patterns of the streets. The novel is something of a captivity narrative with Bayard the captive of the town in which he finds himself a prisoner of expectations which his war experience can no longer allow him to maintain. In the end, Bayard does not escape the tragedy, but he certainly escapes a peaceful one.

After Bayard flees Jefferson and Yocona County, Faulkner includes a telling scene in a bar in Chicago just before Bayard agrees to test pilot the experimental aircraft in which he will die. In the scene, Bayard

was sitting among saxophones and painted ladies and middle aged husbands at a table littered with soiled glasses and stained with cigarette ash and spilt liquor,

accompanied by a girl and two men. One of the men wore whipcord, with an army
pilot's wings on his breast. (384)

This "aviator," as he is described throughout the rest of the scene, is Monaghan, the
same man who in "Ad Astra" wanted to bring a German soldier home with him.
The other man is an older, "shabby" man who is explaining to Bayard the test aircraft that he wants Bayard to fly. The girl is Bayard's companion. She confesses to
Monaghan on the dance floor that she is scared of Bayard and has witnessed him
assault a police officer. She worries that he has no limitations and could harm her
while he is trying to harm himself. She begs Monaghan to help her escape.

The scene in the Chicago bar mirrors much of the scene from the French cafe
in "Ad Astra," though with several significant revisions. The cafe has become a
bar, for starters. The roaring twenties appear in full swing in Chicago, whereas in
France the cafe is a ruin surrounded by the destruction of the war. Monaghan's
male German has become Bayard's girl. The German's seeming willingness
to follow Monaghan to America has transformed into the girl's fear of staying with Bayard. She prefers Monaghan instead. Bayard's relationship with the
girl emulates the trip at the end of "Ad Astra" to the whorehouse. Bayard has a
wife, but this girl allows him to act out a form of violent hypermasculinity that
he could not pursue in the confines of marriage. The girl knows something is
amiss in Bayard's hypermasculine heterosexual courtship of her. In fact, he is
not courting *her*. He is courting death and taking her with him. She recognizes
that his desires are far beyond the pale of mere heterosexuality. Significantly, she
chooses Monaghan, wearing his aviator's wings, to save her. Monaghan teases
her about her fears at first, but only until he can confide in her that Bayard is
dangerous and her desire to leave him could set him off. Monaghan is scared of
Bayard, too. The girl does not court Monaghan as an alternative lover to Bayard.
She only wants his help.

In "Ad Astra," Monaghan needed lessons in how to perform his heterosexual
masculinity properly. He seems not to have learned his lesson, but he does seem to
have developed a healthy fear of overtly challenging the hypermasculine displays
of his fellow pilots. Just as Monaghan was willing to bring his German soldier into
the French cafe in the first place, he is far more well adjusted to his American scene
once he returns home than Bayard. The homophobic reaction that Monaghan's fellow pilots in "Ad Astra," including Bayard, display toward his open homosexuality
reappears in *Flags in the Dust* as Bayard's violent death drive, as if he is trying to
kill part of himself and is completely incapable of re-assimilating into the expectations of home. The girl finally breaks away from Bayard by staying seated when
Bayard gets up to leave the bar. Monaghan never actually agrees to help her, but
instead, when Bayard realizes that the girl is staying behind, Monaghan makes a
point of being "discreetly interested in the bottom of his glass" (388) rather than
making eye contact with Bayard. No words are exchanged.

Of course, Bayard knows that Monaghan has no intention of stealing the girl from him. Monaghan's sexual preference is not for women. The girl is staying to get away from Bayard. Monaghan and Bayard do not need to make eye contact to understand the transaction occurring between them. The girl is abandoning Bayard's violent heterosexuality for Monaghan's calm homosexuality. Bayard was one of several pilots who denied Monaghan his companion in the French cafe by employing a forceful camaraderie to remind Monaghan of his endangered masculinity and the expectations of heterosexuality. Monaghan in turn complies with the girl to deny Bayard the continued erroneous pursuit of his violent exploits under the guise of a heterosexual relationship, though Monaghan prefers a nonconfrontational resolution to an enactment of hypermasculine violence. For Monaghan, the war has ended, but Bayard cannot rest until he is dead. Unlike Monaghan, he cannot accept that the war has damaged his proper heterosexuality by exposing him to its queer disease of homosexuality. As John Duvall explains of Bayard, he panics in the face of this homosexuality. Thankfully, Bayard avoids the "gay panic" defense that might allow him to attack Monaghan as an outlet for his rage. Instead, he leaves the bar with the shabby man who wants him to test pilot his new airplane. He will no longer fight his impulses. He will simply and finally "die." The metaphor of "death" from *Soldiers' Pay* holds in this final scene of *Flags*. "Death" and "dying" are synonymous with the loss of proper heterosexuality that a soldier suffers in the war. He has gone to war and has "died." Bayard's death drive is merely his performance of what he assumes is already accomplished. He is dead already, only he certainly knows it. When he finally leaves Monaghan in the bar in Chicago without challenging him, he is accepting that his masculinity has been "lost." He is effectively accepting that heterosexuality is no longer for him. He certainly does not embrace homosexuality, but he accepts it. Immediately thereafter, he dies.

In "Ad Astra," Faulkner articulated the trauma of the queer soldier by placing Monaghan and Bayard into a dichotomy of homosexual identity: the one who has accepted his desires versus the one who will not. However, the story keeps Monaghan's explicit homosexuality safely in Europe. Bayard returns home after the war and attempts to suppress his latent homosexual desires by performing a proper heterosexual role. That performance proves too difficult to continue, and Bayard finds himself frustrated and driven to acts of extreme violence in a death drive for peace and an end to his increasingly uncontrollable impulses. The heterosexual at home and the *queer* abroad can only maintain at best a tacit separation. When Bayard leaves Yocona County, he even encounters the very person who most embodies his fraught sexuality from abroad: Monaghan, the pilot who wanted to bring his German lover home with him. The queer disease of war cannot be cured by continuing a hollow performance of heterosexuality that attempts to suppress the new knowledge and experiences gained away from home—in the war in Europe for Faulkner's fictional soldiers, in New York and New Orleans for Faulkner himself. As Faulkner began writing *Flags in the Dust*, a novel in which he turned his attention to a county that closely resembled his own hometown, he also returned to that town and began his courtship of Estelle that would culminate in their marriage in 1929. In *Flags*, Faulkner places the conflict of home/away and hetero/homosexual into an apocryphal geographic space but one with clear and significant autobiographical elements. Bayard will have his final encounter with homosexuality in Chicago, however, not in Jefferson. In Jefferson, Narcissa will raise Benbow Sartoris. Bayard's body will find a final resting place in the family plot in the cemetery, his life abroad forgotten, his legacy entombed beside his first wife and child, but also not too far from the remains of his brother.

Location was not the only variable in Faulkner's experiments. His sense of narrative perspective evolved as well through his World War I stories and novels. From his failed *Bildungsroman* about Elmer Hodge, Faulkner crafted narratives of the returning soldier that moved away from the static presentation of Donald Mahon to more complex psychological portraits of soldiers still participating in society, though often that participation reads like a version of shell shock not caused by actual shelling but by attempting to re-submerge oneself in one's home after having experienced the world outside of small-town Georgia, or Yocona County, or Oxford. In *The Sound and the Fury*, the novel he wrote immediately after *Flags*, Faulkner would experiment with internal monologues, with three first-person narrators each with approximately ninety pages of narration followed by an omniscient third-person narrator for the fourth part of the novel. Though not a war narrative, *The Sound and the Fury* does shed light on the evolution of Faulkner's experimental style and would prefigure his next war novel, *As I Lay Dying*, and its formal arrangement. Using fifteen narrators and their shorter monologues, Faulkner would find a way both to explore the complex psychology of the returned soldier from his point of view and to present the deeply woven complexity of the reactions of others to him.

So now we arrive at the last great act of Faulkner's queer drama that began in 1918. In 1927, he returned to Oxford. In 1929, he married Estelle and began to pursue a life much more closely related to the one he diverged from in 1918 to go fight his war. He simultaneously turned his creative attention to Yocona County, though he renamed it for the first time as Yoknapatawpha in the wake of his marriage. In the first novel that he wrote after his marriage, he would bring his soldier home and wind the clock forward. Darl has not just returned home in *As I Lay Dying*; he has been home nearly eleven years. Faulkner would also employ a narrative technique that takes us to the heart of Darl's character. The detail that matters most, however, is the one word that Faulkner relegated to Darl and to Darl alone: *queer*.

Chapter 6

Gay Darl

Darl Bundren is called "queer" five times in *As I Lay Dying*: twice by Cora, twice by Tull, and once by Cash. Darl uses the word himself once to describe Cash in a kind of projection when he remembers Cash giving Jewel a "queer look" as Jewel was sneaking out one night to earn money to buy a horse. This exception to the rule that Darl, and only Darl, is "queer" is the exception that proves it. Otherwise, the word charts in miniature the movement in the novel. As the family moves away from their farm, Darl becomes increasingly "queer." The first appearances of the word come from the Bundrens' neighbors as they report on the general perception of Darl in the community and eventually concede their own feelings toward him as he leaves their isolated, if communal, space. Cash uses the word only in the final pages of the novel, in town, when he, too, sees how his brother, part of the family on the farm, is queer in the city. Thus, Cash determines, "This world is not his world, this life his life," a conclusion he reaches in the final sentence of the penultimate paragraph of the last section of the novel, just before Cash introduces the new Mrs. Bundren (261). The word appears only these six times.

At the end of the novel, Darl seems to have gone insane and is last heard from while he is riding a train south to Jackson to the asylum. Only at this late stage of the novel does Darl allude to "the little spy-glass he got in France at the war" (254). This minor detail does much to explain what might be ailing Darl. He is a "wounded" veteran of World War I, his wound a mental rather than a physical scar. He is a shell-shocked soldier who has returned from the trenches in France. In a larger Faulknerian context, his queerness is not a generic peculiarity. Darl continues a tradition of wounded soldiers beginning with Donald Mahon and continuing in Faulkner's World War I narratives prior to his marriage. These queer soldiers also belong to a specific cultural moment in the history of *queer*. In its late 1920s cultural context, *queer* also meant *homosexual*, a definition it maintains to this day.

On the one hand, Darl is "queer," an adjective which the *Oxford English Dictionary* defines as "[s]trange, odd, peculiar, eccentric. Also: of questionable character; suspicious, dubious." The *OED* even supplies as an example for this definition of the word:

> 1930   W. Faulkner *As I Lay Dying* xxxi. 81   He don't say nothing; just looks at
> me with them queer eyes of hisn that makes folks talk.

Certainly, this definition of *queer* applies to Darl and creates meaning in the novel. No doubt he is peculiar, and people find him strange. The *OED* is incomplete, however, in consideration of the definition of *queer* in the context of *As I Lay Dying*. The *OED* dates *queer* as a noun to identify a homosexual to as early as 1914 and cites adjectival uses of the word ("Of a person: homosexual") also as early as 1914 in relation to "'queer' people [. . .] who sometimes spent hundreds of dollars on silk gowns, hosiery, etc. At these 'drags' the 'queer' people have a good time." A 1915 example of the word as an adjective refers to "[a]n immense reunion of art students, painters, and queer people," also in reference to "homosexual" people. These citations of *queer* are apropos of the Conrad Aiken poetry Faulkner read aloud to Ben Wasson in 1919. Furthermore, as Dan Pigg has noted in his explication of Wilfred Owen's poem "Disabled," as early as 1922 the term was being used in "government-authored documents" to refer to a specific childhood pathology recognizable in young boys who, untreated, might grow up as homosexuals. These examples establish a history of the word as signifying homosexuality well in advance of Faulkner's writing *As I Lay Dying* in 1930, the first novel he wrote after his marriage to Estelle.

The action in *As I Lay Dying* takes place contemporary to Faulkner's composing it. Darl has been home from the war for nearly eleven years when his mother dies. Her death forces him into a confrontation with his "wounds" that his isolated life on the family farm has precluded in the intervening years. Addie's death prompts the family to "get up and move then," as Addie herself puts it (35), and casts each member of the family, with his and her "secret and selfish life," out into the open world (170). Once the family begins moving, each member transforms their secret, selfish desires into the one unified goal of getting her buried, which in turn leads Anse to obtaining a new wife whose presence functions as the "shape to fill [the] lack" caused by Addie's death (172). On the surface, and in traditional readings of the novel, Darl appears to be the exception to this transformation, and he stands out for trying to stop the journey and force the family back to the farm without seeing Addie to her grave nor enabling Anse to find a new wife to replace her. In short, Addie's death is the catalyst; Darl's queerness—that he is antithetical to the goal of his family—provides the tension; the family journeys to Jefferson; and the novel follows this journey to its conclusion with the burial of Addie, the remarriage of Anse, and the removal of Darl, whose presence represents the *queer* tension trying to stop the journey from progressing forward, most dramatically by setting Gillespie's barn on fire.

So, eleven years after the war, a marriage forces out the queer tension to allow the journey to end. One might be forgiven for feeling that the novel bears relevance to Faulkner's actual life, especially in relation to the apocryphal gay identity he fashioned throughout the 1920s. In the structure of the novel is evidence of Faulkner's working out a part of his identity that has always been there in the margins, apocryphal but palpable, only not openly said. I will argue in this chapter for a simple but profound revision of our understanding of Faulkner's shortest novel. Darl is neither "peculiar" nor "suspicious" when we consider what makes him "queer." Because the word is used so specifically and so intentionally to refer to Darl, who proves to be the most significant narrator of the novel with by far the greatest number of narrative sections and often the most important information about events, a revision of our understanding of his queerness greatly shifts the traditional notion of how the novel is structured and what we should find significant in its conclusion. In short, Darl is gay, and reading his queerness as homosexuality moves from the margins a significant aspect of Faulkner's apocryphal world built from realities of actual life in all its complex dimensions.

Meaning, Form, and Misconstruing Darl

Undergirding basically every reading of *As I Lay Dying* are two often unstated assumptions about its structure. First, the form of the novel is intricately bound to the journey at the core of its action. Second, the plot of the novel is fundamentally a marriage plot. As to the former, the novel is composed of fifty-nine interior monologues, told by fifteen different narrators, which span nine days. Told through the private thoughts of private minds, these distinct and discreet monologues create the unified whole of the journey to Jefferson to bury Addie Bundren. Darl narrates nineteen of these narrative sections, including the first. Darl is the second oldest of the five Bundren children, roughly thirty years old, and for much of the novel his is the central voice ordering the chaos of the other narrators by anchoring them to a steady, consistent depiction of the action as it unfolds, including his narration of Addie's death, though he is not present to witness it. The last narrator is Cash, the oldest, who has five narrative sections, including one of the most impressionistic, and who is responsible for explaining what happens to Darl and introducing the new Mrs. Bundren. Vardaman, the youngest, narrates ten sections, second only to Darl, though he is only between six and eight years old and can barely make sense of his feelings or articulate his grief. He famously declares, "My mother is a fish" (84), but he also quite cogently remarks that "*Jackson is further away than crazy*" when Darl is taken away to the asylum (252). To understand Darl and to understand the novel, we must also venture "further away than crazy" in our assumptions about the underlying cause of his surprisingly erratic behavior as the family reaches Jefferson. Other narrators include Dewey Dell, Jewel, and Anse, the surviving Bundrens, and Addie, who narrates her one section some one hundred pages after she dies. An assorted cast of neighbors, including Cora, Tull, and Dr. Peabody, interject their voices to flesh out other details of the rest of the journey. These tangential characters generally narrate sections that coincide with their encountering the Bundrens as the Bundrens move from their farm across the countryside and into town.

Over the course of the actual journey, each of the Bundrens, with the supposed exception of Darl, undergoes a trial by fire and flood that purges them of their individual motives for making the journey and supplants them with the collective goal of burying their mother and reestablishing the lost structure of the family caused by her death. Cash breaks his leg and loses his precious tools; Dewey Dell sacrifices her abortion money; Jewel gives up his horse and suffers severe burns in Gillespie's barn; Vardaman does not get his train set. The whole family does get a gramophone and a bushel of bananas (when we are presented the scene of the Bundrens eating their bananas at the end of their violent journey, we are wise to remember that a marriage plot is fundamentally comic, and in this case, certainly provides a good laugh). Anse gets his new teeth and a new wife. Darl gets sent away to an asylum in Jackson after he tries to stop the journey by burning down Gillespie's barn with Addie's coffin in it. For this destructive (and expensive) act, his family turns him over as crazy to the authorities. His final narrative section seems to prove his insanity, but Cash admits that the family only turned him over to avoid paying for Gillespie's barn, whether he is crazy or not. If they label Darl as crazy, they assume that they will not be considered culpable for the fire and, thus, cannot be made to pay for the lost barn. The Bundrens cannot sacrifice their precious resources to restore Gillespie's barn. All their resources must come together in the pursuit of burying Addie, even to the extent of using Dewey Dell's abortion money and trading Jewel's horse as the only commodities with which they can barter. Darl hinders their progress and might even prevent their returning home if Gillespie were to file charges or sue them. Therefore, Darl must be cast off by the family to bring their journey to fruition. Once the old Mrs. Bundren is buried, Cash introduces a new one. Darl is gone. The family can return home. All is well, despite the extreme suffering to arrive at this restoration of order.

Structurally speaking, Darl represents the tension that must be resolved for the conclusion of the novel to take place—or, more formally, for the disparate voices of the novel to coalesce into a unified plot. While the rest of the family make sacrifices, Darl fails to sacrifice his desire, which seems to be to end the journey that is desecrating his mother's remains. This desire is at such odds with the desire of his family that it cannot be reconciled to it. Since his desire cannot be sublimated into the family's greater good, he must be removed. I will argue later that there is more to his desire than simple opposition and that he does try to contribute to the family's goals. His contributions go unnoticed, however, because, *a priori* to his efforts, he has already been labeled queer. That label precludes any recognition of his efforts because it precludes any discursive space in which to articulate his desire as anything other than "queer," as if he is trapped in a tautology that has doomed him before the journey even begins. In a way, he is the price the family will pay to complete their journey. They need him to be against them to justify that price. They queer him to justify their payment of his physical presence for the attainment of their goal, but they can queer him so easily because he is already queer and has been since he returned from France and the war.

If Darl is insane, then, surely, we cannot trust any of his motives nor any of his information. That we do not discover his "insanity" until his nineteenth narrative section should trouble any reader, but our understanding of the plot is so dependent upon so much of his earlier information that rarely do we discount everything he has said. Despite his unreliability, we still think that we know how Addie died. We still think that we understand the basic family structure. We still trust that the other Bundrens, in their self-serving, insular ruminations, reveal something about how family, love, or sacrifice works, though without the third of the novel Darl narrates, we would have very little framework on which to place Anse's complaining, Jewel's rage, Cash's nearly autistic precision (though his final narrative sections prove to be as surprisingly straightforward as Darl's final section proves to be surprisingly inchoate), Dewey Dell's desperation, or Vardaman's grief. That Darl is the family's ultimate sacrifice never registers as significantly as Jewel's giving up his horse, Dewey Dell's her money, Cash's his tools, or Vardaman's his train set. Readers find themselves willing to sacrifice Darl and his contributions to the journey to make the novel unified and restore familial order, though without Darl the novel would be effectively incoherent. As with "A Rose for Emily," we find ourselves unwittingly participating in the communal opinion that something is not right about Darl. With the journey complete, he must go, though we could not have gotten rid of him any sooner (he even helps dig Addie's grave before the agents take him away). As with Faulkner's prior World War I fiction, we find a community unable to place Darl's queerness into its order. His queerness proves too destructive to the unified ending to which the novel has progressed. The novel resolves itself by ending in a marriage and the promise of a birth in the family—by Dewey Dell if not by the new Mrs. Bundren—thus repudiating any queer elements that might taint it and threaten its internal coherence.

If Darl is not insane, however, then maybe we can trust his lengthy narratives at least as far as we can trust any internal monologue in the novel, but to consider him sane means that his fate reads as deeply tragic, which would be counterintuitive to the nature of a marriage plot. We should be celebrating, or at least laughing at, Anse, with his new teeth, introducing his new wife who lived in the house from which he borrowed the shovels to bury his old wife. We should not be crying our eyes out over the lamentable fate of Darl. We cannot mourn his removal too much, but when we rely on him for much of what we know in the novel, the disintegration of his voice that follows his family's betrayal of him risks being more than we can allow humor to distract us from. Darl is a strange creature in the Faulknerian universe, but if he is not insane, what makes him so strange?

The problem of Darl troubles the heart of the long history of critical responses to *As I Lay Dying*, a problem that surfaces in the foundational work that established its critical significance. Michael Millgate buries his understanding of the novel as a journey below the surface of his criticism, but his default use of this structure emerges in two key places. First, while trying to debunk the idea that Faulkner wrote the novel based on anecdotal material that he collected from the real Lafayette County, Millgate states in an appositive phrase that "the actual plot of the book" is "the story of the slow journeying with the decaying corpse" (111). Second, this understanding of plot-as-journey accounts for Millgate's deductions about Darl's devolution into madness, starting with his opening monologue, the first in the book, that creates the "initial impression of absolute rationality and clarity of vision which is progressively dissolved as the book proceeds" (105). The progress and procession to which Millgate alludes are delineated by the journey of Addie's corpse, and the family's rejection of Darl follows along its trajectory. Olga Vickery also makes the journey subcutaneous to her stated focus. She explores the implications of Addie's separation of word and deed, a separation that Vickery claims "is dramatized in the journey to Jefferson" (55). Darl's knowledge of events that have not been put into words, such as Jewel's parentage and Dewey Dell's pregnancy, makes him a threat to any reconciliation of word and deed the journey can accomplish for the Bundrens. She argues, therefore, that two conditions are necessary for the journey/novel to progress to its nicely unified conclusion: "with [Darl's] departure and the burial of Addie's corpse, the period of tension ends" (63).

Irving Howe focuses more explicitly on the journey as central to meaning, but the implications of the journey challenge his efforts to find formal unity. He calls the novel "[a] story of a journey, an account of adventures on the road," but he adds that "the journey proves exceedingly curious and the adventures disconcert" (127). Key to this disconcerting feeling is Darl's fate, which Howe admits is "excessive," but which he claims stems from how Darl "raises problems" because his madness "does not follow 'inevitably' from what has preceded it" (137–38), which implies that his fate only seems excessive because of the excess of Darl's sudden personal disintegration when we last encounter him. Howe's solution is to invert the terms on which formal unity emerges. He declares that "the book is a triumph of fraternal feeling, and because it is that, a triumph, as well, in the use of idiom" (141), which is to say that a kind of familial bond (fraternity) is

achieved at the end of the novel and justifies Faulkner's use of idiom throughout the novel prior to that end. For this critical move, Howe places the fraternal
bond as primary, as the end justifying the means. He does not declare that the
use of idiom creates fraternity but that the fraternal feeling triumphs over any
disunity implicit in the completing voices, which therefore makes those competing voices triumphant as well, regardless of their implicit inconsistencies.
That the removal of Darl, a brother, could lead to any kind of *fraternal* feeling
is, indeed, disconcerting, but Darl's prolific talking at least allows him to participate in the "triumph in the use of idiom," even if his removal at the end of the
novel is anything but fraternal, unless by fraternal Howe means for everyone
except Darl.

In his landmark study *The Yoknapatawpha Country*, in a chapter titled "The
Odyssey of the Bundrens," Cleanth Brooks identifies a familial bond beyond
the fraternal as fundamental to the narrative and the journey at its heart.
Though Brooks never directly states that the narrative is a journey, his chapter
title alludes to Faulkner's assertion that the title of *As I Lay Dying* derives from
Agamemnon speaking in Hades in Homer's epic poem about journeys, the passage of time, and wives who wait, or do not wait, for their proper husbands
(*AILD* 266, n1.1). Brooks connects the heroic tradition embodied by Odysseus
to the journey of the Bundrens. Notably, Odysseus's twenty-year "odyssey" is
fundamentally a marriage plot in which suitors come to claim Penelope, who
puts them off for twenty years until Odysseus returns and removes the tension of their presence by killing them. Odysseus then reclaims his marriage
bed after a prolonged absence when he was off fighting in a war. The stakes
implicit in this connection are no longer just idiomatic nor brotherly. The world
of Odysseus is one of brutality and violence in the name of maintaining a (hetero)sexual paradigm despite any digressions that might keep the hero from his
one true destination: in bed with his promised and faithful wife.

Brooks attempts to create a rhetorical space for Darl that does not undermine
his significance in the narrative. He is skeptical of Darl's insanity and even goes
so far as stating, "With regards to the burial journey, Darl, the lunatic, is indeed
the only one of the three brothers who is thoroughly 'sane'" (145). Unfortunately,
by the end of the journey "Darl's truth," as Brooks calls it, has become "corrosive
and antiheroic, and in its logic perhaps finally inhuman" (145). According to
Brooks, Darl goes crazy and the other brothers, despite appearing crazy at first,
prove saner for their sacrifices, however absurd or avoidable. Darl corrodes his
claims to "sanity" because he opposes the progression of the heroic journey that
will lead to a new marriage and a reformation of the basic unit of the family.
For the marriage to take place, and the tension in the novel to end, Darl must be
removed, at which point the odyssey of the Bundrens can be complete. Brooks's
connecting the novel to *The Odyssey* suggests that the heterosexual expectations
of the institution of marriage may be "insane," objectively speaking, but Darl's

"sanity" that allows him to see the flaws in the institution and its expectations are not virtues. To expose the "insanity" of a heterosexual order is "corrosive and antiheroic, and in its logic perhaps finally inhuman." Darl is insane for thinking that he can usurp the proper social order, even if that social order is illogical. He undermines his very humanity for opposing its supposedly proper conclusion.

These early giants of Faulkner studies were each critical to establishing his place in the canon of American literature. I do not mean to imply their work is wrong. Rather, in their efforts to mold consistent, coherent meaning from the competing voices of the text, they make decisions about how those voices coalesce into unity. That their efforts are predicated on cultural values is entirely unsurprising. What else would criticism be based on? That a character deemed "queer" would be the prime candidate for exclusion to forge unity is equally unsurprising, at least to people who have been so labeled in their actual lives and, through a long twentieth century of Lavender Scares and Moral Majorities, have centered their lives on the margins and sought new unities, less clearly defined than the compulsory trajectories for gender and sexuality in main-stream American life. Yet, as with the anxiety model of Faulkner and sexuality, these early readings, as the basis for subsequent readings and the interventions of later critical work, transform into grotesqueries when they become so inher-ent in how we read the novel that we can focus on nothing else besides a pre-conceived unity of family as heteronormative, procreative, and worth making certain sacrifices, not other sacrifices, for. Much like Wing Biddlebaum and his queer hands in Sherwood Anderson's first story in *Winesburg, Ohio*, he who touches others in a queer way must go.

The long effects of this distortion remain with Faulkner studies to this day. In fact, Donald Kartiganer not only borrows from the same critical tradition but also makes explicit, if only accidentally, the nature of the cultural values under-lying these earlier works. Kartiganer connects the pressures Faulkner faced in his first few months of marriage with the structure and content of the novel that he wrote in its wake. After marrying Estelle, Faulkner found himself needing a steady income and a real job to support his new family, so he took a job at the coal plant on the campus of the university. He walked there every evening to oversee the boilers, and by his own testimony from his later introduction to *Sanctuary*, he wrote *As I Lay Dying* in the early morning hours—when the boilers needed less attention—over the course of six weeks as one effort, start to finish, with very little revision. Though the job in the coal plant did not last long, it does represent one of the few moments in Faulkner's life when he held regular employment. Especially in the shadow of his bohemian years in New Orleans and throughout the 1920s, such regimented work was in stark contrast to his (queer) pre-marriage life. One assumes he made his evening walk to work on the sidewalks, not by cutting across yards.

Connecting the circumstance of its writing to what Faulkner wrote, Kartiganer identifies the primary impulse in the novel as *Eros*, and the drive that drove Faulkner to write it as his erotic drive. This understanding of erotics comes from Freud's *Beyond the Pleasure Principle* and refers to Faulkner's suppression of his other desires and his pursuit of other pleasures into one central, heterosexual drive for union and familial life, even if that meant working hard in a coal plant rather than devoting unstructured time to writing and extensive revision. Kartiganer finds echoes of Freud's theory in Addie's cryptic statement from her father that "the reason for living was to get ready to stay dead a long time" (*AILD* 169), which does sound strikingly similar to Freud's aphorism, "*the aim of all life is death*" (32). For Kartiganer, the Bundrens undergo the same fundamental process as Faulkner did after his marriage of transforming their multiple individual desires into the singular desire to bury Addie so that Anse can marry his new wife and (re)create the normative family structure in which *Eros* can find its highest fulfillment in licensed, procreative (hetero)sexuality ("By It" 439). Kartiganer even identifies Anse as "'pure' *Eros*" and directly links his pursuits to Faulkner's marriage to Estelle, but this formulation leads Kartiganer to account for Darl as *Thanatos*, the opposite of *Eros*, or the embodiment of the competing death drive:

> Having nothing of *Eros*, Darl has no neurotic need to exploit his inherent masochism in aggressive pursuits. He functions out of a perfect detachment that is the source of his exactingly objective vision that registers the world as it is, divested of desire. (439)

Kartiganer is not complimenting Darl's objectivity. Rather, he removes Darl from any action in the plot because he lacks all desire, a lack that makes him "the supreme agent of violation in the novel. He invades the people around him, not for sex but for secrets, the private interior world, the residue of inanimacy that survives in life not as an intimation of immortality but of the death we all harbor, seek to protect and to delay" (439). Darl is the death to the Bundrens' life, the *Thanatos* to their *Eros*, and so,

> He is expelled in the name of erotic quests: the Bundrens' to complete their mission, however compromised by ulterior motives, to get to Jefferson, to get the body into the ground, no matter its condition or scandalous treatment; Faulkner's to complete the novel, to build what Cash praises as a "tight chicken coop" rather than a court house, "shoddy" or "built well" [*AILD* 234], methodically pushing it out on swing-shift power-plant breaks, the novel of compromise itself compromised by the contract he and Estelle had entered into June 20, 1929. (442)

In short, Darl's expulsion emulates Faulkner's erotic impulses after his eleven years of journeying to the destination of his marriage to Estelle and the establishment of a respectable family. The death drive (Darl) is in opposition to the life drive (Anse), which is also the sexual drive because sex reproduces life for a community if not for the individual. Faulkner's marriage represents his own sexual drive, also a life drive, to raise Estelle's children but also to have his own children in a sanctioned union. The unity of the novel grows out of these deep, subconscious impulses—Faulkner chose life and pushed away bachelorhood, a metaphoric death. The novel comes to reflect these inner dimensions of his psyche. Of course, what Kartiganer does not say is what is just below the surface of Freud's postulations, that the sex drive, in this construction of it, is a model of heterosexual desire (for procreation) as fundamental and natural. Its opposite is death itself, or, in a word, *queer*.

Homosexuality is implicit in Kartiganer's argument, and, by extension, implicit in structuralist reading strategies that view the novel as a journey and Darl as the tension that must be removed at journey's end. Kartiganer's terminology comes directly from *Beyond the Pleasure Principle*. In that book, Freud argues for an erotic drive, which he also calls the life drive and the sex drive, as a condition that has emerged as the natural outcome of bi-cellular reproduction and the instinct for self-preservation. Although no single cell can live forever, Freud deduces, all life nonetheless wants to continue itself, which leads to cellular reproduction. Asexual reproduction among single-celled organisms allows for that "cell" to live forever by duplicating itself—same genetic material, new body. For organisms that do not reproduce asexually, sexual reproduction is necessary and is the central drive that motivates life beyond the simpler drives to attain "pleasure" and avoid "pain." Without a sex drive, an organism would desire to stay completely inert to avoid stimulation, sexual or otherwise. Freud considers this inertia as a metaphoric death, or at least an imitation of death that an organism that opts out of sexual reproduction will pursue until it actually does die. This death drive is a desire to shut down and stop and is figured as directly in opposition to *Eros*, which seeks stimulation. These drives compete for supremacy and, in a properly developed individual, lead to the pursuit of sex as a means of reproduction (heterosexuality) rather than as a means of physical gratification without procreative import (queer sexual acts).

Freud's construction obviously biases heterosexual reproduction as the erotic drive because of its assumption that anything opposed to sexual reproduction must be a manifestation of the death drive. Because it precludes the prospects of sexual reproduction, homosexuality must not have the "intimations of immortality" that motivate properly heterosexual people; rather, homosexuality must be a manifestation of some deep urge for individual, and by extension social, death. According to Kartiganer, the other Bundrens suppress their ulterior desires into the one unified desire to bury Addie, which allows Anse, pure *Eros*, to remarry. This version of marriage is one in which heterosexual reproduction is the goal: man, wife, and kids. The idea that this social and sexual order is necessary for our society has long, deep roots and holds powerful sway over Western ideology. Freud did not invent it; rather, his supposedly objective and scientific ruminations are merely an attempt to justify it. Unfortunately, when literary scholars apply these Freudian terms to their criticism, they tend to carry with them their heterosexist legacies.[1] The New Critics I cited above probably did not mean to invoke this tradition. They did, however, invoke it when they dehumanized Darl to make room not for any conclusion but specifically for the unified conclusion of the novel in the resolution of its marriage plot, with Dewey Dell's pregnancy still viable and intact as no minor detail of that resolution. Unlike Darl, Dewey Dell begrudgingly accepts that she will not have an abortion. When Anse asks for the money that Rafe gave her, she donates it to the family cause. Her pregnancy promises the new birth that will perpetuate the Bundren family. The marriage plot quite unsurprisingly ends with the promise of actual new life. That the new Mrs. Bundren is not yet pregnant is not particularly significant except that the family will make room for Dewey Dell despite her transgression of sex before marriage (her sense of her own precarious relationship to ideal heterosexuality in marriage might account for her extreme violence when the family seizes Darl to turn him over to the asylum agents). The organism that is the Bundrens will reproduce. Meanwhile, the queer element supposedly opposed to that new life and reproduction has been removed.

By the time Faulkner wrote *As I Lay Dying*, *queer* had acquired a clear and known connotation to mean *homosexual*. Walking night after night to his job to turn over a wheelbarrow and punch out a novel to support his new family, why would the Faulkner emerging from his life in the 1920s not have understood the implications of his precise use of so powerful a word? What the Bundren family has removed is homosexuality embodied in their queer brother, Darl, but merely to say that Darl is gay does not resolve the conflict in the novel. This recognition reveals the conflict, but as Darl looks through his spy-glass from the war, we also can now look through a new prism to reread the narrative and account for the effects of this revelation. The problem of Darl is not that he lacks an erotic drive. The problem with Freud's construction and with critical responses that rely on it is that they assume that unity and futurity are heterosexual. This is, alas, a deeply held cultural value that often goes unexamined even by the best of critics. These cultural values seem to be shared by the Bundrens, but we need not participate unwittingly in their reproduction. Evidence exists in the text for a counter-reading that indicts the family's actions and exposes the homophobia of communities near the farm and in the town at the center of Yoknapatawpha. This evidence also points to a simple truth, though one long overlooked by Faulkner scholars. Even in the heart of Faulkner's cosmos, clinging to existence, there are people who are homosexual. When we expand how we understand *Eros*—which is no minor aspect of the human psyche but is also not only what Freud made of it—we can see in Darl a character who is, in fact, motivated powerfully by an erotic drive for union, only his is a *gay* erotics. He was exposed to homosexuality in the war and returned to his home on his isolated farm far removed from interactions with other men who might share his desires. When his mother dies, he faces competing impulses either to enter the broader world again knowing that he desires a sexual union that he does not believe he will find in Yoknapatawpha or to force his family to stay isolated out on the farm where he need not confront his desires at all, as he has done since his return. Admittedly, the tension drives him crazy. Being gay in so rigidly defined a community is more than he can bear.

The Use of the Erotic

To understand Darl's gay erotics requires looking beyond not only Freud but also beyond theories of male homosexuality, in this case by considering an understanding of queer desire articulated by second-wave lesbian feminists in the latter twentieth century. Of course, even Faulkner differentiated between male homosexuality, which did not trouble him, and lesbianism, which did, so looking for concepts in the works of lesbian feminists to articulate Faulkner's vision of male homosexuality is not without its challenges. Generally, it can be problematic to apply concepts across the LGBTQ+ spectrum without pausing to consider if nuance for certain identities carries into application for others. Still, the shape, and possible scope, of gay erotics has already been explored, and it is not difficult to take the premise constructed by these theorists and see in it a broader applicability. Second-wave lesbian feminists saw in *Eros* more than just a heterosexual drive for procreation, and they instead used a new understanding of erotics to claim a kind of power in response to the devaluation of women throughout history, a devaluation that actively sought to sow discord and division among women to keep them from challenging the patriarchal status quo of male-centric heteronormativity. The driving force of life in this model can manifest as sexual desire, but it is not explicitly and entirely bound to a procreative sex act (vaginal penetration as maximal stimulation to produce new life). Rather, the driving force of life is the desire for collective bonds and togetherness represented by acts of devotion, giving, and sharing among a community committed to mutual survival against an order that denies subjectivity to those whom it needs to control.

Audre Lorde and Adrienne Rich have argued for an understanding of erotics that transcends procreative sexual contact and extends to the communities of women that emerge in response to oppressive regimes. In their view, heterosexist erotics are part of the compulsory heterosexuality that limits the full articulation of non-procreative desire and in which women lose many of their basic rights as property passed among men for the propagation of a phallagocentric order. Sometimes, the relationships forged between women in response to oppressive regimes become physically sexual; sometimes they do not. From this perspective, sexual desire is not just a physical act but the root of all desire for action and unity and can exist in familial bonds (mother/daughter, sister/sister), among friends, and among all women. This desire should be viewed as a continuum that erases sexual stigma to allow for a larger sense of union and community forged through bonds between members of the same sex, which can always move toward sexual union and often are originally rooted in sexual desires suppressed by the regimes of compulsory heterosexuality. Lesbianism, thus, ceases to be a pejorative to define a union of two women, usually presented in a butch-femme dichotomy, as something perverse or unnatural. In these formulations, lesbianism is a form of protest in which women find erotic fulfillment in each other and outside of the confines of an erotics that must be focused on reproduction with a member of the opposite sex and is codified in heterosexual institutions such as marriage.

Moving this understanding of *Eros* into a male homosexual context gets ostensibly complicated by how these theorists first explored the erotic through a feminist lens. As an example, Rich's formulations prove difficult to transfer to a gay male context because she purposely ironizes the Freudian assertion that homosexuality in men emerges from too close a relationship between a boy and his mother. Rather than argue that this assertion is false, she argues that if it is true, then the root of lesbianism must also be a girl's close relationship with her mother as well. According to Freud, heterosexual desire is a desire to return to the mother's body, but since incest is taboo and the father prevents the son from competing to take his wife—a tension that Freud famously labeled the Oedipus Complex—then the son directs his sexual desires to other women to replace the mother to whom he cannot return. Rich proceeds from this basic premise to assert that lesbianism is rooted in the mother/daughter relationship and is the origin of all subsequent female sexual expression, if Freud's theories are followed to their logical conclusions. In Freud's theories, it is entirely natural to assume that, since a girl is also forced away from her mother's body, then her natural sexual development will also be a desire for a return to that female body. Therefore, if men are inherently heterosexual, then women must be inherently lesbian.

The obvious problem with transferring this premise to male homosexuality is that Rich's use of Freud is too gendered to allow for that transference. It seems unlikely, however, that Rich intended to uphold Freudian sexual theories, which are generally deeply problematic for all queer and even non-queer identities. More likely, she was attempting to deconstruct the premise that Freud's theories apply across gender lines, and in so doing she implicates the degree to which those theories fail to have universal applicability and, therefore, any applicability at all. If those theories lack universal applicability, then they must only have contingent and exceptionally specific application, which is to say that they really have no applicability except for strictly within a limited Freudian perspective that does very little to explain the complexities of desire that circulate among members of lesbian and gay communities in the contextual ways that those communities conceive of themselves. Basically, she uses Freud to dismiss him, but she nonetheless proceeds to explain a version of *Eros* applicable to lesbian desire. She offers a theoretical framework to justify Lorde's earlier theorizing about the multiple bonds that form between women, which Lorde places under the umbrella term *erotic* and in which she finds a source of power for women to define and shape their lives beyond being bound to men. Lorde and Rich claim *Eros* as a term for lesbian-identified women, and in so doing, they free it from its negative associations with Freud's heterosexist rhetoric and make it a term with applicability to a broad range of desires beyond strictly heterosexual confines.

Though he never calls it *Eros* or *erotic*, John Howard, in *Men Like That*, effectively delineates the same concept for rural gay men when he attempts to explain the dynamism and movement that give "shape and scope" to the "queer life" of mid-century Mississippians (15). Though Mississippians had easy access to the nearby gay community in New Orleans, Howard pauses to explain that for gay men in rural Mississippi,

> a more sporadic, on-the-ground, locally mediated queer experience prevailed. Tracking this experience and integrating the concept of networks with desire and pleasure finally allow a consideration of the human desire for friendship, companionship, love, and intimacy, as well as often unrelated, overtly sexual contact— homo*social* as well as homo*sexual* realms. (15)

This articulation of "human desire" reads as a version of a gay erotics applied to male same-sex identity. This version of gay erotics uses sexual identity and desire to imagine and create new, nonheterosexist communities in a specific place and time. Howard explores how men in rural Mississippi fashioned means of interaction with each other in their seemingly isolated environment. Their erotic desires for unity created a distinct sense of identity. They found each other. They created connections. They did not simply waste away unto death.

Gay erotics are a response for all queer-identified people to the oppressive regimes of compulsory heterosexuality that compel individuals into preset gender expectations and sexual roles. In the case of women (and men) who define themselves as, or find themselves defined as, queer/lesbian/homosexual, these erotics powerfully shape the way that we define ourselves in relationship to our surroundings and articulate our senses of self in relation to our own understanding of community and connection. *Eros* is at the heart of homosexual identity, only this *Eros* is not one of compulsory reproductive utility but of seeking likeness in an environment that defines one's erotic drive as *different*. It is an oppositional drive, but one no less committed, and in fact driven, to unity than the heterosexual erotics articulated by Freud. In that formulation, gay desire is death. In this, it is life. And the outcome of gay desire is neither corrosive nor inhuman; it is, rather, a powerful drive simply to exist.

Darl is a soldier who has returned to rural Mississippi, a site that John Howard identifies as "gay America's closet" (63). "In Mississippi," Howard explains, "spatial configurations—the unique characteristics of a rural landscape—forged distinct human interactions, movements, and sites" that define the "shape and scope" of gay life as a *concept* that differed from the idea of gay culture rooted in a *community* such as the Vieux Carre in New Orleans (15). The other Bundrens seek admittance into Jefferson as members of its heterosexual community bound by its rigid family structure and narrow definition of proper desire. Darl is queer, and his desires do not conform to the communal expectations of the town, which does not mean that he does not seek union with other men like himself. Rather, his journey to erotic unity passes through a different understanding of the landscape connected to the specific rural geography of his home.

In writing *As I Lay Dying*, Faulkner placed Darl into a rural landscape and allowed Darl to shape it through his copious narration. Andre Bleikasten has written on the atmospheric effect of that landscape on the narrative, where he asserts, "The setting of the book is invented in [Darl's] look, created through his words," and continues, "That Darl should see images of uprooting everywhere need not surprise us: they reflect his own rootlessness" (285). Bleikasten prefers to link this rootlessness to Darl's "nonidentity," but as with so many other critics, this claim does not account for the prospect that Darl's "rootlessness" may, in fact, be a mark of a specific identity defined by movement and mobility through the landscape and conceptualized through a specific historical articulation of gay life. That his identity is not the same as the core heterosexual identity to which his family ascribes does not mean that Darl has no identity, only that he has a different one. He desires to find "roots" of his own throughout the novel, though different roots from those his family seeks. His erotics are different from theirs, but he does not lack *Eros*.

Furthermore, Faulkner did not need an advanced theoretical understanding of gay erotics to have experienced it and to have included a version of it in his fiction. From the gravity that drew him to Ben Wasson and drew them to sequestered spaces in their rural environments, to the different lives of Stark Young and William Alexander Percy at home and away from home, to the gay communities in New York and New Orleans, Faulkner had seen and participated in the ersatz configurations that emerged from the shared sense of difference among *queer* men of his time. He would have understood the different performances required by different environments, from the closeted oppositionality of spending time with Wasson at the Stones' home to the reverie of enclaved but communal oppositionality in the Vieux Carre. He would have also understood the tensions caused by moving between these different environments. His actual experiences gave him much on which to base a character such as Darl.

We can begin to access how Darl sees himself in relationship to his surroundings in his famous ruminations about emptying himself for sleep. In his soliloquy, he questions his identity: "I dont know what I am" (*AILD* 80). This statement is not the lament of a man who has no identity; it is the cry of a man who has *lost* his identity and is now seeking to find it. The subtle difference in this perspective pertains to how he ends his ruminations. At the end of the section, Darl offers this deeply moving if enigmatic line: "How often have I lain beneath rain on a strange roof, thinking of home" (81). What roof is he talking about? Just a strange roof, a *queer* roof? That is not the question that needs to be asked, though. Not *what* roof, but *whose*? Whose roof has Darl lain under, thinking of home? Why does this memory make him feel as if, at home, he does not know what he is? Why does home alienate him from what he is? And why would he have longed so much for that home nonetheless, in fact seem still to long for it since it is, ultimately, what he cannot attain except if he can empty himself to dream about it? Darl has memories of a self that he has lost. Deep in the heart of his ruminations lies a desire to find that self again.

We might also ask *where* that roof was in relation to home. Down the road? Just across the county? Or an ocean beyond his limited life on the family farm? We know that Darl has been to war because of his reference to his "little spy-glass he got in France at the war" (*AILD* 254). His exposure to cultures beyond Yoknapatawpha County contributes to his difference from his hill-country family. He returns from France with expressions such as "cubistic bug" (219), which, according to Watson Branch, demonstrate how the war "has so marked [Darl's] view of life and his mode of vision that Faulkner reveals it through his identity: dislocation and disorientation are the reflection of maddening chaos" (Branch 111). Branch also notes that Darl's postwar knowledge "seem[s] highly inappropriate for a country boy" (113). The war played a tremendous role in shaping Darl's separation from the other members of his community. Darl's sense of dislocation and disorientation, however, have resulted less from the world Darl witnessed in France than from the world he returns to in Frenchman's Bend, where he cannot know himself anymore except by his abstractions into memories of a time now eleven years past. His memories have given him access to a "highly inappropriate" knowledge, at least at home where he struggles to find a space for its articulation. His sense of self is suffering from dislocation; the effects of that dislocation are thoroughly disorienting. As Bleikasten asserts, this dislocation may cause Darl's vision to appear "rootless," but such an assertion misses a key element of Darl's character: he is rooted to his home. Darl's problem is that he cannot fathom how both to be home and to be queer. The social order of his home has caused this problem, and he must find a way to bear it. One of his solutions is to empty himself and dream of rain on a distant roof, but now he is home and that distant roof is "strange."

The profound split that his life abroad and his life at home has caused him is fundamentally an articulation of his desire to reconcile an understanding of what he is. Had Darl never left for the war, who knows how his desires and his sense of place in the world would have unfolded. He should be just a backwater country boy on a backwater farm, but the war pulled him out of his isolated life and thrust him into a new world among new men and exposed him to new possibilities for who he could be. As with Claude Wheeler, Darl encountered a way to access and express his homosexual desire in that new world. Indeed, if Darl never names whose roof he lay under while listening to the rain, we know Claude's lover and can even point to the Jouberts' roof. Claude dies, though, and never has to return to the marriage he left or the family farm he was meant to inherit. Darl does return, not to a wife or even to his own farm, but just to the small world of his immediate family. Except for trips to sell goods, such as his and Jewel's when Addie dies, he leaves the farm only on rare occasions, though he is the one who insisted on making that trip away from Addie's deathbed. He meant to avoid the reality of his mother's death by insisting on that trip, but her death is inescapable. He narrates her death as if he is there to witness it. Addie's death forces Darl to confront the secrets that his isolated life on the farm have buried deep in his memories to become the stuff of his dreams. He knows what he is as much as he knows whose roof he slept under in France, but until Addie's death, he can treat this knowledge as abstraction and empty himself for long nights of vague dreams about rain on foreign rooftops. His mother's death forces him to face the reality of his present world. On the journey to bury her, he confronts what it means to be *queer*. The plot of the novel charts the progress of his confrontation.

Darl's Gay Erotics

Darl's journey maps a coming-out story, for himself and in how others perceive him. He moves from farm to city, from life among his immediate family to life in a wider world. On this journey, he encounters people who have long since determined that he is "queer," but who have differing notions about what his queerness entails. By the end of the journey, the competing definitions of *queer* solidify into one meaning: he is a homosexual whose queer desires motivate him to work against the goals of his family. Simultaneously, Darl experiences his identity anew—he has experienced it before, but he has also isolated himself on his family's farm for many years and buried his identity after his previous experiences abroad. When he leaves the farm for Addie's funeral journey, he begins to articulate his homosexual identity again, through memory and through attempts at communion with others. His efforts are thwarted, but he nonetheless attempts to define himself in his immediate geographic and cultural space, not simply be defined by others.

We can trace Darl's journey by mapping the six occurrences of the word *queer* in the novel. The five times the word is used to describe Darl chart his increasing distance from the safe confines of home. They also chart how other people in his community define his queerness. They appear as follows:

1.) Cora: It was the sweetest thing I ever saw. Sometimes I lose faith in human nature for a time; I am assailed by doubt. But always the Lord restores my faith and reveals to me His bounteous love for His creatures. Not Jewel, the one she always cherished, not him. He was after that three extra dollars. It was Darl, the one that folks say is *queer*, lazy, pottering around the place no better than Anse, with Cash a good carpenter and always more building than he can get around to, and Jewel always doing something that made him some money or got him talked about, and that near-naked girl always standing over Addie with a fan so that every time a body tried to talk to her and cheer her up, would answer for her right quick, like she was trying to keep anybody from coming near her at all. (24)

2.) Tull: He [Darl] is looking at me. He dont say nothing; just looks at me with them *queer* eyes of hisn that makes folks talk. I always say it aint never been what he done so much or said or anything so much as how he looks at you. It's like he had got inside you, someway. Like somehow you was looking at yourself and your doings outen his eyes. (125)

3.) Tull: When I told Cora how Darl jumped out of the wagon and left Cash sitting there trying to save it and the wagon turning over, and Jewel that was almost to the bank fighting that horse back where it had more sense than to go, she says "And you're one of the folks that says Darl is the *queer* one, the one that aint bright, and him the only one of them that had sense enough to get off that wagon. I notice Anse was too smart to been on it a-tall." (152)

4.) Cora: Because it is not us that can judge our sins or know what is sin in the Lord's eyes. She has had a hard life, but so does every woman. But you'd think from the way she talked that she knew more about sin and salvation than the Lord God Himself, than them who have strove and labored with the sin in this human world. When the only sin she ever committed was being partial to Jewel that never loved her and was its own punishment, in preference to Darl that was touched by God Himself and considered *queer* by us mortals and that did love her. (168)

5.) Cash: But the curiousest thing was Dewey Dell. It surprised me. I see all the while how folks could say he [Darl] was *queer*, but that was the very reason couldn't nobody hold it personal. It was like he was outside it too, same as you, and getting mad at it would be kind of like getting mad at a mud-puddle that splashed you when you stepped in it. And then I always kind of had a idea that him and Dewey Dell kind of knowed things betwixt them. If I'd a said it was ere a one of us she liked better than ere a other, I'd a said it was Darl. But when we got it filled

and covered and drove out the gate and turned into the lane where them fellows
was waiting, when they come out and come on him and he jerked back, it was
Dewey Dell that was on him before even Jewel could get at him. And then I believe
I knowed how Gillespie knowed about how his barn taken fire. (237)

As Darl moves out from the farm and toward Jefferson, these are the moments
in the novel when his queerness is externally recognized. These five appearances of the word track the shift through which competing notions of his queer
identity condense to a single vision of his queer desire: his lack of proper work
for his family and grief for his mother to his disinterest in being part of the
heterosexual family.

When Cora first uses the word, Addie is still alive and the Bundrens are still
on their farm. This inert state serves as the exposition to the changes wrought
by Addie's death and the subsequent journey. For all practical purposes, this
view of the Bundrens, and specifically of Darl, represents the *a priori* condition.
This general "queerness" is the cloud that has hung over Darl since he returned
from the war. For Cora, she means *queer* as simply a measure of one's work
ethic. The ever-righteous Cora considers that Darl loves Addie most because
he "just looked at her" on her deathbed while Cash and Jewel seem distracted
by their work. Cora's first characterization of Darl's queerness juxtaposes *queer*
with the adjective *lazy*, separating the words by only a comma and following
both adjectives with the participial phrase "pottering about the place no better
than Anse." Meanwhile, Jewel and Cash work too hard, so Cora believes that
they are not properly grieving for their mother. Darl is the queer brother in
this configuration because he stands in opposition to Jewel and Cash, whose
similarities make their response the normative against which Darl's difference
is measured. Cora's moral vision falters, however, in determining which brother
is acting properly. Jewel and Cash are not grieving properly but at least they are
(properly) hard working; Darl is lazy but properly grieves. If queer Darl's grief is
proper, then there is reason to believe that he could function as the moral center of the novel. He could possibly win over either Cash or Jewel or both to his
proper sensibilities in response to death. If the scales do not shift in his favor,
then it will be the (un)grief of his two brothers that stands in opposition to his
grief. The balance of normativity will weigh by consensus. Darl begins the novel
as the queer one. He will end it queer as well.

Tull uses the word next, disconcertingly and in significant contrast to
Cora's moral judgment. For Tull, Darl's "queer eyes [. . .] got inside you,
someway." Tull figures queerness as an ability to penetrate. Equating queerness and penetration sends him into fits of homophobic discomfort similar
to the anxieties Faulkner depicted in "Jealousy" and "Ad Astra." Though Tull
never directly says that this penetration is a sexual violation, he has previously established that Darl's problem is that "he just thinks by himself too

much" (71). Naturally, he agrees with his wife that the solution to Darl's problem is a simple introduction to proper heterosexuality:

> Cora's right when she says all he needs is a wife to straighten him out. And when
> I think about that, I think that if nothing but being married will help a man, he's
> durn nigh hopeless. But I reckon Cora's right when she says the reason the Lord
> had to create women is because man dont know his own good when he sees it. (71)

Tull thinks that marriage would provide Darl with a (female) companion to
keep him from "thinking" by himself so much. Therefore, Tull solves Darl's
problem by proposing that Darl direct his erotic drives into the appropriate
avenue of marriage, rather than getting inside other people, namely Tull. Tull
hardly seems enamored of the idea that a man's only chance of "knowing his
own good when he sees it" is with the help of a woman, but he accepts this status quo as the Lord's judgment, or at least as Cora's wisdom, which he confesses
is probably better than his own simple opinions of what is best for a happy
life. Tull's true opinion is more direct: he would prefer that Darl "sees it" with a
woman, rather than stare him down with queer eyes. If a woman will preoccupy
Darl, Tull is quite pleased to see him marry. Really, Tull just wants Darl to stop
staring at him because Tull thinks that Darl's staring is queer.

Though the third appearance of the word comes from Tull's monologue, he
can only have secondhand credit for it. He is actually quoting his wife, Cora,
who, of course, attributes the word to Tull. Cora still regards the word primarily
as a measure of work (in this case, the effort to get Addie's body across the river)
and equates Darl with Anse in that Darl jumped clear of the wagon, whereas
"Anse was too smart to been on it a-tall." Cash and Jewel, she determines, are still
not acting properly. When Cash and Jewel exert so much effort to save Addie's
coffin, Cora sees their actions as wasted energy, as *cash* spent that should have
been saved or as work done on a system, measured in *joules*, that does not return
the energy invested in it. Her assessment speaks to the fact that Darl, at this
point halfway through the novel, has failed to convince anyone that his actions
are the proper response to Addie's death. He leaps clear of the wagon, which is
effectively a leap away from his brothers. They do not share a desire for similar
ends, and, notably, the crisis of the river crossing fails to sway either Jewel or
Cash, even as it causes the broken leg that becomes the measure of Cash's love
for his mother and willingness to sacrifice for the family. Such a vicious measure
of love would be queer indeed except that it serves to mark Cash's willingness to
sacrifice for the family, misguided journey and all, even to the point of his own
suffering. Thus, his love is not queer. His love is for the betterment of his family,
even in its suffering. Also, since the mules drown in the crossing, and Anse has to
replace them by bargaining away Jewel's horse, this crisis forces Jewel to his first
significant sacrifice as well. Later, he will suffer severe burns while saving Addie's

coffin from the fire. Jewel and Cash suffer together because of the river crossing. Darl jumps clear, essentially denying himself solidarity with his brothers and, by extension, the rest of his family. That his actions are the most practical and logical does not matter. They are the queer actions of a queer man in relation to his surroundings and those surrounding him.

These two appearances of the word come five monologues and roughly twenty-five pages apart, at the beginning and the end of the river crossing scene. In between them, at the point in the narrative when the family should be crossing the river, Darl uses the word himself, as I will explicate below. The river is a boundary between the isolated world of the Bundrens out on their farm and in the open countryside around Frenchman's Bend and the rigidly defined world of Jefferson. Though the family does not physically cross the river, they do cross a threshold represented by the failed crossing in that Jewel and Cash fully commit to the journey, but Darl leaps clear of it. From this moment forward, his queerness begins to transform into something more concrete and troubling.

Cora's and Tull's uses of the word in its first two appearances in the novel allude to how "folks say [Darl] is queer" and his queerness "makes folks talk." Clearly, Darl's queerness has circulated through the community, but not until after the failed crossing do we actually witness the way two people—Cora and Tull—quote each other and bring their different understandings of Darl into a singular meaning. Tull is citing Cora, who measures Darl's queerness in direct relation to his brothers. Cora is attributing the word in this instance to Tull, who measures Darl's queerness as a kind of disconcerting sexual penetration. When Tull quotes Cora, he consolidates the two measurements. Darl's sexual queerness puts him at odds with his brothers, and though he may act properly in terms of logic and reason, his decision to leap clear of the wagon separates him from the aims of the family. He is not willing to work to bring about the proper unity of the family (and its eventual marriage rite) that his brothers are willing to support, even through their own physical pain. *Eros* is, of course, beyond the pleasure principle—the desire for unity exceeds the desire for pleasure, forcing the suppression of that desire if it is counter to the aim of continuing life. At this moment in the narrative, Darl appears to fail to suppress his desires. His brothers properly accept pain for the sake of the quest. As the family passes into the regimented sphere of Jefferson (metaphorically here, though they will cross an actual bridge near Mottstown and pass its gatekeepers in a scene I explicate below), Darl is separating himself from the erotic drive of his family by his sexual otherness.

The fourth appearance of the word technically comes out of time, but it still occupies a central place in the forward progression of the novel. Kartiganer explains, "Each monologue, with the significant exception of Addie's (expressed at no identifiable time) and the two monologues surrounding hers by Cora Tull and Whitfield, follows the previous one in terms of the temporal progress of the action" (433). In the fourth appearance, we have Cora using the word as she might have used it during the exposition of the novel, before Addie's death. We, however, are encountering the word anew, well after that death and after the river crossing. We must, then, reevaluate our original perception of what the word means, even prior to the journey. Cora uses the word again to signify that Darl loves Addie most, but that does not matter. Cora concedes that Darl will not save Addie from her "sin" of preferring Jewel over him. Addie's actions have brought about the necessity of the "punishment" of this journey. Darl cannot save her from it. His lack of working to continue the journey becomes, thanks to Cora, a measure of his opposition to the moral order of the universe: Addie must suffer this punishment and Darl must not save her. If his lack of working is unnatural to the flow of universal causality, that in the aftermath of Cora's timeless words he actively attempts to oppose the journey by setting the barn on fire means that he *does* work in opposition to that natural order. His own sin against the natural order becomes a sin of commission, not a sin of omission. As he works against the supposed natural order—Cora's version of it, anyway— his queerness becomes a direct, acting threat to the unfolding "natural" plot of the novel and any chance for its proper conclusion in Anse's remarriage.

It should come as no surprise that Cash finally concedes that his brother is queer, though only indirectly as if he is just another member of the community who is repeating what everyone knows: "I could see all the while how folks could say he was queer." When Cash states that he "believed he knowed how Gillespie knowed how his barn taken fire," he is acknowledging just how queer Darl appears to other people and how unlikely they will be to forgive his transgressions. Cash and the other Bundrens have no choice but to reject Darl because they can no longer explain away his actions as "the very reason couldn't nobody hold it personal." Now, even Cash understands why people react so personally to Darl's queerness. Cash narrates Darl's violent seizure almost indifferently and effectively replaces Darl as the clairvoyant, rational narrator of the novel at the moment of Darl's rejection. Darl has failed to convince the family that his grief is proper, his failure of which effectively signifying that his love is improper as well. Cash signals the final repudiation of Darl's grief and love by deciding that they are queer. Darl is denied participation in the erotics of the Bundrens, and he never meets the new Mrs. Bundren, whom Cash introduces as a way of accepting her into the family, or at least the family as it stands after Addie's death and Darl's removal.

Though Cash offers the final verdict that Darl's actions are improper and he denies Darl a right to participate in the heterosexual erotics of the family, this verdict does not mean that Darl lacks an erotic drive, only that he lacks the proper heterosexual one. Also, that five of the appearances of the word occur in the monologues of other characters who are effectively queering Darl does not mean that Darl does not also define himself as queer through his own actions and his own perspective, of which we have ample record in his copious narration. If Cash's final use of *queer* marks the moment of Darl's ultimate rejection, Darl's use of *queer* marks the opposite, a primary attempt to bond with his brothers Jewel and Cash and name for himself what he is by finding others who can share in his sense of identity as someone other than the lone *queer*:

> **6.) Darl** (32/11): And so a few nights later I heard Jewel get up and climb out the window, and then I heard Cash get up and follow him. The next morning when I went to the barn, Cash was already there, the mules fed, and he was helping Dewey Dell milk. And when I saw him I knew that he knew what it was. Now and then I would catch him watching Jewel with a **queer** look, like having found out where Jewel went and what he was doing had given him something to really think about at last. But it was not a worried look; it was the kind of look I would see on him when I would find him doing some of Jewel's work around the house, work that pa still thought Jewel was doing and that ma thought Dewey Dell was doing. So I said nothing to him, believing that when he got done digesting it in his mind, he would tell me. But he never did. (133–34)

Darl's monologue would, technically, be the third use of *queer* in the novel, but his use is fundamentally different from the other five. Darl is recounting Jewel's acquisition of his horse, a pivotal episode that prompts Darl's later question, "Your mother was a horse, but who was your father, Jewel?" (212). Darl realizes that Jewel is the queer one, at least as far as queer is strictly a measure of difference, because Jewel is not Anse's son and was conceived outside of the sanctioned nuclear family of the Bundrens' marriage. Certainly, exposing Jewel's paternity could endanger the familial unity of all the *Bundrens* (the father's last name) working together, but only insofar as Jewel is a Bundren instead of a Whitfield, his actual father's name. Darl never outs Jewel. He asks dangerous questions, but he never exposes this knowledge nor participates in the communal transfer of allegations that eventually work to convince people that he, not Jewel, is queer, like folks are always saying.

Though it occurs in a flashback, Darl's use of *queer* appears in a monologue at the height of the river crossing that so profoundly separates him from the rest of the family. This scene includes the moment when Darl jumps clear of the wagon and of the family itself. He is the brother who does not participate in rescuing Addie's coffin. He has made his first active break from the family, but at this moment he recalls a moment of similar disconnection when he had attempted familial unity and failed. Darl claims, "I dont know what I am," but the community calls him queer (80). In this memory, he calls Cash queer. His usage marks the one moment when he tries to take control of the label applied to him and apply it to others—a critical moment of reaching out to find others in his immediate surroundings who are like him in his difference, his fellow "queers." At this moment, Darl is watching the interactions of two other people, his brothers no less, and hoping that he might be included, or that they might be like him. He never is, and they are not.

Cash and Darl originally think Jewel is sneaking out to meet a woman. When Cash finds out otherwise, he violates the work order of the farm. He begins to take over Jewel's chores since Cash knows that Jewel is working in another man's field to make money. Darl does not know what is really happening until later. What he believes is that Cash is taking up Jewel's slack to allow Jewel to pursue sexual experimentations. Darl envies his brothers' transgressions, and he wants to know what Cash knows (and what Jewel is discovering). Darl does not know what Cash knows; he only "knew that [Cash] knew what it was." This scene is not the first in which Darl has felt removed from Cash's sexual knowledge nor the first time he has tried to imagine that Cash and he might *know* the same thing. In one of his earliest monologues, Darl recalls nights in his childhood when he should have been asleep, but stayed awake instead so that he could experience his own nascent sexuality:

> Then I would wait until they all went to sleep so I could lie with my shirt tale up, hearing them asleep, feeling myself without touching myself, feeling the cool silence blowing my parts and wondering if Cash was yonder in the darkness doing it too, had been doing it for the last two years before I could have wanted to or could have. (11)

Darl sees Cash as a repository of sexual experiences since, as far as Darl knows, surely Cash experienced the same sexual awakenings that Darl has experienced, only two years previously since Cash is two years older than Darl. Thus, when Cash follows Jewel, presumably to see whom he is meeting, Darl hopes that Cash is following Jewel for the same reasons that Darl wonders about Cash. Darl calls Cash queer because he wants to see Cash as someone like himself. He waits for Cash to share his knowledge, but Cash never does. Cash and Jewel form a silent, fraternal bond, even as Darl knows the real secret, that Jewel is not actually anyone's brother. Darl remains outside of this bond, too queer for admission into their secret fraternity of work and, as far as Darl ever knows, (hetero)sexual initiation.

Similar attempts to form bonds structure Darl's trip to Jefferson. Leaving the farm, he enters the road, a space outside of the boundaries of the family's isolated home. The family's journey offers Darl the opportunity to meet a larger group of people than he lives among on the farm in Frenchman's Bend. Darl has previously had just such an experience, when he left home to go to war. Now, after Addie's death, he finds himself embarking on what should be a similar journey, but which ultimately proves much more confining. In *Men Like That*, John Howard explains the importance of the road (and the car and the roadside park) as a meeting ground for gay men in the rural South, specifically in Mississippi. Howard explains that "[1]argely homebound, living in familial households, these [gay] Mississippians nonetheless traveled," and that these "queer movements more often consisted of circulation rather than congregation" (xiv). Howard argues that gay men defined their lives by movements and shared interactions, but he does not suggest that merely moving from home guaranteed that one would find gay male companionship. Howard begins his study with an account from rural Jasper County in 1953 when a Methodist preacher picked up a teenager walking alongside the road. After the preacher rebuffed a coded advance from the boy, he let the teenager out and shared the incident with Ted Harrington, a fellow pastor. Obviously, the boy's advances failed, as Darl's do in Faulkner's novel, but Howard suggests that the scenario was not an isolated event. He then explains the desires at work that day in the preacher's car:

> Perhaps through a combination of verbal and body language, utterances and silences—utterances and silences that would be perpetuated and complicated by subsequent retellings, including this one—the young man communicated his desire. But like so many taboo expressions of sexuality at that historical moment, that desire was frustrated. (4)

Though there are many moments when Darl attempts to form communities with his family and with the other people he encounters on the road, I want to highlight two. The first, in particular, parallels Howard's description of the coded gay exchange.

Darl does not set Gillespie's barn on fire to bring about a potential meeting with a sexual partner, but he takes advantage of the opportunity that arises as a result. First, Darl watches Jewel run into the barn to rescue one of the horses. Darl then narrates Jewel's actions with special emphasis on Jewel's body: "Jewel thrusts [the stall door] back with his buttocks and he appears, his back arched, the muscles ridged through his garments as he drags the horse out by its head" (219). By watching rather than helping, Darl alienates Jewel, who "gives [Darl] across his shoulder a single glare furious and brief," a stare to express sever-ance, as opposed to Darl's queer, penetrating gaze. Darl only briefly mentions Jewel's angry look, however, because his attention is distracted by the bodies of Gillespie and Gillespie's son Mack. Gillespie and his son wear "knee-length nightshirts," Gillespie's "rush[ing] ahead of him on the draft, ballooning about his hairy thighs" (219). When Gillespie emerges from the barn, he "passes [Darl], stark-naked, his nightshirt wrapped about the mule's head" (220). If watching male bodies pass into and out of the burning barn has distracted Darl to the point of inaction as he ponders what their nightshirts only suggest, then see-ing Gillespie emerge "stark-naked" pushes Darl beyond the limits of sexual suggestion into the prospect of sexual gratification. Therefore, when Darl sees

Mack struggling with a mule of his own, he "lean[s] to Mack's ear" to tell him, "Nightshirt. Around his head" (220). In response, "Mack stares at [Darl]. Then he rips his nightshirt off and flings it over the mule's head, and it becomes docile at once" (220). Mack's stare is a measure of his uncertainty. He is contemplating what Darl has told him and does not understand Darl's motives at first. Then, as he realizes that Darl might be telling him how to save the mule, he undresses in front of Darl.

Darl breaks more than just a homosexual taboo at this moment. Darl describes Mack with "freckles [that] look like english peas on a plate" (220), suggesting that Mack is still fairly young, possibly in his early teens. Darl is not, however, enacting a simple pedophiliac desire. Such a reading of this scene would not consider the historical context. Darl's sexual arousal exceeds the reductive label of *pedophile* in this instance, and we might remember Howard's account of the teenage boy and the Methodist preacher to contextualize Darl's desires. Age and attraction form a complex matrix in negotiating taboo homosexual desires in the isolated, rural South. Darl actually directs his desires toward Gillespie again after he tells Mack to undress. As Darl watches Gillespie wrestle with Jewel to prevent his returning to the barn to save Addie's coffin, Darl describes, "They are like two figures in a Greek frieze" (221). His reference to art is also a reference to "Greek" love, the two figures engaged in some action, possibly wrestling, and frozen there before him as if before a climactic fall. Faulkner often borrowed imagery from John Keats's poem "Ode on a Grecian Urn." Here he recalls Keats poem bitterly, for though the poem praises the "still unravish'd bride," that this "Bold lover" can never kiss his prize proves tragic, not titillating. Shortly after all the animals and Addie's coffin have been saved, Darl will literally weep for the opportunity that he might have won at this moment with one of the men dancing naked in and out of the flames, but Darl quickly returns to the reality before him with an image of Mack using his nightgown to put out the flames on Addie's coffin as Jewel rescues it. In this scene, Darl's sexual attraction fluctuates between the available men, of any age, but none ever return his attention in their focus on saving the animals (and the coffin) in the barn. Their desires and his do not coincide, but Darl nonetheless cannot take his queer eyes off them. Afterward, Vardaman finds Darl crying. Darl cries most obviously because he has failed to save Addie's body from the desecration of the journey that he wants to end. We are not over-reading, however, to imagine that he is crying because, ever so briefly, he might have forged a connection with Mack, or with any other man in this rural environment. He fails. Darl cries because his desires isolate him. Darl cries because he is alone.

Darl attempts to form one final bond between himself and his brothers, not a sexual bond but an erotic bond nonetheless. As the family enters Jefferson, the only black characters in the novel speak from a porch beside the road to town to exclaim, "Great God [. . .] what they got in that wagon" (229). Darl does not react to this exclamation. After crying over his failure to stop the journey, he seems to have resigned himself to it, despite his supposedly queer desire to stop it. Jewel does react, yelling back, "Sons of bitches" (229). Instead of the poor blacks hearing Jewel's response, a white man passing in the other direction hears it and challenges Jewel. As queer as Darl is and as remote as he is growing from his family, Darl comes to Jewel's defense. Darl steps in to say, "He dont mean anything mister," because the man has a knife and Darl wants to diffuse the situation (230). Meanwhile, Jewel is muttering that the man is "a goddamn town fellow." The family is on the edge of Jefferson. By identifying the man as a "town fellow," Jewel situates him as a gatekeeper who has come out to guard the entrance to the town. Jewel effectively challenges this gatekeeper to a fight. Jewel's reaction to the man could not be more dangerous to the family's immediate goals. Just as they crossed a threshold when they crossed the river, to enter the town the Bundrens must successfully negotiate their way past this gatekeeper to cross the threshold into Jefferson itself. Thus, Jewel's anger will not suffice. A bloody fight could easily bring out the authorities in the town, who would very likely, regardless of whomever they arrest, end the Bundrens' journey and bury the rotting corpse as a danger to public sanitation. Darl proves to be the only Bundren with the guile and skill to disarm and pass the man and so gain access to the town for his family without any problems to the furtherance of the family's goals.

The great reversal that Darl manipulates in this situation is crucial to understanding his attempts for unity and their failures. As soon as Darl convinces the man to pocket his knife, he starts to urge Jewel to apologize, but he stops short. Instead, he turns to the man and asks, "Do you think he's afraid to call you that?" (231). Suddenly finding himself on the defensive, the man can only respond, "I never said that" (231). The disarmed man lets the Bundrens pass. Darl has resolved the situation and gotten past the knife-toting man at the outskirts of the city, but he also defends his brother so that his family will not lose face in front of "a goddamn town fellow." Darl's negotiation of this threshold is brilliant and symbolic. He should at least somewhat regain his family's trust. He has, after all, essentially negotiated their way past a sentinel guarding the border of the town. In doing so, he sacrifices any bond he might form with this new man by putting him on the defensive. Darl's actions should shore up his relationship to the family at this critical moment of their journey, but Darl still fails to form the necessary familial bond that will ultimately include him in the family's reformation with the new Mrs. Bundren. In fact, the very next monologue recounts Darl's seizure by his family. Cash narrates how Jewel and Dewey Dell turn on Darl. Though Darl's handling of the town gatekeeper might not entirely neutralize his burning of Gillespie's barn, Faulkner does not even provide time in the narrative action for us to consider if Darl's presence is as harmful as his barn burning would make it seem. Mere pages before his rejection, Darl works to help the family. So why does no member of his family object to his arrest?

The answer is simple. Darl's fate is the Bundrens' necessary sacrifice, and they must make that sacrifice quickly now, lest queer Darl reintegrate their ranks by these efforts of his to prove that he is not so queer after all. Yes, he still is queer, because even if he wants to be part of the family, his queer desires have no place in that family. He has not merely tried to stop the journey. He has challenged the heterosexual regime that will see its fruition in the proper marriage at the end of that journey. Even if he makes efforts to help to bury Addie—and he does help dig her grave—his queerness is not just a measure of *work for* or *work against*. As Tull has explained, Darl gets inside people and needs to find a wife. He will not take a wife, though. The companion he wants is beyond the realm of possibility in his rural Mississippi, at least from the perspective of his family and other members of the communities in Yoknapatawpha County. He wants it but cannot find it. They want to guarantee that he never will find it and that it will never even have the remotest chance of being found. He is queer. His family queers him. Perhaps in the war he could have had a lover and his masculinity and his place in the community would be safe, but he is home now and has been there eleven years. He is queer, and in this community, there is no place for him. His expulsion allows for a marriage. In a world where two mutually exclusive paths compete for supremacy, there is no middle ground nor room for the rejected path when one chooses the other option. An erotic drive in opposition to what the community deems proper has no place in the community. Darl, and all he represents, must go.

Letters Home through Quarantine

Not surprisingly, when we next encounter Darl in Faulkner's canon, he is simply insane and belongs in an asylum. In "Uncle Willy," written in March 1935, Faulkner recounts the exploits of the town dope fiend, an old bachelor, as told from the point of view of an unnamed fourteen-year-old boy who idolizes Uncle Willy's determination to live for pleasure, even if it might kill him. The young boy from Jefferson who narrates the story never once alludes to Darl's "queerness," but he does know about what happened to Darl Bundren. As that young boy is at a critical age when his own sexual awakening might be on the verge of occurring and as he also finds himself drawn to an older man with a dubious reputation in town, his inability to identify Darl's queer disease speaks to the motive for the expulsion of Darl's homosexuality from the heterosexual expectations of the town.

Generally, the story seems only focused on Uncle Willy, whose main desire is to break free from "the old terrified and timid clinging to dull and rule-ridden breathing which Jefferson was to him" (*CS* 239). Unfortunately for him, Mrs. Merridew and the Reverend Schultz conspire to send him to a sanitarium to clean him up from his bad habits. They succeed in weaning him from drugs, but he returns to Jefferson as an alcoholic, buys a car, has that taken away, then goes to Memphis, and returns married to an obese prostitute, whom the town pays to abandon Willy and return to her job. As if part of a grand card game with the opposing forces countering each other's bets, Uncle Willy ups the ante and manages to buy a plane to replace his lost bride. He wins the game for his freedom when he kills himself in a fiery crash, which the narrator celebrates as emblematic of Uncle Willy's liberation from the confines of Jefferson against which he defined himself.

Uncle Willy marries a woman. His addictions to Dionysian pleasure are manifested in drugs and alcohol. The narrator's idolization of him at times seems motivated by a boyish crush, but the interactions between the boy and Uncle Willy never come to fruition nor are they articulated as sexual. Uncle Willy's appeal to the boy is his free spirit, which does not necessarily mean he is a homosexual, even if his predilection for inebriation makes him stand out in town. The word *queer* never appears in the story. Uncle Willy's inability to fit into the prescribed confines of Jefferson are measured in his addictions, not in his sexual identity, at least until he returns with his overweight "whore" (236) in defiance of Mrs. Merridew and the other "high-nosed bitch[es] in Jefferson" (237) who want to reform him.

In part 2 of the story, however, as he narrates the first intervention by Reverend Schultz and Mrs. Merridew, the narrator makes a curious reference. First, he belittles the patronizing Sunday school lesson of Reverend Schultz as having a tone that "I don't believe even pansy boys like," leaving one to wonder if he is himself a "pansy boy" or if he just cites them as an example (227). When Uncle Willy realizes the lesson is about him and realizes his fellow church members are about to take action to "help" him, he reacts with a resigned terror that makes the narrator "[think] about one day last summer when they took a country man named Bundren to the asylum in Jackson but he wasn't too crazy not to know where he was going, sitting there in the coach window handcuffed to a fat deputy sheriff that was smoking a cigar" (228). As Mrs. Merridew forces Uncle Willy into a car to drive him to his own kind of asylum, the narrator pictures her and Uncle Willy "in the car like Darl Bundren and the deputy on the train" (229). Darl may not have been "too crazy," but the narrator simply assumes that he was crazy, nothing more. His insanity is why he was sent to the asylum, not his "queerness." This knowledge on the boy's part, yet his lack of knowledge about how Darl was queer, rings an ominous note about memory and desire in Jefferson. Darl's particular queerness has been successfully exorcised out of Jefferson, and a young boy on the cusp of puberty has no sense of Darl as sexually other. Darl's queerness has been supplanted by the simpler understanding that he was just insane.

That boy, therefore, can translate Darl into Uncle Willy, Darl's insanity becoming Uncle Willy's addictions and the "pansy boy" narrator becoming an

enabler of Uncle Willy's subsequent attempts at freedom, with no clear reference to gay sexuality and only a defiantly atypical marriage to an obese whore
to challenge the town's heteronormative designs. At the end of the story, the narrator's father explains to his son that "[n]obody blames you" for Uncle Willy's
death, despite the narrator's helping him board the plane that kills him (247).
The narrator closes his story with the frustrated cry, "And now they will never
understand, not even Papa, and there is only me to try to tell them and how can
I ever tell them, and make them understand? How can I?" (247). The problem
the narrator faces is not his lack of effort but his lack of words. He cannot tell us
because he does not even know what he is trying to say. At no point in his story
is he even able to say the word that matters: *queer*. Darl had gained knowledge
in the war that no country boy was supposed to have. With Darl's removal from
Yoknapatawpha, that knowledge has ceased to circulate. The narrator of "Uncle
Willy" cannot even reiterate Darl's conundrum, "I don't know what I am." He
does not even know that he does not know. He cannot make anyone, even himself, understand what has happened or why.

Faulkner seems to have understood even as early as 1918, while he was in
Canada, that there would never be a place for someone deemed *queer* at *home*.
In the letter he wrote home through quarantine in response to the death of
Estelle's sister from Spanish flu, he ruminates on the irony of dying young: "It's
queer how the people one thinks would live forever are the first to go" (*Thinking*
117). Then he pauses and moves outward from the ironies of war and disease to
a greater sense of irony about who loves home and who does not and who ends
up inhabiting that home and at what cost. He ponders,

> Isnt it queer that the ones to whom home life has been everything, beginning and
> ending both, are the ones who go when the time comes [. . .]. It isnt so queer,
> though, for only he whose heart and soul is wrapped about his home can see
> beyond the utterly worthless but human emotions such as selfishness, and know
> that home is the thing worth having above every thing else, and it is known that
> what is not worth fighting for is not worth having. (118)

Away from home in Canada, training to be a pilot in World War I, Faulkner
would return home himself not long after he wrote this letter. But he would not
truly come home until eleven years later, and he would recognize how queer his
journey had been and how far from the path of expectation it had taken him.
So, in 1930, his "heart and soul" fully immersed in Oxford, he would compose an
apocryphal casting out of the queer element that had kept him away for so long.
Darl is the casualty of his acceptance of home, the queer part of himself that
he cannot rectify with his new actual life, at least without profoundly changing
how he performed it.

Chapter 7

La Vita Nuova

William Faulkner's return to Oxford and subsequent marriage to Estelle parallels a shift in his fiction. Both *Soldiers' Pay* and *Mosquitoes* are set outside of Mississippi, but with his third novel, *Flags in the Dust*, he turned his attention to his so-called postage stamp of native soil, which he transformed into a fictional (and apocryphal and mythic) county that he eventually named Yoknapatawpha. He struggled to publish this novel, and he only found a publisher for it thanks to Ben Wasson, who functioned as Faulkner's agent during this period and helped edit the novel as *Sartoris*, the title under which it originally appeared. Faulkner's next novel, *The Sound and the Fury*, is often cited as the significant game-changer for his approach to fiction. He then wrote *Sanctuary* but struggled to publish it, supposedly because of its salacious content, so while he revised it, he turned his attention to *As I Lay Dying* to fill the financial gap as *Sanctuary* floated in limbo. Between beginning draft of *The Sound and the Fury* and publishing *Sanctuary*, Faulkner married Estelle and became the stepfather to her two children by Cornell Franklin and purchased Rowan Oak, which would remain his home on the south side of Oxford until his death in 1962.

The 1930s saw him publish in quick succession a series of novels on which his reputation has been built, including *Light in August*, *Absalom, Absalom!*, *The Wild Palms*, *The Hamlet*, and *Go Down, Moses*, in addition to collections of short stories and the less-critically praised but no-less-innovative novels *Pylon* and *The Unvanquished*. It is hard to underestimate the significance of this literary output in the broader canon of American literature, and these novels still occupy a central place in conversations about that canon and its influence on literatures from around the world. And, as would likely occur for any novels so thoroughly analyzed and canonized, scholars have noticed homosexual themes in these works. James Polchin and John Duvall have both assessed queer sexualities in *Sanctuary* with Polchin focusing on sexuality as deviance and Duvall on intersections in the matrices of racial and sexual identity. No less a critic than Cleanth Brooks has suggested that Joe Christmas in *Light in August* can be construed as a homosexual but ultimately is not. Gail Hightower's unstable relationship with his wife in the novel also leads the town to grow suspicious of his hiring a black female and then a black male cook/housekeeper. Percy Grimm's violent assault on Joe Christmas implicates the unsettling homoeroticism-turned-homophobia that motivates the sexual mutilations of lynching. Gay author James Baldwin signifies on these implications in his more explicitly homosexual presentation of a Percy Grimm-like character in his story "Going to Meet the Man." Most notably, *Absalom, Absalom!* has piqued the interests of critics for what seem to be the unstated homosexual desires between Bon and Henry and, possibly, Quentin and Shreve. As early as 1955, Ilse Dusoir Lind proposed that there may be "affection, mildly homosexual in basis" between Quentin and Shreve (qtd. in Liles 99), but the first essay-length treatment of this "affection," and the first full essay, devoted to questions of homosexuality in the works of William Faulkner, by Don Merrick Liles would not appear until 1983. Along with "A Rose for Emily," *Absalom, Absalom!* has led to one of the few extended critical conversations about homosexuality in Faulkner studies.

This critical conversation about *Absalom, Absalom!* is fascinating for two key reasons.[1] First, though scholars had previously commented on gay elements in the text, this conversation saw its formal inauguration with Liles's essay published in 1983. The inauguration of the critical conversation about "A Rose for Emily" stems from an essay published in 1988. Thus, the two significant conversations about homosexuality in Faulkner's works originated as studies of male homosexual desire in the 1980s, which were also a critical time of expansion in Queer Theory from the political activism of the 1970s to more distinctly academic inquiries influenced by the increased visibility of sexual minority communities but also as responses to setbacks prompted by the social conditions on which that visibility was based, including the damaging court ruling *Bowers v. Hardwick* (1986) and the seeming apocalypse of the AIDS crisis.[2] Second, these conversations developed along cultural and scholarly lines that have not articulated them as clear and coherent gay readings but more often than not as less specific epistemological discussions about the nature of identity writ large or the intersections of race and queer desires. For "A Rose for Emily," as I have described in an earlier chapter, most of the conversation has been warnings away from gay readings of Homer Barron. For *Absalom, Absalom!* the conversation has been considerably more advanced and has followed the trajectory of institutional practice. If the 1980s saw the emergence of more developed studies of gay representation than previous decades of scholarship—passing mention in an essay to the focus of an entire journal article—then the 1990s was profoundly inflected by the turn toward High Theory post-structuralist debates wary of naming with certainty any identity, particularly LGBTQ ones. Thus, Lind's "mildly homosexual affections" in the 1950s transform into what Liles subtitles his essay, "An Exegesis of the Homoerotic Configurations of the Novel" in the 1980s. By the 2000s, no single term seems to suffice, as for example the multiplicity of terms by Michael Bibler in the chapter he devotes to the novel in his longer study of southern queer desires, *Cotton's Queer Relations*. While Bibler does use the word *homosexuality*, he also variably identifies the desires in the *Absalom, Absalom!* as homosociality, homoeroticism, same-sex intimacy, "men's sexual alterity" (Bibler 64), queer relations, and even "homo-ness."[3]

On the one hand, these critical interventions are reflections of their time and of the accepted practice of scholarly inquiry of their cultural moments. It is often best to think of scholarship as an interactive progression wherein later scholars "intervene" into the insights of earlier scholars to add the new insights of our later vision. We learn to see the world differently over time, which, when placed beside older visions, adds to the thing we consider to be "knowledge," and so our knowledge grows. All scholarship (this study included) is a work of its cultural moment as much as it is an assessment of moments in the past. Thus, on the other hand, the difficulty scholars have had in expressing a clear vision of gay themes in Faulkner's novels from the 1930s and into the early 1940s may well be a result of the moment in which Faulkner wrote them and the prisms through which he was re-understanding his relationship to an identity that had become, to an extent, part of his past and not as acceptable in his present.

The 1930s were a time of challenge for Faulkner's understanding of gay identity. Two incidents from the 1930s lend credence to the idea that Faulkner was, in fact, troubled by homosexuality and that its presence caused him psychic friction that can best be described as "anxiety." These incidents matter in understanding how Faulkner's treatments of homosexuality would find a voice in his later fiction, but lesser known connections from this period may have also given Faulkner access to other ways to present gay themes, which can be outlined in two stories from this period of his life, "Golden Land" and "A Courtship."

The Southern Protective Association

In 1931 Faulkner had a new book coming out, *Sanctuary*, his fourth Yoknapatawpha novel, certainly his darkest, and his follow-up novel to *As I Lay Dying*. The novel predates *As I Lay Dying* in terms of when he first drafted it, but he tabled it and returned to it after the publication of that novel. In an introduction to *Sanctuary* that he wrote for the 1933 Modern Library edition, he explained of its creation that after the beautiful but unprofitable aesthetics of *The Sound and the Fury*,

> I began to think of books in terms of possible money. I decided I might just as well make some of it myself. I took a little time out, and speculated what a person in Mississippi would believe to be current trends, chose what I thought was the right answer and invented the most horrific tale I could imagine and wrote it in about three weeks and sent it to [Hal] Smith, who had done *The*

Sound and the Fury and who wrote immediately, "Good God, I can't publish this. We'd both be in jail." (*S* 322–23)

Faulkner then called the novel "a cheap idea, because it was deliberately conceived to make money" (*S* 321–22), and he set it aside and turned his attention instead to *As I Lay Dying*, a decision that Kartiganer claims was directly related to his erotic drive to support his new family. The sale of *As I Lay Dying*, written while he held down a night-shift job to pay bills, led to his purchasing of Rowan Oak, a home in which to create a properly nuclear family. After the publication of that novel, and its repudiation of gay Darl, Faulkner returned to *Sanctuary*, revised it, and saw it to publication. Of all the books that he published prior to his Nobel Prize, *Sanctuary* sold the best.

One must consider Faulkner's Modern Library introduction with a grain of salt. The final version of *Sanctuary* attains a high degree of the Modernist aesthetic that Faulkner valued in his work, even if it usually costs him a popular readership. In that same introduction, Faulkner would admit of the revisions, "I made a fair job of it" (*S* 324), which suggests he was pleased with the final version aesthetically as well as commercially. It might be best to read the 1933 introduction as an attempt to sell the book rather than as an honest history of its production. The introduction works to make the book the tantalizing and illicit object that the introduction claims it is. Publishing it could have even sent Faulkner and Smith to jail! This claim makes the novel sound far more salacious than it ever appears to have been in any stage of its drafting.

Regardless of the veracity of this story, the implicit worry over money to pay bills and support his family does seem to be an honest anxiety on Faulkner's part. Whether or not the introduction is factual, it may contain some truth. He drafted *Sanctuary* originally in 1929, as his marriage was approaching and as the weight of his impending responsibilities began to make their impression on him. His publishers rejected the novel at first, though perhaps not because it could have gotten them arrested. He turned instead to *As I Lay Dying*. Then he returned to *Sanctuary*. He wanted it to make money and pursued multiple opportunities to sell it to a general audience. However, the Modern Library edition of the novel would not come out until 1933. In 1930 in the first year of his marriage, he needed a more immediate marketing strategy to hype his novel and, hopefully, reap some monetary reward. His agent in New York, Ben Wasson, found the perfect platform for a large audience of potential readers in the weekly radio show of the famous critic and member of the Algonquin Round Table, Alexander Woollcott.

Ben Wasson's tenure as Faulkner's agent had no single original moment, but rather evolved over time. As early as 1924, Wasson assisted in promoting *The Marble Faun* by writing to the Billy Levere Memorial Sigma Alpha Epsilon House in Evanston, Illinois, to include it in the SAE published record of alumni accomplishments. He also sent along Faulkner's picture, which he had convinced Faulkner to have taken in Greenville on 29 March, by Willa Johnston, whom Wasson identified in an interview as a lesbian.[4] Wasson had previously introduced Faulkner to William Alexander Percy in Greenville as well. The connections Wasson made on Faulkner's behalf were often with queer members of the artistic communities that Wasson inhabited. This pattern repeated itself in Wasson and Faulkner's friendship and as Wasson moved more formally into the role of agent in Faulkner's career.

In 1927 Wasson decided to give up practicing law in Greenville to move to New York to try his hand as an author and literary agent. Describing his first apartment on MacDougal Street across from the Provincetown Theatre, Wasson brags in his memoir, "I thought when I became an occupant of that room that I had become a genuine Greenwich Villager. When Bill [Faulkner] first saw it, he remarked, 'Ah, the Bohemian life!'" (83). Wasson's family was less thrilled. He recalls, "My mother and father and my sister Mary Wilkinson and her husband were outraged that I lived in that house and neighborhood. Mary wept and called the room disgusting" (83). Did his sister weep because the room was just run-down by the standards of wealthy Greenvillians? Or did she weep because she recognized that her brother's move signaled a more open embrace of his lifestyle that she (and possibly his parents) did not want to face? Wasson deftly leaves the reasons for their objections unclear except to emphasize the proximity of his apartment to Washington Square, the heart of Greenwich Village. In the coded language of his memoir, Wasson is advertising that he lived in the gay epicenter of New York, near Washington Square and not simply on the fringes of the Village in some out-of-the-way alley, but we are left to infer why this detail matters to Wasson's story. He refuses to say it himself.

In this apartment Wasson began working on his own novel, eventually published as *The Devil Beats His Wife*. He also went to work for the publishing house of Cape and Smith after Harrison Smith broke away from Harcourt, Brace to form his own firm. In 1928, when Boni and Liveright rejected Faulkner's third novel, *Flags in the Dust*, Wasson began circulating it to publishers in New York, most notably to the aforementioned Harcourt, Brace, who would accept and publish it with heavy revisions. Thus, Wasson's role as Faulkner's literary agent became a professional one, not just help among friends.

Also, in the late 1920s, another gay associate of Faulkner's moved to New York, a member of the Vieux Carre crowd among whom Faulkner circulated in New Orleans in the mid-1920s. Lyle Saxon took an apartment on Christopher Street, according to Carl and Betty Carmer, two members of the New York set that Saxon established as his personal social milieu once he arrived.[5] In 1928, as Faulkner attempted to find a new publisher for his novel, he found himself in New York, couch-surfing among a fraternity of gay southern men. In a 1966 interview with Blotner, Owen Crump described Faulkner's arrival and nomadic existence in this social sphere:

> WF had stayed with Stark Young. OC [Owen Crump] remembers a discussion at
> Lyle's [Lyle Saxon] about where WF should move. He stayed with Lyle a week, but
> Lyle was so popular that there was usually a crowd there and it wasn't practical,
> presumably, for WF to stay there. Lyle's door was being knocked on day and night.
> He always had Southern drip coffee on, which he served with a big to-do.[6]

A southerner himself, Crump claimed that he took Faulkner in at his apartment on MacDougal Street and 3rd Avenue, just a short way up from the "Provincetown Playhouse." Crump remembered, "We were all poor in those days," but he singled out Faulkner for his being so singularly determined to "try[] to get enough done to get an advance, pay his bills, and go home." Crump also described a practice not explicitly mentioned in memories of Faulkner's previous sojourn in New York in 1921. He recalled "making the rounds of all the speakeasies in the Village." Wasson claims in his memoir that he also tagged along on these adventures, but he qualifies that "I didn't attempt to keep up with Bill's activities" (88). Undoubtedly, Faulkner had very likely visited his share of bars during his previous trips to New York, but no stories of those excursions survive. In 1928, however, he visited bars in the Village, specifically, which often have histories of homosexual clientele, not just generically bohemian customers.[7] He was clearly quite comfortable and mobile in the gay and bohemian set of Greenwich Village, a comfort and mobility that was likely a product of living in the gay quarter of New Orleans if not a product of his previous short stay in the Village in 1921.

The details from Crump and the Carmers are not random tidbits. Rather, they narrate an important transition in Faulkner's publishing life. Faulkner was in New York to sell his manuscript for *Flags in the Dust*. He came to rely on his friend Ben Wasson to help in this endeavor. Without much money, he also needed a place to stay and found a place just a block or so from Wasson's apartment near the Provincetown Theater. He found that place with the help of his friend from New Orleans, Lyle Saxon. The system that assisted Faulkner in New York had a name: the Southern Protective Association, an unofficial fraternity of southern writers and artists committed to looking out for each other in hostile Yankee territory. According to Saxon's biographer James W. Thomas, even in New Orleans Saxon had long served as a den mother for struggling writers. When he moved to New York, he simply transferred his system of fraternal hospitality with him. W. Kenneth Holditch describes the system as follows:

> Saxon's support of writers continued after he moved for a while to New York City
> in the late 1920s and his Greenwich Village apartment became, according to James

W. Thomas, a "clearing house" for authors from the South, Faulkner among them, and was nicknamed "The Southern Protective Association." It is worth noting that the tolerance exhibited in the Quarter in the 1920s and later toward those who were somehow outside the mainstream seems to have been exhibited as well by Faulkner, who numbered among his close friends two gay men, Lyle Saxon and William Spratling. (27–28)

Though he did not emerge as a central figure in Faulkner's life in this period, Spratling also moved to New York during the late 1920s. While I may be over-emphasizing the extent to which the Southern Protective Association was primarily a gay male exchange, its core were gay men, among them Wasson and later, at least briefly, another young gay Mississippian, Hubert Creekmore, who would take advantage of his connections to Faulkner when he moved to New York in 1930 with his own manuscript in hand and a letter from Faulkner recommending it.

Faulkner arrived in New York in 1928 with the manuscript for *Flags* in a satchel. Wasson introduced Faulkner to the editors at Harcourt, Brace, who had accepted the manuscript pending Wasson's extensive revisions. Wasson revised the manuscript into its eventually published form as *Sartoris*. According to Wasson's memoir, Faulkner declared of the revisions, "You've done a good job" (89). He clearly felt that Wasson earned his keep in the hard-scrabble publishing world of New York. The relationship formed in this transaction carried a significant boon for all three parties involved: Harrison Smith, William Faulkner, and Ben Wasson. Smith would soon leave Harcourt, Brace, forming his own company Cape and Smith. Wasson's work on *Flags* as an unofficial agent led to Smith hiring him into his first official job in the publishing industry. Faulkner found in Smith a publisher with faith in him. With Cape and Smith at first and then on his own, Harrison "Hal" Smith would publish *The Sound and the Fury*, *As I Lay Dying*, and *Sanctuary*. Wasson eventually left Cape and Smith to take a job at the American Play Company, which would help smooth the way for his move to Hollywood in late 1932, where Faulkner would follow in the mid-1930s and where he would meet Meta Carpenter, with whom he engaged in his first serious and long-term extramarital affair.

Faulkner did not exactly conquer New York in 1928 (his previous publishers, Boni and Liveright, were New York based and he had lived there previously as well), but it is not overstatement to claim this period as fundamental to all that would follow for him. When Boni and Liveright rejected his novel, Faulkner faced a crisis in his writing and in his prospects for his future as an author with a steady paycheck to undergird his aesthetic intentions. In 1928 he returned to New York to make an entry for himself as he came into his own as the creator of his mythical county and as he approached the new phase in his life as a married man. His success in New York had everything to do with his dependence on the Southern Protective Association, that moveable feast from gay New Orleans held together by his gay friend Lyle Saxon, and his older friend, also a homosexual, who managed to edit his book into a more marketable version that would convince the most important publisher in Faulkner's life to invest in him. Indeed, one can hardly imagine that Faulkner would have ever published *Absalom, Absalom!* with Random House had it not been for the chance Harrison Smith took on *The Sound and the Fury*. Gay men played a not insubstantial role in this success and, thus, the successes that followed.

Still, there is evidence that Faulkner's comfort among these gay men was undergoing a change. When Wasson attempted to edit *The Sound and the Fury* after his success in revising *Sartoris*, Faulkner lashed out at him with his famous invective against Wasson's well-meaning but unwelcome interference. When Faulkner saw Wasson's revisions, he angrily retorted, "And don't make any more additions to the script, bud. I know you mean well, but so do I" (qtd. in Blotner 244). Wasson would make amends for his transgression by recruiting Evelyn Scott to review the novel. Unfortunately, despite her glowing review and numerous acknowledgments from other quarters about the aesthetic brilliance of *The Sound and the Fury*, it was a commercial failure. *As I Lay Dying* met a similar fate. So, no longer the wunder-kind who edited *Sartoris*, Wasson moved on from his role at Cape and Smith. After reading the draft of *The Sound and the Fury*, he even gave up his own career as a novelist, convinced that he could never write a novel as great as those he was helping edit for his old friend. He also realized that he was not helping Faulkner to commercial success, regardless of his literary qualities. Wasson could appreciate Faulkner's aesthetics, but he could not figure out how to make Faulkner's talents pay.

Furthermore, Wasson's endearments as Faulkner's old friend did not hold him in good stead with everyone in the publishing world. In an interview with Joseph Blotner, Leland Heyward would say of Wasson that "Ben was a little shit, arrogant, undependable."[8] Morty Goldman, Wasson's secretary who would eventually replace Wasson as Faulkner's literary agent in New York, complained in his interview with Blotner that "[Ben Wasson] was the social contact man. [I] began doing the marketing. BW was Southern & there was a clannishness, t[h]e Southern Protective Assn. BW was a goodwill ambassador."[9] Blotner included contextual commentary on his interview notes that Goldman "didn't care for BW," and he thought that Wasson handled most clients "badly." Goldman's comments, however, carried with them more than just professional bad blood. They included a sneering contempt for his sexuality. Later in his interview, Goldman singled out as one of Faulkner's friends in New York "a fag librarian from Miss[issippi] at the NY Pub[lic] Lib[rary]—in the Ref. Dept. Lindley something. He knew WF well. BW would know."[10] Even in typed interview notes, the scornful tone of Goldman's insistence that "BW would know" the "fag librarian" comes through loud and clear, though notably the fag librarian from Mississippi was Faulkner's friend, too. Goldman seems to have considered that Wasson's prerequisites as an agent were based on his social skills, not on his business acumen, and that his social contacts were with degenerate types in the southern bohemian colony clinging to its social order in Greenwich Village, people Faulkner also "knew well," if perhaps too well for Goldman's tastes.

These descriptions paint a picture of an embattled Ben Wasson falling out of favor in the New York literary scene in the early 1930s. Wasson's embattlement paralleled Faulkner's commercial failings, but in 1931 Faulkner had a mortgage due. Furthermore, Wasson's reputation as an agent was not bolstered by his failure to capitalize on Faulkner's talents and lead the writer out of the desert of unprofitability. There is no mistaking the tone in Goldman's interview—he thought he could have done better with Faulkner than Wasson had done—so in 1931 Wasson made another attempt to increase Faulkner's marketability. If a review by Evelyn Scott would not increase Faulkner's popular readership, a more populist platform was in order. Wasson chose Woollcott's radio show, *The Town Crier*. What commercial success this platform might have gained the novel aside, the meeting between Faulkner and Woollcott stands at considerable odds with Faulkner's previously comfortable immersion in gay culture.

The Woollcott Incident

In his memoir, Wasson recounts his trying to contact Woollcott to convince him to feature Faulkner's novel on his radio show. Wasson describes Woollcott's "circusy radio program" as consisting of Woollcott "comment[ing] on matters that struck his fancy, his 'fancy fancy,' I should say" (102). When he succeeded in contacting Woollcott's secretary, she drove home to Wasson the point that everyone wanted to be featured on *The Town Crier* and that such attention came with a price. Then, to Wasson's delight, Woollcott "not only mentioned [*Sanctuary*], but devoted almost his entire program to the novel, singing praises as only he could sing them" (103). As Wasson was leaving the studio, however, having watched the recording from the sound booth, Woollcott approached him to exact his payment. Accompanying Wasson to a bar, Woollcott "plied me with questions about Faulkner. I had heard he was notoriously merciless and noted for his chutzpah, and he was asking me highly intimate questions about his favorite new author" (103). As the unsettling interview concluded, Woollcott told Wasson, "If the young genius comes to this Sodom and Gomorrah, you are to introduce him to me" (103). Failure to do so, Woollcott politely insisted, would result in Wasson's "find[ing] yourself in my gem-encrusted dog house" (103). The high-society politics of Woollcott's expectations were driven home to Wasson by the upswing in sales of *Sanctuary* that resulted from Woollcott's show. Wasson knew that he owed Woollcott. He knew that he would have to introduce Woollcott to Faulkner. Faulkner would have to enter this "Sodom and Gomorrah" himself.

In the meantime, Faulkner moved into the Algonquin Hotel in New York, host site for the Algonquin Round Table of which Woollcott was a member, but he seems to have avoided Woollcott until Wasson finally arranged the meeting due as payment, his proverbial pound of flesh. Wasson begins his account of that meeting by excusing the "New Jersey Nero" for "not being on his best behavior on the night Bill and I called on him" (119). Also, Wasson recalls that Faulkner did not want to meet Woollcott but allowed Wasson to arrange the meeting as due payment for *The Town Crier* publicity. Wasson's description of the meeting itself is, quite simply, priceless:

> When we arrived, we were invited into the apartment by one of Woollcott's favorites of the moment. Bill and I were shown into the living room, where a large gathering surrounded our host. He lounged against pillows on a sofa. He was garbed in a rather tattered red brocade dressing gown, the sash untied. His fat belly protruded where the pajama top was not buttoned.
>
> "Ah," he said, arms extended, his head titled upward in an overalert, inquisitive manner. "So, it's Master Faulkner, not looking in the least bit sinister. I observe you don't have your corncob with you." Bill remained silent, as Woollcott looked about to see if those in the room understood the allusion. (119)

What the crowd might have understood, of course, was not merely that Faulkner had written a shocking novel. Decked out in his best hedonist garb, all the better for its tattered appearance invoking a moral decay that the robe could not fully disguise, the sultan was teasing the servant for not coming prepared with his notorious sexual tool.

Faulkner seems to have understood the sexual innuendo, but when he chose silence as his answer, Woollcott directed his salaciousness to Wasson instead and asked, "How much Negro blood do you have?" (120). Wasson claims that Woollcott was disappointed that he played along and guaranteed, "Half" (120). Thus, to Faulkner, who was not playing along, he redirected his attack: "You disappoint me, young Massa. You seem much too harmless to have written that horror of a book. Now, tell me, is Miss Temple a typical Southern belle?" (120). When Woollcott mentioned southern belles, Faulkner revolted. He turned and exited the apartment, leaving Wasson to trail in his wake and offering no words of parting to his host. When Wasson caught up with him outside, Faulkner simply explained, "I'd prefer to keep company with Frankenstein's monster" (120).

The coding in Wasson's memoir here is complicated. Is "one of Woollcott's favorites of the moment" a reference to a house boy or just a generic socialite in his scene? Are we supposed to read his "overalert, inquisitive manner" as suggesting he is a "bitchy queen," a-la Gary Richards's commentary on Faulkner's New

Orleans Sketches? What might Faulkner find so monstrous about this overweight man with his sexually suggestive banter? All these questions can be reduced to something more primal: Was Faulkner disgusted by someone whom he assumed was a fatuous gay man? Wasson's coding makes these questions difficult to answer, as does what we know—and do not know—about Woollcott's sexuality.

In an essay from *Out* magazine, entitled "Inventors of Gay," Joe Thompson considers that Woollcott, though an inventor of gay identity, was "[n]ot technically" gay because "a case of mumps left him impotent." Lacking the ability to perform sex (as an action), Thompson concludes that Woollcott could not, therefore, have a sexual identity as we might recognize it. Thompson places him instead as "gay-adjacent." Of course, failure to be having sex does not necessarily preclude Woollcott's having desires, which also inform identity and self-performance. Surely it is not impossible to imagine that Woollcott was what we would clearly understand as a homosexual who embodied homosexuality as we know it, but there may be more to this quibbling than just a revival of Queer Theory double-talk about *being, doing,* and identity. Woollcott's impotence may have prevented his participating in sexual activities (though as *Sanctuary* graphically illustrates, impotence may limit but does not preclude one's sexual expression). Woollcott, also, never directly declared himself to be homosexual, but perhaps more significantly, Woollcott was of the generation prior to Wasson and Faulkner's and came of age in a slightly less coherent period of gay identity than the one a later generation would inherit and perform. As with William Alexander Percy, Woollcott, born in 1887, belongs to a generation that created the gay identity later generations would consider predetermined, but that Woollcott might have understood as less defined. Nonetheless, gay, gay-adjacent, or something else entirely, given Wasson's description of Woollcott's dress and mannerisms, it is entirely plausible to believe that Faulkner read him as gay, regardless of Woollcott's preferred identity.

Herein lies the heart of the matter of Faulkner's meeting with Woollcott. What Woollcott considered his own sexual identity does not matter very much during this encounter. What matters is what Faulkner *considered* Woollcott's sexuality to be. Faulkner saw him at this moment not simply as gay. Wasson was gay, along with Lyle Saxon, Stark Young, and William Spratling, among others in Faulkner's circle, but Faulkner saw in Woollcott a "monster," not just a gay man. At least according to Wasson, Woollcott's performance of his identity carried with it the markers of a singular and decadent brand of homosexual identity at odds with the self-performance of that identity with which Faulkner had found sympathy prior to this encounter. Even in "Divorce in Naples," his most overtly gay story, neither George nor Carl presents himself as a hyper-effeminate, gender-bending queen. The waiter in "Jealousy" may act prissy at times, but he hardly lounges around in a dressing gown or silk kimono (Charles Bon will prefer the kimono in his college dormitory and his brother Henry will find it quite exotic—Bon, borrowing from Wasson's joke, is a half-blood). Faulkner's World War I pilots confront their fraught masculinity with rage and pain. Hyperbolically effeminate gestures stand in direct opposition to the hyperbolically masculine performances they put themselves through. Darl suffers the burden of isolation rather than pursue, say, the "pansy boys" of "Uncle Willy." His attractions are for men in his local sphere, none of whom present themselves as effeminate. Woollcott is of an entirely different stripe. Thompson claims, "Woollcott's life, work, and acerbic personality formed the basis of a long held negative gay stereotype." When Faulkner encountered this "stereotype" in the flesh in the early 1930s, he flinched because he saw a performance of gay identity too far removed from his comfort level for its outrageous ostentation. Moreover, Woollcott's language in the meeting with Faulkner was clearly intended as a type of race-baiting, calling out the southern writer for his interest in grotesque sexualities by calling him "young Massa" and asking if his friend and companion were part black. Woollcott finally went so far as to insinuating that Temple Drake's nymphomania might be typical of all southern belles. Some part of this encounter, possibly all of it, did not sit well with Faulkner, who turned on his heels and left. His reaction seems striking in relation to his previous queer life and self-performances.

Oddly, Faulkner maintained a modicum of appreciation for Woollcott in spirit, if not in the flesh. This meeting seems to have occurred in 1932. At Christmas of that year, Faulkner wrote to Bennett Cerf, a publisher trying to recruit Faulkner to Modern Library, to thank him for a copy of *The Red Badge of Courage* and to comment on a book by his fellow southerner Erskine Caldwell, *God's Little Acre*, sent to him by Viking Press as an advanced copy before its 1933 publication. He wrote, "I read it with a good deal of interest, but I still think the guy is pulling George Oppenheimer's leg. I believe that Alex Wollcott [*sic*] and Lon Chaney's ghost wrote it."[11] That Faulkner bothered to include Woollcott's name in the letter implies that he was at least comfortable discussing Woollcott in an abstracted way, as a campy sensationalist akin in his literary sensibilities to Caldwell. In the later 1930s Faulkner also enjoyed the company of the Algonquin Round Table, often preferring to stay at the Algonquin when he was in New York. According to Eric and Rita Devine, in 1935 "Dorothy Parker gave a party for WF" for the publication of his novel *Pylon*. Renowned master of ceremonies for the Round Table, Parker had an apartment at the Algonquin. The Devines recounted of the party that "[t]hey went from WF's room down to DP's aptmt [apartment]. Marc Connelly and Woollcott [*sic*] were there. WF was the guest of honor and loved it."[12] The Devines did not recount any specific interactions between Woollcott and Faulkner from that party, at which there were many other sophisticates and intellectuals hovering around Faulkner and praising his new novel. Perhaps this social setting diluted Faulkner's exposure to Woollcott, or else Faulkner had a profound ability to manage context and expectation and he did not want to cause a scene at this party whereas in Woollcott's lair, he was quicker to make tracks. Or, having previously met Woollcott, perhaps he found his presence less disruptive and could enjoy himself. The incident of their first encounter, however, stands out for looking an awful lot like a variety of homophobia on Faulkner's part.

The Bentley Incident

The curious first encounter with Woollcott was not Faulkner's only problematic confrontation with a variety of homosexual performance that troubled him. Immediately following the account of Faulkner's meeting with Woollcott, Wasson's memoir turns to another incident involving Carl Van Vechten and a drag king named Gladys Bentley. Wasson left many of the details of this story unstated in his memoir, though other sources provide salient details significant for the full context. In his memoir, Wasson explains that, after *Sanctuary*, numerous publishers, including the aforementioned Cerf but also Alfred Knopf and Harold Guinzburg, were trying to lure Faulkner to their respective publishing houses. Smith's new one-man firm, which he formed when he broke away from Cape and Smith, was facing financial difficulty. These other publishers could smell the blood in the water and saw an opportunity to secure the up-and-coming talent. After a party that Knopf hosted for him, Faulkner, along with Wasson and the writer Tiah Devitt, decided to follow Van Vechten, who was also at the party, into Harlem for a night on the town. What follows is the only record we have of Faulkner's slumming it at a drag bar in Harlem, but his reaction to this distinctive culture is not commensurate with his previous embrace of gay life.

Wasson includes in his memoir the principal figures: Devitt, Faulkner, Van Vechten, and himself. He innocently recounts how, upon their arrival at a club, Van Vechten showed them the ropes and easily gained admission after "he rang a bell and was immediately recognized and invited in" (122). Van Vechten's love for Harlem is well documented in biographical studies of him and in studies of the Harlem Renaissance, but Wasson's picture of his intimacy with the local drag establishments carries a suggestion of more than merely anthropological investment on Van Vechten's part. They arrived in time to see a show featuring Gladys Bentley, a key figure in the drag scene in Harlem.[13] Wasson describes Bentley "[s]waying and clapping her hands" and "dressed in a tuxedo" in which she "worked as hard as a field hand at her act" (122). Of her songs he remarks, "They were filled with double entendres, but the obscenities were supposedly subtle" (122). In this case, so is Wasson's memoir account. He never mentions that this is a gay bar nor that this is a drag king. In Wasson's version, Bentley becomes just a performer at a Harlem nightclub, and yet Faulkner would have none of the scene played out in front of him. Wasson continues that "Bill

got up from the table" (122), paid his respects to Van Vechten, grabbed Tiah
Devitt's arm, and swiftly left. Afterward, in a cab heading back uptown, Faulkner
declared, "Down in Memphis, I wouldn't spend my time on Beale Street mixing
around socially, and I wouldn't do it in New York's Harlem" (123). He chided
Devitt that "[a] nice, pretty young lady like you hasn't any business in dumps
like that" (123). Considering Wasson's comment about Bentley's "work[ing]
as hard as a field hand" and Faulkner's comparing the trip to "mixing around
socially" on Beale Street, the account acquires a racial, not a sexual, tone. The
social mixing with African Americans in Harlem is the trouble, or so it would
seem, not the queer environment of a drag bar. Devitt did not belong there
because, in addition to being "nice [and] pretty," she was also white. Reading
Wasson's version of the story implies that Faulkner, a southern gentleman, was
protecting her (white) honor.

Whereas often Wasson's memoir provides small gestures that we can decode
for some semblance of queer identity, this story fails to give the necessary
context beyond the racial codes that appeared to trouble Faulkner so much.
Wasson's memoir account is not, however, the best source of what undercur-
rents were really driving Faulkner's reaction. Race certainly played a part, and
Wasson is not just being evasive to dwell on racial concerns rather than on
the homosexuality of the situation, but in his focus on race, and on Faulkner's
courtly (and racist and patronizing) efforts to save Tiah Devitt, the queer context all but dissolves. Wasson's interview with Joseph Blotner from 1965 offers a
more detailed version of events that is much more overtly concerned with race
and (homo)sexuality.

Wasson's interview begins with the same context. Alfred Knopf held a party
at his apartment for Faulkner to try to secure him for his publishing house
if/when Smith's firm failed. The interview involves the same cast, only with
one notable exception, a man Wasson leaves out of his later memoir account.
Blotner recorded Wasson's oral account as follows:

> WF wanted to see Harlem (apparently the party was the Knopfs). Ben Wasson told
> Bennett [Cerf] that WF wanted to see Harlem so Carl Vanvectum [*sic*] and a girl
> Ben knew named Tiah Devitt and Ben and WF went to Harlem. The party before
> they left was the one at which Knopf after dinner asked WF to sign the books
> which he had collected and WF says Ben answered, "Thank you, Mr. Knopf, but I
> only sign books to my friends." The visit to Harlem ended at Gladys's. Gladys was
> an enormous Negress, a lesbian who wore a dinner jacket. She sang a blue version
> of Sweet Violets which made WF so disgusted that he left. Vanvectum's negro
> boyfriend was there with him.[14]

Faulkner's leaving the bar in this story is much more directly attributable not
to his fear of racial mixing or his desire to save a white woman's honor, but to

his "disgust" at the site of "an enormous Negress, a lesbian." He may also have been unnerved not by general mixing but by the specific mixing he witnessed: Van Vechten and his "negro boyfriend." In an odd twist, Blotner included, in decidedly coded fashion, the details of this interview account in his two-volume biography, though he cut it completely from the later one-volume edition. In the two-volume biography, Blotner omitted that Bentley was a lesbian and only referred to Van Vechten's boyfriend as "a young Negro man who was a special friend of Van Vechten's" (Blotner 2 Vol. 743). Wasson left these details out of his memoir altogether. The purest form of the story is Wasson's original interview. This chronology seems backward. Historical studies, and particularly LGBT-themed biographies, tend to progress from less detail to more, from in the closet to out; yet, for this story, its first recorded telling is the most explicit. Over time, it lost its substance in retellings that de-gayed it. It is, now, something of a phantom presence in the life of William Faulkner, or, in a word, apocrypha.

Clues to Faulkner's motivations for leaving the bar shift in each retelling, from possible homosexual anxieties to decidedly racialized ones. Without the "negro boyfriend" and the giant lesbian, Faulkner was cavalierly saving Tiah Devitt's white womanhood. With them, he was performing a brand of homophobia at considerable odds with his previous embrace of gay life and culture (his early poetry implies he did not consider lesbianism and male homosexuality as equal, but the drag bar's clientele was mixed lesbian and gay men, so what, exactly, set Faulkner off is hard to deduce). A more accurate understanding of his motivations would seem to be that racial and homosexual anxieties infuse each other in his exiting the drag bar in Harlem that night. Perhaps in New Orleans, fancying himself a sexual pioneer, Faulkner could join Spratling while he cruised for (white) hobos in Jackson Square, and he could ignore the implications of a douche bag hanging in their shared bathroom. Faulkner certainly felt comfortable in the (white) bohemia of Greenwich Village—if nothing else, the Southern Protection Association was a white collective of writers, in fitting with the Jim Crow world they carried with them to the (also segregated) North. Harlem was, and is, a black space in the American imagination. If, in the early 1930s, Faulkner wanted to visit Harlem, it follows that he may not have previously gone there. This line—a racial line—may be one that he had not crossed in his previous explorations. When he crossed it, he apparently found more than he bargained for.

Why he would perform such anxious responses to homosexuality in these two circumstances proves a difficult quandary. Woollcott was a loud and popular voice on the radio. Surely Faulkner was at least somewhat aware of his personality before he met him. Faulkner went to the drag bar with Wasson, Van Vechten, and Van Vechten's boyfriend. Surely he knew what kind of bar he was going to and what kind of performance he was going to see there. Yet in both cases, he flinched when his gaze took in the full scene laid out before him. It is hard to ascertain the source of his anxieties, especially because we do not have his accounts of these incidences. We have Wasson's accounts, sometimes mediated through Blotner's biographies.

If these incidences proved troubling, we also know that not all of Faulkner's gay encounters in this period were so fraught with anxiety. In the mid-1930s, Faulkner went to Hollywood. He was joined by Ben Wasson. While there, he met and befriended Clark Gable, whose sexuality included an attraction to women but also included a closeted appetite for men. The difference between Faulkner's sojourn in Hollywood and his previous trips to New York or New Orleans is that he never liked Hollywood and always, quite famously, did nearly everything in his power to work from "home," even when he was employed by studios there. In one famous instance when he asked for permission to work from home, his studio boss, who thought he meant his hotel in Los Angeles, agreed only to find out that Faulkner actually went home to Oxford to work on a screenplay. Of course, home meant Estelle and his children, which may account for why his time in Hollywood never seems to have elicited from him the zestful embrace of a queer life away from home that he had previously enjoyed before his marriage. His time there elicited something else. He engaged in a heterosexual affair with Meta Carpenter, but he also refused to divorce Estelle for fear of losing Jill, his daughter by Estelle who survived and would grow to adulthood. He also had a daughter by Estelle, named Alabama, who would die shortly after her birth, a heartbreaking loss for any parent of any orientation. Faulkner's sense of self was clearly changing in these years, but if they were not in the spotlight, his connections to a gay world were nonetheless present.

The Curious Case of Clark Gable and William Faulkner

Faulkner did not exactly follow Wasson to Hollywood, but Wasson preceded him in moving there and eased Faulkner's own move there in 1933, where he would find work as a screenwriter. Faulkner was never happy in Hollywood, but Wasson's experience was considerably more positive. Upon arriving, "a Hollywood friend" helped him find a good house to rent, and "[a] New Yorker lived in the house across from mine, and together we employed a houseboy, a friendly, shy Philipino, Paul Pagurayan" (Wasson 130). Wasson also recounts that he had "[t]wo friends, Dan Totheroh and George O'Neil" who "had a black woman cooking for them" (133). Such subtlety misdirects from the implications of this living arrangement. The cook is employed in Dan and George's shared house. Maybe they were just roommates, though even that word, *roommate*, has loaded implications in the rhetorical closets of homosexuality, as does, for that matter, *houseboy*, but Wasson does not dwell on additional detail.

In Hollywood Wasson remained a close friend of Faulkner's even though his role as Faulkner's agent was diminishing. In early 1933 Faulkner wrote to Wasson about hoping to approach Howard Hawkes when he arrived in Hollywood. At the end of the letter, Faulkner teased Wasson: "Are you married yet? Cho-cho is quite interested; she thinks Thia [*sic*] is quite beautiful; 'cute,' she calls it. But that's the same word she uses for a bouquet of roses or the burning of Rome, so she cant say more."[15] Faulkner was not asking if Wasson was married. He knew Wasson too well to suspect that Wasson had a romantic interest in Tiah Devitt. Cho-Cho wanted to know, not Faulkner. In 1933 Cho-Cho, or Victoria, Estelle's daughter, would have been in her early teens. Faulkner's brief rumination about her use of "cute" implies that he was faulting her lack of astute observation— "Thia" is cute like a bouquet of roses, which is to say Cho-Cho had not learned how to distinguish subtleties yet. She, apparently, was still in the dark about Uncle Ben. Faulkner's asking about "Thia" Devitt had an ulterior motive as well. Morty Goldman, who was just becoming Faulkner's literary agent in New York, clarified in his interview with Blotner that Faulkner, not Wasson, "liked Thia Devitt."[16] If Goldman's assessment was accurate, then Faulkner's motive for asking about her was likely to keep track of her for his own romantic interests, not to hold out for Wasson's heterosexual conversion. Those romantic interests may also elucidate Faulkner's reason for acting so chivalrous and protective of Devitt's virtue at Gladys Bentley's drag show. Saving Devitt from the drag club in Harlem may have derived from his hope to impress her as a suitor. Surrounded by Wasson, Van Vechten, and Van Vecthen's boyfriend, he may have found courting her difficult without an excessive gesture of his sexuality (perhaps he was even worried that in that group, he would be confused as Wasson's boyfriend and Tiah as their mutual fag hag).

At times Wasson and Faulkner's intimacy in Hollywood would prove problematic, especially regarding Faulkner's attempts to woo other women. Wasson found himself at the center of Faulkner's first serious infidelity to Estelle in his affair with Meta Carpenter, whom Faulkner had introduced to Wasson in the early stages of their relationship. Wasson understood that Faulkner was pursuing Meta despite his being married. That Faulkner would share such a potentially damaging piece of information with Wasson, who was also friends with Estelle, suggests that Wasson and Faulkner's relationship, even after Faulkner married Estelle, maintained much of the same tenor as it had during the 1920s. As Wasson confessed to Faulkner that he had kissed Estelle, Faulkner showed Wasson that he was having an affair with Meta. Perhaps Wasson was supposed to respond to Faulkner as Faulkner had once responded to him: "Remember, bud, that Eve wasn't the only woman who handed out an apple, just the first one" (Wasson 81). In that earlier scene, however, Wasson was unaware of any special connection between Estelle and Faulkner. In this later scene, he would have known that Faulkner was breaking his vows to Estelle. It proved a hardship for Wasson.

The crisis of this relationship occurred when Estelle and Jill visited from Oxford. Estelle hosted a party, and Faulkner decided he wanted Meta to attend.

Faulkner's motives for this decision prove difficult to determine. He seems to have wanted a confrontation, but rather than force that confrontation explicitly, Faulkner arranged for Wasson to attend as Meta's date. In his memoir, Wasson details what ensued. While she served martinis, Estelle sized up Meta. A veiled exchange of challenging pleasantries passed between the two women. Though Wasson was intended to play the part of Meta's lover, he does not suggest that he fooled anyone, especially Estelle. The next morning, Estelle called Wasson. She was "infuriated" and proceeded to explain: "You didn't fool me for a second, you and Billy. I know that the person you brought to my house last night is Billy's girl out here and not your girl at all! I know about that movie actress you're so crazy about" (149). Estelle was particularly appalled since "all these years you've been like a member of the family" (149). The movie actress of Estelle's accusations was likely either Miriam Hopkins or Claudette Colbert, both of whom Wasson names in his memoir as acquaintances, neither of whom he identifies as a girlfriend or lover. These women replace Tiah Devitt as his possible romantic interest. Cho-Cho and Estelle were the two people assuming these women were Wasson's lovers. Aside from Cho-Cho and Estelle wondering aloud about Wasson's relationship, no evidence suggests that his relationships with any of these women advanced to intimacy. In the coded language of his memoir, he reports when other people assumed he was having relationships with women. He does not verify these assumptions.

Faulkner knew Wasson well, yet he used him as cover for his affair with Meta. Wasson was obviously poor cover, and Estelle immediately saw through him. This forced confrontation suggests that Faulkner was not very good at lying about his life to the people most intimately involved in it even if he could tell elaborate falsehoods to acquaintances and strangers. As an example of his ineptitude, he chose his gay friend to pose as Meta's date. Given Wasson's Oxford connections, it seems unlikely that Estelle would have fallen for the gambit. It is entirely likely that she knew that Wasson was gay. Her accusation about his having some other actresses "you're so crazy about" is carefully worded in Wasson's memoir. He did not record her saying that "you are dating some other actress." Rather, it seems more likely that Wasson was supposed to introduce Meta as his "date" in the sense that they were friends and Wasson wanted a friend at the party. Estelle seems to have been inquiring why he did not bring someone more famous and beautiful to be more believable in his deceit. Instead, Estelle realized that Meta, an office worker in Faulkner's studio, was connected to her husband, not his gay best friend. Of course, Wasson proves throughout his memoir to be an adept manipulator of the veil of knowledge, which is to say that Wasson knew how to negotiate the closet. Faulkner does not appear to have mastered those intricacies, at least by the evidence of this story, but the other side to this story is that Wasson was not Faulkner's only gay acquaintance, nor his only access to the ways that gay men manipulated the closet in their personal lives and in their public personae. For that, he had another model in Clark Gable.

Faulkner was a denizen of Hollywood off and on for most of the 1930s and 1940s. He met many artists, writers, movie stars, and other members of the cinema production world while there, from nameless masses of men and women with whom he crossed paths to much more influential figures who would factor into his life more definitively. One of the latter was Howard Hawkes, a director who appreciated Faulkner's talents and remained friends with him for the rest of his life, including through several of Faulkner's later alcoholic binges in Hollywood, Egypt, and elsewhere. Meta Carpenter worked for Hawkes, and Faulkner first met her in Hawkes's office, but another of Hawkes's friends also provided a colorful story for the biopic of Faulkner's life. Sometime in early 1933, Hawkes introduced Faulkner to Clark Gable. The two enjoyed each other's company immensely and even went hunting together in the hills around Los Angeles. Hawkes would recall one of these hunting expeditions when Gable asked Faulkner for advice on some good books to read. When Faulkner included himself in the list of worthy living authors, "Gable took a moment to absorb that information. 'Oh,' he said. 'Do you write?' 'Yes, Mr. Gable,' Faulkner replied. 'What do you do?'" (Blotner 310). The humor of this story belies the friendliness of the exchange. Bruce F. Kawin, Blotner's source for the anecdote, explained of the encounter "that Gable's and Faulkner's ignorance of each other's career may have been feigned" (n. 735). In context, the two men were both jibing each other, and their friendship would survive the feigned ignorance. During Estelle's visit to Hollywood with Jill, "Clark Gable occasionally dropped in for a drink" (Blotner 374). Blotner reports that as late as 1942 Faulkner and Hawkes continued to hunt together with Gable often joining them as a companion and a drinking buddy. Hawkes's wife would recall a 1942 incident after one such hunting expedition when "Faulkner and Gable shared a bottle of bourbon—very jolly and then very sleepy" (445). If Wasson's interactions with Faulkner in Hollywood turned into family dramas, Gable's seem to have been less given to deceitfulness.

Gable was very likely not the only man engaged in closeted homosexual activities whom Faulkner met in Hollywood, but the friendly interactions between the two make him a good example for a general type of Hollywood homosexual. Understanding Gable's sexuality and self-performance helps open the closet door of Faulkner's purgatorial tenure in that golden land. Though Faulkner's coterie of gay male friends in New York and New Orleans were, to varying degrees, nationally famous, those worlds of bohemian writers stand at some odds with the glamor and public spectacle of the life of a Hollywood leading man. In his biography of Gable, David Bret describes his sexual maneuvering and labels him bisexual because Gable had as many affairs with women as with men and even married more than one woman. Bret also details how Gable's father constantly derided his son for his interest in "sissy" activities, such as the arts and his early penchant for theater, which recalls something of Faulkner's being labeled "quair" in his hometown for his interest in the arts as well. Gable's father also taught him to hunt, which Bret suggests Gable embraced to prove his masculinity to his father. Faulkner's love for hunting may well have also grown out of his own sense that it affirmed a masculinity that his youthful persona failed to present. Growing up, Gable inherited from his father a disdain for effeminate homosexuality, but nonetheless he willingly engaged in numerous homosexual affairs throughout his life, from his earliest years in small community theaters to the height of his career as a major movie star. Faulkner was apparently troubled by Alexander Woollcott's ostentatious queening, but he nonetheless maintained gay friendships. All in all, Faulkner and Gable had ample grounds to relate to each other and become friends, except that Gable's pursuit of roles in films would not follow Faulkner's own struggles for publication.

Gable represents what Bret calls the "lavender ladder," or a well-established sexual trade in Hollywood in which a man such as Gable, trying to advance his career in the business, would trade sex for money or for better theatrical roles. Moreover, despite Gable's disgust with effeminate homosexuality, Bret offers numerous stories that lead him to the conclusion that Gable preferred the passive role in his homosexual relationships. Bret quotes from several of Gable's former male sexual partners to establish that Gable was a "bottom," a role often associated with the effeminate partner in a homosexual relationship and, generally, with effeminacy. According to John Duvall, Bayard Sartoris in "Ad Astra" is motivated by his fear of the emasculating power of anal penetration, so it is likely that Faulkner understood the negative associations of being the passive partner in gay sex and how that role produced assumptions of effeminacy. Gable, alas, engaged in this most emasculating of gay sexual practices, but he preferred that his sexual life not become the focus of popular media attention. Nonetheless, according to Bret's biography, his predilection for being the passive partner in anal sex was well known among his closest friends.

Gable did not engage only in homosex. He married women, but he was openly promiscuous even when he was married and many of his relationships were with women attempting a "lavender marriage" (or at least lavender date) to cover their own preference for women. Similarly, many of Gable's male sexual partners were themselves in lavender marriages to women to cover up their homosexuality, at least according to Bret. Gable's sexual practices were part of a well-established system in Hollywood. By the early 1930s, after he had been in Los Angeles for five years, Gable had mastered the system to the extent that his private life remained beyond the purview of the public eye but was well known among other Hollywood stars. Of course, those stars would not out Gable because they, too, were involved in the system of public/private sexual exchange. The system was Hollywood's open secret.

Gable's place in that system largely found its outlet in hyperbolic masculinity. His fear of perceived effeminacy led him to craft an increasingly hypermasculine persona to distinguish himself as a "regular guy" rather than a "fluff" (Bret 26–27). Still, Gable utilized the lavender ladder to advance his career and engaged in many homosexual relationships despite their negative associations. The extent to which any Hollywood star in this period defined themselves as gay or straight probably varied tremendously, but their identities were not, as with Stark Young or Faulkner's other gay friends in Mississippi, based on a geographic division. The line these movie stars negotiated ran between public image and private life without much deference to geographic location. These stars mostly lived in Hollywood, a geographic location that allowed them much more leeway than the small towns where people would watch their films, but even within the confines of Hollywood, as Bret repeatedly insists, the stars were allowed much sexual license but only if they were discreet about it in press releases and publicity shoots.

Faulkner's friendship with Gable points to his awareness of this "secret" Hollywood sexual world. Within Hollywood the sexual exploits of movie stars circulated openly, but always well out of the earshot of newspapers and RKO reporters. Faulkner lived in this environment and knew men, such as Clark Gable, who were immersed in it. Unlike Woollcott and Bentley, these men preferred discretion, or at least tried to maintain a public persona of being "regular guys." Around a sybarite or a drag king, Faulkner may have faltered in his embrace of gay culture. Around a man who could at least act "regular," with an emphasis on *act*, he was much more comfortable. In fact, Ben Wasson's acting the part of Meta's boyfriend when Estelle came to visit could easily represent Faulkner's own attempt to pull the (lavender) curtain over Estelle's eyes for his female lover the way he had observed other Hollywood men do for their "other" lovers as well. If this were the case, his failure would seem to be that he did not understand that a lavender wife always knew what her husband was up to in private. The public eye, not the private family, was whom the optics of normalcy were meant to fool.

A New Life in Stories

The backdrop of these two seemingly homophobic incidents and stories from Hollywood about affairs and the lavender ladder is, of course, Faulkner's extraordinary literary output during this period. His novels from these central years of his aesthetic accomplishment have led to critical conversations about homosexual themes, but those conversations have generally struggled to see a coherent vision for those themes, even as those novels explore other themes in profound and powerful ways. Two shorter works from this period, however, provide useful insights into how Faulkner was reevaluating the place of homosexuality in his fiction.

In 1935 Faulkner published "Golden Land." In the story Ira Ewing is a former Nebraska farm boy, born in a sod-roofed house, who has moved to Hollywood and made himself rich as a realtor. The problem is that the hard-edged, scrape-and-save-every-cent life that he was born into in Nebraska is not commensurate with the life of wealth and decadence that he encounters (and adopts) in his new home. Faulkner infused into the story two scenarios that seem to have derived from his understanding of the sexual economy of famous movie stars. First is a situation involving Ira's daughter Samantha, who is on trial throughout the story. Her name appears in the newspapers as April Lalear. As Ira explains to his mother, Samantha had to change her name to get better opportunities in Hollywood, but changing her name was not enough. To get more parts in films, she also has had to sleep with casting directors, but when she is caught in what the police deem an "orgy," she finds herself exposed to a gawking press. This casting director has two girls in his hotel room at once. When he is caught, all three are charged with indecent behavior.

Though the story never describes what sexual activities occurred in the hotel, that the casting director wanted two girls somewhat queers the situation, but the sex may have had less to do with desire than with self-debasing opportunism. Samantha seems willing to do what is necessary to advance her career, including having sex with a presumably male casting director or acting out lesbian scenarios with the other woman likely also seeking career advancement under the prurient eye of an eager male gaze. In "Golden Land," Faulkner depicts the sexual economy of Hollywood, wherein decent sexual conduct is less important than advancing a career. The catch, however, is not that Samantha should not have engaged in the orgy but that she should not have gotten caught. Following from the model of the lavender ladder and lavender marriages, the goal is to keep private sex private, lest it influence carefully crafted public perception. Samantha makes the best of her bad luck. She later makes a scene in the courtroom to try to capture some media attention to help revive her career. Given that she broke the code regarding keeping sexual practices private, she might as well try to keep the spotlight on herself in case that spotlight leads to better opportunities. In this attempt she is simply emulating her father, who has no qualms about using Samantha's trial to advertise his realty company. Her downfall is his capital gain. Ira Ewing did not get rich just by selling houses. He knows a good opportunity when he sees one, even if that opportunity involves exploiting his own daughter to attain it.

Second is Ira's son Voyd and the private family consequences of a revelation about Voyd's sexual life that escalates into a disturbing image of abuse. At some point prior to the action of the story Voyd was deposited at home one afternoon "drunk and insensible by a car full of occupants [Ira] did not see" (706). Ira took Voyd inside and began to undress him to put him to bed, but while he undressed Voyd, "he discovered [Voyd] to be wearing, in place of underclothes, a woman's brassiere and step-ins" (706). Ira proceeded to beat Voyd violently, ostensibly to revive him from his drunkenness but more likely motivated by a fit of homophobic rage. Ira's wife intervened when she heard the beating, and she refused to listen to his explanation about Voyd's underclothes. She only wanted to protect her son. After this encounter, we are told that "the son had contrived to see his father only in his mother's presence" (706), guaranteeing that any future interactions between father and son will be mediated by her continued intervention between his homosexuality and Ira's homophobia.

On the morning when Samantha—as April Lalear—appears in the newspaper for her pending trial, Ira and his wife get into an argument about what is wrong with their children. Ira shouts at his wife that he did not make Samantha what she has become, though he suspects that his wife "will tell me next I made my son a f—" (708). He means to say "fag." Even censored into "f—," the word Ira means is unambiguous. Clearly, Faulkner had a broader discursive experience of homosexuality than just the word *queer*, though Ira's rejection of his son and slur to refer to him should not be confused with Faulkner's opinions about homosexuality (and, notably, to refer to Voyd as a "fag" aligns his cross-dressing with effeminate homosexuality rather than broader categories of gender expression). Voyd may seem like a bit of a rich wastrel. He might even grow up into the kind of Frankenstein monster Faulkner saw in Alexander Woollcott, but Ira is the true monster of the story who is willing to sacrifice his children for his personal gain. He will exploit his daughter. He will beat his son in a rage of homophobia. The duality presented in these situations is stark and telling. Ira can go so far as to use the publicity about his daughter's sexual transgression to advance his own marketability. As for his son's sexual deviance, that must be beaten out of him in the privacy of the son's bedroom. The son quite literally attempted to hide his gender-bending, but his father discovers his "underclothes" anyway. He assaults his son. His wife must intervene to save him. The implication is that there are some acts of perceived deviance that even attention-craving Hollywood types cannot allow to be exposed.

In 1942 Faulkner wrote "A Courtship," one of his Indian stories.[17] In it, David Hogganbeck and Ikkemotubbe compete against each other for a girl only identified as "Herman Basket's sister." She has no name nor any identity beyond being simply the unnamed object of male attention for her beauty, though aside from some general statements that she was exceptional in some vague way, the story provides no physical description of her beyond noting her sex. Hogganbeck and Ikkemotubbe compete for her nonetheless. Ikkemotubbe shows interest first, but unlike Spratling and the unnamed narrator of "Out of Nazareth," his attention does not give him primacy of place in the courtship. Hogganbeck arrives, and with very little direct discussion that they are competing for her, he and Ikkemotubbe find themselves racing each other and challenging each other's endurance and masculinity for Herman Basket's sister's hand. They challenge each other so exhaustively, in fact, that the first night after they race, "they both slept in Ikkemotubbe's bed in his house that night" (369). The next night they wear each other out again and "both [slept] in David Hogganbeck's bed in the steamboat" (369). They challenge each other to drinking and eating contests, and even engage in a dancing contest, but Ikkemotubbe cannot bring himself simply to kill his challenger. He likes Hogganbeck too much just to get rid of him. He enjoys the elaborate courtship and considers Hogganbeck a worthy adversary, and even starts to consider him a dear and close friend.

Their courtship climaxes when they challenge each other to an old Chickasaw ritual wherein they will race each other to a cave that is a hundred and thirty miles away. The cave is notorious for its roof, which will collapse with any sound more than a whisper or from any sudden movement. The first to arrive at the cave must enter and fire a pistol, thus bringing the roof down on himself and killing the "victor," whose victory lies in proving his superior manhood even as he loses his chance at the girl because he is, alas, dead (but very masculine!). The loser will get to marry Herman Basket's sister, but he will always know that he lost. Ikkemotubbe arrives at the cave first, but as he fires his pistol, Hogganbeck rushes in and holds the collapsing roof up to save him. Ikkemotubbe in turn rushes out of the cave to find a strong cane to hold up the roof and allow Hogganbeck to escape. They both nearly die, but they both also live. On their way back to the Indian village, they learn that Herman Basket's sister has taken as her husband a harmonica-playing Indian named Log-in-the-Creek, whom neither saw as competition during the courtship and who is presented throughout the story as comically inert and useless.

The relevance of the story to gay themes is that it is ultimately about an open secret. "A Courtship" never specifies which courtship is the most central to its narrative structure. Ikkemotubbe and David Hogganbeck seem to be courting Herman Basket's sister, but really, they are courting each other. She is just their excuse because they cannot express their desire for each other in the confines of the structured courtship rituals of their isolated Mississippi world. If "Golden Land" depicted the dread of exposing possible homosexual desire in the glamorous world of Hollywood, "A Courtship," written as it was late in the central period of Faulkner's career, brings a thinly veiled homosexual relationship back into Yoknapatawpha County, or what will soon become Yoknapatawpha County in the fictional history of its purchase from native peoples and settlement by white families as described in major works like *Absalom, Absalom!* and *Go Down, Moses.* The story hints at a primal presence of gay desire in that apocryphal county, as if maybe the expulsion of Darl Bundren in a contemporary story about it did not fully rid this fictional cosmos of a gay presence. It remained in Faulkner's universe. It simply took on a different form.

The story ends with a depiction of a successful "marriage" of sorts, or maybe what we would better consider a partnership of two men who have come to understand each other in a way a man and a woman never can, at least according to a younger William Faulkner, who wrote as much in a letter to an editor of a New Orleans newspaper in 1925. Ikkemotubbe and Hogganbeck at least have each other at the end of the story, even if they have lost the object of desire that supposedly animated their quest. They sail away together on Hogganbeck's steamboat. While they pass the new home of Log-in-the-Creek and his wife, they take turns pulling the "crying-rope" that measures the steam in the steamboat's engine. One might erroneously assume the "crying-rope" represents their tearful recognition of defeat. Quite the contrary, it signifies their departing together as a couple with enough steam to forge ahead. John Duvall, in his seminal essay on homophobia in Faulkner's work, considers his World War I stories as the "crying game" of his fiction, a reference to the 1992 film about homosexual desires embodied in a femme queen whose undressing in the privacy of her bedroom shocks her partner into an act of violence but that does, eventually, progress to recognition, acceptance, and love. Perhaps Duvall missed the mark in the stories, or story, to which he applies that pop culture reference. David Hogganbeck and Ikkemotubbe's departure in "A Courtship" is Faulkner's real crying game, not in an image of homophobia but in an image of discovering that love has outmaneuvered their otherwise heterosexual inclinations. At the end of the story, we see them moving toward a future together that, in retrospect, it seems they had been seeking all along, including on the nights when they shacked up together, first under Ikkemotubbe's roof, then under Hogganbeck's. Yet neither are listening to rain on strange rooftops because maybe beyond the unnamed woman whose courtship brings them together, they have found their own new home. They pull the "crying-rope" to announce their own wedding to everyone in the Indian village, including Herman Basket's sister and her new husband. Their misguided heterosexuality at the beginning of the story has become their homosexual desire for each other, now converted into steam to power an exit from that social order at the conclusion of *the* courtship most important to the story about *a* courtship, but which leaves unclear until this final image which of the many possible courtships it means to endorse.

Endorse might seem too strong a word for what is happening to representations of gay desire in Faulkner's fiction through the 1930s and into the early 1940s. However, while there is evidence in this period of anxious or troubled responses to gay people and gay culture, even through this period, to prefer words like *anxiety* or *phobia* to describe his depictions of gay themes would be equally inaccurate, at least if applied holistically rather than just to the specific incidences wherein Faulkner clearly expressed discomfort with certain gay individuals while simultaneously surrounding himself with gay men to whom he felt more akin. Prior to his marriage to Estelle, Faulkner led what looks an awful lot like a gay life, even if he was just performing that persona as one of many guises he donned in his youth and early adulthood, and even if that gay identity was, and is, primarily apocryphal. He seems to have worked through a psychic removal of that part of his identity in his fiction culminating in the removal of Darl in *As I Lay Dying*, but continued research into his life, especially through the 1950s, suggests that if this element of his identity was less a part of his self-performance, it remained a community and an identity from which he never could venture very far. He maybe even found peace with it. Finding that peace just took a while.

Chapter 8

The Faulkner We Know and Do Not Know

After publishing *Go Down, Moses* in 1942, Faulkner fell relatively silent for six years, though it was during this period that Malcolm Cowley approached him to begin the collaboration that would result in *The Portable Faulkner*. In 1948 Faulkner published *Intruder in the Dust*. Shortly thereafter, he swiftly published another barrage of works including *Requiem for a Nun* and the short story collections *Knight's Gambit* and *Collected Stories*. Cowley first proposed that Faulkner collect his previous stories and even provided suggestions for the framework of that collection, which survives in Faulkner's organization of the stories under the general thematic titles such as "The Country" and "The Village." Faulkner chose to include among those stories "Divorce in Naples" and "Golden Land," two narratives with clear gay elements, as well as "A Courtship," with somewhat less clear but nonetheless present gay themes. *Collected Stories* won Faulkner the National Book Award. This significant award would almost be a highlight in Faulkner's career had it not nearly exactly coincided with his winning the Nobel Prize in 1950 (though actually for the year 1949). Also, in response to Cowley's *Portable Faulkner*, the great writer found himself increasingly the center of critical attention and his works increasingly discussed as exemplary of American cultural values and achievement. The Nobel Prize, two National Book Awards, and two Pulitzer Prizes from 1950 to 1963 attest to the emergence of Faulkner not only as a great American writer from the first half of the twentieth century but as *the* great lion of American letters whose fiction would inspire literary movements around the world and whose Nobel Prize speech is still regarded as perhaps the greatest speech given in the history of the award.

In the march to place Faulkner at the center of the American canon, however, many of the queer elements of his narratives disappeared into the folds of what critics wanted to claim as his larger, grander universal vision. The coincidence of the great William Faulkner encountering openly gay men in the 1950s became, accordingly, a history of his revulsion and discomfort. The surviving biographical record of Faulkner's life in the 1940s and 1950s provides evidence to support such a view, much as his reactions to Woollcott and Bentley in the early 1930s stand out for his uncharacteristic rejection of their expressions of sexual identity despite his continued relationships with Wasson and other gay men in the Southern Protective Association and his friendship with Clark Gable. In his research, Joseph Blotner reached out to several prominent gay literary figures from mid-century whom he learned had encounters with Faulkner and might have a story to tell. Though sometimes there is more to their stories than meets the eye, sometimes there is no way around admitting that Faulkner rejected homosexuality, and not always by quietly turning and exiting the room. On the one hand, Blotner uncovered stories concerning Christopher Isherwood, Truman Capote, Thornton Wilder, and Tennessee Williams. Faulkner's encounters with each of these authors form a complex narrative of his interactions with gay men in the latter years of his life—not a full narrative, but also not an extraneous one. On the other hand, Blotner left a trail of proverbial bread crumbs in his biographical notes that point to a much more complex history of gay interaction and gay literary borrowing than has heretofore been considered in Faulkner's later works. In the 1950s, Faulkner did not cease to perform his apocryphal homosexuality. Instead, he simply found new ways to perform it by using the latest literary models from significant gay authors whose works have been forgotten in American literary history. Nevertheless, these men and their works provided models for Faulkner as he maintained his insidious and challenging critiques of society and its rigid expectations.

These Famous Gay Men

Faulkner met Christopher Isherwood at least twice. In 1955, he, Jean Stein, Isherwood, and Gore Vidal saw Tennessee Williams's *Cat on a Hot Tin Roof*. After the play Vidal and Isherwood engaged in a "desultory conversation [that] convinced Jean that the day of the literary salon was over," but Faulkner remained distinctly aloof from this conversation and hardly spoke to the others about the play (Blotner 597). Later, no longer in company with Isherwood and Vidal, Faulkner admitted to Stein that he did not care for the play. That the play is about a broken marriage caused by the possibility of repressed homosexuality and the obvious alcoholism of the husband certainly could have been the source of Faulkner's response. Aloud, however, he would only say that he felt that it dealt with childish themes, which was an enigmatic criticism to be sure.[1] That Faulkner attended the play with Vidal and Isherwood suggests at least some degree of friendship among these men, but little else survives of this interlude to shed light on their interactions. Attending a production of this play, however, was not the first time that Faulkner and Isherwood met.

Faulkner first met Isherwood in Hollywood at a party in 1945. Isherwood would recall that, despite being warned not to talk about literature with the reticent Faulkner, he and Faulkner had a pleasant conversation "about Auden and Spender, about their work, with a distant politeness in what sounded like a very British accent" (Blotner 2 Vol. 1192). Faulkner later insisted to Malcolm Cowley that the meeting had proceeded quite differently:

> The night before I left Hollywood I went (under pressure) to a party. I was sitting on a sofa with a drink, suddenly realised I was being pretty intently listened to by three men whom I then realised were squatting on their heels and knees in a kind of circle in front of me. There were Isherwood, the English poet, and a French surrealist, Helion; the other one's name I forget. I'll have to admit though that I felt more like a decrepit gaffer telling stories than like an old master producing jewels for three junior co-laborers. (Cowley 35)

Superficially, Faulkner had little to say about this meeting. On closer inspection, however, this recollection proves extremely revealing of a private side of Faulkner that he often worked to hide in interviews and letters. Faulkner seems to have wanted to convey the impression that he vaguely remembered the three men, despite naming two of them and identifying their work, which also implies he was probably familiar with that work. Isherwood's recalling a conversation with Faulkner about W. H. Auden and Stephen Spender, gay poets and friends of Isherwood, implies that Faulkner had also read them, which implies that he was generally well read in the works of contemporary writers, including homosexual ones. Ever fretful about revealing too much about himself, however, Faulkner transformed his literary discussion about gay poetry into the "stories" of a "decrepit gaffer" when he reported the encounter to Cowley. One might almost miss the acknowledgment that, though he felt like a decrepit gaffer, he was actually the "old master producing jewels for three junior co-laborers." He may have been just "sitting on the sofa with a drink," but Faulkner still engaged in a deep and memorable conversation, despite his efforts to pretend for Cowley that he had been accosted by total strangers and had nothing really to say about the party at all.

Obviously, Vidal and Faulkner met when they went together to see *Cat on a Hot Tin Roof*. Knowledge of this connection probably prompted Blotner's inquiry letters addressed to Vidal asking if he might have other recollections about Faulkner. Vidal declined, politely claiming that he had nothing much to add. Similarly, Blotner collected numerous stories about Faulkner and Tennessee Williams, but Williams never seems to have responded to Blotner's inquiries. Blotner was forced to tell the story of Williams and Faulkner's most famous encounter entirely through third-party interviews.[2] That both men were from Mississippi, both heavy drinkers, and both chroniclers of the South—one in novels, one on the stage—would suggest that they shared at least a kindred spirit that would make a meeting between them mutually positive. A meeting of like minds never seems to have occurred, and the famous meeting between them was anything but positive. Rather, that meeting is one of the most damning stories about Faulkner's interactions with gay men and is certainly a story that exacerbates the critical impression about Faulkner's sexual anxieties.

Approximately six months after seeing *Cat on a Hot Tin Roof*, which would go on to win the Pulitzer Prize for drama in the same year in which Faulkner won for *A Fable*, the two writers met at a party hosted by Jean Stein. Blotner records in his two-volume biography that Williams attended with "a young friend of his from Italy" (1576). Monique Lange, who was present at the party, would be less evasive in her interview with Blotner about the evening. She told him plainly that "Tennessee Williams and his Italian boyfriend were there."[3] The "boyfriend" identified in the interview transforms into only the "young friend" in Blotner's first published biography. He disappears altogether from the later one-volume revision. The broader story about the party remains in all three sources, however, complete with Faulkner's devastating dismissal of Lange and Williams later that night. According to Lange, Williams made Faulkner very uncomfortable when they met. Lange attributes this discomfort to "a question Williams asked him about Negroes in the South. He refused to answer and remained silent for what seemed two hours" (Blotner 611). Williams's question troubled Faulkner probably much as he had been previously troubled by Alexander Woollcott and his perceived decadence and race-baiting in 1932 and by Van Vechten and his negro boyfriend at Gladys Bentley's drag show, but in this encounter with Williams, Faulkner would not just turn and leave the party as he had extricated himself from those previous confrontations. Nor would he stay silent all night. Later, when Lange decided to leave the party, "she asked [Faulkner] if he minded if she went with the others to another party" (611). The "others" were Williams and his boyfriend. Faulkner apparently "laughed" at her for asking his permission to leave and dismissed her, saying, "Go with your queers" (611).

No reading of Faulkner's response to Lange can escape the invective in those four words. Those words articulated what Faulkner merely acted out in his rejection of Woollcott and Gladys Bentley. No understanding of gay Faulkner can be complete without admitting that in this well-documented account from this party we have evidence of his using a word to identify homosexuals and using it as a slur. Ample evidence readily suggests that throughout his life, Faulkner was quite comfortable around homosexuals. The few examples of his rejecting homosexuality come with caveats: Woollcott's hedonism and Bentley's and Van Vechten's racial crossings. Faulkner's reaction to Williams stands out, though. Something about Williams got under Faulkner's skin as deeply or more deeply than anything else in the surviving record, apocryphal or not. Perhaps the question about "Negroes" bothered Faulkner. Perhaps Williams's Italian boyfriend was the problem. Whatever it was, Faulkner assigned to Williams a pejorative for his sexual orientation in a word that Faulkner had also been called at various times in his life and for which he undoubtedly understood its sting. Whatever his motive, Faulkner acted out a clear homophobia toward Williams. No fancy critical contortions can deny that Williams caused Faulkner deep psychic discomfort. That discomfort appears to be directly related to Williams's homosexuality.

With Truman Capote and Thornton Wilder, similar, if less contemptuous, patterns of discomfort emerge. In a lengthy interview with Blotner, Albert Marre recounted arranging a meeting between Faulkner and Wilder at Wilder's apartment and at Wilder's request. When Marre approached Faulkner about the meeting, Faulkner established the tone that the meeting would eventually take by asking Marre, when he named Thornton Wilder, "Who's that?" (Blotner 2 Vol. 1401). Marre understood the insult and called Faulkner's bluff. When the two writers met, Faulkner continued his insolent performance. The "disastrous interview" consisted of Faulkner's putting on his "super Southern country boy routine" and sitting at some distance and at an angle from the partially deaf Wilder. Faulkner's spatial manipulation forced Wilder to lean in and cup his hand over his ear to hear Faulkner, who intentionally spoke in a low voice in response to Wilder's questions (1401). When Wilder tried to explain what he thought was the meaning of the title *Light in August*, Faulkner rudely rejected his interpretation. Marre explained that he "saw Wilder flush. He rose and departed," clearly upset that his praise of Faulkner elicited such a boorish response. Marre's anger at Faulkner only increased when Wilder wrote Marre a few days after the incident to ask, "Why did he hate me?" (1402). Many surviving stories demonstrate that Faulkner never felt comfortable around praise or literary discussions, but in this instance, Wilder's homosexuality may have influenced Faulkner's treatment of him. Faulkner may have recalled Woollcott's desire to meet him in 1932. As with that previous meeting, perhaps Faulkner saw something that went beyond his comfort level, though Wilder is not described in Marre's version of the story as presenting himself in the exaggerated trappings that Woollcott had. Though there may be more to this story than merely a manifestation of Faulkner's discomfort around gay men, the open secret of Wilder's sexuality deserves consideration in accounting for Faulkner's actions. Similar discomfort motivated his name-calling and fretful interaction with Williams. Similar discomfort marked his most significant interaction with Truman Capote.

Faulkner's treatment of Capote paralleled his treatment of Wilder, though with the slight variance that with Wilder Faulkner was interacting with a well-established literary giant in the wake of his Nobel Prize, whereas with Capote Faulkner took on the role of correcting mentor to Capote's less disciplined posturing. In 1950, after a party at the home of Leo Lerman, Ruth Ford, Truman Capote, and William Faulkner shared a cab to her apartment to have a drink.

Blotner describes what ensued. In a familiar role, Faulkner sat silently while Capote carried on his endless chattering, but when Capote turned the conversation to Ernest Hemingway's *Across the River and into the Trees* to lampoon it, Faulkner suddenly spoke up. "Young man," Faulkner patronized, "I haven't read this new one. And though it may not be the best thing Hemingway ever wrote, I know it will be carefully done, and it will have quality" (514). Blotner concludes his retelling of this exchange, "For a few moments there was silence in the taxi" (524) It was an impressive silence, to be sure, given Capote's reputation for loquaciousness.

Faulkner's rejoinder of Capote with the title "Young man" situates himself as the superior in relation to Capote's aesthetic taste and level of maturity. Given Capote's reputation, however, there are other implications to consider in Faulkner's response. Just two years earlier, the elf-like Capote's first novel, *Other Voices, Other Rooms*, appeared, complete with an image on the back cover of Capote "languidly sprawled on an ornately carved Victorian settee" and "turning a provocative, pouting face to the camera," as Gary Richards describes the pose in his study *Lovers and Beloveds* (32). Richards asserts that this image was meant to present "a brazen performance of one of the most frequently recurring gay types: the passive, effeminate, foppish gay man" (32). The extent to which this posture formed the basis for Capote's public performance of himself would also allow that Faulkner's "Young man" was meant to belittle Capote's effeminate foppery, especially in comparison with Hemingway's hypermasculinity. Faulkner's rebuke of Capote may have stemmed from his sense that this young, prissy man did not have the right to critique the older, established, manly Hemingway and his manly aesthetics. Capote would later claim that he had no recollection of this incident. The two men would not meet again and certainly never struck up any friendship.[4]

Faulkner did return to Capote in the abstract, though, if not in the flesh. In 1954, while acting as cultural ambassador for the United States on a visit to Brazil, Faulkner remarked, "Generally, I don't read my countrymen's books. In fact, I read little." Faulkner was lying when he claimed he did not read his countrymen's books, but he compounded his lie by inadvertently rebutting it to single out Truman Capote. In the same comments, Faulkner added: "The few times I've tried to read Truman Capote, I had to give up . . . His literature makes me nervous."[5] To read *one* author—an *American* author with a huge popular following—a *few* times undermines Faulkner's claim that he read little and did not read books by his countrymen. Indeed, when Faulkner corrected Capote in that taxi in 1950, he claimed that he had not read "this new one" by Hemingway, but he certainly implied his awareness of Hemingway's works, one novel of which he had adapted as a screenplay in the 1940s while he worked in Hollywood. Still, in his few attempts to read Capote, Faulkner claimed that "[h]is literature makes me nervous." Although not all of Capote's "literature" is as explicitly gay as his first novel, his short stories and *Breakfast at Tiffany's* certainly contain their share of effeminate men with easily identifiable gay characteristics. That Faulkner's "nervousness" was a response to Capote's hyperfeminine homosexual self-performance and literature seems a reasonable conclusion to make. Faulkner's "nervous" reaction to Capote implicates a latent homophobia. Capote's hypereffeminate foppery was a performance of sexuality that made Faulkner anxious, much as Woollcott's sybaritic display had bothered Faulkner nearly twenty years previously.

When Faulkner encountered these gay men certainly accounts for some of Faulkner's reaction to them. American culture progressed between the 1920s, when Faulkner first submerged himself in large gay communities and nurtured his most intimate gay relationships, and the 1950s, during the Cold War and at a time of ideological crisis for the United States as it assumed its position as the dominant capitalist nation in the world. Capote in particular, but to varying degrees Williams, Vidal, and Isherwood as well, all participated in a cultural movement of gay visibility that paralleled the cooling national entry into the Cold War with the communist Soviet Union. Hard-right conservatives did not fail to see a connection between increasing gay visibility in cultural productions, particularly in the fine arts, and a plot by communist infiltrators to undercut the strength of masculine capitalist American industrial might. Two strains converged in a peculiar cultural perception of gay artistic production. On the one hand, gay artists rose to places of prominence in the 1940s and 1950s as leading figures in the arts. In *Gay Artists in Modern American Culture*, Michael Sherry goes to great lengths to explore the ubiquity of known gay men who functioned as arbiters of American culture during this period, despite cultural myths, mostly a product of later decades, that revise homosexuality out of history and pretend that the closet door was as tightly fastened or almost as tightly fastened in the 1950s as it was in the 1960s and 1970s. On the other hand, with increased visibility came increased criticism, culminating in the appropriation of the term Comintern as "Homintern," or the belief that gay men secretly meant to take over American culture and acculturate the youth of America to their perverted designs. Thus, the communist witch hunts of the McCarthy era, Sherry explains, were as often as not gay witch hunts in addition to looking for supposed Soviet spies.

The increasing anxiety over the ever-present threat that gay men were suddenly everywhere led to the perpetuation of the medical establishment and government officials classifying homosexuality as abnormal and attempting either to treat it or to punish it. That anxiety also led, of course, to its own self-perpetuating problem: the more people discussed homosexuality, the more homosexuality became a topic of discussion. These anxieties would develop, in literary representation anyway, into increasingly problematic presentations of feminized, and even hyperfeminized men, the representative homosexual so perfectly crystalized in Capote's infamous book-jacket picture. Thus, depending on how one views homosexuality, Joel Knox, the protagonist of *Other Voices, Other Rooms*, finds himself either at the mercy of a grotesque queen intent on corrupting him or in the nurturing care of a parental figure emblematic of his own nascent desires. In the cultural milieu of the 1950s, the former impression far outweighed the latter. "Degenerate" homosexuality came to threaten healthy masculinity. The crisis manifested itself in depictions of men emasculated by the confines of the new, postwar world of domesticated masculinity always one step shy of putting on the wife's frilly-laced apron and cooking neatly prepared meals. Robert Corber explores this phenomenon in the works of Williams, Vidal, and James Baldwin, and Susan Donaldson has argued that V. K. Ratliff from the latter two Snopes novels embodies Faulkner's own anxieties over this crisis in masculinity. *The Town* and *The Mansion* are certainly properly read as Cold War novels, and Faulkner's comments about Capote's works making him nervous lend credence to Donaldson's argument. There is, however, more to Faulkner's statement about Capote than meets the eye.

As with all his public statements, the complexities of Faulkner's comments about Capote mount on closer examination. Capote's works made him nervous, yet he tried to read them a few times. Why did he keep trying to read them if they made him nervous? Maybe he tried to read them but failed because they made him nervous, but if they made him nervous in the first place, why did he try again? Similarly, Faulkner claimed that he did not want to attend a party in Hollywood, but he did attend and had a pleasant conversation with Christopher Isherwood. He also acted as if he did not want to meet Thornton Wilder, but he met with him anyway, and he owed him no thanks for helping market a novel as he did to Woollcott for this radio show promoting *Sanctuary*. He acted out his discomfort and alienated Wilder, but he still met with him, privately and upon request, not at any party as a chance encounter. These comments and encounters present conundrums that do not provide clarity so much as suggest that Faulkner was hiding something in his answers and performing a role that attempted to shield him from the implications of reading certain novels or appreciating the chance to meet his fellow artists who were, also, gay.

Throughout this period of his life, Faulkner clearly had trouble negotiating the gay identity of these men in relation to his own sense of identity. Yet, for someone so "nervous" about homosexuality, he quite often found himself in the middle of it, thinking about it, and reading about it (or trying to anyway). Faulkner's evasiveness regarding his conversation with Isherwood, his boorishness when he met Wilder, his haughtiness (and nervousness) toward Capote, and his dismissal of Williams and his "queers" all portray a man surrounded by and reacting to homosexuality. Surely, if Faulkner genuinely hated gay men, he could have found some way to avoid some, if not all, of these encounters, but Faulkner seems to have been as immersed in gay life in the 1950s as he had been in the 1920s, though his new immersion was not necessarily *living* with gay men but *reading* and, at times, *working* with them. Upon deeper inspection of some lesser explored biographical details of Faulkner's life, the Faulkner we know from the 1950s runs headlong into a Faulkner we do not yet know. The Faulkner we do not know proves to be an elusive and enigmatic figure, certainly, but not always as homophobic a figure as these famous stories imply.

And These, Who Were Homosexuals, but Who Were Not Famous

While Faulkner had brief interactions with Williams, Capote, Isherwood, and Wilder, these men were not the only gay men with whom he had contact. Evidence suggests that Faulkner read other contemporary writers in addition to Capote, including Calder Willingham and Charles Jackson, met other gay figures, such as Thomas Hal Phillips and Charles Henri-Ford, and possibly even helped start the career of one gay author from the nearby town of Water Valley, about twenty miles south of Faulkner's Oxford. While Faulkner's connections to these men (and their sisters) differ from his participation in gay culture while he was living in New Orleans or courting Ben Wasson, they provide evidence for a continuing influence in his life and in his work. Beyond the documented reports of anxious homophobia, a small sea of other gay voices surrounded him.

An off-hand photocopy in Blotner's notes suggests that Faulkner owned a signed first edition of Calder Willingham's novel *End as a Man* (1947).[6] Though this novel is not exclusively a gay novel—rather, it details a variety of "perverse" sexual practices at a military academy in the Deep South—it is often listed alongside gay novels in bibliographic studies of the genre. Also, Willingham was not a homosexual, at least not openly so. That Faulkner might have read this lesser-known novel proves an enigmatic intersection between Faulkner and gay literature in the 1940s and 1950s, but that Faulkner seems to have owned the novel—a signed first edition no less—suggests that he did, in fact, stay abreast of contemporary fiction, including fiction adjacent to the rising genre of gay novels that was developing through this same period. Of course, Faulkner not only owned lesser-known books with homosexual themes by contemporary writers. He also knew more openly gay men than the current biographical record includes. Christopher Isherwood recalled a longer guest list from the night in 1955 when he, Faulkner, and Vidal went to see *Cat on a Hot Tin Roof*. He included Carson McCullers and Marguerite Lamkin as well. Blotner identifies Lamkin as an employee of the director Elia Kazan, whom Kazan "had hired to coach his actors in simulating Southern accents" (Blotner 2 Vol. 1529). Perhaps her southern background led to Faulkner's interest in her, though Lamkin ultimately makes only minimal appearance in the biographical record. No evidence suggests that they engaged in an affair, but Shelby Foote claimed that Lamkin was responsible for introducing Faulkner to Jean Stein, whose friendship would prove significant in Faulkner's life thanks in large part to Stein's interview of him for the *Paris Review* in 1956.[7]

Stein journeyed to Mississippi in late 1955 along with Lamkin, who was working with Kazan on his film *Baby Doll*. Faulkner introduced both to Ben Wasson and another famous Greenville native, Hodding Carter. Stein would recall how highly she regarded Carter. Conversely, she explained of Wasson that he "seemed very effeminate, homos[exual], old when she saw him."[8] Faulkner did not share her disregard for his old friend; nor, for that matter, would Lamkin have shared Stein's opinions either. According to Foote, Lamkin had a reputation for being part of a gay social milieu: "Her brother, Speed, the writer, was apparently King of the perverts. Apparently she was the Queen." Although Blotner's notes include that Foote's wife "admired [Lamkin] extrav-agantly," Foote himself "seemed to think she was disgusting."[9] Foote's disgust clearly emanated from his opinion of her sexual taste, an opinion he extended to Lamkin's brother.[10] Foote's and Stein's homophobic comments—recorded in interviews ten years after the Greenville trip but nonetheless edged with keen vitriol—suggests that Wasson's homosexuality and Lamkin's acceptance of "per-version" were no minor sidelines to this excursion South. Conversely, no report survives that suggests that Faulkner was bothered by Wasson or Lamkin on this trip, which only seems natural given Faulkner's long history of friendships with openly gay men. Nor does any surviving evidence suggest Faulkner read Speed Lamkin's books, which, though they are salacious, are not as explicitly gay as many other works to which Faulkner was exposed. Lamkin's novel *The Tiger in the Garden* (1950) gained enough success that Faulkner may well have heard of it. Having met Speed Lamkin's sister on more than one occasion might even have prompted him to read it, or at least try to, but as with Willingham's novel and the photocopy in Blotner's notes, the evidence only gets us so far in our speculations. The link between the Lamkins and Faulkner is, at best, a near miss in Faulkner's interaction with gay culture and literature during this period.

Another near miss occurred in 1950 at Faulkner's home, Rowan Oak. Shortly after being awarded the Howells Medal in American Literature, Faulkner received as visitors Thomas Hal Phillips and Ernest E. Leisy, faculty members at Southern Methodist University, in Dallas, Texas. Phillips wrote about the visit for the *Dallas Morning News*.[11] A native of Mississippi himself, Phillips described a view of Faulkner completely in line with his public persona as a shy, reclusive farmer living a simple life in the Mississippi hill country. Phillips's only subjective appraisal of the great man in what is otherwise a narrative of his visit depicts Faulkner as free from the confines of being "tamed into a drawing room lion: He remains an individual, a great one I think, a lover of the Deep South who has seen more clearly than anyone else the South's virtues as well as its social disintegrations and decay." Significantly, these themes also inform Phillips's own novels, primarily *The Bitterweed Path*, which was published almost simultaneously with his visit to Rowan Oak. In fact, a review of Phillips's novel was scheduled to appear in the *Dallas Morning News* the week after his Faulkner essay, according to the editor's note that appeared with Phillips's story.

The Bitterweed Path takes the implicitly homoerotic material Faulkner explored in *Absalom, Absalom!* between the generations of male Sutpens and makes it the focus of an explicitly homosexual narrative. John Howard identifies the main theme of Phillips's novel as "the trope of brotherhood" as the two male protagonists, though of different class backgrounds, love each other and channel their same-sex desire into a desire to be actual brothers. The conflict is tentatively resolved when Darrell, the tenant, marries Rogers's sister, thus entering the white planter class through marriage as "brother-in-law," which is metaphorically a kind of marriage, the *de jure* union that links "in law" a familial unit with no other means of legal articulation (Howard 190–91). Though he removed the racial element from Faulkner's narrative to craft his own, Phillips managed to bring about the same-sex union *Absalom, Absalom!* denies when, unable to bear Bon's intentions to marry Judith, Henry shoots him at the gates of Sutpen's Hundred. Given Phillips's praise for Faulkner in his essay, we can easily trace the influence of Faulkner on Phillips. What proves more difficult is tracing whether Phillips would have influenced Faulkner in return, assuming Faulkner would have read the forthcoming book by the Mississippian who visited him at his home in the spring of 1950.

Throughout his life, Faulkner undoubtedly read contemporary fiction. In fact, the most recent trade paperback versions of Faulkner's novels published under the imprint of Vintage International all include the following quotation from Faulkner about how he consumed literature and how it influenced him:

> Read, read, read. Read everything—trash, classics, good and bad, and see how they do it. Just like a carpenter who works as an apprentice and studies the master. Read! You'll absorb it. Then write. If it is good, you'll find out. If it's not, throw it out the window.

Although his major influences included Dostoyevsky and Conrad, Shakespeare, the Bible, Balzac, and any number of other literary figures from generations prior to his own emergence as a literary giant in his own right, Faulkner continued to read other authors and continued to grow and experiment with his writing throughout his long and prolific career. While Faulkner greatly influenced a whole generation of southern writers, rarely do scholars contemplate that Faulkner, in his long career, might have found material that influenced his fiction in return. The length of his career and his prolific literary output allows for one to explore how even books by authors from as late as the 1940s and 1950s— who may well have read their share of Faulkner—in turn found their way back into his sphere and provoked his creativity as well. Though Willingham,

Lamkin, and Phillips prove minor footnotes in Faulkner's life, their presence signals the ubiquity of younger writers in the life of the old master, and stories about these younger writers begin to point toward a remarkable conclusion. Faulkner did not just record a dead past or write in antiquated narrative forms. He changed and grew as literature did, including as new genres developed and new ways of writing about older themes found sturdy legs and a stronger voice.

An often-overlooked coincidence of Faulkner's literary career was that it paralleled the development of another literary genre, the gay novel, which began to take a toe-hold in American letters in the early 1930s with such books as Henri-Ford's *The Young and the Evil* and books by Richard Meeker, Lew Levinson, and Andre Tellier, among others. Through the 1930s and 1940s this genre grew until, in 1948, it reached its cultural apex with the publication of Vidal's *The City and the Pillar* and Capote's *Other Voices, Other Rooms*. Explicitly gay narratives about explicitly gay lives formed a niche market in the mid-1940s and onward until well after Faulkner's death. Willingham, Lamkin, and Phillips were among just a few of the writers of that genre whose paths would cross Faulkner's. If these three men prove elusive in their possible influences, then three others would seem to have played a much greater role in Faulkner's late career.

The Lost Week(end)

In 1948 Faulkner published a new book, *Intruder in the Dust*. His publishers were so pleased that they asked him to come to New York to celebrate its publication. Though in the late 1920s and early 1930s, Faulkner regularly visited New York, in 1948 he had not been to New York in ten years. Bennett Cerf not only invited Faulkner to New York to celebrate *Intruder*, but he also went so far as to extend an invitation to Faulkner to stay at his home while he was in town. Faulkner accepted the invitation to New York, but he declined the invitation to stay with the Cerfs. Instead, he wrote to request that Cerf book him a room at the Algonquin Hotel. Cerf complied with Faulkner's wishes and made the arrangements. Faulkner then wrote to Cerf that he had tentative plans to meet "a Mississippi friend, an actress, Ruth Ford" when he arrived.[12] Faulkner's friendship with Ford had a long history, which I will detail shortly. For now, I will focus instead on this particular trip, the record of which was compiled and detailed by Blotner and also told in outline by Malcolm Cowley in his memoir, *The Faulkner-Cowley File*.

Thanks to Cowley's memoir, we can date the trip precisely. Faulkner arrived in New York in late October. On Saturday, 23 October, Cowley noted that he had joined Faulkner for dinner on the previous "Tuesday [19 October] evening at the Park avenue apartment of Robert Haas" (103).[13] On 25 October, Cowley composed a brief sketch from a personal interview with Faulkner that he conducted at his home in Sherman, Connecticut. In the meantime, Faulkner had arrived at Cowley's home for unfortunate reasons. On the evening of 23 October, Cowley was called to New York to retrieve Faulkner from the Algonquin. On 26 October, three days after his arrival at the Cowleys' home, Faulkner returned to New York. According to Cowley, Faulkner took with him Cowley's copy of *The Lost Weekend*, by Charles Jackson. On Saturday, 30 October, Cowley's wife received a dozen long-stemmed roses that Faulkner ordered from the nearby town of New Milford on his way home to Mississippi. By the time these arrived, Faulkner had already boarded a train to Oxford, his celebratory trip to New York concluded. Faulkner sent these roses in gratitude to the Cowleys for the time he spent in their home, which even included Faulkner's borrowing clothes from their son while he was there since he had none of his own to wear besides those in which he arrived.

In interviews with Ruth Ford, Blotner was able to reconstruct what happened on Saturday, 23 October, that led to Faulkner's arrival at Cowley's house. After dinner on Tuesday night at Haas's apartment, Faulkner began drinking alone in his room at the Algonquin. Ford called on him the next day to invite him out, but, as Blotner explains, "When he declined she thought his voice sounded strange. She called him the next day, and again he wouldn't go out, and his voice sounded even stranger. There was no answer at all when the operator rang his room on Friday" (498). Recognizing that something was wrong, Ford went to check on Faulkner with the help of her friend Harvey Breit. She found Faulkner in his room, semiconscious from his extreme drinking, and called an ambulance. The doctor insisted on hospitalizing Faulkner, but Faulkner begged not to be confined to what he called a "cage," or the alcoholics' ward (498). Given Faulkner's condition and his desire to avoid a hospital stay, Ford devised a plan: send Faulkner to the Cowleys' home in Sherman where he could recuperate for a few days and dry out under the watchful eye of Malcolm and Muriel Cowley. The Cowleys agreed. As a sort of payment for their kindness, Faulkner allowed himself to be interviewed at length by Cowley. He even signed many of Cowley's copies of his novels, still largely out-of-print but soon to make a hugely successful commercial comeback.[14] He also began reading a book on Cowley's bookshelf ostensibly about an alcoholic on a five-day bender but implicitly about a closeted homosexual attempting to numb his erotic desire for other men. Faulkner asked Cowley if he might borrow the book, but Cowley gave it to him instead. *The Lost Weekend* is one of the few novels that we know, thanks to Cowley's memoir, that Faulkner not only read but by which he seems to have been deeply and genuinely moved. In fact, he would try to write his own version of it.

By 1948, when he read the novel, there is good reason to believe that Faulkner was already aware of its basic premise. Upon its publication in 1944, *The Lost Weekend* became something of a cultural phenomenon. In 1945 it was made into an immensely popular and critically acclaimed film. That Faulkner was a denizen of the Hollywood community in the mid-1940s increases the likelihood that Faulkner had at least heard of the story before he found the book on Cowley's shelf, but he had not read the book until his 1948 stay with the Cowley family. If he had, by chance, seen the movie prior to reading the book, he would not necessarily have known about the homosexual narrative embedded in Jackson's novel. The screenwriters, following the Hayes Code that led to the excision of explicitly gay themes in film for a generation of Hollywood cinema, conveniently buried that element of the plot and instead secured a heterosexual salvation at the end of the film that is not present in the novel. Whatever the case may have been, Faulkner found *The Lost Weekend* on Cowley's shelf, read it, asked to borrow it, and kept Cowley's copy as a gift.

Two works pull into focus the homosexuality underlying the case study of alcoholism in Jackson's most famous novel. First, in a biography of Jackson, Blake Bailey teases out the origins of Jackson's bait-and-switch wherein alcoholism serves as a stand-in for homosexuality and homosexuality a stand-in for alcoholism. Jackson was himself both an alcoholic and a homosexual, and he used his own experiences with psychoanalysts—applying the general perception at the time that alcoholism was a problem of will, homosexuality a mental disorder—to craft his complex portrait of Don Birnum, the novel's protagonist. Bailey explains the connection as follows:

Though it may be correct to assume that compulsive drinking is symptomatic of an underlying neurosis, the symptom meanwhile evolves into a separate and no less pressing problem—chemical dependency—which in turn may be exacerbated by the analyst's efforts to address the neurosis. Saint-Exupery's tippler in *The Little Prince*—who drinks because he is ashamed, and is ashamed because he drinks—is a nice illustration of the conundrum, one that Jackson struggled with in life and art. "He knew what no one else knew, no one he had ever met yet," Jackson wrote in a discarded passage from *The Lost Weekend*: "His 'disease' [i.e., alcoholism] was not disease, or at least not the principle thing from which he suffered." This was meant to reflect the Freudian notion of an underlying neurosis, though perhaps it pointed too directly at what Freud himself considered almost a constant among alcoholics: repressed homosexuality. According to Freud, male homosexuals drink because of their failed relations with women, and because it provides an excuse to seek the company of men. Don Birnum, for his part, implicitly blames his drinking on the more fearful "disease" of homosexuality, though at other times it's precisely the other way around: "What Bim"—the male nurse at Bellevue—"did not see was that the alcoholic is not himself, able to choose his own path, and therefore the kinship he seemed to reveal"—i.e., their common homosexuality—"was incidental, accidental, transitory at best." Thus Don is a homosexual because he drinks, and drinks because he is a homosexual. (90–91)

We may know better now, in the twenty-first century, about the causes of alcoholism and the naturalness of homosexual desire, but Faulkner's time had not reached our higher plateau on these matters. Of course, Faulkner's experiences from the 1920s would have given him access to evidence to rebuff the idea of homosexuality as a neurosis inevitably tied to alcoholism in his friends and other acquaintances (though many of the men in his life, homosexual and not, were heavy drinkers), but his own alcoholism could have made it difficult for him to assess objectively whether or not some alcoholics drank because they were homosexuals and were, in fact, identifiable as homosexuals because they drank. In the middle of his own bender, Faulkner's reading *The Lost Weekend* could easily have challenged his assumptions about his own queer identity, apocryphal or otherwise, and its reflection he might have seen written in such detail before him.

Second, in a literary study of Jackson's works, Marc Connelly explores the references to homosexuality in the novel beyond just the medical discourse of the novel that used alcoholism as a closet for the homosexuality subcutaneously motivating the character to his drinking habits. Connelly reads the novel not as a study of a five-day binge by an alcoholic but as a gay chronology wherein Don Birnam reenacts the critical moments of his developing homosexual desires in the internal monologues that motivate so much of the action. One of two key moments in Birnam's life where his interior desires take external form include his recounting of his expulsion from his college fraternity for having an inappropriate crush on a fraternity brother. The novel returns to this incident as the cause of Don's drinking repeatedly and leaves little doubt that Don was, in effect, accused of being a homosexual, even if that word was not said by his former fraternity brothers. The other key moment is his confrontation with Bim, the nurse in the alcoholics' ward, who secures Birnam's address under the auspices of testing his memory, forces Birnam to dress in front of him, and then provocatively comes on to Birnam while he is leaving the ward: "'Listen, baby.' The voice was so low and soft he could scarcely hear it. 'I know you'" (Jackson 139). Mixed with these moments are memories of a precocious childhood, including masturbatory fantasies about other men, his horror at his sexual maturity during adolescence, and a nightmare about his being bullied by the boys at school. Don's interior monologue recalls these memories while he, in the five-day time frame of the novel, bar hops primarily through the former speakeasies in Greenwich Village in the first years after the end of Prohibition (the novel was published in 1944 but is set in the early 1930s). Throughout the novel, Don constantly finds himself watching other men in the bars that he inhabits, as Connelly points out, always with an eye toward their physiques and sexualities. The additional element in the novel that might most have appealed to Faulkner is that Don Birnam harbors dreams of literary greatness. He couples his memories of his sexual development with memories of being a bookish, literary youth. He conglomerates his failures as a writer with his mishaps among other boys/men, primarily his embarrassed withdrawal from college, and his constant need for a drink to steady himself. He has a sometime-girlfriend, Helen, but she functions primarily as nothing more than a mother-figure to help take care of him when he is deep in a binge.

According to Connelly and Bailey, the autobiographical elements in the novel parallel Jackson's own struggles with alcohol and his homosexual desires, but those parallels extend as well to Faulkner's life, especially in 1948 as he finally published a novel after a long drought in his publishing career and when, generally, his other novels, with the exception of *Sanctuary*, were out of print in the United States (until he won the Nobel Prize anyway). That Don drinks to avoid facing his literary failures would certainly register with Faulkner, the alcoholic writer struggling through his own recent writer's block, though unlike Faulkner, Don only dreams about the great books he would write but never writes them. Faulkner had produced a wealth of fiction that struggled for sales in the literary market but certainly had received its share of critical praise. Nonetheless, Faulkner's reading *The Lost Weekend* while he was recovering from his own lost week of heavy drinking clearly suggests that he saw the parallels between the action of the novel and the events of his own life, and Don's awareness of his homosexual inclinations would not have been lost on Faulkner, nor on any reader paying even mild attention to the details of the story. Perhaps unlike many readers of Jackson's novel, however, Faulkner had spent the first half of his life labeled "quair" and queer and often immersed himself in gay cultures to the extent that, even while he was courting his own Helen (Baird), his social set would take for granted that his roommate William Spratling might also be his lover much as his college peers had given him queer looks for reading Conrad Aiken to Ben Wasson on the verdant campus of Ole Miss.

The Lost Weekend had such an effect on Faulkner that by 1953 he had written a short story based on it. Originally titled "Weekend Revisited," but later retitled as "Mr. Acarius," the story follows a much older man than the thirty-three-year-old Don Birnam as he meets with his doctor to plan a weekend binge, an intentional relapse into his old ways.[15] He tries to let himself "revisit" his former habits, but being in a bar overwhelms him and he drinks far more than he should have allowed himself. He regrets his decision to go on a planned drinking binge after "accidently" getting in a police car when he flees the bar and when he meets men who are clearly alcoholics with no control over their impulse to drink, but the darkly humorous story does not succeed in painting a realistic picture of alcoholism. Mr. Acarius has far too much control over his urge to drink, or at least believes he does, and his planned binge may provide comedy but points to the unsettling reality about the compulsive behavior of alcoholics. Don Birnam believes that he plans his actions while he is drinking, but Jackson clearly demonstrates that Don's sense of self-control is entirely an illusion. Faulkner depicted Mr. Acarius as having control, which is not an accurate depiction of the compulsions of alcoholism. Also, Mr. Acarius, significantly older than Don Birnam, is not haunted by memories of adolescent homosexual impulses. The omission of this element costs Faulkner any underlying motive for Mr. Acarius's actions and makes Mr. Acarius read as a character driven by a plot rather than a character driving a plot, as Jackson's protagonist proves to be.

That Faulkner left the homosexual elements out of his story inevitably leads to questions about what motivated the omission. "Mr. Acarius" lacks the homosexual subplot so entirely as to suggest that Faulkner very consciously recognized that element of Jackson's novel and removed it from his own retelling. Perhaps this omission speaks to Faulkner's wish that his own drinking did not harbor in it any implication of homosexuality, much as Mr. Acarius's sense that he can start and stop drinking whenever he chooses might represent hopes for Faulkner unrelated to sexuality and purely a matter of his long, troubling history of alcoholism. Maybe, in the years after his reading of *The Lost Weekend*, Faulkner had determined that he did not approve of a literary model that wed alcoholism and closeted homosexuality so intrinsically, which might also explain his comments about Williams's *Cat on a Hot Tin Roof* and his criticism of it. Maybe he had come to see such heavy-handed psychology as not indicative of homosexual identity or experience after all. Whatever his motivations as an author, he excised homosexuality from his retelling of Jackson's novel in short story form.

In an interesting twist, and for whatever motive, Faulkner's omission led to a good outcome, at least in terms of representations of homosexuality, even as it hurt his ability to write a memorable story with a clear motivation for its protagonist. Faulkner failed to find a suitable replacement to fill in the void left behind by the absence of a motive for Mr. Acarius's behavior. Contemporary medical diagnostics would firmly declare that alcoholics do not need a motivation to drink, but the absence of "motivation" for a character can seriously disrupt good narrative, even if that motivation is erroneously tied to its action. Faulkner's "failure" in regard to "Mr. Acarius" stems from a depiction of alcoholism that was ahead of its time. Mr. Acarius's sense of control is misplaced, but the randomness of his decision making, lacking a source in repressed desires, proves intriguingly, if incidentally, accurate.

After the Lost Weekend

Jackson's gay-themed novel would not be the only gay-themed influence on the apocryphal creations that Faulkner fashioned from the results of his difficult New York trip. The other central figure from this episode in 1948 also provided Faulkner access to close bonds with gay life in the post–World War II decades. Ruth Ford's connection to Faulkner did not begin in October 1948, though her actions during Faulkner's lost weekend lionized her presence in his life. Ford entered Faulkner's life much earlier, as a coed at the University of Mississippi in 1929–1930. A native of Hazlehurst, Mississippi, Ford attended Ole Miss at approximately the same time as Faulkner's brother, Dean. Estelle claimed that Dean and Ford dated and that Dean, a talented painter, had Estelle and Ford sit for him. Victoria (Cho-Cho), barely a teenager at the time, disputed that any relationship existed between Dean and Ford, but Estelle would tell Blotner in 1963 that this relationship, though it "never became truly serious apparently," is why Faulkner not only wrote *Requiem for a Nun* for Ford, but also why he gave her the stage rights with very little requirement on her part for payments to option it until it finally appeared ten years after his initial offer.[16] Ford told Blotner that Dean introduced her to his brother, a struggling writer at the time. Barbara Izard, whose work on the history of the production of *Requiem* also serves as a biography of Ford, recounts, however, that Faulkner introduced himself to Ford, roughly around the time he was composing *As I Lay Dying*. According to Izard, Faulkner approached Ford in the local Oxford landmark, the Tea Hound, to tell her "'You have a very fine face.' Then without further comment, he turned and went back to his table" (31). Though these are, techni-cally, competing narratives, all accounts establish that Ford and Faulkner knew each other in Mississippi in the late 1920s and early 1930s, even if they do not agree on how, precisely, the two met.

Ford would consistently claim that Faulkner promised to write her a play during that week in October 1948, but his earlier acquaintance with her prob-ably also helped lay the groundwork for that promise. Certainly, Ford was a beautiful woman, and if memories of what precisely transpired in Oxford in 1929–1930 are inconsistent, what emerges of Ford is an image of her as a popu-lar campus socialite who attracted Faulkner's eye. In Hollywood in the 1940s, Faulkner would again encounter Ford, this time embodying the idealized south-ern girl expatriated from the South toward whom he gravitated in his extra-marital courtships. Ford would go so far as to claim that, during this period in Hollywood, Faulkner tried to court her. Blotner's interview notes include: "They were never quite lovers, but once he said to her, 'I've been your gentleman friend for quite a while now. Ain't it time I was promoted?'"[17] Faulkner also gave Ford's daughter, Shelley, a hand-bound copy of his unpublished children's book, *The Wishing Tree*.[18]

In 1948 Ford was living in New York and working in Broadway produc-tions but traveling often to Boston to work for the Brattle Theater Company, where, in the early 1950s, she would first attempt to stage *Requiem* with the help of her brother's lover as the set designer. The novel was published in 1951. On 15 September 1951, the *New York Times* announced that Faulkner was work-ing with producer Lemuel Ayers on a stage version of the play to feature Ruth Ford, whom, according to the columnist, Faulkner "had in mind for his leading feminine character."[19] Unfortunately, the production was profoundly delayed. Albert Marre, who was supposed to direct the production in 1951, would cite trouble between Ford's vision and the Brattle's interests as the source of the problem. Ford insisted that her brother's partner, Pavel Tchelitchew, be the set designer.[20] According to Marre, in the spring of 1952 Tchelitchew, Ford's brother Charles, and Ford had a falling out over their creative differences, which led to the death of this first attempt at producing a stage version of the play.[21] Concerning all this theater drama, Marre claimed that "W[illiam] F[aulkner] didn't concern himself" with Ford's decision to turn over set design to her brother's homosexual partner.[22] Other sources do not substantiate Marre's version of events.

In early 1952 Faulkner wrote to Saxe Commins about the play and its production costs, which he asserted that he would cover for a run of the play in Europe. In a detailed discussion of the financing involved in the production, Faulkner paused to write: "The old-Russian painter, [Tchelitchew], will design the sets, getting back to my original version of the script." Faulkner even spelled the difficult name correctly. He took such concern to get it right that, in the typescript of the letter, he left a blank for the name and went back in pencil to write in the name by hand. He went so far as to claim that his faith in the investment to produce the play was based in part on Tchelitchew's involvement: "I am inclined to risk it, since the Russian's idea sounds like me, but mainly on Miss Ford's account, who to an extent has suffered from the delay."[23] The delay and the disagreement that caused it was financial. The creative differences, however, were between the management of the Brattle Theater Company and the Fords (including Charles's life partner Pavel), not between Ford and Tchelitchew. Faulkner not only involved himself with the production, but he also sided with Ford and Tchelitchew.

Through the years-long process of producing the play, Faulkner ultimately let Ford make the decisions about its production. Ford probably told Faulkner that she wanted Tchelitchew to design the sets. Faulkner was happy to agree and put that decision in writing with his own endorsement. Indeed, Faulkner had surely met both Tchelitchew and Charles Henri-Ford during his frequent trips to New York from 1948 to 1952, most likely at the famed social gatherings hosted by the couple in their apartment. Izard charts the history of the weekly salons hosted in Henri-Ford's apartment in the New York landmark, the Dakota, where Ruth Ford would also live until her death in 2009. Though these salons originally started as low-key gatherings of friends, they eventually "included Salvador Dali, Carl Van Vechten, William Carlos Williams, John Huston, and Virgil Thomson" (Izard 38). Modeled after the weekly salons that Gertrude Stein and Alice B. Toklas hosted in Paris, which Henri-Ford had attended in the early 1930s, these salons became legendary, so much so that in her memoir *Just Kids* Patti Smith would lament that by the time she attended the salon in the 1970s, it had lost the luster that made her so excited to attend in the first place (Smith 150). Faulkner had the luxury of attending the salon in its prime. There he would have met Henri-Ford, the young pioneer of surrealism whose first novel, written with his homosexual friend Parker Tyler, stands as one of the original novels of the gay genre in American literature, *The Young and the Evil* (1933). The reputation of that novel would precede it, having been praised by no less than Djuna Barnes and Gertrude Stein. The playful stream-of-consciousness in the novel aligns it with the other great American novels with similar experimental structures from the same period: Jean Toomer's *Cane* (1923), Faulkner's *The Sound and the Fury* (1929), and Barnes's *Nightwood* (1937).

The Young and the Evil details aspects of a gay life in Greenwich Village and Harlem with which Faulkner would have been all too familiar. His own lifelong gay friend Ben Wasson was in the center of that life when Faulkner stayed with him in the late 1920s and early 1930s to revise his novels. We also know that Faulkner slummed it in Harlem at least once in the early 1930s with Carl Van Vechten and his boyfriend. We cannot absolutely verify that Faulkner read this landmark of gay fiction, but he certainly met its author at a salon devoted to discussions of art at that author's home. What most stands out about Faulkner's interactions with Henri-Ford and Tchelitchew is that nothing stands out about them. He was comfortable with the bi-national gay couple and trusted them to "get[] back to my original version of the script" of *Requiem*. Charles Henri-Ford was a key figure that linked Faulkner to Ruth Ford (to Charles Henri-Ford) to Pavel Tchelitchew. So pervasive was his place in this relationship that in both instances where Blotner references Tchelitchew in his biography of Faulkner, he includes Henri-Ford as a collaborator on the project, not just as Ruth's brother or as an anonymous "special friend" (Blotner 2 Vol. 1409, 1419).

Faulkner's interest in Charles Jackson's gay-themed, alcohol-themed novel and his professional relationship with Charles Henri-Ford and Pavel Tchelitchew provide evidence that Faulkner was not singularly homophobic in the latter decades of his life. Perhaps the most immediate influence on Faulkner's life, however, was much closer to home, in fact just twenty miles south of Rowan Oak on the railroad, just across the Yocona River (Yoknapatawpha on hand-drawn maps of Faulkner's mythic postage stamp). In 1948 Faulkner published *Intruder in the Dust*. In 1948 two landmarks of the American gay novel were published, *The City and the Pillar* and *Other Voices, Other Rooms*, the latter a southern gay novel that might have made Faulkner "nervous." Another gay-themed novel was published in 1948, however, by an author from Water Valley, Mississippi, a gay author whom Faulkner not only knew but had once even endorsed to his then-publisher Harrison Smith. In 1948 Hubert Creekmore published *The Welcome*. More than his other influences, this novel may have most influenced Faulkner's depiction of homosexuality in the 1950s because it provided an element lacking in Faulkner's previous works and in the other major gay fiction of the period and was perhaps even lacking in Faulkner's inner life and sense of self since his return to Oxford to marry Estelle. *The Welcome* placed open homosexuality in the heart of Faulkner's immediate South, just a little way down the road, in a town that is even willing to accept it from two boys who grew up there, even if they do not realize that acceptance until too late.

The Nearby Gay South

The Welcome tells the story of Don Mason and James (Jim) Furlow, two young men from the fictional town of Ashton, Mississippi. As teenagers in the late 1920s, Don and Jim were best friends and always together. In the mid-1930s, as the novel begins, Jim is married to Doris, a coed from Ole Miss, though they sleep in separate beds. Don has been living in New York, where he moved just before Jim and Doris's wedding, but he is returning to Ashton to take care of his ailing mother. We discover over the course of the novel that Don's flight was a product of Jim's rejection. As young men, they had fallen in love but could not articulate that love. Don, finally, tried to express it, but only after Jim had met and courted Doris. Don flees to New York, that bohemian city not unfamiliar to Faulkner, to escape his desires when Jim fails to acknowledge that he feels the same way. In the wake of Don's departure, Jim comes to realize too late what he felt for Don. He marries, but his marriage is horrifying. Doris turns out to be a monster, representative of all the worst aspects of heterosexual unions between two people who marry because marriage is expected rather than because they love each other. Jim and Doris's relationship speaks directly to Faulkner's letter from 1925 on what is the matter with marriage. If Creekmore never read that letter, his novel nonetheless shared the spirit of its thesis.

When Don returns, Jim's marriage is coming apart. Don, however, has returned not only for his mother, but also because he could not make a life for himself in New York. To return, he has decided to accept the life of expectation in his small Mississippi town. He courts Isabel, the local tomboy-turned-woman, who was also Jim's girlfriend in high school before he married the more conventional Doris. As Jim comes to accept and articulate his love for Don, Don in turn rejects Jim for the comfortable, quiet life of the institution of heterosexual marriage in Ashton that Jim has realized is not what he ever wanted, but now he finally knows that he wants Don. The final scene of the novel is one of utter tragedy. Don leaves with his new bride, but Jim must return upstairs to Doris, who has grown increasingly grotesque in her representation of all the evils of a conventional "woman." Jim's misery has been amplified by Don's return. He makes one last move for Don, a move that signifies his willingness to leave Doris, but Don's rebuff at that critical moment relegates Jim forever to the stifling confines of the marriage he had chosen long ago, before he realized the true love of his life, Don, was slipping away.

The Welcome is a novel of error and punishment. Creekmore begins it with a quotation from Marlowe's *Faustus* and ends it with the living death of Jim sinking into the inescapable confines of the inflexible conventions of small-town life, as if swallowed up by the earth itself for his transgressions against his true desires. The homosexual element of the novel becomes its fulcrum, despite its not being the focus of the novel in Creekmore's original drafts. When Creekmore first began *The Welcome*, under the title *Fulcrum*, he wrote as part of the synopsis of the novel for his publishers that

> The theme of the novel is the responsibilities of the man and the woman in a marriage, to each other and to their contract. A second but equally important theme will be the relation of marriage to the environment in which it occurs, in this particular case a small southern town. These themes will be objectified by the attitudes of two couples, *one* already married and *another* moving toward marriage.[24]

Creekmore apparently did not originally intend for the plot to revolve around the problem of articulating homosexual desire, but around the crisis of marriage by contract rather than marriage by love in a town stifled by convention and forcing young men and women into a preset mold that does not always fit them. After completing the novel, Creekmore was more direct about the central problem that he included as he wrote it—not the loveless marriage of a man and a woman, but the loveless marriage of a man and a woman when the man loves another man. In a summary of the novel from shortly after he finished it, Creekmore explained that "the choice of *not* marrying" was predicated on "submerged homosexuality to dramatize the negative choice" of marrying without love or even desire.[25] Creekmore's shift from a general critique of marriage to a critique predicated on homosexual desire developed simultaneously to his other significant editorial decision as he wrote the book. He decided to revise the setting.

Originally, Creekmore set the action after World War II, contemporary to when he wrote the novel, but in drafting it, he changed that setting to the prewar 1930s. This decision parallels Creekmore's own life to the extent that he graduated from Ole Miss in the late 1920s and would have been, therefore, about the same age as Don and Jim, his two protagonists, in their fictional time frame. Creekmore's actual life was probably closer to Don's than Jim's fictional biography. Creekmore attempted to move to New York in 1930 but returned to Mississippi in the early 1930s. His attempt to move to New York was motivated by a manuscript for a novel he wrote in the years after his graduation. It appears he showed this manuscript to William Faulkner and his old friend Phil Stone because of deep connections between Stone, Faulkner, and the Creekmore family from even earlier, in the first years after Faulkner returned from the war. The extent of these connections is deep enough that it provides reason to believe Faulkner may have followed Creekmore's career well into the 1940s and read

The Welcome, and possibly even recognized the similarities between it and the plot of that earlier, ultimately unpublished manuscript.

The late 1920s and early 1930s found Creekmore in Oxford working on a novel he would title *The Elephant's Trunk*. The story follows the rebellion of Ruth Anderson, who explores her sexuality with her first boyfriend, Walter, falls in love with a young man named Robert at the university, but ultimately marries the lower-class Drake Mullins. The novel is set in Mississippi primarily in the town wherein is located the state university. Rather than name that town Oxford, however, Creekmore called the town Lowry.[26] Walter and Ruth part ways when Walter leaves to fight in World War I. The novel ends approximately ten years later, in the late 1920s, contemporary to when Creekmore wrote it, with Ruth having two young sons whose ages place the climax of the novel around 1928. Ruth has married Drake out of pure lust because he represents the proverbial "bad boy" of whom her parents would not approve. He also looks very much like Robert, Ruth's second boyfriend who replaced Walter as the object of her affections, only Drake has rougher edges and stronger hands. Ruth embraces the scorn of her town and the rejection of her parents in her delight that she has broken away from convention and married "the wrong man." Of course, after the initial romance wears off, she finds herself poor and miserable. After years of a miserable, abusive marriage, she begins to fantasize about Robert, the emblem of a more polished version of Drake, whom she could have married instead. When she runs away to Jackson to find Robert, Drake follows her and kills her in a fit of jealous rage.

The moral of the story is that marriage is a contract, and an inescapable one. In his first novel, Creekmore devastatingly critiqued this contract, especially when a couple enters into it for the wrong reasons. Ruth attempts to escape the expectations of a "proper" marriage by making an "improper" marriage, but her biggest mistake is that she marries at all. Once she has married, the town expects her to follow through with her obligations, even if they kill her. Those obligations do, in fact, kill her. Robert, her "proper" beau, refuses to help her when she tries to run away from Drake. He contacts Drake when Ruth appears in Jackson to re-court him. His sense of the proprieties of marriage—Ruth belongs to Drake in his view—directly causes Ruth's death. That death, then, is the inescapable fate that Ruth chose when she married in the first place. Creekmore closely repeated this critique of marriage in *The Welcome*, only Ruth becomes Jim and Robert becomes Don. The prior heterosexual relationship that might have proven better for Ruth becomes the prior homosexual desire that could have saved Jim from his disastrous marriage and signals impending tragedy for Don for not recognizing that his own marriage will probably be similarly flawed. Don refuses Jim and instead decides that he will marry Isabel and, so, will leave Jim to his chosen fate, though the bitter irony is that Robert's punishment of Ruth and Don's of Jim stem from their own slighted feelings from before Ruth married Drake or Jim married Doris. In both novels the chosen marriage is a responsibility that stifles the free expression of a better, prior love.

The key difference is that Ruth *could have married* Robert. Don and Jim could not marry, but Creekmore does not suggest that Don and Jim could not find peace together. In fact, they might find more peace than Ruth would ever attain even with Robert. In both novels, marriage is the problem, not love. Even between two people who love each other, marriage confines expectations and demands the performance of rigid duties and obligations. Marrying Robert would not have saved Ruth from the tragedy of her life. Robert's decision to inform Drake about Ruth's presence in Jackson does more than simply make him a maintainer of the status quo. Ruth dies. Robert helps bring about her death. Don's marriage implicates his decision to maintain the status quo, but he does not kill Jim, at least not literally. Oddly, Don clearly understands the problem with marriage. Early in *The Welcome*, he summarizes the tragedy of (married) life as he walks around his town in the wake of his return, before he begins to court Isabel:

> All around his horizon, the houses he no longer felt close to, the houses that must already have shut him away, lifted their roofs above the trees along the two ridges of Ashton. They secretly guarded their inhabitants and held them silent in their walls and made those mysterious in the night who in the day were trivial. The warm breeze brushed over the town, like an ineffectual blessing; in the east the deep yellow arc of the moon had thrust above the hills. But only he saw it tonight. And only he saw the houses imprisoning the people, the people imprisoning each other and each person imprisoning his own heart in the dark silent fear of community. (79)

Unfortunately, Don believes he can reenter the mystery of his hometown by embracing the very expectations that he recognizes as the prison of the heart. Don's sensibilities address the same anxieties that Ruth Anderson encounters, but transferring them to a homosexual couple alters the implications of Don's actions and makes them truly tragic, in the classical sense of the word. Unlike for Ruth, who would have married someone, Don and Jim could have escaped and could have made a new world for themselves. Don even sees the nature of the tragedy before him and then inexplicably embraces it for himself. That Don can recognize that there is a way out for him and Jim—a way for the two of them to save themselves—signals the "recognition" of classical tragedy. The conclusion, wherein Don departs for his honeymoon while Jim returns to his wife upstairs, models the "reversal." Don's blindness—his *hamartia*—prevents his connecting his recognition to his own fate. His fault is a form of *hubris*. He thinks he can make a better marriage and not find himself as shattered as Jim. In truth, he and Jim together have the best chance at happiness, but they miss the proverbial mark. As a tragedy, *The Welcome* is masterfully constructed on a simple flaw in the universal order: these two men cannot see the love right in front of them because theirs is a world that hides love in an institution and closets desires into the illicit or unspoken realms of the seemingly impossible. The town survives on the sacrifice of its youth to its prescribed order. Everyone stays on the sidewalks. No one cuts across the grass.

The first question, of course, is, did Faulkner read *The Welcome*? The second question is, did it influence his own writing? He read *The Elephant's Trunk*— in fact, he seems to have offered to recommend it to his own publisher. Proof that Faulkner read Creekmore's first novel comes from a letter that Creekmore wrote to Phil Stone, and the background that led to that letter might well answer both questions, at least as far as speculation allows for making reasoned inferences. Hiram Hubert Creekmore Jr. was born in 1907 in Water Valley, the third son of an established family (his father was a judge). As a thirteen-year-old, Creekmore would watch a series of events unfold on the Ole Miss campus in the fall of 1920 from the safe distance of the neighboring county. The events significantly influenced the course of Faulkner's life and involved Creekmore's father and his two older brothers, both students at the university. The ripples of those events would eventually reach Creekmore, and so they deserve some consideration to establish why these events would have played such a role over such a long period of time.[27]

The connection between Creekmore and Faulkner began in a fraternity and extended to the Southern Protective Association. When Faulkner enrolled at Ole Miss on a special dispensation for returning veterans, he befriended Ben Wasson, a young man whom he had met briefly before the war. Wasson subsequently left Ole Miss to attend Sewanee for the remainder of his undergraduate career. At Sewanee, Wasson joined the Sigma Alpha Epsilon fraternity. He returned to Ole Miss for his law degree after the war, where he also reestablished his friendship with Faulkner and began to pressure Faulkner to rush SAE. Faulkner was also pressured to rush SAE by his other close friend in Oxford, Phil Stone, a member of the fraternity from his own undergraduate days at Yale. In fact, the entire Stone family, the male members anyway, were all SAEs and active in the Ole Miss chapter even after their matriculations. Furthermore, Faulkner's uncle John Wesley Thomas Falkner Jr. had rushed SAE while attending Ole Miss for Law School. Family pressures convinced Murry (Jack) Falkner to rush SAE when he enrolled at Ole Miss in 1919. William joined his brother and went through the initiation ceremony at the home of Jim Stone, Phil Stone's father, just north of the campus. As I have previously argued, the walk back through the woods with Ben Wasson after the initiation ceremony would inform Faulkner's early poem "Portrait," but William and Jack were not the only two young pledges initiated that night. They were joined by Rufus Creekmore, a star tackle on the Ole Miss football team and, generally, a campus socialite and former member of the extremely exclusive Red and Blue Club. Rufus was beginning his law degree when he rushed SAE. His younger brother Wade joined him. Two Creekmores and two Fa(u)lkners rushed SAE at the Stone home, also site of Faulkner's "musical sessions" with Ben Wasson when the Stones were away.[28] The deeply ingrained commitments to fraternity brothers forged in the uniquely hierarchical world of Ole Miss is difficult to explain to outsiders—one really must witness it firsthand to believe it—but in the case of the bonds forged among this group of Ole Miss SAEs, more would come to link them than their mere attendance at Ole Miss and a predilection for a common social group.

The reason this initiation occurred off campus was because in 1919, fraternities were banned at Ole Miss. This ban extended from a 1912 law passed by the state legislature barring all "secret societies" on the campus. The ban itself had its origins ten years earlier, in 1902, when a young country boy from Lafayette County named Lee Russell attended Ole Miss for his own law degree before going to work for a local lawyer and politician in Oxford, Faulkner's grandfather, J. W. T. Falkner Sr. In 1902, Russell had been denied entry into the campus system of elite social clubs because, despite his admittance to Ole Miss for Law School, he was a poor white who lacked the appropriate social status. Enraged at being snubbed, Russell began a campaign to ban what he called "secret societies" on the campus. By 1912, he managed to get a law passed to that effect, but the *de jure* limitations on active practices by these societies simply resulted in a *de facto* continuation of their practices in a "sub rosa" capacity. A perfect example of this sub rosa activity was the fraternity SAE, which continued to initiate members but did so off campus at the home of a well-to-do lawyer and SAE alumnus, Jim Stone.[29]

Lee Russell was not fooled by the de facto situation on the campus. When he completed his meteoric political rise in 1920 by winning the governorship of Mississippi, he traveled to Ole Miss to exact his revenge. Understanding the system that had spurned him all too well, Russell went after members of the legal campus group, the Red and Blue Club, a group of twenty seniors chosen by the previous year's twenty senior members and sponsors of a university dance. The head of this group, Lowery Simmons, found himself the brunt of a blistering attack by Russell in a private interview in the chancellor's office that quickly turned from a discussion of the Red and Blue Club to an assault on the elitist fraternity system. At one point, Russell, now governor of the state, asked if he would be allowed entry into any of these clubs given his current status. Simmons assured him that he would not with the insolent but marvelously witty rejoinder: "Governor, you still wouldn't get in."[30] In response, Russell greatly curtailed the plans for the Red and Blue dance, a staple event of the campus social scene. Outraged by Russell's actions, the student body rose up in protest and burned the governor in effigy in the Grove, the famous green space on the eastern edge of campus overlooking the railroad depot at the bottom of the hill. In response to the protest, Russell pulled his ace out of his sleeve. Simmons was also a member of SAE. Despite lacking proof that any one social group was responsible for the burning, Russell proceeded to declare that the "secret societies" he abhorred, namely the sub rosa fraternities, were responsible for the protest and demanded that all students sign a pledge stating that they were not members of any such groups. Russell's ace was that he knew the same gentlemanly code that refused to grant him entry into these societies would also bar students from swearing an oath that they were not members of a society when, in fact, they were. Failure to sign the pledge would result in dismissal from Ole Miss.

With their backs against the wall, the SAEs met nightly at the home of Jim Stone. Central to these meetings was the nightly presence of Hiram Hubert Creekmore Sr., a local judge who came up from Water Valley to advise his sons and the other members of SAE on the wisest course of action.[31] Finally, as the 10 November deadline for signing the pledge approached, Judge Creekmore advised the SAEs to withdraw from the university rather than be dismissed. His own sons withdrew, both transferring to the University of Alabama for the remainder of the school year.[32] Wade returned to Ole Miss for his junior year and listed his membership in SAE with his yearbook picture, relying on the claim that he had joined legally at Alabama though he had, in fact, joined the fraternity while he was at Ole Miss. Rufus would transfer to Yale in the fall of 1921 to finish his law degree. Legally an SAE from Sewanee, Ben Wasson was not obliged to withdraw. William and Jack Fa(u)lkner withdrew under the advice of Judge Creekmore. Jack later reenrolled and finished his degree. William Faulkner never returned to Ole Miss as a student, though he did maintain his close ties to the theater group on campus, the Marionettes. In the fall of 1921, when he first attempted to leave Oxford for New York, with the encouragement of Stark Young, Faulkner found himself temporarily in New Haven, Connecticut. While there he reencountered Rufus Creekmore and wrote home to his mother that, "I saw Rufus Creekmore across the street yesterday. Law school, I imagine" (*Thinking of Home* 148). In later interviews, Rufus recalled spending time with Faulkner in New Haven during that fall semester.[33] Their shared rebellion and exile gave them much in common beyond the usual fraternal bonds.

Faulkner made little effort as a student, and he likely did not feel as strongly as his fellow SAEs did about the crisis of 1920. His walk back to campus through the woods with Ben Wasson following his initiation, along with Wasson's account of Faulkner's reaction to the ceremony, suggest that Faulkner was not particularly dedicated to the fraternity itself. He seems to have joined at the behest of his friends and family. He certainly did not speak of his membership or the crisis that forced his withdrawal very often in his later life. One of the few times in his later life when he would mention his SAE membership, however, came in 1951 when Jeff Hamm, another SAE from 1920, asked Faulkner to convince a young student, Billy Ross Brown, to rush SAE at Ole Miss. Brown would recall Faulkner's advice years later in his interview with Blotner. "[F]raternities didn't mean a whole lot," and "you got out of fraternities what you put into them," Faulkner told Brown, yet despite this seeming indifference, Brown also claimed that Faulkner added, "if he [Faulkner] had any influence on [Brown], he'd appreciate his going SAE."[34] Faulkner's tacit acceptance of his commitments to fraternity brothers would extend to more than just Brown. He also extended that commitment to the younger brother of his fellow SAEs Rufus and Wade Creekmore. Their younger brother Hubert attended Ole Miss from 1923 to 1927. When Hubert made his own attempt to conquer New York in 1930, with a manuscript of a novel in hand, he turned to Faulkner for assistance.

The extent of Hubert Creekmore's relationship with Faulkner at Ole Miss proves as enigmatic to detail as Faulkner's relationship with Ford from her undergraduate days. Creekmore attended Ole Miss beginning in the fall of 1923, during William Faulkner's tenure as the university postmaster. Faulkner's job would have made him a central figure on the campus (one can only surmise how important the postmaster was on a university campus without wireless Internet and e-mail). As for Creekmore, he would establish himself on campus as something of a literary nerd, even earning a reputation akin to Faulkner's "Count No 'Count" nickname. Creekmore fashioned himself as the campus "literary vagabond,"[35] but whereas Faulkner rushed the social fraternity SAE with Creekmore's brothers, Hubert Creekmore preferred to join the campus literary fraternity, the Scribblers, which had rejected Faulkner during his days as a student. Creekmore did not rush SAE, or at least he did not claim that he had on his list of affiliations in the yearbook even though fraternities were allowed back on campus while Hubert was still a student there. During Creekmore's tenure on campus from 1923 to 1927, Faulkner was in and out of Oxford, and no evidence remains of a meeting between the two in the Tea Hound or the post office, but Creekmore did contribute to and eventually assistant edit the campus humor magazine *The Scream*, to which Faulkner contributed three drawings in 1925. He also joined the Marionettes and acted in several of their productions.[36]

By 1930, three years after his graduation, Creekmore had completed a novel and wanted to sell it to a publisher in New York. Notably, he did not turn to Ben Wasson, a former SAE with connections to the Marionettes and also active in the Southern Protective Association in New York. Wasson left Greenville for New York in 1927, the year Creekmore graduated. From 1927 to 1930, Wasson spent little time in Mississippi. Conversely, Faulkner spent much of his time in Oxford during those years, returning from New Orleans in 1927 to begin his serious courtship of Estelle. Faulkner's only significant trips away from Oxford from 1927 to 1930 included his honeymoon and his trips to New York to work

on drafts of his novels *Sartoris* and *The Sound and the Fury* for his publisher
Harrison Smith (Faulkner's regard for Hal Smith survives in the dedication to
As I Lay Dying), but generally, Faulkner was in Oxford for those three years.
Still haunting Oxford himself, Creekmore befriended Phil Stone and William
Faulkner, friends of his brothers from SAE and literary men with whom he
could discuss the latest literary trends and share drafts of his novel. In fact,
in *The Welcome*, Creekmore depicted Stone's influence on his writing in the
character of Horace Saxon, the town newspaper editor. Saxon refused one of
Don Mason's childhood poems to protect him because "[t]hink what might
have happened if [Saxon had] printed that poem" in all its youthful ineptitude.
Rather, when Saxon realized that Don had a taste for literature, he "gave [Don]
books to read instead of encouraging him to write bad ones" (103). These books
and other reading materials included "*The New Republic*, and a literary [maga-
zine], *The Dial*, and *Poetry* and other strange and wild publications" (26). Don
dutifully shared these materials with Jim during their courtship as teenagers,
part of their shared dreams about moving on to bigger places than Ashton and
its provincialism. The reading list is curious, of course, because of its similarities
to the one Stone also shared with a young William Faulkner in the 1910s and
early 1920s. Significantly, Horace Saxon's name blends two influences, though
it suggests a third. The first, Lyle Saxon, was the central figure in the Southern
Protective Association in New York in the early 1930s. In 1930, Creekmore was
headed in Saxon's direction. The second, Phil Stone, appeared in Faulkner's fiction originally as the character Horace Benbow, though he reappeared later
and much more fully as Gavin Stevens. Stone was the man in Oxford who was
trying to help Creekmore make his big move. In the reference to Stone, however, Faulkner's presence emerges. Horace Benbow was a central character in
Faulkner's 1928 novel *Flags in the Dust*. The bridge between Saxon and Stone is
Faulkner. He was also the bridge between Mississippi and New York.

As Creekmore finished his manuscript, Stone asked Faulkner for help introducing his new local protégé to the publishing world in New York. Faulkner
apparently read Creekmore's manuscript and offered to introduce the young literary vagabond to Harrison Smith. Writing from the Stevens Hotel in Chicago
on 24 May 1930 on his way to New York, Creekmore reminded Stone that he
still needed that letter:

Dear Phil:

I meant to write to you just before I left to ask Bill Faulkner to send me the
letter to Harrison Smith. But I got off in such a rush that I hadn't time. I have my
book completed and typed and am now on my way to New York to storm the
publishers. I'd never know how to thank both of you enough if you could help
me with Mr. Smith. I can imagine it's a pretty hard task for an outsider to break
through the book publishing game. At present I don't know where I shall stay in

New York but you can address me in care of Miss Judith Page, 11 Van Dorn Street, until I wire you where I am.

> Hastily but sincerely,
> Hubert Creekmore[37]

Faulkner's role in this relationship was to play the mediator between Oxford and New York. He took an interest in Creekmore and seems to have offered to help smooth his transition. This help very likely included introductions to Wasson and Saxon, who very likely helped solve Creekmore's other problem that he mentioned in his letter: where he would stay once he arrived. Though Wasson would not have been in Oxford during Creekmore's maturation toward his first novel from 1927 to 1930, he would have been the contact man in New York. Lyle Saxon would have provided the slow-drip coffee. Faulkner provided the glue that held these pieces together. Though it requires significant speculation, I think it is entirely plausible to conclude that Creekmore appreciated the help.

Recommendation aside, Creekmore's first and eventually his second manuscripts would not be accepted for publication. He would spend most of the 1930s in Jackson, Mississippi. He would publish poetry, if not fiction, including selections in a 1933 volume *Mississippi Verse*, where his poems would appear alongside a selection of Faulkner's poems. He would eventually pursue a master's degree at Columbia University. In 1946 he would finally "break through the book publishing game" with his first published novel *The Fingers of Night*. In 1948 he would follow that novel with *The Welcome*, and then publish a third novel in 1952, *The Chain in the Heart*. It is entirely reasonable to assume that Faulkner followed the career of this former fellow literary vagabond from Ole Miss. It is equally reasonable to assume that when Faulkner read *The Welcome*, he recognized the themes of marriage that Creekmore included in all his novels, beginning with his first novel, which Faulkner recommended to the most important publisher in his life. In *The Welcome* the problem of marriage revolves around a fulcrum of suppressed homosexual desires deep in the heart of north Mississippi, the landscape with which Faulkner was so familiar, with which he is now so universally associated, and in which, on a hillside in Oxford, he has come to his eternal rest.

What makes Creekmore's gay novel so thematically pertinent to Faulkner's writing is a matter of geography. Creekmore modeled Ashton after his hometown of Water Valley, just over the border from Lafayette County in neighboring Yalobusha County. On Faulkner's map of Yoknapatawpha, he transforms Water Valley into Mottstown, the next town south on the railroad and over the Yoknapatawpha River. The real Water Valley lies slightly to the southwest of Oxford, over the Yocona River, but it is the next incorporated town south on the now-defunct rail line. Don and Jim inhabit a town wherein nearly everyone owns a car (Gus Traywick, their mutual friend, owns a car dealership); where jazz music plays in the movie theater before the nightly show begins; where townswomen meet at the drugstore during the day to drink ice-filled Coca-Colas; and where Isabel nonchalantly displays on her walls prints by Marie Laurencin, a French Cubist painter. These mass-market prints serve as something of a stark contrast to Darl Bundren's utterly out-of-place reference to a "cubistic bug" during the river crossing scene of *As I Lay Dying* (the Bundrens were attempting to cross the Yoknapatawpha/Yocona River). *As I Lay Dying* and *The Welcome* are set in the same temporal moment, the former in approximately 1929, the latter in the early 1930s. In the former, Darl is alone and cannot find someone else like him to share his life and his desires. In the latter, two men almost find happiness together but miss it because they are too blind to see the love that they could embrace. Darl searches for union but never finds anyone close to his home to unite with. Jim and Don fail, and their story is a tragedy, but that tragedy is rooted in the hope that they *could* be together, if they could escape their blind acceptance of tradition. Jim and Don are not alone.

The utter modernity of Ashton is striking, especially in comparison to Faulkner's nearby Jefferson, but Ashton also remains a town clearly rooted to its traditions. What Faulkner would have been able see in Ashton was a reflection of Jefferson, a town troubled by the same conventions and equally inescapable for the rigidity with which one must adhere to its expectations. If, however, Faulkner could never find a way to place homosexuality in his Jefferson without also having to represent its troubled presence and its (often violent) removal from the community, in Creekmore's novel, he would see a different possibility. In Creekmore's novel, the setting is thoroughly modernized, and the young people are eager to embrace a new world. Jim even comes out to Gus Traywick on a hunting expedition to explain the tension between him and Don since Don's return. Though Gus is surprised by the revelation, he nonetheless continues to consider both Don and Jim as his friends. The problem in *The Welcome* is not that gay people attempt to live in the rural South at all, but that they fail to realize that they could find each other in that landscape if they would only open their eyes to the possibility that someone else there feels the same way—not only feels that way but maybe even realizes that they do not have to care if anyone knows about it, to paraphrase the youth in "Out of Nazareth" as he praised the poetry of A. E. Housman to two gay men cruising in Jackson Square. In Creekmore's gay novel, Faulkner would find homosexuality at the heart of a narrative set in his own backyard. His own gay narratives set in New Orleans or Europe or his "queer" characters beaten down and sent away by their families in Jefferson had never been so daring. Explicit gay narratives, such as Capote's *Other Voices, Other Rooms*, made Faulkner nervous, or so he claimed. Creekmore's novel would have allowed Faulkner to face homosexuality in rural north Mississippi and not be made nervous by it, for this world *is* his world, this life *his* life.

Given Faulkner's gay exposure in the 1940s and 1950s, we should not be surprised that he would return in his later career to the themes of his early prose and poetry, only revised into a new vision connected to the latter half of his life and the cultural moments he lived through during it. He had before him numerous models. He did not warrant all these models as correct and some of them even made him "nervous." Some, however, exposed possibilities for how to view and express homosexuality that were not so burdened by rigid spatial dichotomies. These influences created an imaginative space in which to place homosexuality despite the challenges that seem to encumber it there, in that South, in the heart of Yoknapatawpha. When he had at his disposal a basis to return to his explorations of homosexual themes in the latter 1950s, he embarked on a project to complete his great epic of his mythical county and evolved in that epic a character whose implicit critique of the rigid structures of sexuality saturates *The Town* and *The Mansion*. As a character present in the earliest stories that Faulkner wrote about his apocryphal county, V. K. Ratliff is an ever-changing but ubiquitous figure thoroughly at the heart of his small community and, in his final incarnations, decidedly emblematic of Cold War homosexuality. Ratliff is one of Faulkner's greatest achievements, his Falstaff with a pressed shirt and apron, and even Faulkner would admit that he simply fell in love with him.

Chapter 9

V. K. Ratliff, a Biography

The character who would become V. K. Ratliff is as old as Yoknapatawpha County, there from its conception in one form or fashion, there in the major works of the 1930s, and there finally in his own novel in 1940, *The Hamlet*, and again a major character in the latter two Snopes novels, *The Town* and *The Mansion*, the third to last and second to last novels of Faulkner's career. Of all Faulkner's characters, Ratliff is the most ubiquitous, though his ever-changing presentation makes him more the great trickster figure of Yoknapatawpha than its vicar or its spokesperson. Originally named Suratt, Ratliff came to occupy such a central place in Faulkner's imagination that in 1945 Faulkner would explain to Malcolm Cowley that, as he began laying the groundwork for what would become *The Hamlet* in the mid-1920s, this character stood out:

> [It] was incepted as a novel. When I began it, it produced "Spotted Horses," went no further. About two years later I had "The Hound," then "Jamshyd's Courtyard," mainly because "Spotted Horses" had created *a character I fell in love with*: *the itinerant sewing-machine agent named Suratt*. Later a man of that name turned up at home, so I changed my man to Ratliff for the reason that my whole town spent much of its time trying to decide just what living man I was writing about, the one literary criticism in town being "How the hell did he remember all that, and when did it happen anyway?" (26, italics added)

This explanation is, in miniature, the process of apocryphization for William Faulkner, with one minor detail misremembered. A man named Suratt did not show up after the character. Rather, the character was based on a man named Suratt. When the real Suratt objected to Faulkner's using his name, it forced the crucial shift when Faulkner changed Suratt into Ratliff, for legal as well as literary reasons, sometime in the late 1930s. The moment of that critical change sparked a revision of Ratliff so compelling that even Faulkner may not have realized at the time what he had done, though by the late 1950s, he seems to have understood it. When Faulkner changed Suratt to Ratliff, he created a gay character fully realized in a southern landscape and central to its very existence.

In the Beginning

J. M. Coetzee offers a succinct, if somewhat reductive (though only somewhat), overview of the moment when Faulkner first realized the artistic vision that would become his mythic county. Describing the young writer after his return from Europe in 1925, Coetzee epitomizes the general impression of Faulkner as a "would-be writer of unusual doggedness but no great gifts" (192). Although *Soldiers' Pay* and *Mosquitoes* proved he could write novels, the lightning bolt of genius had not built up the charge in these early works to impress as more than just potential. Then, as if out of nowhere, Faulkner "would sit down and write a 14,000 word sketch bursting with ideas and characters which would lay the groundwork for the series of great novels of the years 1929–1942. The manuscript contained, in embryo, Yoknapatawpha County" (192). Coetzee's summary elides a few key details. First, that groundwork would people novels until 1962, not just 1942. Second, those 14,000 words were just broad brushstrokes for a collage that would change much and to which Faulkner would add a great deal, in characters and history, as the mood struck him for each new novel that he produced. Those 14,000 words were not in themselves the entirety of Yoknapatawpha. Nonetheless, Coetzee's implicit comparison between Faulkner's sketch and the Big Bang holds true. In that sketch, Faulkner's vision emanated as a proverbial series of subatomic particles and other loose radicals that would, as they cooled in the expanding ether, condense to form larger, more complex particles that would, in turn, support the structure of a cosmos all his own.

That original manuscript was the outline of a never-completed novel called *Father Abraham*, a story about the rise of poor whites into positions of power in the South, primarily in the figure of Flem Snopes. At roughly the same time, Faulkner began working on the inverse story, the decline and fall of an old aristocratic southern family, the Sartorises. The former he put aside to pursue the latter, which became *Flags in the Dust*, though it was rejected by his publisher Boni and Liveright. With the help of Ben Wasson's editing, that "first" Yoknapatawpha novel appeared under the impress of Cape and Smith as the much-shortened *Sartoris*. Faulkner then turned his attention to newly created characters for newly conceived novels set in the same geographic location—the Compsons, the Bundrens, Temple Drake, Joe Christmas, the Sutpens—few of whom ostensibly featured in that original manuscript but all of whom grew from it much as the biblical tradition explains that God promised to Abraham of his descendants that they would number more than the stars. Yet, alongside the novels he wrote in the 1930s, Faulkner also continued to tinker with stories directly related to the original manuscript of *Father Abraham*. This tinkering eventually produced a series of stories from the late 1920s and into the mid-1930s that would become, after numerous and extensive revisions, the picaresque novel *The Hamlet* in 1940.

The central influence in the creation of the Snopes/Sartoris material, originally two sides of one larger story of the "South," was Phil Stone, in whose front
office of his law firm on the Square in Oxford Faulkner would spend many
an afternoon trading and embellishing stories of the townspeople whom he
and Stone observed around them every day. Although especially later in his
life, Faulkner was reluctant to credit Stone's influence too emphatically, he dedicated both *The Town* and *The Mansion* to Stone, the former with the note: "To
Phil Stone: He did half the laughing for thirty years" (*T* 352).[1] Elements of Stone
informed the creation of Horace Benbow in the early novels, but Stone's greatest
presence in Faulkner's apocryphal county is clearly reflected in Gavin Stevens,
not only the counterpoint in Jefferson to Flem Snopes and "Snopesism" but
also the confidant and co-conspirator of V. K. Ratliff. The suggestive relationship between the apocryphal Stevens and Ratliff implicates the degree to which
Ratliff, the man Faulkner fell in love with, was, in large part, an apocryphal version of Faulkner himself.

From the collusion of these two minds in that front office, the young writer
of "unusual doggedness" created Yoknapatawpha. Though the two men talked
Yoknapatawpha into existence in the late 1920s, Faulkner would finally articulate his creative process from that earlier time in 1955 in marvelously poetic
language that has been central to Faulkner studies and extensively informs the
structure of the study of his life and works you are currently reading:

> Beginning with *Sartoris* I discovered that my own little postage stamp of native
> soil was worth writing about and that I would never live long enough to exhaust
> it, and by sublimating the actual into apocryphal I would have complete liberty to
> use whatever talent I might have to its absolute top. It opened up a gold mine of
> other peoples, so I created a cosmos of my own. I can move these people around
> like God, not only in space but in time too. (*Lion* 255)

In considering this genesis moment of Faulkner's creative vision, Coetzee
explains the debt that Faulkner owed for the philosophical origins of this
perspective not just to Stone but to a book Stone recommended to him, *The
Creative Will*, by Willard Huntingdon Wright. In that book, Wright claimed that
the artist must be "an omnipotent god who moulds and fashions the destiny of a
new world" (qtd. in Coetzee 192). Intriguingly, Coetzee establishes that Wright's
aesthetic principles derive from his being "a disciple of Walter Pater," the nineteenth scholar of same-sex desires in Renaissance art (192). This genealogy—
Pater to Wright to Faulkner—found subcutaneous to the original inspiration of
Faulkner's genius implicates the degree to which the entire so-called Southern
Renascence, of which Faulkner is considered a prime progenitor, can trace parts
of its origins to same-sex erotic influences. Such a genealogy, an erotics of aesthetic patrimony, lends credence to Eve Sedgwick's claim that we will recognize

a renaissance by "where and how the power in them of gay desires, people, discourses, prohibitions, and energies were manifest" (*Epistemology* 58). In Ratliff/
Suratt's "bland and affable" but ever-changing face, Faulkner would produce a
manifestation of these "desires, people, discourses, prohibitions, and energies."
Thus, in the twilight of *The Mansion*, at the end of Faulkner's brilliant career,
as Ratliff leads Gavin Stevens to find Mink Snopes, we can recognize that this
cosmos of Faulkner's own is a gay cosmos and the heart of Yoknapatawpha is a
gay voice still talking beyond the end of its world and into ours.

Conception

V. K. Ratliff was born on 27 April 1894, in the pages of the now-defunct local
newspaper, the *Oxford Globe*, when "a wholesale dealer in sewing machines
advertised for a local man with a suitable rig of horse and wagon to become
his traveling agent in the countryside around Oxford" (Williamson 133). A man
named James Suratt answered that ad, though in town he seems to have gone
by the nickname Junius, or June for short.[2] Maud Faulkner would remember in
an interview in 1953:

> We had a June Suratt here who sold sewing machines in Lafayette County from
> about 1910 to 1925. He lived in a little house just off the Square. On the bed of
> his wagon, he had a little doghouse painted to look like a sewing machine as
> advertising. We used to see his wagon whenever he was in town. Billy used him
> in quite a few of his early stories. Later, I guess he thought he ought to change
> the name to Ratliff.[3]

Though only minimally useful for identifying a person's living situation, census
records imply that this man was a family man, that he was probably not native
to Lafayette County but rather an itinerant worker, and that he left little trace
of himself in Oxford after his death in the early 1930s. He had several children,
one of whom, Hugh Miller Suratt, born sometime in the early twentieth century, would significantly factor into the life of the character. That June Suratt
was married and had several children does little to prove or disprove whether
he might have carried on extramarital affairs, with either men or women, but
at least from a distance, which seems to be how Faulkner observed him, his
large family and marital status does not make him a likely candidate for a gay
character in a novel. The part of this real man that Faulkner apocryphized into
the character Suratt, however, was not his family ties but the wagon that James
Suratt used to sell his sewing machines. The fictional Suratt appears in a hand-
ful of short stories: "Spotted Horses," "Lizards in Jamshyd's Courtyard," "Fool
about a Horse," and "A Bear Hunt." He also appears in *Flags in the Dust*, *As I Lay
Dying*, and *Light in August*. "A Bear Hunt," which was published in 1935, marks

the final appearance of Suratt as Suratt, though when Faulkner published the story in *Collected Stories* in 1951, he retroactively changed the name to Ratliff to signify the change that actually came about in the late 1930s as he was composing *The Hamlet*. This change demonstrates that Suratt and Ratliff are, effectively, the same character, only revised with a new name, but, regardless of name, one characteristic remains for both: the housing for selling sewing machines.

Suratt first appears in "Spotted Horses," the short story Faulkner eventually composed out of a fragment of *Father Abraham* and published in 1931, but earlier versions of the story have survived that predate the heavily revised 1931 version. The oldest version of "Spotted Horses," as its own story, after Faulkner sprung it from the head of *Father Abraham*, is actually a short narrative entitled "As I Lay Dying." Suratt appears in that story as a witness who explains to the narrator the events of a botched horse trade. That narrator describes his first view of Suratt/Ratliff with an accoutrement that will define him for the next thirty years of Faulkner's career:

> Tethered to a veranda post was another rig: a sturdy mismatched team and a
> buckboard, to the rear of which was attached a thing like a sheet-iron dog-kennel.
> "There's Suratt," my uncle said, "with his sewing machine." The sewing machine
> was his demonstrator. It fitted neatly into the dog-kennel, which was painted to
> resemble a house with two windows in each side, in each of which a woman's
> painted head simpered above the painted sewing machine. "Something can hap-
> pen forty miles away, but he'll be there by the next morning." (174)

With one minor change of detail, this description matches the appearance of Suratt in Faulkner's 1928 novel, *Flags in the Dust*. In the novel, the third-person omniscient narrator describes an automobile that young Bayard has "impressed" into service for his purposes of drinking corn liquor with the boys and then serenading Narcissa's bedroom window with a jazz band:

> It was a ford body with, in place of a tonneau, a miniature one room cabin of sheet
> iron and larger than a dog kennel, in each painted window of which a painted
> housewife simpered across a painted sewing machine, and in it an actual sewing
> machine neatly fitted, borne thus about the countryside by the agent. The agent's
> name was V. K. Suratt and he now sat with his shrewd plausible face behind the
> wheel. (131)[4]

Both descriptions come from material Faulkner wrote around the same time, but the difference between the two pertains to when the action of the stories takes place. The events in "As I Lay Dying" are set at the turn of the century, when the events in *The Hamlet* also takes place.[5] *Flags in the Dust* is set immediately after World War I. Between the two stories, Suratt trades his buck-board and team for a car, but he keeps the housing for his sewing machine.

The implicit danger of deciphering these details is that Faulkner so pro-foundly revised so much of the material that appears in the various Snopes novels and Frenchman's Bend stories that clear connections between earlier and later versions can prove difficult to trace or trust. Thirty years after these two descriptions, in the late 1950s, Faulkner's editors had no end of trouble attempting to edit the inconsistencies of *The Town* and *The Mansion* to fit, at least modestly, with *The Hamlet* and the earlier Snopes material. Faulkner even went so far as writing an *apologia* at the beginning of *The Mansion* to assuage their fears about his faulty memory, offering that, though the characters might have changed some, it is only because the author "knows the characters in his chronicle [now] better than he did then" (*M* 677). Nonetheless, one detail stayed consistent throughout: on the first page of *The Town*, Chick Mallison pauses to explain that, in the past, Ratliff "had to spend most of his time in his buck-board (this was before he owned the Model T Ford)" (353–54). Though there are many inconsistencies between the early and later Snopes material, it is striking that Faulkner remembered and repeated this detail so accurately, not just the painted dog-kennel but the consistency of its appearance across time and atop different modes of transportation. Indeed, from the moment of his first appear-ance in Yoknapatawpha, one feature most clearly defines V. K. Ratliff under any name and at any time. His buckboard or his car carries his housing for his sew-ing machines, but both carry him because, above all else, the central feature of Suratt/Ratliff is his mobility.[6]

Much else about the man changed over the course of his fictitious life, largely because of Faulkner's continual revisions of the stories about him. In his early incarnations, Suratt proves to be more of a sarcastic commentator in the early stories than a shrewd participant in the economic dealings of Frenchman's Bend like the later Ratliff would become. In her aptly titled essay "Suratt to Ratliff: A Genetic Approach," Joanna Vanish Creighton argues that the Suratt who appears in the early stories failed to prove up to the task of outwitting Flem Snopes. Especially in relation to Suratt's commercial dealings, Creighton asserts emphatically that the events of *The Hamlet* and of the earlier stories do not match because "the extent of the complications that Faulkner introduces into [the confrontations between them] is a measure of the shrewd-ness he attributes to Ratliff and Flem, shrewdness Suratt clearly lacks" (103). Creighton argues that the Suratt of the early stories, though a humorous local figure whose colloquial expressivity allowed Faulkner to explore a coun-try idiom, could not fill the role of the keen and purposeful character that Faulkner would need him to fill to craft the story of the dangers of Snopesism. Snopesism would not seem so insidious nor dangerous just because it could outwit a country bumpkin. Therefore, Creighton offers that the name change of Suratt to Ratliff coincides with Faulkner's attempt to craft a more keenly intellectual and subtly thoughtful character as he composed *The Hamlet*. The new name stands in for the new man. Faulkner changed the name to break with the past versions of the character and their attendant shortcomings. This new Ratliff, though *genetically* kin to and in fact spawned from Suratt, would become his own being, separate from Suratt, whom Faulkner could maneuver more deftly while revising his early stories than he could by anchoring the character to a real man and his stylized buckboard. The buckboard remains, however, beyond just the genetic links between the characters and even as Ratliff's intellect surpasses the limitations of his ancestor.

Notably, Creighton limits her argument to only the stories that eventually became *The Hamlet*. In so doing, she does not consider Suratt's appearances in any novels from prior to 1940 nor his role in "A Bear Hunt," a story wherein he does appear more directly involved in the action and as capable of manipulating a situation with calculation and subtlety. In the novel *As I Lay Dying*, Suratt appears briefly as a man whom Darl claims that "Cash aimed to buy that talking machine from" (190), a reference to the gramophone that Cash wants to buy on the journey to town. This reference suggests that Suratt functions as a general salesman in the rural parts of the county, not only as a sewing machine agent, so perhaps Cash could have bought a gramophone from him rather than go to town for it. Joel Williamson off-handedly mentions that, at the end of *Light in August*, we find "V. K. Suratt comfortably settled in bed with his wife telling her about Lena and Byron between episodes of making love" (367). The driver at the end of that novel has no name in the text, but Williamson's deduction that the man is Suratt makes sense. The driver seems to be a traveling salesman on his way north to Jackson, Tennessee, on the old highway that passes Grand Junction. By 1932, Faulkner had already established that Suratt was his token traveling salesman in his apocryphal cosmos, so this traveling salesman is likely Suratt. Of course, since the driver at the end of *Light in August* is "in bed with his wife," he would make for a pretty poor homosexual, though perhaps the omission of his name in that novel wherein this traveling salesman is presented as a heterosexual belies the flat characterization of Suratt even at this early moment. Maybe Faulkner already had a sense that Suratt—and later Ratliff—was more complicated than the bedroom recitation of Lena and Byron's courtship allowed. Maybe Faulkner already knew Suratt had something queer about him, so he opted against repeating his name in this context. Thankfully, as Williamson also points out, "When V. K. comes on stage again as a major character in 1940, his family name had shifted to Ratliff, and he was and always had been a bachelor" (367). From general salesman to possibly married, these versions of Suratt (if they are Suratt) show elements of his character with which Faulkner may have been experimenting. In each, however, his mobility remains.

Suratt, as Suratt, last appears in "A Bear Hunt," at least in the early versions of the story from the mid-1930s, though he is transformed almost seamlessly into "Ratliff" for the versions of the story that appear in *Collected Stories* and *Big Woods*, both of which transcribe *Ratliff* for *Suratt* as a retroactive revision. "As I Lay Dying/Spotted Horses" and "Lizards in Jamshyd's Courtyard" were not revised for publication with this change except as Faulkner subsumed them into and greatly altered them for *The Hamlet*, a process of revision that Faulkner seems to have begun in the late 1930s for two reasons. First, as Creighton argues, the character of Suratt from the early stories did not possess the keen and subtle characteristics Faulkner needed as a match for Flem Snopes; and if Suratt in these other stories was, in fact, mildly changing, to complete that change as radically as Faulkner needed to for *The Hamlet* required the name change. Second, Hugh Miller Suratt threatened to sue Faulkner.

Blotner suggests that Hugh Miller Suratt, not his father, might have been the primary source for Faulkner's character (Blotner 2 Vol. 545). The son was a local salesman who sold "Home Comfort Ranges," rather than sewing machines. Hugh Miller Suratt would have been roughly the same age as Faulkner and a contemporary denizen of Oxford through the 1930s. His proximity to Faulkner could have made him a likely candidate for Faulkner to transform into his fictional character, or perhaps Hugh reminded Faulkner of June and his sewing machines so Faulkner subsumed parts from both men into his fiction. Evidence is hard to find, but Emily Whitehurst Stone claimed that the father, June/James, was the real "prototype" and a local named Joe Parks was the prototype for Flem Snopes.[7] Joseph Blotner, of all people, had his own theory entirely separate from either Hugh or June. He determined a possible source for the character was a man named Rusty Patterson, whose "English was colloquial but grammatical, and some said that Rusty and V. K. Suratt had the same kind of aphoristic style" (Blotner 2 Vol. 658).[8] Faulkner hired Patterson to help restore Rowan Oak in the early 1930s, so if Patterson figures into the genetics of Ratliff, he very likely did so from the earliest stages of Ratliff's development as Suratt in the early stories from the 1930s. Nonetheless, Hugh Miller Suratt ultimately threatened to sue Faulkner for using his name, regardless of the source of the character. As Blotner explains,

> Hugh Miller Suratt had heard about his namesake and decided the resemblance was too close. It was intimated, Faulkner would later say, that if a sewing-machine agent named V. K. Suratt of Yoknapatawpha County appeared again, the next voice he would hear would be that of a lawyer representing H. M. Suratt of Lafayette County. (2 Vol. 1010)

The specious element of this account comes from Blotner's own admission that "Faulkner would later say." Faulkner was given to embellishing and apocryphizing details of his life and experiences (we might recall his story about staying in Stark Young's apartment in Greenwich Village in 1921). Therefore, it is worth verifying whether such a threat ever occurred and what pressure it might have had on Faulkner to revise the name for practical reasons, not just as a matter of characterization or narrative structure. Concerning this threat, Oxford judge Taylor McElroy confessed to Blotner, "Maybe [Hugh] didn't actuall[y] intend to sue [William Faulkner], maybe he just hoped to get a little money."[9] That the local judge remembered Hugh Miller Suratt's threats implies that those threats were real, not simply later Faulknerian embellishments. Still, no biographer has found evidence that anyone filed a lawsuit against Faulkner about the name Suratt. Faulkner changed the name and a few key details anyway. Perhaps Hugh Miller Suratt threatened legal action but never actually filed a motion with the court, so Faulkner's decision to change the name resolved the matter before any legal action was taken. Maybe his decision to change the name was purely motivated by a threat of possible legal action, even if that action had limited chance of success, but with the name change, Faulkner found opportunities for other changes as well, as Creighton has argued.

In *The Hamlet*, Faulkner transformed Suratt into Ratliff and his origins entered the realm of speculation and local legend, leaving the townspeople to wonder, "How the hell did [Faulkner] remember all that, and when did it happen anyway?" The key element of Suratt that survived into Ratliff was his mobility. The one key element that changed was that Ratliff had always been and would always be a certified bachelor. Among other benefits of his bachelorhood, this change would effectively prevent any Oxford locals from ever claiming that Ratliff was his father since Ratliff had no children. However, in this revision is room for excessive significance of which Faulkner may have been unaware in 1940 but which nonetheless greatly altered the shape of the Ratliff to come.

Adolescence (or "Conception," Part 2)

John Howard defines the movement and patterns of gay life in Mississippi in the 1940s as a "concept" rather than as a single, rooted community. After Faulkner conceived of the revisions of Suratt to Ratliff, he depicted a character whose basic patterns substantially approximate the concept of gay life that Howard explores. From that concept(ion), gay Ratliff was born. The Ratliff that emerges in *The Hamlet* bears a striking resemblance to a pattern of gay life in the 1940s and into the later twentieth century explicated in *Men Like That*. Howard uncovers how gay men in rural southern environments—specifically in Mississippi—used mobility and the liminal space of the road as an avenue to pursue their erotic lives.

To an extent, this pattern is relevant to understanding Darl Bundren as a homosexual. Howard places the beginning date of his study roughly ten years after Darl emerged in Faulkner's canon, but by 1940, as Howard's study begins, his evidence suggests that the patterns of mobility were already established, so there is reason to believe that those patterns elucidate gay life from a decade earlier or more, with variations due to the type of transportation available (such as a team and buggy as opposed to a car). Certainly, by the time Faulkner revised Suratt as Ratliff, those patterns were stable and discernible, even if they offer contemporary readers only the outline for understanding the earlier patterns that shape Darl's sense of place and identity. The Bundrens only had a wagon and a team of mules. Jewel had a horse, and the efforts it took him to get it were significant enough to parallel with the challenges a teenager fifty years later might face in financing an automobile on their own. Darl did not own his own horse and rarely left the farm except for his previous journey as far away as France during World War I. Upon his return, his isolation afforded him a way to cut off his desires, but his mother's death forced him out on the road and into the patterns of mobility that defined gay life in his rural space—to find a lover required movement and sanctioned spaces to meet, such as the back seat of a car on a roadside. Darl looks for but never finds that sanctioned space. He goes crazy, and his family casts him off to preserve their heterosexual order. In his time and place, Darl's challenges, or at least the way in which Faulkner presents them, sketch the edges of the mobility and conception of space necessary for gay life that Howard finds in more developed form in the decades after Darl's removal from his community. For Ratliff, however, who makes his first appearance in a novel published in 1940, his mobility and conception of space fit Howard's model much more clearly. That Faulkner depicted these patterns as early as 1930 suggests that he was at least minimally aware of how they shaped the trajectory and performance of gay desire, or gay *erotics* as I termed it in discussing Darl. By 1940, Faulkner seems perhaps more aware of this "concept" of mobility, desire, and identity, and if he never named it as queer explicitly, he nonetheless shaped Ratliff's character by its contours in *The Hamlet*. Ratliff's mobility frames him as a homosexual whose conception of his native landscape is tied to his sexual identity.

Ratliff first appears midway through the first chapter of *The Hamlet*. He is still "a sewing machine agent," but though "[h]e live[s] in Jefferson" in a house with his widowed sister, he is also a bachelor who "travel[s] the better part of four counties with his sturdy team and the painted dog kennel into which an actual machine neatly fitted" (*H* 16). Ratliff's introduction continues:

> On successive days and two counties apart the splashed and battered buckboard and the strong mismatched team might be seen tethered in the nearest shade and Ratliff's bland affable ready face and his neat tieless blue shirt one of the squatting group at a crossroads store, or—and still squatting and still doing the talking apparently though actually doing a good deal more listening than anybody believed

until afterward—among the women surrounded by laden clotheslines and tubs and blackened wash pots beside springs and wells, or decorous in a splint chair on cabin galleries, pleasant, affable, courteous, anecdotal, and impenetrable. (*H* 16)

From the onset of his emergence with this new identity, Ratliff is presented as a complex character, one who seems to talk, but who really listens, one as at home among a group of men as among a group of women, and one constantly on the move. As David E. Evans explains, "Throughout *The Hamlet*, [Ratliff's] greatest resource is his mobility—at once his capacity for bodily movement and his discursive shiftiness, his sense of the provisional and revisional character of his stories and relations" (470–71). Ratliff's mobility defines both his literal capacity to move and, as Evans explains, his capacity metaphorically to alter his self-presentation. According to Evans, "[Ratliff] constantly shifts and revises, resisting a single, definitive version" of the stories he carries across the country-side, making them over for each new audience and for each new setting to give what information is necessary and to gain the most information in return (470). To further Evans's reading, one can imagine Ratliff as a chameleon of sorts, able to blend in for being "pleasant, affable, [and] courteous" but at the same time "impenetrable," as if there is something below the surface of his character that he does not want his audience in Frenchman's Bend to discern. His shape-shifting capacity allows him to retain final control of knowledge, including the secrets of his own identity. His shrewd demeanor does not reveal the deeper nature of his desire. He is just the salesman who appears all over the place.

At first glance, Ratliff's "shrewdness" is almost as notable a characteristic as his actual mobility. Ratliff can hardly appear on a page without the nearly ubiq-uitous description of his "shrewd brown face" and "shrewd impenetrable eyes" (*H* 18), his "shrewd intelligent eyes in his smooth brown face" (19), "his pleasant, courteous, even deferent voice" (28), his "shrewd humorous voice" (68), and "the smooth, impenetrable face with something about the eyes and the lines beside the mouth which they [Bookwright and the other men in front of the store] could not read" (156). Clearly, there is more to Ratliff than meets the eye, but Ratliff remains "shrewd" enough in his rural southern environment not to show what lies beneath the surface because he is shrewd enough not to announce it to just anybody. Though only a slight reference, *The Hamlet* provides a reason for Ratliff's reticence. When the Texas horse trader Buck Hipps trades Flem for the "runabout buggy with bright red wheels and a fringed parasol top" (88), he reveals a peculiar anxiety about the buggy. Given its effeminate appearance, he "ought to have a powder puff or at least a red mandolin to ride it with" (184). Though he traded for it, he decides not to ride in the buggy on his way home to Texas. As he explains, "I wouldn't get past the first Texas saloon without start-ing the vigilance committee" (184). Making a spectacle of oneself, especially an effeminate spectacle, can draw unwanted, sometimes hostile, attention. Buck

Hipps recognizes this problem immediately, but that there are vigilance committees at all suggests that communities in general are on the lookout for queer spectacles. In this case, "vigilance" does not signify acceptance—they are not on the lookout for queer spectacles to welcome queer energies into their communities. The vigilance committee keeps queer elements out, unless those elements have learned to mask themselves into the shrewd, discerning impenetrability of a man like, per se, V. K. Ratliff. The presence of such committees means that keeping a low profile would be part of having a gay identity, at least in extremely rural settings, unless one's goal was to be rejected and suffer the kind of violent removal Faulkner depicted in *As I Lay Dying* and from another family native to Frenchman's Bend. Though Ratliff seems all too pleased to advertise his sewing machines with the display on his buckboard, he otherwise guards himself against revealing too much about his desires. In this regard, he differs from the talkative Suratt of the early stories who often blurts out more than he means to say, making him less than a fitting rival for the reticent Flem Snopes.

The narration does give one look at the inner Ratliff behind his impenetrable face. As Ratliff looks through the spy-hole to see Ike Snopes having sex with his beloved cow, Ratliff's shrewd character undergoes a telling reversal:

> He did look, leaning his face in between two other heads; and it was as though it were himself inside the stall with the cow, himself looking out of the blasted tongueless face at the row of faces watching him who had been given the wordless passions but not the specious words. (*H* 188)

The novel does not support a reading that would argue that Ratliff wants to have sex with a cow, thus prompting his moment of empathy with Ike. Rather, as Mrs. Littlejohn challenges, and Ratliff does not deny, the viewing, the publication, of the act troubles Ratliff. "It's all right for it to be," she asserts, "but folks mustn't know it, see it" (190). Ratliff empathizes with the spectacle of being found out, not the bestiality. For Ratliff, sexual expression is not meant to be a spectacle. Behind Ratliff's impenetrable face, he empathizes with Ike's outing to the point of putting "himself inside the stall with the cow," looking out on the faces gathered to watch him. Despite Ratliff's shrewd inscrutability, he demands scrutiny at this moment. Something about his new characterization does not fit, or rather, too much about his characterization does not fit. There is something excessive about his empathy, and something excessive about his character, beyond what meets the undiscerning eye. A discerning eye can spot immediately the enigma of V. K. Ratliff: he is a bachelor with a buggy, so there is no reason to believe that he spends his nights alone.

Noel Polk's essay "Ratliff's Buggies" explores many of the aspects of Ratliff pertinent to understanding him as a gay character. Polk ultimately defers from Ratliff as a possible homosexual, however, positing that Ratliff "simply opted out of sexual life" (187) because he cannot find evidence of Ratliff's sexual encounters, even though the title of his essay so strikingly names precisely where Polk should look. Polk's essay predates Howard's landmark study, which makes visible what previous histories ignored about gay male erotic practices, and which, when put alongside Polk's essay, reveals what has lain in plain sight all along. Howard's study discusses the ways in which "mobility—both physical and social—[was] linked to sexual practices, meanings and regulations" and the ways in which "homosexual desire manifested" in rural southern environments between World War II and the 1980s (4). As he argues, there developed "a dialectical relationship between historical actors and their surroundings" (xix), which in the rural South led to a gay culture marked by its congregation and circulation, "but more often consisted of circulation than congregation" (xiv). Dually, the sense of space and place in the South led to the uses of certain sites for homosexual encounters and the sense of isolation for rural gay men led to a need for movement, or mobility, for gay men to navigate socially sanctioned places in their environment and maintain anonymity, while also finding other men like themselves. As Howard explains, "[f]riends and sex partners, longtime acquaintances and strangers relied on technologies of transport to enable not just congregation but circulation" (78). He also documents that this movement is "constant," "multidirectional," and "enabled by multiple means of conveyance" (79). Furthermore, he includes that "just as the car moved between sites and was itself a site, roads served as avenues and venues, as arenas of circulation and congregation" (101) for gay men. Therefore, if "the rural South—rural space generally—functions as gay America's closet" (63), there is also no doubt that "[e]ven in Mississippi's smaller cities and towns, queer sex seemed to be going on with great frequency" (86). Indeed, if we substitute buggy for car as the mode of transportation that could allow for this circulation, Ratliff's relationship to this gay social pattern overflows from the novel. Also, as I have explained elsewhere, that the novel is set at the turn of the century does not preclude applying Howard's study about the 1940s to the patterns that emerge in it. Faulkner published the novel in 1940. As with all historical novels, *The Hamlet* is much more attuned to its specific cultural moment than it is an accurate portrayal of the past (though, thankfully, Ratliff will eventually trade his buggy for a car, because, alas, Faulkner's gaze was truly unflinching).

Polk never makes this leap in his interpretation of the novel. He describes Ratliff with his buggy as the "roving vicar of Varner's economic tradition" (169). Polk means to explain that Ratliff is the high priest of the sexual economy of Frenchman's Bend in which Will Varner means to use his daughter Eula to secure a financially fortuitous alliance (marriage), but the bachelor Ratliff never shows interest in Eula himself. So, Will Varner turns to Flem Snopes instead. In response to this marriage, Polk notes, "Ratliff is more upset about Varner's loss of the Old Frenchman place than about what nearly everybody in *The Hamlet* would call Eula's shame" (180), and throughout *The Hamlet* no solid evidence implies that Ratliff is ever sexually attracted to Eula, as it seems that every other man in all of Yoknapatawpha County is or will be at some point. That he notices her is not the same as saying that he desires her. That she marries Flem only bothers Ratliff to the extent it involves a house passing on to someone he does not much like. Ratliff cares about the house, not the heterosexuals who will live in it. Polk does point out how "Ratliff thinks about those courting buggies" parked outside of the Old Frenchman place to court Eula, which, according to Polk "evoke in Ratliff all of youth's dangerous passions" (186–87). However, the language that appears in the novel about those buggies offers a view of Ratliff's reaction in decidedly more ambiguous terms: "That would have never been for [Ratliff], not even in the prime summer peak of what he and Varner both would have called his tomcatting's heyday" (*H* 153). Despite his "tomcatting," Ratliff has remained a bachelor, and only conventional assumptions, but no actual evidence, suggest that he tomcatted with women instead of with young men. That he never married does not mean he courted women and failed. Perhaps he never courted women at all and has remained unmarried, which is not the same as saying he has remained eternally single. His courtships were simply not the marrying kind.

Beyond his buggy, Ratliff is also an eternal bachelor. Polk discusses Ratliff's "perennial bachelorhood," but he does not pause to explain that Ratliff is not the only bachelor in Frenchman's Bend. There are different types of bachelors, and each seems to be a bachelor for different reasons. Bookwright is a bachelor and a close friend of Ratliff's who even joins Ratliff's economic venture at the end of the novel when he and Ratliff are duped by Flem Snopes. Uncle Dick Bolivar is also a bachelor, though on his mantle at home he has "a faded daguerreotype of a young man in a Confederate uniform which was believed by those who had seen it to be his son" (*H* 328). If the young man was his son, perhaps Uncle Dick is simply a widower, not a bachelor, but people only "believe" the young man was Uncle Dick's son. No one knows for sure. In 1861, forty to fifty years prior to the action of the novel, the relationship between Uncle Dick and the young man could have been of a number of different kinds, including homosexual. The novel leaves the reader to believe what they will about the young man and the hermit bachelor Uncle Dick. Also, in the first description of him in the novel, Jody Varner "emanate[s] a quality of invincible and inviolable bachelordom" (*H* 10). Like Ratliff, Jody is a bachelor, but he's not necessarily the same kind of bachelor as Ratliff. As the narration explains of the "bridgeless difference" between Jody and Ratliff:

> [Jody] would become an old man; Ratliff, too: but an old man who at sixty-five
> would be caught and married by a creature not yet seventeen probably, who

would for the rest of his life continue to take revenge upon him for her whole sex; Ratliff, never. (*H* 303–4)

The difference between bachelors in Frenchman's Bend is that some will marry and just have not yet managed to do so while some never will. Ratliff is the latter kind of bachelor, a genuinely perennial bachelor. In fact, he does not even seem to be the marrying kind at all.

That the other "bachelors" live far and wide across the landscape of Yoknapatawpha County proves no difficulty for a man like Ratliff. In the very first description of him in the novel, Ratliff is "the man in the buckboard" (*H* 16), as perennially sitting atop his buckboard as he is perennially a bachelor. He is a man "moved by his itinerary" whose "route embraced four counties" (55) but takes him as far north as Tennessee at times. He knows every back road in the county, from the "little-travelled section near Frenchman's Bend village" (67) where he spots the goats with which he tries to outwit Flem, to the path to Uncle Dick Bolivar's isolated cabin. Even more tellingly, when Ratliff gets sick and is bed-bound for several months during his recovery, what most pleases him about the end of his confinement is "the sheer happiness of being out of bed and moving once more at free will" (68). More than the illness, what Ratliff explains that he minded most about the ordeal was the doctor's order that he "spend so much time setting down" (77). The list goes on; descriptions of Ratliff's shrewd face and impenetrable eyes are only half as ubiquitous as references to his "buckboard." Even when no one knows that Ratliff is in Frenchman's Bend, someone is bound to spot not Ratliff but his buckboard and then realize that Ratliff, in his travels through the countryside, has returned. When Ratliff is not moving, he is unhappy. Perhaps his displeasure with stasis stems from his erotic desire for union with other perennial bachelors like himself. Unlike Darl, who prefers to isolate himself out on the farm rather than confront the complex challenges of his queer life, Ratliff celebrates his mobility and the *community* it forms for him in his environment—though his *concept* of community is contingent upon understanding the cultural and geographic landscape of his native region. We never see him with those other bachelors in a compromising act, but Ratliff is too shrewd to be caught doing his tomcatting. We know how he feels about people discovering and watching certain private acts. We know, as well, that he is incredibly mobile. Seeing beyond the shrewd calculations of his mobility may well be the secret to understanding his inner life.

When Faulkner first saw a married man named Suratt with his odd painted dog-kennel for selling sewing machines, he probably did not intend, years later, to make that man emulate in outline a mode of homosexual life that, though actually quite common, remained subcutaneous to more visible histories for a great many years (in an academic sense, Howard's study is a landmark, even if, from the perspective of gay men living in rural communities, it simply let a well-kept cat out of the proverbial bag). A keen observer of his surroundings and recorder of his moment in history, Faulkner continually revised Suratt/Ratliff through the 1930s. When he arrived at *The Hamlet*, Faulkner's revisions included signifiers of gay identity in his rural southern space. To make the actual into the apocryphal, he fashioned in outline the image of a gay character actively engaged in a gay cultural practice for which we now have a recorded history to make it visible to our critical eyes. This circumstance should not shock us. Faulkner began the long evolution to create Ratliff in the mid-1920s, when he was heavily invested in queer/gay-themed creative endeavors. He continued to revise Ratliff through the 1930s, when he was troubled by some aspects of gay identity but also embroiled himself in the rigors of marriage (and perhaps Faulkner's decision to make Ratliff a bachelor stemmed from nothing more than his frustrations about depicting men interacting with women in various romantic and heterosexual scenarios, which does, admittedly, get old after a while). That bachelor did not opt out of sexuality. He simply acquired a different sexuality than a heterosexual one, though somewhat more shrewdly presented than the flamboyance of Woollcott or sojourning in public with a boyfriend, "negro" or Italian, like men in New York.

To the extent to which Ratliff can be read as a homosexual in *The Hamlet*, he points to the presence of homosexuality in rural southern environments—a theme Faulkner would also see explored in Hubert Creekmore's 1948 novel *The Welcome*, where Jim and Don court each other in high school in a car, driving all over the back roads near Ashton (Mottstown? Water Valley?), Mississippi. In fact, Creekmore's novel makes much use of this concept of gay life. Don and Jim's courtship takes place mostly in a car on afternoon drives, which, at one point, leads them to an abandoned church in the country where they are almost able to articulate their feelings for each other. As I said in the previous chapter, the novel is set around the same time as *As I Lay Dying*, and their exploits in a car would have taken place in the late 1920s, at the same (fictional) time as Darl Bundren lives out his days on an isolated farm just over the Yoknapatawpha River. The Bundrens are presented as living a lifestyle anachronous to their world, though at one point a car appears on the road where they trudge along with their wagon and mules. There is much more mobility in his world than Darl lets on in his narrative sections. Arguably, Darl (and probably the writer who gave him a voice) intentionally excludes a sense of how much more possibility for mobility existed even in such an isolated, rural space as the farm on top of the giant hill that Faulkner depicted in his novel. Darl's isolation and desire to avoid movement is heightened in the novel by the seemingly un-modernized space he moves through, which very possibly stems from his awareness of what mobility, the road, and means of transportation represent—(homo)sexual community even where it seems like it cannot and does not exist. Such a possibility has the potential to ignite all sorts of dangerous desires (and surely there is some joy in imagining the slash fiction wherein Darl, in the late 1920s but just before his mother falls ill, somehow wanders into the soda fountain in nearby Mottstown/Ashton for an ice-cold Coca-Cola and meets Jim, before he marries Doris, and they get to talking and go buy a car from Jim's friend Gus Treywick and drive off into the sunset together).

When Faulkner wrote *The Hamlet*, Creekmore had not yet written, much less published *The Welcome*, though if that novel gave Faulkner an ability to see homosexuality within his rural environment and native space, his understanding of movement in it and, in his own life, away from it, was well established long before he revised Suratt into V. K. Ratliff and long before Creekmore came of age himself in north Mississippi. Or, if Faulkner was unaware of the excess in his novel that can be read as Ratliff's latent homosexuality, in *The Town* and *The Mansion*, he not only seems to have become aware of it, but he also intentionally crafted it as an ever-present and fundamental aspect of the plot of both. For the final appearances of this apocryphal gay character, however, Faulkner also infused in his representation a specific Cold War context to layer his critique through a nexus of signifiers for difference.

Maturation

Faulkner turned out to be a victim of his own success in his transformation of Suratt into Ratliff. In the Snopes trilogy, Flem *must* beat Ratliff so that he can move from Frenchman's Bend to Jefferson, where he will compete with Gavin Stevens for supremacy. The latter two novels of the trilogy depict this conflict, and Ratliff seems to become a minor character with little or no direct participation in the plot that unfolds in either *The Town* or *The Mansion*. The problem is that Faulkner was so successful in creating a smarter, subtler Ratliff for *The Hamlet* that Flem's old "salted mine" trick, which fools him into buying the Old Frenchman Place, is far too simple a trick to fool the sophisticated Ratliff. The ending of the novel feels unbelievable. Ratliff is too shrewd to have fallen for Flem's con.

Fifteen years later, when Faulkner returned to the Snopes trilogy, this inconsistent characterization of Ratliff from the earlier novel troubles his depiction in the latter two. Faulkner wrote *The Hamlet* over the course of the 1930s and published it in 1940, before World War II. He did not return to the trilogy until well after the end of World War II and well into the early years of the Cold War. Susan Donaldson rightly places the latter two novels in a Cold War context in her essay "Ratliff and the Demise of Male Mastery," but she predicates her reading of Ratliff's "defeated manhood" (240) on the ending of the earlier novel and asserts that all three novels paint "a somewhat unsettling picture of Faulkner's own complicity in the discourse of cold war masculinity" (236). She reads Ratliff's well-pressed clothes and other signs of his domestic self-sufficiency in a Cold War context as signs of "a masculinity signaling in some respects an acknowledged loss of mastery." Donaldson even goes so far as to conclude that the "loss of mastery" in question signals a loss of mastery for "the men in the Snopes novels and for Faulkner himself" (236). Her premise is that in the 1940s and 1950s, commodity culture and mass-market capitalism threatened to emasculate strong, manly soldiers returning from World War II and transform them into soft, middle-class, and thoroughly domesticated husbands. The Cold War amplified the paranoia about domesticated masculinity because of the continued martial sense that during this "war" the United States needed to prove its dominance over the world, primarily over the communist Soviet Union, by its masterful and unbridled masculinity. Weak and effeminate men (and effeminate men are always weak in these American mythoi) could not lead American cultural expansion nor defeat America's enemies. Thus, depictions of men who were domesticated by consumer culture and who subsequently could not demonstrate masculine mastery over their home environments represented the negative outcome of American consumer culture. A sewing machine salesman who sews his own shirts, Ratliff does not prove to be up to the task of defending American values and, in fact, represents precisely the fearful domesticated consumerism that Donaldson means to explicate. Regarding masculinity, Ratliff represents, in a word, anxiety, or that Faulkner was anxious about emasculation and its toll.

There is much merit to Donaldson's argument, but her argument assumes that the excess of Ratliff in the trilogy, namely his domestication and defeat, is beyond Faulkner's control and so, as the title of her essay asserts, represents the demise of Ratliff's economic mastery. Also, since Ratliff's domesticity proves to be beyond Faulkner's control, it represents Faulkner's loss of formal narrative mastery as well. Basically, Faulkner's inability to create a convincing conclusion to *The Hamlet* implicates the demise of his formal mastery, which is later embodied in Ratliff's hyper-domesticated presentation. Although there is excess signification in *The Hamlet*, I would counter that, by the time Faulkner wrote *The Town* and *The Mansion*, he had control over that excess and used it to critique the very aspects of Cold War paranoia that Donaldson finds him complicit in advancing.

The unstated sideline of Donaldson's argument is that effeminate men were often equated with homosexuality and homosexuality was often equated with effeminate men. As Michael Sherry argues, this fear of effeminate gay men proved to be a touchy subject in the mid-1950s. Sherry emphasizes the large degree to which gay men were cultural icons during this period. This seeming ubiquity of gay men in the arts led to consternation by conservatives who *imagined* that homosexuality posed a threat to American masculinity and dominance and that gay men were taking over the arts and, of course, corrupting it and the Americans who consumed it. In this period, Sherry finds a rhetoric of homophobia with parallels to fear of communist infiltration. In the 1950s, he explains, the Red Scare had as its corollary the Lavender Scare. Just as one communist in the CIA, per se, was one communist too many, one fag in the cinema or theater or literary marketplace was one fag too many as well. Also, just as certain politicians believed that anyone might be a communist and that they were everywhere, many conservatives genuinely believed that the artistic community was replete with homosexuals and needed to be flushed clean of their insidiously prurient influences. In reality, the reactionary fear of communists and homosexuals rarely reflected the actual effects gay men and communists were having on the country. As Sherry argues, much of our contemporary sense that the 1950s were a time of intense worry and crisis has slightly later roots, as the so-called closing of the American mind tightened strictures on sexual difference in the later 1950s and into the 1960s. In the late 1940s and early 1950s, he contends, these fears were significantly less pervasive and much more formless.

All of this is to say that evidence of an effeminate man in two of Faulkner's novels does not mean that Faulkner feared effeminate (or gay) men or was complicit in a cultural resignation about lost mastery. He likely included a presentation of one such man as his own addition to the cultural prevalence of such characterizations in other fiction of the time, but our sense that such a presentation was necessarily a manifestation of anxiety is a product of a later period of fearmongering and angst. Those angst are not Faulkner's. We are wiser to read Faulkner's handling of an effeminate, and therefore gay, character as we should read many of his gay characters, as an indictment of the homophobia of its day, in this case of Cold War masculinity and its hyperbolic demands on identity. Indeed, when Faulkner presented the paranoias of the Cold War in his fiction, the results were not reactionary, nor, for that matter, even terribly conservative. For example, if we read *The Town* or *The Mansion* as Cold War novels, we are immediately faced with the obvious conundrum that Linda Snopes Kohl, a good southern girl, moves north, marries a Jew, fights on the side of the communists in the Spanish Civil War, where her husband is killed and she loses her hearing, and returns to Jefferson intent on helping to educate rural African Americans. It would be difficult to find a more specific representation of everything feared by southern conservatives in the post–World War II civil rights era, nor a more explicit critique of that conservatism because Linda, after all, is ultimately responsible for the defeat of Flem Snopes. Without her, Mink would never have managed his revenge. In fact, in all their efforts to defeat Flem Snopes, neither the foppish Gavin Stevens nor the affable V. K. Ratliff succeed as well as Eula in *The Town* and Linda in *The Mansion*. The former is an unfaithful wife who repeatedly and unapologetically cuckolds her husband. The latter is a "nigger-lover" who was once married to a Jewish communist freedom fighter. Neither implicate Faulkner's woeful sense of lost masculinity as much as they implicate his interests in depicting intensely powerful female characters whose proficiency in attaining their goals vastly outshines the lesser concern in the novel with the inability of the male characters to do more than talk to each other about the dangers of Snopesism. More specifically, if Flem embodies the cut-throat and less-than-virtuous side of cold-blooded capitalism, then when the communist sympathizer Linda finally brings about Flem's demise, we see the outcome of the novel as possibly endorsing the idea that his version of capitalism and any association it has with overwrought masculinity will not win the day. Flem's demise critiques assumptions about the virtue of a purely acquisitive capitalism, and the woman who finally arranges his death represents the possible virtues in supporting communism, at least as a fellow traveler and freedom fighter in a struggle against pernicious fascism. At the very least, the novel does not dwell on a fear of communist infiltration; instead, the entire plot of the trilogy relies on it. If this reading of Linda seems reasonable, then it follows that the novel generally might contain other criticisms of mainstream American ideology. Thus, Faulkner's using communism as a plot device to produce a narrative critical of a Cold War Red-phobia suggests that he could as easily have used homosexuality to produce a narrative critical of Cold War homophobia as well.

Little evidence suggests that Faulkner was radically liberal, much less communist, in his actual political beliefs. He very likely voted Democratic because he was a southerner and in the 1950s, southerners voted Democratic. He once told Phil Mullens, however, that he was going to vote for Eisenhower for president. Asked why, Faulkner responded, "You give us another president on the left and Joe McCarthy will be our next president."[10] What emerges in this response is Faulkner's desire for a moderate middle ground rather than radicalism on either side of the political spectrum. On the one hand, in August 1955, speaking to the Tokyo Correspondents Club, Faulkner was adamant that "there is a general 'misunderstanding' of how much Communists do to win their points."[11] On the other hand, at almost the same moment he was beginning to write a novel in which he made V. K. Ratliff the descendant of a Russian veteran of the Revolutionary War. The key to understanding the degree to which Faulkner had mastery over the signifiers that he used for V. K. Ratliff in the latter two novels of the Snopes trilogy is in his refiguring of Ratliff's name and the very conscious way in which Faulkner specified his origins in *The Town*. Despite his public statements, Faulkner maintained a thoroughly complex political philosophy, and his fiction bore out the finer points of its liberal leanings more than his public statements ever did, almost as if his fiction allowed him to create an apocryphal political identity wherein he could explore something beyond the extremism he seemed to fear.

Between *The Hamlet* and *The Town*, Faulkner did much to explore the characters of Chick Mallison and Gavin Stevens, primarily in the stories collected in *Knight's Gambit* and the novel *Intruder in the Dust*. He did not leave Ratliff by the wayside, however. Ratliff, or at least one of his progenitors, appears in *Requiem for a Nun*, which Faulkner published in 1951 and turned over to a gay Russian set designer for its eventual stage production. The Ratliff that appears in *Requiem* is actually named Ratcliffe, and he is very distinctly identified as "Ratcliffe, son of a long pure line of Anglo-Saxon mountain people and—destined—father of an equally long and pure line of white trash tenant farmers" (37). This "destiny" is ungenerous of Faulkner. One of this Ratcliffe's descendants would be a traveling salesman, not just a white trash tenant farmer. Roughly six years later, in *The Town*, Faulkner made the decision to revise this "long pure line of Anglo-Saxon mountain people." He transformed that blood line into a female line in which a man of Russian descent named Vladimir Kyrilytch Radcliffe fought for the British army in the Revolutionary War, was captured, then:

> —[he] was sent to Virginia and forgotten and Vla—his grandfather escaped. It was a woman of course, a girl, that hid him and fed him. Except that she spelled it R-a-t-c-1-i-f-f-e and they married and had a son or had the son and then married. Anyway he learned to speak English and became a Virginia farmer. And his grandson, still spelling it with a c and an e at the end but his name still Vladimir Kyrilytch though nobody knew it, came to Mississippi with old Doctor Habersham and Alexander Holston and Louis Grenier and started Jefferson. Only they forgot how to spell Ratcliffe and just spelled it like it sounds but one son is always named Vladimir Kyrilytch. Except like you said, nobody named Vladimir Kyrilytch could make a living as a Mississippi country man—. (628)

Unless, of course, his name was simply V. K. Ratliff, and nobody knew the truth about him because that would change entirely how we perceive him in his rural southern environment as the master of his mobile world. Among the secrets that Ratliff hides behind his shrewd face is that he is not descended from a male Anglo-Saxon line. He is the descendant of a Russian with an English surname. His "American" heritage stems from an unnamed woman who bore a child for that Russian and established a tradition of naming one son in each generation after his progenitor. The "joke" embedded in this history of his name, though, is that in late 1950s, when Faulkner wrote the novel, a (communist) Russian probably would not succeed in business in Mississippi. In the time of the novel, only a generation or two prior, that name may not have been as much a liability. Eula suggests that Ratliff's reticence in telling people his name is simply that it would sound funny with a colloquial Mississippi accent. V. K. has a nicer ring to it.

This genealogical change to Ratliff suggests that Faulkner consciously meant to critique trends in the arts and letters and in rhetoric by men like Joseph McCarthy. Gavin Stevens even laments about the rise of organizations within American society with seemingly fascist intentions: "the ones right here at home: the organizations with the fine names confederated in unison in the name of God against the impure in morals and politics and with the wrong skin color and ethnology and religion" (*M* 823). It is hard not to believe that Gavin means the Ku Klux Klan and the House Un-American Activities Committee, which he equates with each other. If Faulkner's conversion of Suratt to Ratliff gave him an opportunity to craft a more complex character with excess that he could channel into a more dynamic figure in his postage stamp of native soil, then giving that Ratliff this new, seemingly impure history allowed him even more excess to work with. He could tie the critique of Red-phobia to a critique of homophobia in the character with a Russian name dressed up in very well-hemmed and pressed Mississippi clothing. In *The Town* and *The Mansion*, Faulkner intentionally crafted Ratliff as a gay man to critique a discourse of fraught masculinity.

Fruition

As he appears in the latter two Snopes novels, Ratliff differs from his predecessor in the degree to which Faulkner crafted him as an overly feminized, domesticated male. This shift in his character follows from Faulkner's masterful maneuvering of Ratliff into a role as a recognizable gay figure in a mid-1950s Cold War context and serves to critique the extreme conservatism of the cultural moment, though the critique is subtle enough to avoid being itself a radical liberal vision. In *The Town* and *The Mansion*, Faulkner re-dressed Ratliff and even sent him to Greenwich Village. He also made Ratliff the driving figure— literally the *driving* figure—of unity and coherence in both plots.

In his Cold War emanation, Ratliff no longer only wears the faded blue tieless shirts, as he did in *The Hamlet*, but he makes, washes, and presses them himself. He does the same for "the immaculately clean, impeccably laundered and ironed handkerchief" that he hands to Stevens in the final scene of *The Mansion* (*M* 1061). This Ratliff no longer lives with his widowed sister. He lives on his own in a house with "a tea tray and Ratliff had a teacup and a cucumber sandwich" at four in the afternoon as a small meal. These accoutrements in his home and the delicacy of his palate are signifiers of a refined domesticity that is alien to "the country where Ratliff came from" (*T* 446). He is also now "a damned good cook, living alone in the cleanest little house you ever saw, doing his own housework" (*M* 863). He makes a habit of sitting in "the immaculate room he called his parlor, with the spotlessly waxed melodeon in the corner and the waxed chairs and the fireplace filled with fluted green paper in the summer but with a phony gas log in the winter" (*M* 885). He does his cooking and cleaning while wearing "a spotless white apron over one of those neat tieless faded blue shirts which he made himself, cooked the meal, cooking it damned well, not just because he loved to eat it but because he loved the cooking, the blending up to perfection's ultimate moment" (*M* 885). These elaborate descriptions transform Ratliff into a housewife over the course of the latter two novels, but another way to view these descriptions is to consider Ratliff not merely as domesticated but urbane, a model of clean sophistication in his rough, rural world, or, in short, as a gay man. His alien virtues register as distinctly queer in his immediate environment. His version of effeminacy signals his queer sexuality, a stereotypical but nonetheless germane sexuality compounded by the cultural context when Faulkner wrote these descriptions in the 1950s, at a time of severe anxiety about their significance.

Ratliff's urbanity is put to the test, though, not in Yoknapatawpha, but in Greenwich Village. While in Greenwich Village for Linda's wedding, he meets Barton Kohl and is given a statue of an Italian boy doing something that the text never reveals but that Ratliff recognizes. As in "Out of Nazareth" when the young man praises A. E. Housman's *The Shropshire Lad*, this statue of an Italian boy is meant to signal to readers what perhaps cannot be stated aloud but should be easily inferred. It represents the open secret of homosexuality permeating the scene. The Italian boy in the statue is probably naked, which would make him an object of homosexual fascination, and probably in a suggestive pose that Ratliff, as a homosexual, recognizes, but that others—namely Gavin Stevens and Chick Mallison—do not. In his Greenwich Village apartment, Barton Kohl pulls Ratliff aside at the wedding reception to show Ratliff his sculptures, including the one of the Italian boy. Ratliff is neither "[s]hocked" nor "[m]ad" at what he sees, only surprised because he has "never seen it before" (*M* 833). Barton responds in disbelief that someone "at [Ratliff's] age" (833) has not seen something like this before. Barton then decides to give the sculpture to Ratliff in his will because, as Stevens explains, "Bart liked him. He said he hadn't expected to like anybody from Mississippi, but he was wrong" (858). Then, as Stevens continues to explain,

> You remember it—the Italian boy that you didn't know what it was even though you had seen sculpture before, but Ratliff that had never even seen an Italian boy, nor anything else beyond the Confederate monument in front of the courthouse, knew at once what it was, and even what he was doing? (858)

What Barton likes about Ratliff is that he gets to show Ratliff an aspect of life in Greenwich Village that Gavin does not—and probably cannot—show him. When Ratliff says that he has "never seen it before," he means the statue, or the open display of homosexual desire, in fine artistic expression no less. In Mississippi, the signifiers between men are much less overt, such as the daguerreotype in Uncle Dick's cabin with its somewhat ambiguous sense that maybe it is Uncle Dick's long-lost son, maybe not. Ratliff's entire sense of gay identity would be vastly different from what he witnesses in Greenwich

Village. Rural Mississippians had a concept of gay identity related to the multiple spaces in which they expressed their (often closeted) desires. Greenwich Village was a gay *community*, and it did not have the same strictures on visible gay expression as Mississippi, where Ratliff explores his sexual identity through his knowledge of back roads and through his constant mobility. In Greenwich Village, one can express and view much more explicitly what in Mississippi one is not allowed to show to the world. The statue stands out to Ratliff because it embodies a variety of gay experience that, until that moment, he has not known so openly.

Of course, Faulkner was well aware of the cultural value of Greenwich Village and used it as his own version of the "open secret" in this scene. Just as Ratliff's special eye can see something in the Italian boy that others cannot, discerning readers can detect something in the setting of this scene that Faulkner quite deftly left unstated. In the penultimate novel of his life and career, Faulkner returned to the setting in which he made his first attempts to define his own apocryphal gay identity away from Mississippi. Faulkner pulled his characters from the confines of Yoknapatawpha County and placed them in Greenwich Village, a site that Stevens describes as "a place with a few unimportant boundaries but no limitations where young people of any age go to seek dreams" (*T* 652), and a site that historian George Chauncey identifies at length as a center of gay culture from as early as the 1910s. As Chauncey also demonstrates, Greenwich Village was so popularly acknowledged as a center of gay culture that by the late 1940s, magazine guides to New York City had to point out that "not all New York's queer (or, as they say it, 'gay') people live in Greenwich Village" (qtd. in Chauncey 20). No, they probably did not, but if a magazine had to go so far as to clarify that misimpression, then it is likely that a great many people held that impression in the first place. In this (easily recognizable and gay) setting, Barton Kohl recognizes something about Ratliff. After first mistaking him for a Texas oil millionaire because of his seventy-five-dollar Allanovna necktie, Kohl realizes that Ratliff is no ordinary Mississippian and wants to show him a collection of private sculptures, but Kohl is "a sculptor so advanced and liberal that even Gavin couldn't recognize what he sculpted" (*M* 866). That Barton, in his will, should send the statue to Ratliff to be placed in Ratliff's splendidly refined home is only fitting. Barton's decision metaphorically moves to America's gay closet an emblem of the open secret of homosexuality from one of America's gay epicenters. The statue links Ratliff's domesticated home to the gay space of Greenwich Village and makes that home, for all practical purposes, a little bit of Greenwich Village in Mississippi. Once the homosexual leaves Mississippi and becomes visible within another gay space, when he returns to Mississippi, we can follow him back there and recognize what the signs have been pointing to all along as having been present in that landscape since its inception: the confident, comfortable gay man.

Most significantly, Faulkner did not craft Ratliff as a gay, somewhat Russian figure merely for the purposes of demonstrating his representational mastery to no useful end. By crafting Ratliff in this way, he also pulled a masterful slight-of-hand to make good the seeming incongruity of the ending of *The Hamlet*. In *The Town* and *The Mansion*, Ratliff may seem to function primarily as a commentator and may never seem to involve himself directly in the battles between Flem Snopes and Gavin Stevens. He even seems to be a secondary figure in these novels, mostly present as the glue that binds Flem's former life in Frenchman's Bend to his current life in Jefferson (few characters from *The Hamlet* appear in the latter two novels). Thus, as Donaldson argues, he has been defeated and now plays a minimal role in the remaining action, or so it would seem. These assertions, however, while superficially true, do not account for the utter centrality of Ratliff's role in both latter novels. That role is laid bare at the ends of both novels when Gavin Stevens seeks to understand how first Eula, then Linda, with Mink's help, manage to defeat Flem, each in their own fashion and each without his knowledge of how they managed what he has been trying to do all along in his own fashion as well.

In *The Town*, Gavin cannot quite understand what, precisely, Flem is after in Jefferson. Ratliff supplies the answer: Respectability. He has understood this goal all along and has simply waited for Stevens to work it out for himself. Moreover, Ratliff proves to be more than just a residual character linking the hamlet and the town symbolically. He actually transports Flem out to Will Varner's store in chapter 18 of *The Town* for the fateful meeting that will prompt Eula to play her trump card in the complicated game between her lover, Manfred de Spain, and her husband, Flem. She will commit suicide to rescue Linda if not herself. Gavin watches these events unfold in stunned horror. Ratliff participates in them. He invites Flem to join him on his ride out to Frenchman's Bend, where Flem will work to secure his share of the Varner family fortune now that he has evidence to use against Eula and force himself into a major share of the local bank. Eula, who has long since considered Ratliff a confidant and has even managed to find out his real name, goes to Stevens to explain the situation before going home to kill herself. Stevens fails to understand what has transpired between these major players on the stage of Jefferson's economic fortunes. Ratliff arrives and explains to him all the extraneous detail that he—Ratliff—has collected and that the forensic Stevens needs help compiling into the proper conclusions. As with the matter of respectability, Ratliff has tried to allow Stevens to reach his conclusions on his own, but Stevens would not be able to do so were it not for Ratliff's assistance. Ratliff knows the whole score, not just the partial highlights. When he finally tells Stevens the missing details from Stevens's narrative, the novel itself can conclude.

In *The Mansion*, after Linda has duped Gavin into helping her free Mink, Ratliff arrives—his timing as perfect as always—to escort Gavin through the ritual of realization, the *peripeteia* of the mammoth revenge tragedy at the heart of the Snopes trilogy. In the final pages of *The Mansion*, Ratliff is the one who first reasons through Linda's motives for freeing Mink to kill Flem. Then he leads Stevens down the overgrown road to Mink's cabin to find Mink, a procession emblematic of his role in the entire trilogy as the guide who helps bring others to the knowledge they will need to allow the events their full conclusion. Gavin is overwhelmed by the sheer gravity of what has occurred and how it has all finally played out on the vast mythic stage of Yoknapatawpha County. So, as they leave Mink's cabin, "[g]entle and tender as a woman, Ratliff opened the car door for Stevens to get in" (*M* 1063). Throughout the latter two novels Ratliff is the all-knowing seer and guide, but also an effeminate one. In this final description of him in all three novels, Faulkner uses those three telling words to describe him: "as a woman." Not only has he guided Stevens to his final understanding of events, but he also gently guides Stevens back to his home and back to the peace of the denouement necessary at the end of this grand tragedy. Though the ending of the Snopes trilogy is chilling in its brutality, the ending also restores the modicum of order necessary for the proverbial "All is well" of an Aristotelian structure. Ratliff's womanly touch is the sign that all is well now that all has ended. Mink will lay down on the earth to rest in a symbolic death. The rest of the characters will go home and continue their lives. Ratliff has guided them through the horror and signaled the proverbial Fortinbras on the horizon. He has done so "tender as a woman" because the deep knowledge that he carries throughout Yoknapatawpha is a queer knowledge. His touch is needed. That touch is a queer, which is to say gay, touch.

In the context of Cold War paranoia over communists and homosexuals, Faulkner places at the heart of his great trilogy a coded gay figure as the one who brings about the vital revelations necessary to the plot and ultimately the conclusion of each novel and the conclusion of the trilogy as a whole. *The Reivers* would be Faulkner's next and final novel. *The Town*, *The Mansion*, and *The Reivers* are, collectively, the long swansong through which Faulkner sang his cosmos to a close from its beginnings in *Father Abraham*—the first two novels the proper conclusion of that early draft, the latter his final novel before his own death in 1962. Ratliff may, then, be less Faulkner's Falstaff reappearing in his affable way in several novels, more his Prospero, letting us know our revels have ended and now the play must close. The knowledge and control exhibited by Ratliff over the significant events of these novels makes him the great purveyor of truth and finality in Yoknapatawpha, and as a side note, Faulkner also chose to craft him as a character who becomes, over the course of his biography, legibly gay.

In the long arc of Faulkner's career, in the long arc of Faulkner's life, Ratliff's presence and identity in the closing pages of *The Mansion* are a fitting tribute to the span of that arc and a fitting conclusion to a long and complex story of Faulkner's own aprocryphal gay life. Ratliff's biography is perhaps the best apocryphal autobiography Faulkner ever wrote. For the young man who could never quite fit in in his hometown and sought to make himself different from it, and the young man who once saw two paths, seemingly irreconcilable, before him and so started on a long and complex journey, beyond the eleven years of his queer life and into the thirty-three years of his marriage and fatherhood, but really across the whole span of his sixty-five years until his death, the one feature of Faulkner's life that most defined him was that he was always, not despite but because of his gestures, a man who entirely belonged to and masterfully recorded the actual history of his home. In his way, Faulkner was always the insidious guide through the epic of his apocryphal creation. In the extraneous details of the apocrypha of his life, a new and dynamic figure emerges to suggest to us new possibilities of interpretation and to leave clues to an open secret about the actual man that have been overlooked for too long.

Notes

Chapter 1

1. See Williamson and Karl for the most detailed accounts of William Clark Falkner. Both agree that while the Civil War ruined numerous white landowners in Mississippi, W. C. Falkner capitalized on the war and its aftermath.

2. See Blotner and Williamson for the geography of these local areas. There is currently a historical marker in Oxford, Mississippi, marking the house of Maud Falkner, which stands on part of the large corner lot on which once stood "the Big Place." Also, Blotner, Williamson, and Karl explore the often-romanticized culture of the Mississippi frontier both before and after the Civil War. Karl refers to W. C. Falkner as a "man on the make" in this landscape of new opportunities. However, in his history of the nearby Mississippi Delta, Cobb cautions against assumptions that men who settled in Mississippi were destitute and without inherited resources. He establishes that most settlers brought with them some degree of inherited wealth and resources (often in the form of slaves).

3. Van Buren Avenue was previously called Depot Street and appears by that name in numerous biographies and, of course, on contemporaneous maps.

4. See Williamson for a detailed history of the street-making in Oxford. The original sidewalks were made from wooden boards and would not be replaced until the early twentieth century (in Faulkner's life) with concrete.

5. See Karl and Snell for the best accounts of Faulkner and Stone's relationship and reciprocity of influence.

6. See Pilkington. Also, Young's memoir *Pavilions*. Young was born in 1881 in Friars Point, Mississippi (and is now buried in Como, where he spent his early youth). Young's father, Dr. A. A. Young, moved the family to Oxford in 1895, the same year Young enrolled at the University of Mississippi. In his memoir, Young refers to Oxford as his hometown, though in 1925, both his father and stepmother died within days of each other and his subsequent trips to Oxford became less frequent. The Young House, now the Walton-Young House and part of the University Museum, borders Bailey Woods, a short walk to Rowan Oak and to the "Big Place."

7. Of Young and Faulkner, Blotner would write, "There were tastes they did not share, as with the work of D'Annunzio" (104). Blotner's source for this information were interviews with Emily Whitehurst Stone now collected in BP.

8. Crowell goes one step further and places the source of gay male identity in Mississippi in this time period squarely on the shoulders of Oscar Wilde, whose American Tour in 1882 included stops in Memphis on June 12 and Vicksburg on June 14 (see Ellman). Young would have been too young to attend, Percy not yet alive, but as a matter of six degrees of separation, surely someone who attended one of Wilde's lectures later met Young, Percy, or both, and they both met and (in a manner of speaking) befriended William Faulkner. Thus, we can trace a

direct line from Wilde to Faulkner, who later visited Wilde's grave in Paris. But at this moment in our story, the gay men Faulkner knew and from whom he could be influenced are Stark Young and W. A. Percy.

Chapter 2

1. BP, Letter, Paul Rogers to Joseph Blotner, 7 April 1980.
2. BP, Letter, Joseph Blotner to Paul Rogers, 21 May 1980.
3. BP, Letter, Paul Rogers to Joseph Blotner, 3 June 1980.
4. Ibid.
5. The idea that gay people cannot live comfortably if at all in rural and/or southern spaces is a deeply ingrained myth of American life. Unfortunately, it is difficult to gauge the number of "gay" people who lived in Mississippi (or anywhere) at the turn of the twentieth century largely because no one bothered to count. The 2010 census was the first significant federally funded survey of LGBT populations, primarily as a measure of shared households that the Defense of Marriage Act precluded from federal recognition in the tax code. Writing for the Williams Institute at UCLA, Gary J. Gates and Abigail M. Cooke noted that the data on "same-sex marriage" defied many expectations. Mississippi ranked sixth in the nation in terms of the highest percentage of same-sex couples who identify as "spouses," with 30 percent of same-sex couples preferring this designation (1,050), as opposed to identifying as "unmarried partner couples" (2,434). These numbers put Mississippi ahead of California (seventh) and the five states ahead of Mississippi (Massachusetts, Vermont, Connecticut, Iowa, and New Hampshire) had all taken steps to legalize same-sex marriage by 2010. California had briefly done the same in 2008.

This data is important for at least two reasons: these numbers quantify actual living people; also, these numbers imply that many LGBT people make a life for themselves even in Mississippi. Not everyone flees or hides. We can too easily assume that there was no gay life in a place like Mississippi in the past because we have no statistical data to support it and very few open and explicit firsthand accounts to describe it. When one bothers to do statistical data on LGBT life and identity, the numbers rarely support myths about gay isolation or lack of distinctive communal identities and connections. LGBT people did not arise from the earth fully formed as if sown from dragons' teeth planted in a field somewhere. We have been here for quite some time, even in Mississippi.

6. BP, Letter, Paul Rogers to Joseph Blotner, 3 June 1980; "pundonor" appears in original.
7. BP, Letter, Hunter McKelva Cole to Joseph Blotner, 2 July 1982.
8. BP, Interview, Robert Farley to Joseph Blotner, 3 April 1965.
9. BP, Photocopy of Essay, Ben Wasson, *Delta Democrat-Times*, 1962. All quotations from Wasson in this paragraph come from this account, which Wasson later expanded in his longer memoir.
10. Faulkner's familiarity with Malory directly is hard to verify. For Tennyson, see Blotner, Parini, and Signal, all of whom establish that Faulkner was well read in *Idylls of the King*.
11. See Duvall, "Faulkner's Crying Game," for more on this scene.
12. See Howard (*Men Like That* xvii) for the term "homosex" to describe homosexual acts and separate them from the identity we now describe as "homosexual."
13. BP, Article, *Oxford Eagle*, 15 September 1921.
14. BP, Article, *Oxford Eagle*, 8 September 1921, with accompanying note by Blotner.
15. BP, Interview, Emily White Hurst Stone and Joseph Blotner, 30 November 1965.
16. Ibid.
17. BP, Undated note, Joseph Blotner.
18. BP, Article, *Oxford Eagle*, 6 March 1924, with accompanying note by Blotner.
19. BP, Summary of article, Stark Young, *Oxford Eagle*, 30 November 1950.

20. BP, Photocopy, Essay, Stark Young, "New Year's Craw," *New Republic*, 1938. As verification that he had long been a central figure in Faulkner's life, Young wrote this piece before Faulkner's reputation was lionized by his Nobel Prize.

21. Wasson does not provide a date for this incident; the editors at UPM were unable to reconstruct an exact date and instead included this story at the end of a chapter in the memoir titled "Greenville," which covers Wasson's life from 1921 until approximately 1927. Blotner cites this incident in the one-volume biography in a chapter from "October 1926–June 1927," as an influence on a scene in *Flags in the Dust*, not because it occurred in those months.

I assign 1924 as the date of this incident because of textual and contextual evidence. First, from Sensibar's *Faulkner and Love*, we have a clear timeline of Estelle's visits to Oxford. In his memoir, Wasson describes Cho-Cho (born in 1919) as still small enough to be picked up but also old enough to walk on her own. He makes no mention of Estelle's second child Malcolm (born in 1923). When Estelle visited Oxford in 1924, Cho-Cho was with her, and the editors of Wasson's memoir include a picture of Cho-Cho, Estelle, and Cho-Cho's Chinese nursemaid from 1924 with Wasson's description of this incident. Certainly, by 1927, Cho-Cho would have been older and less easy to pick up; Malcolm would have been young enough and small enough to be the accidental intruder in this scene.

22. Williamson, Gwin, and Polchin have also explored the homosexual influence in Faulkner's work from New Orleans.

23. BP, Photocopy, Newspaper article, "Marriage Is Not at Fault," *New Orleans Item-Tribune*, 4 April 1925. All quotations from the same. This letter is collected by Meriwether, in *ESPL*, but Meriwether identifies the newspaper as the *Times-Item* and does not include the introductory material published in the newspaper when the letter first ran. Also, this letter is only included in Meriwether's revised edition.

24. I am citing the book-length version of Spratling's memoir. Both Williamson and Blotner relied on the shorter version, "Chronicle of a Friendship," that Spratling had published in *Texas Quarterly* while he was writing his longer book. Unlike Wasson's essay-turned-memoir with a twenty-year gap, Spratling's accounts are so similar as to be interchangeable.

25. BP, Interview, Ben Wasson and Joseph Blotner, 28 March 1965.

26. The Blotner Papers are thorough and extensive, but despite repeated efforts, I have so far been unable to find the reference to Spratling's homosexual encounter that Blotner included in the revised one-volume biography. Blotner cites his interview with Spratling, which proved to be his only interview with Spratling, who died in a car accident shortly afterward and before Blotner published his original two-volume version. Blotner typed up the notes from the interview on six pages, none of which include mention of the homosexual encounter. The handwritten interview notes total nine pages and contain information that did not make it to Blotner's typed notes, but they make no mention of this homosexual encounter either. The short-hand notes Blotner took during his interviews in small pocket steno-books are illegible. Nonetheless, Blotner included this information in his revised biography as credible information from William Spratling.

27. See *UC*, notes (p. 710) for Blotner's fullest account of the history of this story.

28. BP, Interview, Harold Levy and Joseph Blotner, 5 February 1965.

29. BP, Interview, William Spratling and Joseph Blotner, 28, 29, and 30 January 1965.

30. BP, Ibid.

Chapter 3

1. I am citing most of the poetry from Collins's edited collection of Faulkner's early work because it is a standard volume with most of Faulkner's early works in it. However, Sensibar

has overseen the reprinting of much of Faulkner's early poetry and quotes that poetry at length in her work. Close inspection of the poems as they appear in Collins and in Sensibar shows no significant alterations except for occasional spelling changes from Faulkner's original, highly stylized, and handwritten poems.

2. See Hemingway, *A Moveable Feast*.

3. Monroe's column was nationally syndicated, and she was herself a lesbian, which may have influenced her (dis)regard for Percy's Sapphic poems. Faulkner likely read her columns in the *Commercial Appeal* from Memphis, Tennessee, which was the largest circulating regional paper in the Mid-South during Faulkner's life. Even if Faulkner did not take the *Commercial Appeal* himself, it is reasonable to assume many people around him did (such as Phil Stone) and he could have read it and discussed the opinions on literature published therein.

4. For more on homosexuality in hobo culture, see Chauncey.

5. This sentence appears in the novel, but Gwin points out that in the original typescript, a subsequent conversation between Julius and Fairchild is deleted.

6. BP, Interview, Ben Wasson and Joseph Blotner, 28 March 1965.

7. In the one-volume edition, Blotner cites John Falkner's assertion that his brother was primarily working on short stories in the early months of 1926. Blotner says of "Divorce in Naples," "It would be years before [it] appeared, but as the manuscripts show, there were several versions" of the story from this period.

8. A version of this argument appears in slightly altered form in *Faulkner and Warren*, under the title "Naples Re-Visited: A New Perspective on Same-Sex Desire in 'Divorce in Naples.'"

9. In the one-volume edition, Blotner explains that Faulkner and Estelle moved into 803 University Avenue in Oxford shortly after their marriage. Faulkner likely wrote "A Rose for Emily" there, first referring to it in a letter on 7 October 1929, the publication date of *The Sound and the Fury*. Faulkner had already written *Sanctuary*, and would begin the manuscript of *AILD* on 25 October 1929 and finish it on 12 January 1930. "A Rose for Emily" was published in *Forum* in April 1930. Therefore, Blotner concludes that Faulkner wrote "A Rose for Emily" and *AILD* at the same time, between October 1929 and January 1930.

10. See Fick and Gold, Blythe and Sweet, and Robertson.

Chapter 4

1. There are two slips in Faulkner's rhetoric during this letter exchange. First, he referred to his service in the RAF, or Royal Air Force, though when he had enlisted, that branch was still the RFC, or Royal Flying Corps. Faulkner used the abbreviations more-or-less interchangeably, as it seems Cowley did. It is hard to tell if this was just a normal rhetorical shift or if it represented Faulkner's own ambivalence because his service was so minimal in the first place. Second, in a study of gay Faulkner, that Faulkner used the phrase "bugger up," which borrows the slang "bugger" from "buggery," another way to refer to sodomy, should strike readers as odd. Perhaps, in his agitation with Cowley, Faulkner just was not thinking and used the phrase without meaning it as a queer signifier. However, his use of a phrase with connotations for queer sexuality lends itself to the general themes of all his war writings: there is always the touch of something queer in them.

2. See Ellman, 390, 436–37, and 446–47. See Ovid, *Metamorphoses*, Book X.

Chapter 5

1. According to notes in BP, Oxford suffered at least two cases of the flu in 1918. In newspaper clippings from around north Mississippi that Blotner collected in his research, he found evidence of towns in the area considering imposing quarantines when outbreaks occurred

nearby. Thus, foreign though the flu may have been and its global impact heightened by the war and the pathways for spreading opened thereby, the flu was not purely foreign. It infiltrated even the heart of Faulkner's rural, native world.

2. BP, Photocopy of Review: William Faulkner, *The Road Back*, by Erich Maria Remarque, *New Republic*, 20 May 1931.

3. From "Disabled," lines 11–12. Line 13 contains the reference to the invalid's "queer disease."

4. This moniker for the novel comes from a series of telegraphs between Phil Stone and Faulkner. See Blotner 135.

5. See Blotner 169, for a sense of the time frame for the writing of this strange story. Also, Catherine Kodat offers an alternative "queer" reading of this story in "Unhistoricizing Faulkner."

6. In the one-volume biography, Blotner provides that the story was influenced by a serialized anonymous war diary titled *War Bird*, published in 1926, so it was probably written after 1926. In the two-volume biography, Blotner offers that the story was told from the point of view of 1930 in a frame narrative, which would suggest that Faulkner wrote the story around that time himself, which would place the story after he wrote *Flags in the Dust*. I place it here for thematic purposes, but I may be misplacing it chronologically.

7. See Bruhm; also, Ovid, *Metamorphoses*, Book III.

8. For more on "non-sense" and minstrelsy, see Baker.

Chapter 6

1. Two other touchstones worth considering here are Peter Brooks's *Reading for the Plot* and Lee Edelman's *No Future: Queer Theory and the Death Drive*.

Chapter 7

1. For the key additions to this conversation, see Crowell, Jones, Peterson, and Entziminger. For a recasting of this mold into a productive discussion of lesbian themes in the novel, see Harker.

2. See Stockinger for a significant manifesto on LGBTQ literary theory from this period.

3. See Bersani.

4. BP, Interview, Ben Wasson by Joseph Blotner, 28 March 1965. All the details of this paragraph stem from one notecard that Blotner dated as "1925," though he subsequently crossed out that date and concluded in pencil that these events pertain to 1924.

5. BP, Interview, Carl and Betty Carmer by Joseph Blotner, 23 August 1965.

6. BP, Interview, Owen Crump by Joseph Blotner, 9 June 1966; all subsequent quotations in this paragraph Ibid.

7. See Chauncey—in the index to his book (p. 474) he includes under the entry for "speakeasy" both "as gay meeting places" and "in Greenwich Village."

8. BP, Interview, Leland Howard by Joseph Blotner, 21 January 1965.

9. BP, Interview, Morty (Morton) Goldman by Joseph Blotner, 21 February 1967.

10. Ibid.

11. BP, Letter, William Faulkner to Bennett Cerf, undated. Blotner supplied in pencil on the side, in reference to *The Red Badge of Courage*, that it was autographed by Faulkner at "Xmas 1932." At this time, Cerf was courting Faulkner to publish an edition of *The Sound and the Fury*, a proposal which Faulkner alluded to in the letter and which helps date it.

12. BP, Interview, Eric and Rita Devine by Joseph Blotner, 15 August 1965.

13. An image of Bentley in her white tuxedo, top hat, and cane appeared on the cover of the May 2009 edition of *PMLA*. Editor Patricia Yeager called Bentley an embodiment of the "Cluster on Queer Metaphor" featured in the volume. Additionally, Martha Vicinus placed Bentley

into a lesbian context in her essay "They Wonder to which Sex Do I Belong," where she quotes the lesbian-themed lyrics Bentley sang in her shows.

14. BP, Interview, Ben Wasson by Joseph Blotner, 28 March 1965.

15. BP, Letter, William Faulkner to Ben Wasson, 12 February 1933. Faulkner spelled Victoria's name as "Cho-cho" whereas in almost all other instances in biographies and memoirs it appears as "Cho-Cho."

16. BP, Interview, Morton (Morty) Goldman by Joseph Blotner, 21 February 1967.

17. Published in 1948. For more, see Blotner, 2-volume edition, pp. 1101, 1253.

Chapter 8

1. While writer-in-residence at the University of Virginia, Faulkner explained, "I saw *Cat on a Hot Tin Roof* and that was about the wrong people—the problems of children are not worth three acts. The story was the old man, I thought, the father. That's all I know of Williams." See *Faulkner in the University*, 13.

2. BP contains letters from Blotner to Williams (2 March 1966) and Blotner to Vidal (28 September 1969). There are no significant responses from either included in BP. In both versions of the published biography, stories that include Williams and Vidal come from other interview sources.

3. BP, Interview, Monique Lange by Joseph Blotner, January 1964.

4. BP, Interview, Truman Capote with Joseph Blotner, 29 December 1967.

5. BP, Photocopy, "Faulkner Speaking," *Time Magazine*, 23 August 1954.

6. Scattered throughout his notes, Blotner made lists of novels, usually from cut-outs of book lists from publishing houses. Their placement generally coincides with what evidence would suggest that Faulkner might have read a certain book at a certain moment. The photocopy for Willingham's novel is from a folder from 1947.

7. See *Lion in the Garden*, 237–56.

8. BP, Interview, Jean Stein by Joseph Blotner, 10 November 1964. Wasson did not think highly of Stein either. From his interview with Blotner from 28 March 1965, Blotner recorded:

Jean Stein was a salonier, liked to collect names. She finally turned WF against Ben. She was with the company shooting BABY DOLL. She said she was going to go to E [Estelle?] and scratch her eyes out, or something of the sort. Ben quickly phoned WF with a stratagem to avoid trouble. He said, "Can we come over?" Then he filled in a group around her and got them out as soon as he could. She was hoping to linger to the end to make a scene.

In his memoir, Wasson mentions Stein in passing and even records a lunch he had with her and Shelby Foote in New York after the filming of *Baby Doll*. He neither affirms friendship nor vilifies her. Of Lamkin's visit to Greenville, he simply mentions that she was present for the filming (195).

9. BP, Interview, Shelby Foote by Joseph Blotner, 20 November 1965.

10. Lamkin would eventually marry and no evidence in these interviews suggests that she was a lesbian. Rather, Foote likely meant to indict her as what we might now call a "fag hag," or a woman who surrounds herself with the company of gay men (and which can be used as a pejorative).

11. BP, Photocopy, "Faulkner of Oxford: A Brief View." This one-page facsimile has no date on it. To date the story, I have relied on internal clues—the reference to the Howells Medal, which prompted Blotner to write in the margins, "Spring 1950, WF didn't go." Also, *The Bitterweed Path* was published in 1950, and the editor's note identifies that "first novel"

and that it will be reviewed the following week. On the facsimile, the paper refers to itself as "The News" and contains a pen-and-ink drawing of Faulkner "by Dallas artist Ed Bearden." SMU is in Dallas as well. It seems likely that the *Dallas Morning News* is the paper in which this story appeared.

12. BP, Letter, William Faulkner to Bennett Cerf, 1948. The details of this paragraph are compiled from a series of letters between Faulkner and Cerf from 1948. Most are undated and informal in tone, as if to suggest a personal, not professional, exchange, which accounts for the lack of precise datelines.

13. In his memoir, Cowley's dates do not add up (he misidentifies 23 October as being on a Sunday). Blotner was able to reconstruct the dates more accurately through additional interviews and letters. I have amended the dates to accord with Blotner's corrections.

14. The copy of *Absalom, Absalom!* that Faulkner signed for Cowley is now part of the Brodsky-Faulkner Collection at Southeast Missouri State University, along with BP. Faulkner's handwriting was unique, consisting of a microscopic, almost cramped precision that can prove difficult to read. His signature, under normal circumstances, was in the same script but is clear and easy to read. The one known exception is this copy he signed for Cowley on the weekend he was recovering from his bender at the Cowley's home. The signature appears shaky and unsteady, distinctly Faulkner's but also an imprint of his condition at the time. This signature—literally a product of Faulkner's own hand—is a powerful and chilling testament to his alcoholism. It is, in its way, a witness to these events on this lost weekend in 1948.

15. Blotner includes "Mr. Acarius" in *Uncollected Stories* and includes its drafting and publication history in his endnotes there.

16. BP, Interview, Estelle Oldham by Joseph Blotner, August 1963; Interview, Victoria Fielden by Joseph Blotner, 27 October 1964; additional letters between Faulkner and his publishers also collected in BP offer a full account of the financial leeway Faulkner allowed Ford for the rights to the play, including his request that she be given special options for a payment schedule while a theatrical version was still in development.

17. BP, Interview, Ruth Ford by Joseph Blotner, June 1964.

18. Izard's book contains a portrait of Faulkner holding Shelley, dated to 1942 while Faulkner was in Hollywood, while Ford was married to Peter Van Eyck.

19. BP, Photocopy, Lewis Funke, "Gossip on the Rialto," *New York Times*, 9 September 1915.

20. BP, Interview, Albert Marre by Joseph Blotner, 22 September 1967.

21. In his diary, published as *Water from a Bucket* in 2001, Henri-Ford recounted his and Tcheltichew's departing for Europe in 1952 and hinted at a family drama, but he offered no account of specific details related to the production of *Requiem*.

22. BP, Interview, Albert Marre by Joseph Blotner, 22 September 1967.

23. BP, Letter, William Faulkner to Saxe Commins [January 1952]. Blotner appended the date to the undated letter.

24. From the Hubert Creekmore collection at the Howard Gottlieb Archival Research Center at Boston University, underlining in original.

25. Ibid.

26. HC, Typescript of *The Elephant's Trunk*. At times in the typescript, Creekmore mistakes his location and writes Oxford when he means Lowry. Elsewhere in the typescript, Water Valley is identified as the town just south of Lowry (it is, in truth, the town just south of Oxford).

27. There is no authorized biography of Creekmore. I gathered the data that follows from a variety of sources, including BP, Suzanne Marrs's biography of Eudora Welty, and the yearbooks for the University of Mississippi from the years 1915–1930. I identify my sources as accurately as possible in the notes that follow.

28. Wade's son, Jimmy Creekmore, has confirmed to me that his father did rush SAE at Ole Miss before the showdown with Governor Russell in 1920. It is difficult to ascertain if Wade was initiated in fall 1919 as a freshman or fall 1920 as a sophomore. I chose the earlier date because his family connections to SAE would likely have encouraged him to rush at the earliest possible time. Also, evidence in BP suggests that certain dorm rooms on campus were occupied by secret SAE members during this period and became locations for smaller secret meetings. Wasson and his roommate were both SAEs and their dorm room was supposedly one such secret meeting place.

29. The story of this crisis of 1920 exists in several places, most of them collected in some form in BP. In the folder for 1920, Blotner compiled interview notes with several members of the fraternity, including with Rufus and Wade Creekmore, whom he interviewed in Jackson, Mississippi, on 25–26 March 1965. Additionally, BP includes what appears to be a term paper, most likely written in the mid-1960s, by a student either at Ole Miss or at the University of Virginia named Sarah Eva Furr Butts, entitled "Lee Maurice Russell and His Attempt to Democratize the University of Mississippi." To my knowledge, this paper has never been published and its provenance is difficult to ascertain. Therefore, I do not quote from it directly (nor did Blotner), but the details in that paper seem to be a significant source of the information in chapter 18 of the original two-volume biography.

30. BP, Interview, Lowery Simmons by Joseph Blotner, 15 November 1966.

31. Creekmore Sr.'s role in these meetings is confirmed by three different interview sources in BP.

Interview, Jeff Hamm by Joseph Blotner, 16 November 1966: "Creekmore and other fathers come over & decided it was best for the boys to withdraw."

Interview, David Callahan by Joseph Blotner, 25 March 1965: "Wade and Russell [sic] Creekmore got their father to come up and talk with them about the situation. Mr. Creekmore advised them to withdraw from school before they were dismissed and thus avoid losing credit for work they had done."

Interview, Lowery Simmons by Joseph Blotner, 15 November 1966: "Mr. Hiram Creekmore was the father who would come up every night during the crisis and give advice. SAE was the only fraternity to carry out initiation and pledging there [the Stone home/Ole Miss]. The Kas and others wouldn't initiate there. There was a move under way to bring the fraternities again. Creekmore would come up from Water Valley every night."

32. In his interview notes, Blotner records that Rufus went to the University of Alabama immediately after his withdrawal, but he mistakenly identifies Wade with a group that transferred to Mississippi State and in the two-volume biography claims both brothers transferred to Mississippi State. However, Wade completed his sophomore year at the University of Alabama (his affiliations in the 1922 Ole Miss yearbook confirm this, as has his son, Jimmy). Wade returned to Ole Miss for his junior year. Rufus transferred to Yale to complete his law degree.

33. BP, Interview, Rufus Creekmore by Joseph Blotner, 25 March 1965.

34. BP, Interview, Billy Ross by Joseph Blotner, 27 November 1965.

35. University of Mississippi Special Collections, Image, "Glorifying the American Male," *Ole Miss Annual*, 1926.

36. University of Mississippi Special Collections, Images of Creekmore dressed as a dapper young courtier in suit and tie and as a clown, *Ole Miss Annual*; the three drawings can be found in *William Faulkner: Early Prose and Poetry*; one of these drawings was chosen as the image for the annual Faulkner and Yoknapatawpha Conference, *Faulkner's Sexualities*.

37. William Faulkner Collection, Harry Ransom Center, Letter, Hubert Creekmore to Phil Stone, 24 May 1930. The letter is part of the "Burned Papers" that were recovered from the Stone home after a fire in the 1940s.

Chapter 9

1. See Snell, whose biography of Phil Stone not only documents the life of Faulkner's close friend but also explores the complexity of their relationship.

2. My reconstruction of the real person who materialized from this newspaper ad is based on some online hunting through various genealogy websites. While those websites—often maintained by family members—are not necessarily reliable, they do provide some census data to back up their claims. Also, certain names recur and are verified by commentary from surviving family. I attempted to find grave sites to correspond to names that appeared in these online searches, including long days surveying as entirely as possible the main cemeteries in Oxford, Abbeville, and Water Valley, as well as several cemeteries in the county when they were accessible from the road (some of these near Sardis Lake on the northern and western edge of Lafayette County were marked as private property, so my searches were limited to what felt respectful and safe). I have not found the graves of June Suratt or any of his children as their names appears on census records. It is possible that their grave stones have disintegrated beyond legibility in the rough north Mississippi climate.

3. BP, Photocopy, "A Faulkner Reminiscence: Conversations with Maud Faulkner," by James Dahl, *Journal of Modern Literature* (April 1974).

4. Despite other revisions to the novel as Wasson winnowed it down to *Sartoris*, this description survived verbatim.

5. The chronology established in *The Hamlet* does not accord with the chronology of the other novels in the Snopes trilogy. I tend to rely on Cleanth Brooks's reconstruction of a logical timeline in *William Faulkner: The Yoknapatawpha Country*, but the dates are plainly inconsistent in the trilogy.

6. The original description of Suratt's buckboard disappears entirely from the published version of "As I Lay Dying." This deletion is probably a result of Faulkner's changing the narrative perspective from the unnamed speaker of the earlier story to Suratt for the 1931 version he published under the title "Spotted Horses" (*As I Lay Dying* had by then been transferred to the title of a novel, also set in Frenchman's Bend). It would be nonsensical for Suratt to pause to describe his own buckboard, so when Faulkner made Suratt the narrator of the story, he traded the external signifier so vital to his character for the intimacy of crafting a first-person narrative voice.

7. BP, Interview, Emily [Whitehurst] Stone by Joseph Blotner, 18 November 1967.

8. BP, from a series of articles, titled "Moonbeams," which appear to have been a weekly column in the *Oxford Eagle*. The unidentified author wrote on 21 May 1936, "Paperhanger Rusty Patterson by ruse drops an overgrown catfish into my shirt pocket and says something about not writing him up. I am told that Rusty has been written up by one much more adept in the art than myself. Much of his homily wit—they say—can be found between the covers of Faulkner's books." Beside this entry, Blotner wrote in the margins "Suratt."

9. BP, Interview, Judge Taylor McElroy by Joseph Blotner, 18 November 1967.

10. BP, Interview, Phil Mullens by Joseph Blotner, 18 November 1966.

11. BP, Photocopy, "American 'Misunderstanding': Faulkner Speaks on Reds," from the *New York Times*, 23 August 1955.

Bibliography

Archives and Special Collections

In addition to the sources below, I cite material from the following archives:

The William Faulkner Collection in the Harry Ransom Center at the University of Texas at Austin.

The Hubert Creekmore Collection in the Howard Gotlieb Archival Research Center at Boston University.

The Special Collections at the University of Mississippi.

The L. D. Brodsky/Faulkner Collection at Southeast Missouri State University. The L. D. Brodsky/Faulkner Collection houses the Blotner Papers.

Works Cited and Selected Bibliography

Aiken, Conrad. *Turns and Movies and Other Tales in Verse* (1916). Philadelphia: Richard West, 1976. Print.

American Experience: Influenza 1918. Prod. Rocky Collins. PBS, 2006. DVD.

Anderson, Sherwood. *Winesburg, Ohio* (1919). New York: Bantam Dell: Random House, 2008. Print.

Backman, Melvin. *Faulkner: The Major Years*. Bloomington: Indiana UP, 1966. Print.

Baker, Houston A. *Modernism and the Harlem Renaissance*. Chicago: U of Chicago P, 1987. Print.

Bannon, Ann. *Beebo Brinker*. San Francisco: Cleis Press. 1962. Print.

Barr, James. *Quatrefoil* (1950). Boston: Alyson, 1982. Print.

Bersani, Leo. *Homos*. Cambridge, MA: Harvard UP, 1995. Print.

Bibler, Michael. *Cottons Queer Relations: Same-Sex Intimacy and the Literature of the Southern Plantation, 1936–1968*. Charlottesville: U of Virginia P, 2009. Print.

Bleikestan, Andre. "The Setting." *As I Lay Dying*. Norton Critical Edition. Ed. Michael Gorra. New York: W. W. Norton, 2010. 276–85. Print.

Blotner, Joseph. *Faulkner: A Biography, One Volume Edition*. New York: Vintage, 1991. Print.

———. *Faulkner: A Biography, Two Volume Edition*. New York: Random House, 1974. Print.

Blythe, Hal. "Faulkner's 'A Rose for Emily.'" *Explicator* 47.2 (1989): 49–50. Print.

Blythe, Hal, and Charlie Sweet. "A Rosey Response to Fick and Gold." *Eureka Studies in Teaching Short Fiction* 8.1 (2007): 108–14. Print.

Branch, Watson. "Darl Bundren's 'Cubistic' Vision." *William Faulkner's* As I Lay Dying: *A Critical Casebook*. Ed. Dianne L. Cox. New York: Garland, 1985. 111–29. Print.

Bret, David. *Clark Gable: Tormented Star*. New York: Carroll and Graf, 2007. Print.

Bronski, Michael. *Pulp Friction: Uncovering the Golden Age of Gay Male Pulps*. Ed. Michael Bronski. New York: St. Martin's Griffin, 2003. Print.

Brooks, Cleanth. *William Faulkner: First Encounters*. New Haven, CT: Yale UP, 1983. Print.

———. *William Faulkner: The Yoknapatawpha Country*. Baton Rouge: Louisiana State UP, 1990. Print.

Brooks, Peter. *Reading for the Plot: Design and Intention in Narrative*. New York: Knopf, 1984. Print.

Bruhm, Steven. *Reflecting Narcissus: A Queer Aesthetic*. Minneapolis: U of Minnesota P, 2001. Print.

Capote, Truman. *Other Voices, Other Rooms* (1948). New York: Vintage International: Random House, 1994. Print.

Carpenter Wilde, Meta, and Orin Borsten. *A Loving Gentleman: The Love Story of William Faulkner and Meta Carpenter*. New York: Simon & Schuster, 1976. Print.

Carryin' on in the Lesbian and Gay South. Ed. John Howard. New York: New York UP, 1997. Print.

Cather, Willa. *One of Ours* (1922). New York: Vintage Classics: Random House, 1991. Print.

———. *The Selected Letters of Willa Cather*. Ed. Andrew Jewell and Janis Stout. New York: Knopf, 2013. Print.

Chauncey, George. *Gay New York: Gender, Urban Culture, and the Making of the Gay Male World 1890–1940*. New York: Basic-Perseus Books, 1994. Print.

Cobb, James. *The Most Southern Place on Earth: The Mississippi Delta and the Roots of Regional Identity*. New York: Oxford UP, 1992. Print.

Coetzee, J. M. *Inner Workings: Literary Essays 2000–2005*. New York: Penguin, 2007. Print.

Cohler, Bertram J. *Writing Desire: Sixty Years of Gay Autobiography*. Madison: U of Wisconsin P, 2007. Print.

Connelly, Marc. *Deadly Closets: The Fictions of Charles Jackson*. Lanham, MD: UP of America, 2001. Print.

Corber, Robert J. *Homosexuality in Cold War America: Resistance and the Crisis in Masculinity*. Durham, NC: Duke UP, 1997. Print.

Cowley, Malcolm. *The Faulkner-Cowley File: Letters and Memories 1944–1962*. London: Chatto & Windus, 1966. Print.

Creekmore, Hubert. *The Welcome*. New York: Appleton-Century-Crofts, 1948. Print.

Creighton, Joanne V. "Suratt to Ratliff: A Genetic Approach to *The Hamlet*." *Michigan Academician: Papers of the Michigan Academy of Sciences, Arts, and Letters* 6 (1973): 101–12. Print.

Crowell, Ellen. "The Picture of Charles Bon: Oscar Wilde's Trip through Faulkner's Yoknapatawpha." *MFS: Modern Fiction Studies* 50.3 (2004): 595–631. Print.

Delaney, Samuel. "Some Queer Notions about Race." *Queer Cultures*. Ed. Deborah Carlin and Jennifer DiGrazia. Upper Saddle River, NJ: Prentice-Hall, 2004. Print.

Donaldson, Susan V. "Ratliff and the Demise of Male Mastery: Faulkner's Snopes Trilogy and Cold War Masculinity." *White Masculinity in the Recent South*. Ed. Trent Watts. Baton Rouge: Louisiana State UP, 2008. 234–50. Print.

Dubermann, Martin. *Stonewall*. New York: Dutton, 1993. Print.

Duvall, John. "Faulkner's Black Sexuality." *Faulkner's Sexualities: Faulkner and Yoknapatawpha, 2007*. Ed. Annette Trefzer and Ann J. Abadie. Jackson: UP of Mississippi, 2007. 131–47. Print.

———. *Faulkner's Marginal Couple: Invisible, Outlaw, and Unspeakable Communities*. Austin: U of Texas P, 1990. Print.

———. *Race and White Identity in Southern Fiction: From Faulkner to Morrison*. New York: Palgrave Macmillan, 2008. Print.

———. "Faulkner's Crying Game: Male Homosexual Panic." *Faulkner and Gender: Faulkner and Yoknapatawpha, 1994*. Ed. Donald M. Kartiganer and Ann J. Abadie. Jackson: UP of Mississippi, 1994. 48–72. Print.

Edelman, Lee. *No Future: Queer Theory and the Death Drive*. Durham, NC: Duke UP, 2004. Print.

Ellmann, Richard. *Oscar Wilde*. New York: Vintage Books: Random House, 1988. Print.

Entzminger, Betina. "Passing as Miscegenation: Whiteness and Homoeroticism in Faulkner's *Absalom, Absalom!*" *Faulkner Journal* 22.1 (2006): 90–105. Print.

Evans, David E. "Mobile Home: Pragmatism and *The Hamlet*." *Mississippi Quarterly: The Journal of Southern Cultures* 58.3–4 (2005): 463–93. Print.

Faulkner, John. *My Brother Bill*. New York: Trident Press, 1963. Print.

Faulkner in the University: Class Conferences at the University of Virginia 1957–1958. Ed. Frederick L. Gwynn and Joseph Blotner. New York: Vintage, 1965. Print.

Faulkner, William. *Absalom, Absalom!: The Corrected Text* (1936). Ed. Noel Polk. Modern Library, 1993. Print.

———. "As I Lay Dying." *As I Lay Dying*. Norton Critical Edition. Ed. Michael Gorra. New York: W. W. Norton, 2010. 173–83. Print.

———. *As I Lay Dying: The Corrected Text* (1930). Ed. Noel Polk. New York: Modern Library, 2000. Print.

———. *Collected Stories* (1950). New York: Vintage International: Random House, 1995. Print.

———. *Elmer*. Ed. Dianne Luce Cox. Foreword by James B. Meriwether. *Mississippi Quarterly* 36 (Summer 1983): 343–447. Print.

———. *Essays, Speeches, and Public Letters*. Ed. James B. Meriwether. New York: Modern Library, 2004. Print.

———. *Flags in the Dust*. Ed. Douglas Day. New York: Vintage: Random House, 1973. Print.

———. *Helen: A Courtship and Mississippi Poems*. Ed. Carvel Collins and Joseph Blotner. New Orleans, LA, and Oxford, MS: Tulane UP and Yoknapatawpha Press, 1981. Print.

———. *Intruder in the Dust* (1948). New York: Vintage International: Random House, 2011. Print.

———. *Light in August: The Corrected Text* (1932). Ed. Noel Polk. New York: Modern Library, 2002. Print.

———. *Lion in the Garden: Interviews with William Faulkner 1926–1962*. Ed. James B. Meriwether and Michael Millgate. New York: Random House, 1968.

———. *Mosquitoes* (1927). New York: Liveright, 1997. Print.

———. *New Orleans Sketches* (1958). Ed. Carvel Collins. Jackson: UP of Mississippi, 2002. Print.

———. *Requiem for a Nun* (1951). New York: Vintage: Random House, 1975. Print.

———. *Sanctuary: The Corrected Text* (1931). Ed. Noel Polk. New York: Vintage: Random House, 1993. Print.

———. *Selected Letters of William Faulkner*. Ed. Joseph Blotner. New York: Random House, 1977. Print.

———. *Soldiers' Pay* (1926). New York: Liveright, 1997. Print.

———. *The Hamlet* (1940). *Snopes*. New York: Modern Library, 1994. 1–350. Print.

———. *The Mansion* (1959). *Snopes*. New York: Modern Library, 1994. 673–1065. Print.

———. *The Marble Faun and a Green Bough* (1924/1933). New York: Random House, 1960. Print.

———. *The Marionettes*. Ed. Noel Polk. Charlottesville: UP of Virginia, 1977. Print.

———. *The Sound and the Fury: The Corrected Text with Faulkner's Appendix* (1929/1946). Ed. Noel Polk. New York: Modern Library, 1992. Print.

———. *The Town* (1957). *Snopes*. New York: Modern Library, 1994. 351–672. Print.

———. *Thinking of Home: William Faulkner's Letters to His Mother and Father 1918–1925*. Ed. James G. Watson. New York: W. W. Norton, 1992. Print.

———. *Uncollected Stories* (1979). Ed. Joseph Blotner. New York: Vintage International: Random House, 1997. Print.

———. *Vision in Spring*. Ed. Judith Sensibar. Austin: U of Texas P, 1984. Print.

———. *William Faulkner: Early Prose and Poetry*. Ed. Carvel Collins. Boston: Atlantic Monthly Press: Little, Brown and Company, 1962. Print.

Fick, Thomas, and Eva Gold. "'He Liked Men': Homer, Homosexuality, and the Culture of Manhood in Faulkner's 'A Rose for Emily.'" *Eureka Studies in Teaching Short Fiction* 8.1 (2007): 99–107. Print.

Foucault, Michel. *The History of Sexuality, Volume 1: An Introduction.* Trans. Robert Hurley. New York: Vintage, 1990. Print.

Freud, Sigmund. *Beyond the Pleasure Principle. The Complete Psychological Works of Sigmund Freud, Vol. XVIII.* Trans. and ed. James Strachey. London: Hogarth, 1955. 3–64. Print.

Fussell, Paul. *The Great War and Modern Memory* (1975). New York: Oxford UP, 2000. Print.

Gates, Gary J., and Abigail M. Cooke. *United States Census Snapshot: 2010.* The Williams Institute, UCLA School of Law. Web. 21 June 2013.

Godden, Richard, and Noel Polk. "Reading the Ledgers." *Mississippi Quarterly: The Journal of Southern Cultures* 55.3 (2002): 301–59. Print.

Gordon, Phillip. "Naples Re-Visited: A New Perspective on Same-Sex Desire in 'Divorce in Naples.'" *Faulkner and Warren.* Ed. Christopher Reiger and Robert W. Hamblin. Cape Girardeau: Southeast Missouri State UP, 2015. 114–24. Print.

Gwin, Minrose C. "Did Ernest Like Gordon?: Faulkner's *Mosquitoes* and the Bite of Gender Trouble." *Faulkner and Gender: Faulkner and Yoknapatawpha, 1994.* Ed. Donald M. Kartiganer and Ann J. Abadie. Jackson: UP of Mississippi, 1994. 120–44. Print.

Harker, Jaime. "'And You Too, Sister Sister': Lesbian Sexuality, *Absalom, Absalom!,* and the Reconstruction of the Southern Family." *Faulkner's Sexualities: Faulkner and Yoknapatawpha, 2007.* Ed. Annette Trefzer and Ann J. Abadie. Jackson: UP of Mississippi, 2007. 38–53. Print.

Henri-Ford, Charles. *Water from a Bucket: A Diary 1948–1957.* New York: Turtle Point, 2001. Print.

Henri-Ford, Charles, and Parker Tyler. *The Young and the Evil* (1933). The New Traveller's Companion Series: Olympia Press. Print.

Holditch, W. Kenneth. "William Faulkner and Other Famous Creoles." *Faulkner and His Contemporaries: Faulkner and Yoknapatawpha, 2002.* Ed. Joseph R. Urgo and Ann J. Abadie. Jackson: UP of Mississippi, 2004. 21–39. Print.

Howard, John. *Men Like That: A Southern Queer History.* Chicago: U of Chicago P, 1999. Print.

Howe, Irving. *William Faulkner: A Critical Study.* New York: Random House, 1951. Print.

Irigaray, Luce. *This Sex Which Is Not One.* Trans. Catherine Porter. Ithaca, NY: Cornell UP, 1985. Print.

Izard, Barbara, and Clara Hieronymus. *Requiem for a Nun: Onstage and Off.* Nashville, TN: Aurora, 1970. Print.

Jackson, Charles. *The Lost Weekend.* New York: Modern Library, 1948. Print.

Jones, Norman W. "Coming Out through History's Hidden Love Letters in *Absalom, Absalom!*" *American Literature: A Journal of Literary History, Criticism, and Bibliography* 76.2 (2004): 339–66. Print.

Karl, Frederick R. *William Faulkner: American Writer.* New York: Weidenfeld and Nicolson, 1989. Print.

Kartiganer, Donald. "'By It I Would Stand or Fall': Life and Death in *As I Lay Dying.*" *A Companion to William Faulkner.* Ed. Richard Moreland. Malden, MA: Blackwell, 2007. 429–44. Print.

———. "The Farm and the Journey: Ways of Mourning and Meaning in *As I Lay Dying.*" *Mississippi Quarterly* 43 (Summer 1990): 281–303. Print.

Kerr, Douglas. *Wilfred Owen's Voices: Language and Community.* Oxford: Clarendon Press, 1993. Print.

Kodat, Catherine Gunther. "Unhistoricizing Faulkner." *Faulkner's Sexualities: Faulkner and Yoknapatawpha Conference 2007.* Ed. Annette Trefzer and Ann J. Abadie. Jackson: UP of Mississippi, 2007. 3–20. Print.

Liles, Don Merrick. "William Faulkner's *Absalom, Absalom!:* An Exegesis of the Homoerotic Configurations of the Novel." *Literary Visions of Homosexuality.* Ed. Stuart Kellogg. New York: Haworth, 1983. 99–111. Print.

Limon, John. "Addie in No-Man's-Land." *Faulkner and War: Faulkner and Yoknapatawpha Conference 2001.* Ed. Noel Polk and Ann J. Abadie. Jackson: UP of Mississippi, 2004. 36–54. Print.

Lindemann, Marilee. *Willa Cather: Queering America.* New York: Columbia UP, 1999. Print.

Lorde, Audre. "Use of the Erotic: The Erotic as Power." *Sister/Outsider: Essays and Speeches by Audre Lorde* (1984). Berkeley, CA: Crossing Press: Ten Speed, 2007. Print.

Lowe, Nell, and Andrea L. Suratt. "Surratt, James 'Junius.'" *Sarrett/Sarratt/Surratt Families of America: Mississippi Queries.* Ancestry.com. rootsweb. Web. 21 June 2013.

Mallarme, Stephane. *Collected Poems and Other Verse: With Parallel French Text.* Trans. E. H. Blackmore and A. M. Blackmore. Oxford: Oxford UP, 2006/2008. Print.

Marrs, Suzanne. *Eudora Welty: A Biography.* New York: Harvest; Harcourt, 2005. Print.

Maupin, Armistead. *Tales of the City* (1978). New York: Harper Perennial, 2007. Print.

Meriwether, James B. *The Literary Career of William Faulkner: A Bibliographic Study.* Columbia: U of South Carolina P, 1971. Print.

Michaels, Walter Benn. *Our America: Nativism, Modernism, and Pluralism.* Durham, NC: Duke UP, 1995. Print.

Millgate, Michael. *The Achievement of William Faulkner.* Lincoln: U of Nebraska P, 1978. Print.

Minter, David. *William Faulkner: His Life and Work.* Baltimore, MD: Johns Hopkins UP, 1980. Print.

Mississippi Verse. Ed. Alice James. Chapel Hill: U of North Carolina P, 1934. Print.

Oates, Stephen B. *William Faulkner: The Man and the Artist.* New York: Perennial Library: Harper & Row, 1987. Print.

Owen, Wilfred. *The Collected Poems of Wilfred Owen.* Ed. C. Day Lewis. London: Chatto & Windus, 1964. Print.

Parini, Jay. *One Matchless Time: A Life of William Faulkner.* New York: HarperCollins, 2004. Print.

Percy, William Alexander. *In April Once.* New Haven, CT: Yale UP, 1920. Print

———. *Sappho in Levkas and Other Poems.* New Haven, CT: Yale UP, 1915. Print.

Peterson, Christopher. "The Haunted House of Kinship: Miscegenation, Homosexuality, and Faulkner's *Absalom, Absalom!*" *CR: The New Centennial Review* 4.1 (2004): 227–65. Print.

Phillips, Thomas Hal. *The Bitterweed Path* (1949). Intro. John Howard. Chapel Hill: U of North Carolina P, 1996. Print.

Pigg, Daniel F. "Owen's 'Disabled.'" *Explicator* 55.2 (Winter 1997): 91. *Academic Search Premier.* EBSCO. J.D. Williams Library, Oxford, MS. 31 July 2007. Web.

Pilkington, John. *Stark Young.* Twayne's United States Authors Series. Ed. Kenneth Eble. Boston: Twayne, 1985. Print.

Polchin, James. "Selling a Novel: Faulkner's *Sanctuary* as a Psychosexual Text." *Faulkner and Gender: Faulkner and Yoknapatawpha, 1994.* Ed. Donald M. Kartiganer and Ann J. Abadie. Jackson: UP of Mississippi, 1994. 145–59. Print.

Polk, Noel. "Ratliff's Buggies." *Children of the Dark House: Text and Context in Faulkner.* Jackson: UP of Mississippi, 1996. 166–95. Print.

Reed, John Shelton. *Dixie Bohemia: A French Quarter Circle in the 1920s.* Baton Rouge: Louisiana State UP, 2012. Print.

Rich, Adrienne. "Compulsory Heterosexuality and Lesbian Existence." *Blood, Bread, and Poetry: Selected Prose 1979–1985.* New York: W. W. Norton, 1986. 23–75. Print.

Richards, Gary. *Lovers and Beloveds: Sexual Otherness in Southern Fiction, 1936–1961.* Baton Rouge: Louisiana State UP, 2005. Print.

———. "The Artful and Crafty Ones of the French Quarter: Male Homosexuality and Faulkner's Early Prose Writings." *Faulkner's Sexualities: Faulkner and Yoknapatawpha, 2007.* Ed. Annette Trefzer and Ann J. Abadie. Jackson: UP of Mississippi, 2007. 21–37. Print.

Robertson, Alice. "Response to Fick and Gold's 'He Liked Men': Homer, Homosexuality, and the Culture of Manhood in Faulkner's 'A Rose for Emily.'" *Eureka Studies in Teaching Short Fiction* 8.1 (2007): 115–16. Print.

Schwartz, Lawrence H. *Creating Faulkner's Reputation: The Politics of Modern Literary Criticism.* Knoxville: U of Tennessee P, 1988. Print.

Sedgwick, Eve Kosofsky. *Between Men: English Literature and Male Homosocial Desire.* New York: Columbia UP, 1985. Print.

———. *Epistemology of the Closet.* Berkeley: U of California P, 1990. Print.

Sensibar, Judith. *Faulkner and Love: The Women Who Shaped His Art.* New Haven, CT: Yale UP, 2009. Print.

———. *The Origins of Faulkner's Art.* Austin: U of Texas P, 1984. Print.

Sherry, Michael S. *Gay Artists in Modern American Culture: An Imagined Conspiracy.* Chapel Hill: U of North Carolina P, 2007. Print.

Signal, Daniel J. *William Faulkner: The Making of a Modernist.* Chapel Hill: U of North Carolina P, 1997. Print.

Skaggs, Merrill Maguire. "Cather's War and Faulkner's Peace: A Comparison of Two Novels and More." *Faulkner and His Contemporaries: Faulkner and Yoknapatawpha 2002.* Ed. Joseph R. Urgo and Ann J. Abadie. Jackson: UP of Mississippi, 2004. Print.

Smith, Henry Nash. "A Troubled Vision." Rev. of *As I Lay Dying. As I Lay Dying.* Norton Critical Edition. Ed. Michael Gorra. New York: W. W. Norton, 2010. 160–61. Print.

Smith, Patti. *Just Kids.* New York: Ecco: HarperCollins, 2010. Print.

Snell, Susan. *Phil Stone of Oxford: A Vicarious Life.* Athens: U of Georgia P, 1991. Print.

Somerville, Siobhan B. *Queering the Color Line: Race and the Invention of Homosexuality in American Culture.* Durham, NC: Duke UP, 2000. Print.

Spratling, William. *File on Spratling: An Autobiography.* Boston: Little, Brown and Company, 1967. Print.

Stockinger, Jacob. "Toward a Gay Criticism." *The Homosexual Imagination.* Spec. issue of *College English* 36.3 (1974): 303–11. Print.

Stokes, Mason. *The Color of Sex: Whiteness, Heterosexuality, and the Fictions of White Supremacy.* Durham, NC: Duke UP, 2001. Print.

Swinburne, Algernon Charles. *The Best of Swinburne.* Ed. Clyde Kenneth Hyder and Lewis Chase. New York: Ronald Press, 1937. Print.

Thomas, James W. *Lyle Saxon: A Critical Biography.* Birmingham, AL: Summa, 1991. Print.

Thompson, Brock. "Where the Action Is: Interstate Rest Areas, the Creation of Gay Space, and the Recovery of Lost Narrative." *White Masculinity in the Recent South.* Ed. Trent Watts. Baton Rouge: Louisiana State UP, 2008. Print.

Thompson, Joe. "Inventors of Gay: Alexander Woollcott." *Gay.net.* OUT Magazine, 26 April 2011. Web. 17 October 2012.

Vicinus, Martha. "'They Wonder to which Sex I Belong': The Historical Roots of Modern Lesbian Identity." *The Lesbian and Gay Studies Reader.* Ed. Henry Abelove et al. New York: Routledge, 1993. Print. 432–52.

Vickery, Olga. *The Novels of William Faulkner.* Baton Rouge: Louisiana State UP, 1973. Print.

Wallace, James M. "Faulkner's 'A Rose for Emily.'" *Explicator* 50.2 (1992): 105–7. Print.

Wasson, Ben. *Count No 'Count: Flashbacks to Faulkner.* Jackson: UP of Mississippi, 1983. Print.

Watson, James G. *William Faulkner: Self-Presentation and Performance.* Austin: U of Texas P, 2000. Print.

Weinstein, Philip. *Becoming Faulkner: The Art and Life of William Faulkner*. New York: Oxford UP, 2010. Print.

Wells, Dean Faulkner. *Every Day by the Sun: A Memoir of the Faulkners of Mississippi*. New York: Crown, 2011. Print.

William Faulkner of Oxford. Ed. James W. Webb and Wigfall Green. Baton Rouge: Louisiana State UP, 1965. Print.

Williamson, Joel. *The Crucible of Race: Black-White Relations in the American South since Emancipation*. New York: Oxford UP, 1984. Print.

———. *William Faulkner and Southern History*. New York: Oxford UP, 1993. Print.

Willingham, Calder. *End as a Man*. New York: Vanguard, 1947. Print.

Wise, Benjamin E. *William Alexander Percy: The Curious Life of a Mississippi Planter and Sexual Freethinker*. Chapel Hill: U North Carolina P, 2012. Print.

Wittenberg, Judith Bryant. *Faulkner: The Transfiguration of Biography*. Lincoln: U of Nebraska P, 1979. Print.

Yaeger, Patricia. "Editor's Note: Bulldagger Sings the Blues." *PMLA* 124.3 (2009): 721–26. Print.

Index

About the Author

Photo courtesy of Katlyn Churchill

Phillip "Pip" Gordon was born in Memphis, Tennessee, and grew up just north of Faulkner's Yoknapatawpha County. He is currently assistant professor of English and Gay Studies coordinator at the University of Wisconsin-Platteville, where he lives with his dog, Scout.